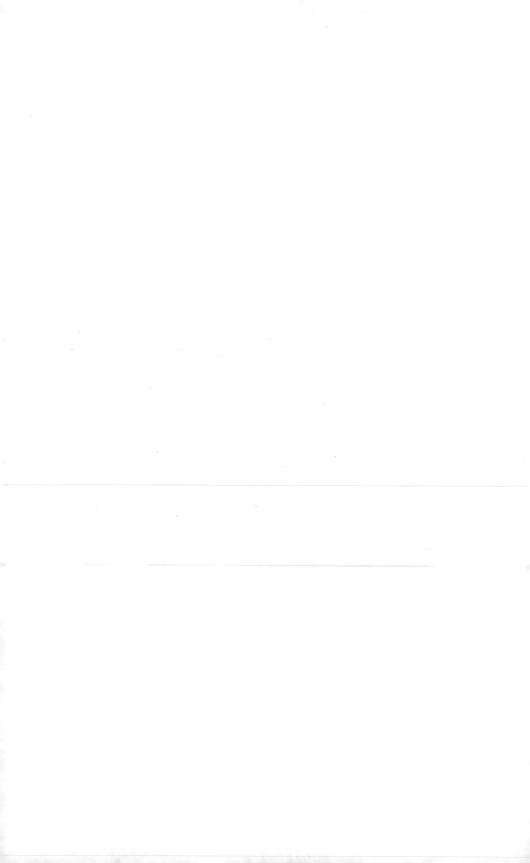

Noble Lies, Slant Truths, Necessary Angels

University of North Carolina
Studies in the Germanic Languages
and Literatures

Initiated by RICHARD JENTE (1949–1952), *established by* F. E. COENEN (1952–1968), *continued by* SIEGFRIED MEWS (1968–1980) *and* RICHARD H. LAWSON (1980–1985)

PAUL T. ROBERGE, Editor

Publication Committee: Department of Germanic Languages

For other volumes in the "Studies" see pages 239–40.

Number One Hundred and Eighteen
University of
North Carolina
Studies in the
Germanic Languages
and Literatures

Noble Lies, Slant Truths, Necessary Angels: Aspects of Fictionality in the Novels of Christoph Martin Wieland

Ellis Shookman

The University of North Carolina Press
Chapel Hill and London 1997

The paper in this book meets the guidelines for permanence and
durability of the Committee on Production Guidelines for Book
Longevity of the Council on Library Resources.

Library of Congress Cataloging-in-Publication Data
Shookman, Ellis.
    Noble lies, slant truths, necessary angels : aspects of
fictionality in the novels of Christoph Martin Wieland / Ellis
Shookman.
        p.   cm.—(University of North Carolina studies in the
Germanic languages and literatures ; no. 118)
    Includes bibliographical references and index.
    ISBN 0-8078-8118-X (alk. paper)
    1. Wieland, Christoph Martin, 1733–1813—Criticism and
interpretation.   2. Fiction—Philosophy.   3. Fiction—History and
criticism.   I. Title.   II. Series.
PT2571.S56   1997
838'.609—dc20   96-30545
                                                                CIP

Portions of this work appeared earlier, in somewhat different form,
in "Fictionality and the *Bildungsroman*: Wieland's *Agathon*,"
Michigan Germanic Studies 13, no. 2 (1987); "Intertextuality,
Agathon, and *Ion*: Wieland's Novel, Euripides's Tragedy, Plato's
Dialogue," *Lessing Yearbook* 22 (1990); and "Pseudo-Science, Social
Fad, Literary Wonder: Johann Caspar Lavater and the Art of
Physiognomy," in *The Faces of Physiognomy: Interdisciplinary
Approaches to Johann Caspar Lavater* (Columbia, S.C.: Camden House,
1993) and are reprinted here with the permission of the publishers.

01 00 99 98 97   5 4 3 2 1

Denn ein aus Mittelmäßigkeiten konstruierter Charakter macht sich über die Fiktivität der Dinge und Erkenntnisse wenig Gedanken . . .
—Hermann Broch, "Methodologische Novelle" (1918)

Contents

Preface

The first three concepts cited in the title of this book—noble lies, slant truths, and necessary angels—derive from Plato, Emily Dickinson, and Wallace Stevens, respectively. They suggest three aspects that the fourth—fictionality—assumes in the novels of Christoph Martin Wieland, where the idea of being (or at least seeming) made up pertains to myths sustaining political life, the obliqueness of narrative verities, and the human need for elevated messages. The following chapters explore these matters and explain how they are related.

This book first began as a doctoral dissertation at Yale. Since then, it has been significantly revised and expanded. For readers unfamiliar with Wieland's novels, it includes summaries of their plots, some general remarks on previous studies of them, and quotations that spell out the evidence for its thesis. For specialists, it also regards those stories, secondary sources, and textual proofs in greater detail. Brief passages of the introduction and of Chapter 2 appeared in articles listed in the bibliography. They are reprinted with the permission of their earlier publishers.

I wish to thank Bruce Duncan, Dennis Mahoney, and Steven Scher for reading my manuscript—and Paul Roberge for facilitating its publication.

Noble Lies, Slant Truths, Necessary Angels

Introduction: Fictionality, Wieland, and the Eighteenth-Century German Novel

Diese erlogene Wahrheit, die ganz allein Wirkung
hervorbringt, wodurch ganz allein die Illusion
erzielt wird, wer hat davon einen Begriff?
—Goethe, *Wilhelm Meisters Lehrjahre* (1795–96)

I

The concept of fictionality is crucial to the modern novel. Ever since Cervantes, there have been narratives showing concern with the fact that they are invented, that they describe characters and events at least partly imaginary, rather than real or literally true. This concern can be playful, but it also answers serious charges that such stories are made up or false. Authors, scholars, and critics accordingly have long considered the logical difficulty as well as the aesthetic appeal of distinguishing creative writing from fanciful deceit in narrative prose "feigned" instead of corresponding to actual fact. Their arguments betray a venerable ambivalence, recalling both Plato's suspicion of poets as inspired liars and Aristotle's claim that poetry describes what is possible and *might* happen, not what is historical and already *has*. Indeed, despite defenses of fiction as such an art of the possible, early European novels were often faulted for being counterfeit, rejected by learned detractors as delusive fabrication. Nowhere was the resulting skepticism more extreme than in Germany, where novels were long decried as sinful flights of fancy and reading them was censured as an immoral waste of time. Authors such as Christoph Martin Wieland (1733–1813), who tried to justify the genre, therefore confronted critics and had to cultivate readers still unused to taking prose fiction seriously. Wieland met this challenge by writing nine novels that show and tell much about their own fictional nature. In those novels themselves, he examines the imagination needed to read and write them, their capacity to convey utopian ideals, and their problematic illusory effects. These topics involve fictionality defined in literary as well as epistemological, ontological, and anthropological terms, since the nature of Wieland's storytelling closely

1

parallels his larger psychological, ethical, and social themes. The present study suggests both that his novels cohere by treating fictionality in such broad terms and that they help us understand the significance of fictionality even now, nearly two centuries after the last of them was written. This suggestion combines interests in literary theory and the history of the German novel, hoping to prove how each can illuminate the other.

Such a reading of Wieland's novels also requires combining approaches to fictionality taken in current theoretical work. Although implicitly as old as Plato's and Aristotle's more or less severe definitions of mimesis, that concept has only fairly recently become an explicit object of academic study. Philosophers frequently view it from semantic or ontological angles, investigating the meaning of fictional sentences, for example, or the names of fictional characters or the existence of fictional objects.[1] Literary theorists tend to prefer historical and aesthetic categories established by their own notions of narratology, speech acts, reader reception, and similar subjects.[2] The interests of these two camps seldom coincide, and their adherents can seem mightily at odds. According to one scholar on the philosophers' side, "Literary critics have not hesitated to use the concepts of fictionality, of truth in/of literature, truthfulness to life, etc., but the theoretical standard of critical discourse is rather low in this domain."[3] By contrast, it has been observed that "logicians rush in where Leavis fears to tread."[4] The depth of this scholarly rift may be measured by comparing Käte Hamburger's *Die Logik der Dichtung* (1957) with John Woods's *The Logic of Fiction* (1974). Despite their equivalent titles, these two books address strikingly different topics. Hamburger relates her "phenomenology of fictional narration"—an explanation of prose fiction according to its inherent logical structure—to the traditional literary genres of epic, dramatic, and lyric poetry, whereas Woods proposes a "semantic structure of fictional discourse" that expressly ignores aesthetic considerations.[5] Studies of fictionality from either point of view, moreover, rarely interpret individual literary texts. Paying close attention to Wieland's narrative ways and means not only invites aesthetic as well as logical inquiry, then; analyzing his novels one by one also avoids a shortcoming common in much prior research. In turn, those novels help put that research in new perspectives, implying a conception of fictionality applicable to life far beyond that of the academic mind alone.

Such research itself has shown that fictionality has many facets. While analytic philosophers study its logical implications, other theorists consider fictionality a literary and aesthetic issue pertinent to the modern novel, or recount its semiotic history, or see it in terms of linguistic communication, not necessarily between authors and readers. These judgments can have familiar yet far-reaching consequences. Fictionality has been called both the central problem of literary semantics, for example, and a fundamental category of literary theory.[6] It has also been said to imply less a negation of references to reality than an aesthetic consciousness of fictional texts as being self-contained imitations of linguistic utterances, an awareness of inauthenticity manifest in all modern art, that is, above all, in the novel.[7] Baring "historical roots of the modern dilemma of fictionality" has shown how concepts of it have changed along with our religious and intellectual models of reality.[8] Fictionality has also seemed a form of communication in which readers, like moviegoers, ignore artistic media, and has been traced to such readers' reception of literary texts as well as to authors' semantically and rhetorically enhanced speech acts.[9] Even as such a way of producing poetic texts, however, it has been likened to Aristotle's concept of mimesis, for the fictional character of what those texts signify, though they may be aesthetic in senses other than fiction proper, determines their signifiers.[10] Moreover, it has recently resurfaced in a study regarding all representational art as fiction, a project entailing a "unified account of fictionality" as a property of propositions meant to be imagined in games of make-believe and analogous to truth, though not a species of it despite our inclination to think so.[11] This attempt to reconcile metaphysical and aesthetic theories of fiction confirms that defining the terms "fictitious" and "fictional" helps prove the ironic, complex power of imagination.[12] In these several ways, fictionality has seemed an important, multifarious, and promising concept.

Reading Wieland mindful of current theories of fictionality would seem anachronistic, however, without a sense of its history. That history is long, and his place in it is prominent. Both authors' and readers' consciousness of fictionality are said to have changed over time, having spread since the sixteenth century and culminated in the irony of the German romantics.[13] This historical process started in antiquity, when such consciousness first emerged between the eighth and fourth centuries B.C., as written literature and individual reading gradually supplanted the public oral tradition of Homer.[14] Awareness of fictionality has also been found in Neoplatonic as well as vernacular writings of the Middle Ages, when distinctions between epic fiction and historical truth were rediscovered and then reinforced the autonomy of art.[15] Similar results have accrued from analyses of poetic terminology, textual practices, and authors' self-images in the sixteenth century.[16] One historian of the English novel likewise suggests that such literary issues inform William Congreve's *Incognita* (1692): "In Congreve's amused subversion of verisimilitude there is the groundwork for a view of probability as a kind of 'aesthetic' truth, aware of its own fictionality and detoxified of crude empiricist illusion."[17] In eighteenth-century Germany, such awareness was encouraged by critics like Johann Christoph Gottsched, Johann Elias Schlegel, and Gotthold Ephraim Lessing, who all helped define aesthetic autonomy by facing the problem, character, and consciousness of fictionality. Bit by bit, they appreciated its import in the theater, thereby making it more respectable.[18] A quantum leap in this slow process was the Leibnizian concept of fictionality refined by Christian Wolff, Alexander Baumgarten, Johann Jakob Bodmer, and Johann Jakob Breitinger, who all furthered the notion that novels describe possible, not actual, worlds.[19] Subsequent theories of artistic creation developed this suggestive notion and did indeed culminate in romantic irony, which has been said to reflect fundamental conditions of fictionality.[20] As both a student of Bodmer and a poet often noted to be a forerunner of romanticism, Wieland assumes an important position in this historical spectrum. Indeed, his novels are repeatedly cited, albeit only in passing, in a recent study of readers' consciousness of fictivity and the problem of fictionality in the eighteenth century.[21] Talk of virtual reality and cyberspace confirms that the history of fictionality is far from over and that its aspects revealed in those novels still concern us.

Wieland's place in the history of fictionality may also be explained by comparing his novels to modernist "metafiction," twentieth-century texts seeming self-conscious or self-reflexive by indicating their own narrative artifice and thus suggesting an awareness of their shaky ontological status. One concise definition tells why such qualities matter: "*Metafiction* is a term given to fictional writing which self-consciously and systematically draws attention to its status as an artefact in order to pose questions about the relationship between fiction and reality. In providing a critique of their own methods of construction, such writings not only examine the fundamental structures of narrative fiction, they also explore the possible fictionality of the world outside the literary fictional text."[22] Such self-critical stories have even been said to expose "the fictionality of reality" itself.[23] By contrast, most popular texts "suppress their own fictionality," though they can foreground a cliché so that "an awareness of its fictionality sets in which changes . . . not only our reading of the popular text, but also its aesthetic function."[24] Television, too, has been seen as a self-reflexive medium justifying "the fictionality and style of even its most extravagant programs."[25] To be sure, some modern authors dislike thus stressing the differences between artistic conventions and life, tired of stories about writers writing stories in what seems a decadent *regressus ad infinitum*.[26] To call "metafiction" nothing more than narcissism, however, is to limit its scope as severely as if one takes it to mean merely novels about readers reading other novels. A recent treatment of the German *Bildungsroman*, for example, regards the genre as metafiction because its heroes often act on what they read in fictional texts, but omits Wieland because he almost never alludes to German literature.[27] The present study considers his novels "metafiction" more broadly defined. Although they are not as self-conscious as Pirandello's plays, say, where a character can realize its own fictionality,[28] they do convey an awareness of their medium and message that is often attributed only to more recent, more radical literati.

Besides Plato's and Aristotle's old definitions of mimesis, then, reading Wieland's novels as studies in fictionality involves recent developments in philosophy and literary theory as well as established trends in the history of fictionality and the meaning of "metafiction." As the following chapters demonstrate, such reading raises issues that determine not only the extent to which serious novels constitute reality rather than simply reflect it,[29] but also the cognitive value of many other logical and linguistic constructs. At stake, in other words, is the efficacy and validity of literary and other, related "fictions" as modes of knowledge. Wieland's novels all pose such general questions, and the answers they suggest still seem pertinent today. Finding those answers requires reading each of them meticulously, but doing so shows why they remain of more than just historical interest. Far from being clever games about nothing more than their narrative form, elaborate Chinese boxes that turn out to be empty, they display what John Hollander has called the "fictive character of form itself" in poems that tell stories about their own formal elements, about what they mean and what to make of them.[30] They also show how Wieland dealt with all novelists' dilemma of fusing fiction and life, which Frank Kermode traces to tension or dissonance between "paradigmatic form" and "contingent reality."[31] In numerous ways, they prove Kermode's contention that the history of their genre is one of "antinovels" written in attempts to "evade the laws of what Scott called 'the land of fiction'—the stereotypes which ignore reality, and whose remoteness from it we identify as absurd."[32] Such generic evasion, dissonance, and tension often attend Wieland's sojourns in this same land of fiction, lending them historical import as well as lasting appeal. Using a pair of terms proposed by Henry James in "The Art of Fiction" (1884), one might say that the German novel was not *naïf* after Wieland, who made it *discutable*. Linking his several novels to the concept of fictionality, which they themselves subtly define and develop, helps show why this was so.

II

The general literary and aesthetic issues cited so far are raised in many remarks on fictionality *avant la lettre*, but they are complicated by recent treatments of three specific concepts studied in terms of fictionality per se: the opposition of fiction to nonfiction, the nature of fictional reference, and the character of fictional truth. All three may be traced to Aristotle, who not only drew the line between poetic mimesis and historiography but also found poetry graver and more philosophical than history, explaining that it concerned "universals" rather than the "singulars" examined by historians. The first has also been addressed in research on narratology, speech-act theory, and sociolinguistics — important sources of inspiration for literary scholars. For Aristotle, the difference between approximating the general and analyzing the particular overrode the fact that poetry was written in verse and history in prose. Similar attempts to separate narrative fiction from nonfiction have been made by Gérard Genette, who notes conceptual differences between narrators and authors, their stories and discourse, and textual indices as well as "paratextual" markers in what Dorrit Cohn calls a search for "narratological criteria of fictionality."[33] Cohn has sought such signs of fictionality herself, and a few colleagues have followed her lead by distinguishing history from fiction, or fictionality in historiography and the novel, or fictionality, historicity, and "textual authority."[34] Aristotle's old distinction between two basic modes of writing has thus been refined by efforts to correct recent academic trends neglecting narratology, which, as Cohn observes, has been "largely disregarded by modern theorists in the ongoing discussion of fictionality."[35] Such efforts show that Hamburger's focus on stylistic details of fictional dialogue and description — for example, on verbs that express subjective feelings and thoughts, on interior monologue, and on free indirect discourse — has started to enjoy a certain revival.

The concepts of fictionality that Genette, Cohn, and others oppose have often been advanced in the name of speech-act theory and sociolinguistics. Proponents of the former maintain that literary fiction is a "fictive use of language" or "fictional discourse" suspending some of the many pragmatic assumptions shared in nonliterary communication.[36] They read novels as representations of natural discourse and thus as fictive utterances, so "the essential fictiveness of novels . . . is not to be discovered in the unreality of the characters, objects, and events alluded to, but in the unreality of the *alludings* themselves."[37] Some claim that "fictivity" is not exclusively or directly literary, holding that literature can be defined "without reference to literariness or fictionality."[38] Others say that the extent of fictionality in nonliterary instances depends on attitudes taken by the speakers and listeners who evoke and perceive it.[39] Similarly, fictionality is sometimes thought to be a matter of linguistic or aesthetic convention. It is a socially determined and relative phenomenon, that is, a pragmatic game played by interlocutors who observe a general "fictionality convention,"[40] which has been explained as "a *dynamic* concept where contextual factors have to be regarded in terms of semantic *conventions* pertaining to social groups of actors behaving in fictional discourses."[41] Thus stressing the contexts of everyday language often neglects or rejects traditional aesthetic concerns, as it does in a study lamenting that debates about fictionality are confined to literature.[42] Research on readers' reception of fiction, though, defines such concerns in new ways. Johannes Anderegg has written that the term "fictionality" denotes ways of communicating in a "functional aesthetics," for example, and he also distinguishes merely playful fictions from more aesthetic experience, developing insights into the alienating, fictive frame of reference that texts can establish for their readers.[43] Christian Berthold similarly differentiates between *fictivity*—the assumption and modality of being invented—and *fictionality*—an attitude that makes internal coherence seem paramount and any text the potential object of "fictional reading."[44] Fictionality has also seemed to result from a rhetorically guided reading of figurative language.[45] The issue of dividing fiction from nonfiction thus persists, pitting some ideas of fictionality against others.

Another issue recently raised together with fictionality concerns reference. It, too, lends itself to various scholarly treatments. Introducing a volume of *Poetics Today* entitled "Reference and Fictionality," Peter Brooks notes that we are no longer innocent about what literature refers to and how we can know such a referent, two questions that he finds neglected in narratology, with its focus on formal elements.[46] That recent research on this issue is indeed not simple may be gleaned from one study explaining how literary texts have not only internal fields of reference that they simultaneously construct and refer to, but meanings tied to external fields of reference as well, whence fictionality is not just a matter of invention and "literature is not simply art in language but, first of all, art in fictionality."[47] Another result of tying fictionality to reference is accounts of how fictional texts refer to themselves. According to Dieter Henrich and Wolfgang Iser, the organizers of a think tank that has studied this and other, related aspects of fiction, self-referentiality is indispensable to *fiction*, in which the *fictive* must be recognized as such.[48] Others reject the idea that literary fiction refers to itself or else to nothing at all, citing the greater or lesser extent to which it borrows items from the outside world as proof that fictionality is a question of degree and that every text is characterized by more or less of it, by a certain *"taux de fictionalité."*[49] Degrees of reference are difficult to assess in "mixed" discourse, however, which mentions fictional characters and events along with historical ones. Fictionality can also seem a result of an author's aesthetic competence, since "the fictionality of literary works dealing with real events . . . is connected with the skill the author exhibits in *using* the events he chooses to describe in such a way that a meaningful imaginary world is created," and distinctions between the inner and outer references of a literary work do not always involve the "fictionality of its report sentences," statements about the world beyond it.[50] Like questions of how writing fiction differs from reporting facts, the issue of its shadowy referents thus divides scholars who consider its fictionality.

The idea that fictional literature refers to imaginary worlds is far from new, moreover, but it nonetheless informs many recent efforts to explain reference in terms of fictionality. Some scholars even propose a semantics of "possible worlds," a notion especially useful, as noted above, for reading Wieland. Lubomír Doležel predicts that mimetic semantics will be replaced by *"possible-worlds semantics of fictionality,"* arguing that fictional worlds are sets of possible states of affairs, that the set of such worlds is unlimited and maximally varied, and that they are accessible from the actual one via semiotic channels opened by literary texts.[51] This model "legitimates the sovereignty of fictional worlds," he adds, so literature is no more restricted in theory than in practice simply to imitating the actual one.[52] As Doležel comments, such a possible-worlds semantics revives a Leibnizian idea also cited by others who note its significance for literature such as novels.[53] Such fiction describes worlds that do not exist, Leibniz wrote, in the sense that God did not choose to realize them. Events recounted in novels could thus be regarded as possible, even though they do not occur in the actual world. In *Fictional Worlds* (1986), Thomas Pavel similarly proposes a semantics of fictionality that does not measure fiction against the real world but rather reflects both internal workings of fiction and readers' understanding of it. This "flexible definition of fictionality" includes semantic and pragmatic as well as stylistic and textual factors, he explains, adding that fictionality is not always a matter of textual semantics, as in the case of myths that are regarded as fictional only when no longer believed, proof that "fictionality is in most cases a historically variable property."[54] Pavel also notes that texts "always flirt with the self-referential temptation and the intoxicating games of higher-order fictionality," games that contribute to the "playful fictionality" of narratives such as Jorge Luis Borges's *The Garden of Forking Paths* (1941) and *Artifices* (1944).[55] Current interest in possible-worlds semantics, then, helps relate Wieland's novels to modernist "metafiction."

In addition to figuring in studies that distinguish fiction from nonfiction and define reference, fictionality also informs recent work on a third issue: truth. Fiction and truth often seem mutually exclusive since fiction cannot, strictly speaking, correspond to actual incidents, objects, or people. If it is nonetheless true, some say, its truth must be considered together with its aesthetic character, rather than measured against external reality. What to call that truth, however—historical, logical, moral, empirical, or internal, for example—is a difficult question. In *Fiktion und Wahrheit* (1975), Gottfried Gabriel tries to reconcile the extremes of fiction and truth, explaining how important it is to grasp each of them separately. To decide whether and how literature can claim to be true despite being fictional, he writes, one must first determine what constitutes its fictionality, then clarify how that claim is to be understood. He does so himself by using a semantic method derived from both analytic philosophy and speech-act theory to define the concept of fictional discourse and then to compare the "truth claim" made by fictional literature with that of science. He argues that literature rightly claims to be true, that its truth is more than just an emotive or rhetorical effect, even though it consists of fictional discourse, which lacks certain characteristics of assertions and referentiality. He insists that literature cannot be reduced to this truth claim, though, and in the end his argument turns on literary realists' ideas of showing the general or universal in the particular. In this attempt to bridge the gap between analytic philosophy and literary theory and to demonstrate how fiction can convey knowledge, the only literary text that Gabriel discusses at length is Wieland's *Agathon* (1766–67), a novel that he commends for its explicit defense of empirically verifiable verisimilitude, which it claims to offer in place of historical truth. This selection confirms that Wieland's novels are key to discussing literary truth in terms of fictionality, though the preliminary remarks that Gabriel quotes from *Agathon* are hardly Wieland's last word on their relationship.

Fictionality and truth are also closely connected in Michael Riffaterre's *Fictional Truth* (1990), an "analytical approach to the fictionality of fiction" noting how "fiction emphasizes the fact of the fictionality of a story at the same time it states that the story is true."[56] Regarding the semiotic codes and arbitrary conventions of verbal mimesis, Riffaterre examines narrative signs "pointing to the fictionality of fiction," thereby correcting research on narratology that he thinks has neglected "the coincidence between textual features declaring the fictionality of a story and a reassertion of the truth of that story."[57] Those signs include figures and tropes inconsistent with narrators' or characters' specific situations as well as stylistic traits such as humor. Literary form, he explains, "being obviously contrived, betrays the hand of its maker and signals fictionality."[58] Form thus draws attention to the gap between narrative verisimilitude and real factuality, indirectly pointing to truth beyond flawed fictional mimesis. In other words, Riffaterre's indices of fictionality both expose artifice and presuppose the real, since even ironically speaking about an object assumes its existence. Following such ambiguous signs, moreover, readers perform a hermeneutic task, creating a "metalinguistic" frame of reference, so the truth of fiction is semiotic and symbolic, a matter of linguistic perception prompted by literary texts. As Christopher Norris has cautioned, the history of fictionality prior to postmodernism makes at least some such judgments about textual reference and truth seem passé. Semiotic fissures between signs and their referents have been part of self-conscious fiction all along, Norris warns, and fiction has always been "more or less aware of its own fictionality."[59] Riffaterre's argument that fiction points to truth by exposing and transcending its own figurative language is also reminiscent of Friedrich Schlegel's remarks on irony. Wieland's novels are further proof that fictionality was known long before it became a poststructuralist preoccupation. Reading them should therefore help correct critical myopia about its close ties to fictional truth.

The foregoing survey of recent research demonstrates how the concept of fictionality helps decide what is fiction, what it refers to, and how it can be true. Scholars also debate how widely that concept can be applied, not only to literature but also to other arts and to life. Hamburger restricts the probability described by Aristotle to literary fiction, calling it an aesthetic question only in the realm of fictionality, from which she excludes the fine arts along with lyric poetry. Only narrative and dramatic texts, she insists, include the category of fictivity.[60] Others admit that the lyric and novel share "a common fictionality," or they find different kinds of fictionality in novels and plays, which makes such generic distinctions less restrictive, for "a novel can usually be transformed into a drama (and vice versa) without fundamental difficulties, and this will not change the *fact* of fictionality but obviously only the *kind* of fictionality involved."[61] A few cast fictionality in even broader terms. Doležel, for example, approaches fictional worlds in ways potentially useful for discussing "fictional existence in other semiotic systems and for the problem of fictionality in general."[62] Such a synthetic conception recalls Hans Vaihinger's *Die Philosophie des Als Ob* (1911), the neo-Kantian phenomenological study of theoretical, practical, and religious fictions—artificial logical constructs, that is, that human beings use to orient themselves in reality, which is otherwise unknowable. Vaihinger himself recognizes the value of such ideas posited to meet human intellectual and ethical needs, accounting for empirical facts as well as abstract ideals with an idealistic positivism based on this concept of fiction. His subject is the *fictive* activity of the logical function, he states, and the products of that activity are *fictions*.[63] Proving the fictivity of such heuristic constructs does not diminish their usefulness, since unlike hypotheses meant to be tested, they are known to be false but are nonetheless accepted. They thus resemble legal fictions: assumptions of facts that may not be true, made to advance the ends of justice. In this nominalistic sense, which Vaihinger derives not only from Kant but also from Nietzsche, fictional*ity* involves philosophical fictional*ism*.

Such encompassing concepts of fictionality are sometimes rejected, but precisely their scope makes them suggestive for reading Wieland's novels. Vaihinger says surprisingly little about literary fiction, and his remarks on it are downright philistine, but Kermode suggests that such fiction is much like Vaihinger's "consciously false" mental structures.[64] Citing the human *need* for fiction, moreover, Iser adds that literary fictionality has profound anthropological implications since it conveys the "ec-static" and duplicitous human condition.[65] Fictions like Vaihinger's play a major role in knowing, acting, and living in the world, he explains, while literary texts differ from such general, larger fictions, which are often not acknowledged as such, by exposing their own fictionality.[66] The extent of such fictionality has also been limited by rejecting the confusion of narration with metaphysics and by pragmatically arguing that "in the relevant sense, fictionality resides in a special kind of institutional and rule-governed relation between writer, text and reader."[67] Nonetheless, "fiction" is a term that has been taken to mean both the fictitiousness of entities created in fictional narration and the fictional character of that narration itself.[68] This ambiguity suggests why even limited ideas of fictionality cannot ignore its larger implications. Wieland's novels constantly explore such implications. While reading them does not solve abstruse problems of modal logic nor resolve disputes about the nature of fictional entities, they do involve issues such as "ethical pan-fictionalism."[69] At the same time, they all address the three fundamental questions here adduced from recent research concerned with fictionality: What is fiction and what is not? How and to what does it refer? How can it be true? Wieland answers such questions in ways showing how well he had learned the "art of framing lies" first defined in Aristotle's *Poetics* and mastered in so many arresting ways ever since. Indeed, his novels reward close reading because they pose such questions in engagingly broad terms.

III

Grasping the full importance of fictionality in Wieland's novels requires knowing not only both its general and specific connotations but also its role in the history of the German novel and its significance in others' studies of his work. During the first half of the eighteenth century, that history had been one of theory rather than practice. The religious, moral, and aesthetic climate of the Enlightenment seldom favored fiction. Older romances were rejected, their stories of fanciful adventures set at aristocratic courts being considered sinful, depraved, and improbable. Such books were thought to be dangerous and to distract their readers from religious belief as well as historical truth. Only gradually did new ways of defining fiction overcome their opponents' qualms and reservations. Such qualities were recognized as critics' thinking evolved from a normative concept of mimesis, defined in neoclassical poetics as imitating nature, into a more refined aesthetics of fictional illusion, which left more room for writers to use their imagination. This evolution depended less on German novels than on more progressive French and English ones, however, and German narrative practice prior to Wieland lagged considerably behind the theory advanced to make it more modern. Indeed, it has been noted that "he had almost to create the genre of the German novel in which he was to work so successfully."[70] This was not an easy task. As late as 1767, even a Lessing could not praise *Agathon* without apologizing for calling it a *Roman*.[71] By 1774, however, Friedrich von Blanckenburg ranked it as the supreme model of the modern novel.[72] The innovative form that Wieland gave the genre has also been related to Hegel's dictum that novels oppose poetry of the heart to prosaic reality.[73] At any rate, a reviewer writing in 1791 agreed that Wieland helped make the German novel more than just a means of killing time.[74] Other German authors had hinted at the fictivity of their novels, and simplistic concepts of fictionality distort their accomplishments, but their pragmatic concerns ignored its complexity, which Wieland was the first to convey.[75]

The strong resistance that he encountered may be gauged by recalling the religious strictures and moral limitations imposed on novels in the late seventeenth and early eighteenth centuries. Grave doubts were expressed by Gotthard Heidegger, who had inveighed against novels from a Calvinist's point of view in his *Mythoscopia romantica* (1698). Novels were all lies, he argued, citing a biblical passage (1 Tim. 4:7) to support his ban on reading such old wives' tales.[76] Heidegger rejected novels so flatly because they were so popular, and he abhorred their seductive appeal. One of his critics was subtler, careful to distinguish between speaking falsely and speaking mendaciously, between making up (*fingere*) and lying (*mentiri*).[77] Even pietism, however, which encouraged its followers to record their contrition and thereby paved the way for the novel as autobiography, dismissed the genre as telling inauthentic, godless lies. Gottsched proved slightly more tolerant, admitting that novels were a kind of poetry but limiting them to teaching unmistakable lessons in virtue.[78] Like Heidegger, he borrowed such notions of the novel from Pierre-Daniel Huet's *Traité de l'origine des romans* (1670). Huet, too, thought novels effective vehicles for conveying moral values, and Gottsched wrote that they must show virtue rewarded and vice punished. He made such rules according to rational assumptions about verisimilitude, which he elaborated in his *Versuch einer Critischen Dichtkunst* (1730).[79] Establishing the close similarity of fiction to nature requires demonstrating its causality, he explained, and novels seem more credible if they conform to historical likelihood. Wieland probably learned this lesson in his youth, when Gottsched, for a time, was his literary idol.[80]

Other critics were more attuned to the effects of fiction and its readers' psychology. Wieland's Swiss mentor, Bodmer, together with Breitinger, for example, defined verisimilitude and historical truth in ways far more conducive to imaginative fiction. Bodmer, too, thought that fiction should correspond to nature, but he found its apparent failure to do so a pleasant surprise, since readers perceived that correspondence more clearly after overcoming their initial confusion. He also thought that novels could approximate historical truth, which he regarded as less than absolute.[81] Defining historiography, too, in terms of probability, he cast the difference between it and novels as one of degree. Poetic truth could never be as certain as that of history, he admitted, but the gap between them could be put to good use since it gave the initial appearance of falsehood that made novels seem marvelous and more rewarding. Novels could therefore compete with history, moreover, as a means of learning about life. By also positing a logic of suppositions—a special "Logik der Vermuthungen"[82]—Bodmer relaxed Gottsched's rules for imitating nature, and by having fiction differ intentionally from history he encouraged poetic creativity. His claim that fiction should seem marvelous (*wunderbar*) also resembles Breitinger's general aesthetic comments. Like Gottsched, Breitinger regarded art as mimesis, but he extended its scope, as noted above, to include the imitation of worlds that God had not made. By respecting laws that nature conceivably *might* have decreed, even though they did not actually obtain, good fiction was simply a history (*Historie*) or narrative (*Erzählung*) from another, possible world.[83] Breitinger was still convinced that fiction had to be true, declaring that the marvelous should not be mixed with lies, but he also defined the marvelous as verisimilar, as something new and thus suited to catch judicious readers' attention. Such substitution of possible worlds for historical truth has been said to make a virtue of fictionality.[84]

Wieland's debt to Bodmer and Breitinger has often been acknowledged, especially as it affected his general views on art and poetry and his work in genres other than the novel. How aesthetic innovations like theirs also pertain to his prose, though, is a question that has sparked disagreement. He is said to have conceived of art less as imitation than as imagination, as something creating reality rather than imitating nature, an attitude that at once harks back to Bodmer's and Breitinger's poetics and looks forward to the concept of aesthetic autonomy favored during German classicism and romanticism.[85] Indeed, his novels have been hailed as the turning point in the emancipation of artistic *Phantasie* since they show reality to result from subjective imagination, though they also give mimetic accounts of its intellectual products.[86] His novels also seem prime examples of rhetorical *imitatio*, and his conception of fiction appears to require writing according to rules.[87] While his fairy tales and verse epics give freer reign to fancy and the marvelous, however, his artful mix of irony and illusion transcends specific genres.[88] What is more, his narration can be studied in those tales and epics, and tension between fictional facts and characters' consciousness found in his verse is also at work in his novels.[89] The playful attitude that he takes toward fiction in his tales, moreover, has been called symptomatic of the shift from enmity to irony that occurred as awareness of fictionality increased in the eighteenth century.[90] His comic poems similarly are said to convey irony that shatters his fiction and keeps his readers conscious of it and that parodies yet also justifies narrative fancy.[91] The marvelous in his novels likewise appears both confined to characters' subjective views and meant to protect them from the leveling clutches of reason,[92] and his gift for describing it has seemed to belie his own enlightened principles.[93] That he uses creative writing to criticize flighty imagination has seemed a fatal paradox, in fact, and he is said to have abandoned his Swiss mentors and embraced an empirical poetics.[94] Similarly, that he turned to writing novels has suggested that he came to regard reality along the lines of the natural sciences.[95] Nonetheless, the forms that poetic fantasy takes in his work make him seem a precursor of romanticism,[96] and his narrative skill is said to have raised readers' consciousness of fiction as an art form, as do his own introductions to his novels, where he often makes a show of citing purely fictional sources.[97] Eighteenth-century novels like his accordingly suggest the psychological and social effects of fictional, other realities.[98]

Similar differences of opinion mark the few previous studies that treat more than one or two of Wieland's novels. These studies seldom mention fictionality as such, though their authors occasionally imply its significance. Heinrich Vormweg has considered Wieland's narrative treatment of time, a topic related to the present study only insofar as his novels reveal levels of human existence less transient than plot in dialogue constructed to obscure its own fictionalness (*Fiktionshaftigkeit*).[99] Gerd Matthecka has examined the precursors and principles of Wieland's theory of the novel, explaining how his personal narrators disappear in his later novels, which are related more directly, yet no less subjectively, by characters who communicate in dialogues and letters. Matthecka thus demonstrates a logical development and a unity of form and content in Wieland's writing, linking its aesthetics and epistemology, but also observing that he "capitulated" when faced with contradictions between ideals and reality.[100] Jürgen Jacobs has praised Wieland's novels as civilizing influences, finding their fictionality exposed in an ironic game played with readers whose manners and social graces he tried to refine.[101] Jan-Dirk Müller has studied the narration and narrated reality of Wieland's last three novels, which he reads as fiction rather than philosophy, seeing in their subjectivity and ironic attitude toward anything supernatural an attempt to transcend the limits of reason while remaining within them.[102] Finally, John McCarthy has demonstrated the interplay of fantasy and reality in three of Wieland's novels, illuminating the intuitive aspect of his epistemology and the lofty enthusiasm of his heroes, complex subjects that his narrative style conveys.[103] In spite of McCarthy's insight that Wieland therefore resembles some German romantics, the idea that he embraced empiricism persists in a more recent study of "fictional readers" in his novels.[104] While some studies suggest the power of fiction itself in those novels, then, others limit it to an ancillary role in Wieland's life. By broadly applying the concept of fictionality, one can resolve such disputes.

The historical and scholarly moment of fictionality in Wieland's novels would thus seem obvious, but it remains to be fully explained. To be sure, some mention of fictionality is made in studies limited to only one or two of those novels. Such studies will be quoted below, whenever appropriate. Its recurring urgency in all of them, however, requires taking a longer and more inclusive view. His treatment of it does not consist of merely playful irony, resigned aestheticism, or hope that falls short of philosophical rigor, as one can read in remarks by literary scholars who—oddly enough—appear hostile to fiction themselves. Instead, he makes coherent statements and uses consistent techniques that help suggest its larger ramifications. Some of the foregoing comments on the concept of fictionality help put his novels in such challenging perspectives. The theoretical and epistemological kind of approach taken by Matthecka and McCarthy also seems worth pursuing. According to McCarthy, the fictional reality shown in Wieland's novels is a "mixture of fantasy and reality, just as each individual perception of the world is an intermingling of the two."[105] Current research on fictionality helps explain such narrative facts. Jan-Dirk Müller, moreover, writes that Wieland betrays his oblique idealism by drawing analogies between events described in his novels and art.[106] This insight will likewise be developed in the chapters that follow, which examine how his thoughts on fictionality often emerge in passages about painting, sculpture, music, and the theater. Those thoughts confirm what Michael Beddow has written about *Agathon* as well as other *Bildungsromane*: "The narrative of the hero's experiences, *precisely insofar as we perceive it to be a piece of fiction*, offers insights into human nature which could not be adequately conveyed either in the form of discursive arguments or through a rigorously mimetic, non-self-conscious fictional work."[107] Offering further insights thus sharpened by an awareness of fiction itself, Wieland's other novels, too, show why they need to be understood in such general terms of fictionality.

IV

The forms that the concept of fictionality takes in those several novels, as well as the consequences that they all imply it has, are also suggested by three of Wieland's essays: "Unterredungen mit dem Pfarrer von ***" (1775), "Über die Ideale der Griechischen Künstler" (1777), and "Versuch über das deutsche Singspiel" (1775). He initially published all three under slightly different titles in his *Der teutsche Merkur* (1773– 1810), one of the most successful literary journals in eighteenth-century Germany. Wieland also wrote many other essays on philosophical, literary, and political topics, of course, showing himself to be not only a consummate stylist but also an astute observer of current events, especially of the French Revolution. His essays on literary matters include "Briefe an einen jungen Dichter" (1782–84), which discusses poetic gifts such as a vivid imagination as well as the often strained relationship between poets and their readers, and "Über die Rechte und Pflichten der Schriftsteller" (1785), which argues that political reporting should be truthful and impartial, and that authors should enjoy freedom of the press. The former essay has been called a major document in German literary history, though Wieland had already raised some of its subjects in an earlier lecture titled "Theorie und Geschichte der Red-Kunst und Dicht-Kunst" (1757).[108] These treatments of poets and authors from a sociological angle, moreover, attest to Wieland's didactic concern with his audience. As McCarthy has observed, "An acute awareness of the need to teach readers how to read via the writing process itself permeates all of Wieland's journalistic and essayistic writing."[109] The three essays cited here help tell how this need to teach includes refining common notions of fictionality, and they do so in remarks on three issues associated with that concept in Wieland's novels: imagination, ideals, and illusion.

Imagination is paramount in "Unterredungen mit dem Pfarrer von ***," which examines it from readers' as well as authors' standpoints. The essay specifically defends Wieland against the charge that his salacious *Komische Erzählungen* (1765) undermined their readers' morals, but the ethical and aesthetic questions that it raises also pertain to his novels. Wieland poses such questions in two rambling conversations between a certain "W**," who apparently speaks for him, and an unnamed country parson who objects to all literature written without a clear moral purpose. Wieland thus submits himself to a test that W** calls an "Untersuchung der Güte und Nützlichkeit meiner Schriften" (30:435).[110] In the first of the two conversations, W** maintains that his writings are moral, claiming that he would have burned the *Komische Erzählungen*, had he known that their rococo eroticism would inflame some readers' imagination. He denies responsibility for all such ill effects, though, adding that neither those stories nor his heroic-comic poem "Idris" (1768) could harm the imagination of readers belonging to the beau monde, albeit he would not give either to his own daughters. The parson is dissatisfied with these dubious arguments, and he censures products of the imagination (*Einbildungskraft*) that he thinks would surely tempt even the coldest fancy (*Fantasie*). W** nonetheless excuses giving lewd descriptions as a fault easy to commit when one has an ardent imagination: "Wie leicht kann einem Dichter von warmer Einbildungskraft so etwas begegnen! . . . wie leicht kann eine lebhafte Einbildung mitten im Feuer der Komposizion den Dichter da oder dort ein wenig über die Grenzen der *Vorsichtigkeit* wegführen, womit moralische Schilderungen dieser Art verfertigt werden sollten!" (30:479–80). A poet's vivid imagination, that is, can inadvertently exceed the aesthetic limits imposed by a prudent sense of morality. Such reasoning notwithstanding, W** remains on the defensive, and he ends the first conversation by admitting that he and the parson have failed to solve tricky "aesthetic-moral" problems. Such problems result from fiction that seems more powerful than is good for its readers, who— like its authors—sometimes get carried away by their imagination.

Both the parson's moral qualms and W**'s self-defense recall a tradition of polemics surrounding the European novel, but W** also relies on notions of fiction that legitimate authorial imagination by limiting its scope. When absolving authors of blame for their readers' misinterpretations, he echoes Huet, who had defended them similarly over a century earlier.[111] He also explains their writing in terms borrowed from more recent research in the natural sciences, which he thinks such authors of fiction should emulate to describe characters true to real life. Indeed, he favors a taxonomic kind of fiction that requires showing people as they really are, rather than as some moralist would simply like them to be. True "historians" must even report events occurring in dissolute times and places, he adds, so as to make their readers better and wiser. Their writing itself is not at all immoral, though it must show causes and effects of characters' actions in detail sufficient to achieve its didactic purpose. Professing good intentions, W** thus defends the fictional kind of "history" related in novels like *Agathon*. In his second conversation with the parson, W** reinforces this defense of fiction, which he ties to recent developments in the European novel. The two men differ when they discuss what kind of fiction is morally most useful. The parson prefers Samuel Richardson's *Charles Grandison* (1753–54), but W** wants to describe people as they really are—"*wie sie sind*"—and therefore rejects such books, which he thinks show them merely as they should be—"*wie sie seyn sollten*" (30:491). Instead, he proposes Henry Fielding's *Tom Jones* (1749), which he regards as more realistic. When the parson objects that fictional figures must be good to improve readers' morals, moreover, W** answers that the effect of dubious ones is sometimes better, alluding to Claude Prosper Jolyot de

Crébillon's tale *Les égarements du coeur et de l'esprit* (1736), thereby confirming his faith in down-to-earth "historians." Such writers seem more useful to him than enthusiastic "Prometheuses," a name for the angry young men of German letters whose charges of moral laxness prompted Wieland to write this essay. The restrained imagination that it recommends is also less exalted than the irrational kind they liked.

The moral and aesthetic criteria of fiction noted by W** seem pertinent to Wieland's novels and suggestive for reading them as intersections of his own and his readers' imagination. Moral accusations have been leveled at those novels from many quarters. Nearly a century later, their racy scenes were faulted for being lewd and effeminate and offending the best minds of his day.[112] This low opinion was shared by the scholar J. G. Robertson, who wrote that Wieland appeared to approve of hedonism, thus revealing "the absence of . . . an ethical backbone" behind Wieland's "cynical delight in depicting the highest ideals and virtues succumbing to the charms of sensuality."[113] These moralistic criticisms show why Johann Heinrich Voß was not alone when he labeled Wieland's poems smutty *Buhlgesänge*.[114] Wieland tried to outflank such attacks by not relying on literary evidence alone. His W** draws support from the visual arts, too, defending William Hogarth's satirical portraits. This tactic underscores Wieland's similarity to Fielding, who likewise cited Hogarth to justify the "comic" prose of *Joseph Andrews* (1742). Wieland's parson says that illustrations (*Abbildungen*) like Fielding's advocated by W** are often caricatures that distort human nature and neither amuse nor instruct their readers. W**, too, objects to outright distortions of human nature, but he labels them "grotesques," and he reserves "caricature" for likenesses that are either recognizably true or only slightly exaggerated. His point is that Hogarth's drawings are accurate caricatures, not distorted grotesques, and that human nature—as shown by artists and writers alike—can be ugly yet true.[115] The parson has higher hopes for humanity, and he firmly rejects grotesques as products of a wild imagination, but he understands that W**'s defense of Hogarth applies to authors, too, and he goes home persuaded that readers themselves are to blame if they misconstrue fiction like W**'s. He thus sets a docile example for Wieland's real readers, but W** himself finds that the "aesthetic-moral problems" of their first conversation remain unsolved. W** also observes that artists like Hogarth involuntarily idealize their subjects, so his apology for comic fiction raises as many questions about imagination as it answers.

The stakes of the debate about human nature and artistic ideals staged in "Unterredungen mit dem Pfarrer von ***" are raised in "Über die Ideale der Griechischen Künstler." This second essay also treats imaginariness in terms more conducive to fictionality. W**'s defense of caricatures opposes the parson's observations on unflattering portraits by Hogarth that were reproduced in Johann Caspar Lavater's *Physiognomische Fragmente* (1775–78), and Wieland's remarks on Greek artists disagree with the enthusiasm for the ancient Greeks and their art that Lavater himself expresses in the fragment entitled "Über Ideale der Alten; schöne Natur; Nachahmung."[116] Echoing Johann Joachim Winckelmann's similar paeans, Lavater asks why the beauty of Greek sculpture surpasses that of all other art. His answer is simple: Either the ancient Greeks had far loftier ideals and imagined more perfect human beings than any other nation, or they lived in a nature itself more perfect than ever existed elsewhere. In other words, their artworks are either products of their own, nobler imagination or imitations of a nature itself much more beautiful then than now. Lavater emphatically embraces the latter explanation, calling Greek sculpture a faithful reproduction of human beings who outdid all others in beauty. Assuming that art naively mirrors nature, he reduces the activity of artists to a minimum, conceding that nature must inspire them for art to occur, but also insisting that their genius simply transforms ingredients given in its surroundings. Artists' ideals are merely the sum of their visual experience, then, and art cannot make nature more beautiful than it already is. Such statements reveal the empirical, Lockean definition of experience and imagination that underlies Lavater's views on art, aesthetic ideals, and the Greeks. Moreover, just as he saw in human faces visible evidence of hidden characteristics, outward proof of inner moral qualities, Lavater views art as a transparent sign of its sitter's physique and of physical traits typical of an entire civilization. His thinking is thus consistent with his dubious science of physiognomics.

Wieland disputes Lavater's idyllic view of the Greeks and disproves his notion that their art more or less slavishly mimicked nature. Wieland, too, admires the Greeks, but he argues that they were neither better nor more beautiful than eighteenth-century Europeans. The high ideals embodied in Greek art are therefore not copies of more perfect people or more beautiful nature, he writes, but poetic creations that never existed, except in artists' imagination. He knows that not all ancient Greek art was so abstract, but he thinks that the very best of it must have been: "Wenn ich also von den so genannten *Idealen* der Griechischen Künstler als *dichterischen* Werken oder Geschöpfen ihrer Imaginazion spreche, so ist meine Meinung: daß *einige* ihrer Werke *weder Kopien noch Karrikaturen der im Einzelnen sie umgebenden Natur* gewesen, sondern Nachbildungen von *Urbildern,* die *außer der Imagi-*

nazion des ersten Erfinders nirgends in der Natur *so* da gewesen; und von *diesen Werken allein* behaupte ich, daß sie einen Grad von Schönheit, oder Größe und Majestät gehabt haben, dessen kein einzelnes menschliches Wesen sich rühmen konnte" (24:148–49). Wieland does not deny that the Greeks and their artists both saw and made strong connections between art and nature, but he insists that nature can be no more than an occasion or a model for ideas embodied in artworks and that the source or archetype of such ideas is always imaginary. Thus stressing imagination instead of imitation, Wieland construes the relationship of art to nature more loosely than Lavater, refuting Lavater's simplistic concept of visual art along with his specious reasoning about the ancient Greeks. This stress on artistic creativity has led some scholars to see in Wieland's plea for imagination an aesthetic idealism also pertinent to his novels, but others are more reserved.[117] In two related essays—"Über eine Stelle des Cicero, die Perspectiv in den Werken der griechischen Mahler betreffend" (1774) and "Die Griechen hatten auch ihre Teniers und Ostaden" (1777)—he himself explains ancient portraits in technical terms and describes how the Greeks themselves sometimes tired of idealistic art.

Three points made in "Über die Ideale der Griechischen Künstler" leave no doubt, however, that the essay has larger aesthetic implications. First, Wieland argues that nature and art are not strictly opposed, since human subjectivity limits the perception of both: "Die *Natur*, von der diese ganze Zeit über die Rede war, ist ja wahrlich *nicht die Natur selbst*, sondern bloß die Natur, *wie sie sich in unsern Augen abspiegelt*—und dieß rückt Natur und Kunst um ein beträchtliches näher zusammen" (24:219–20). Nature itself, that is, can never be known immediately. Second, he explains that imagination—especially artists' and poets'—is obscure and unfathomable. One can never know the causes and forces at work in it: "Die *Imaginazion* eines jeden Menschenkindes, und die Imaginazion der *Dichter* und *Künstler* insonderheit, *ist eine dunkle Werkstatt geheimer Kräfte*, von denen das *Abc*buch, das man *Psychologie* nennt, gerade so viel erklären kann, als die Monadologie von den Ursachen der Vegetazion und der Fortpflanzung. Wir sehen Erscheinungen—Veranlassungen—Mittel—aber die wahren *Ursachen*, die *Kräfte* selbst, und *wie* sie im Verborgenen wirken,—über diesem allen hängt der heilige Schleier der Natur, den kein Sterblicher je aufgedeckt hat" (24:228–29). Third, Wieland respects modern artists, unlike Lavater, who dismisses them as hopelessly inferior. Finding the decisive factor in art to be imagination, not nature, Wieland thinks that modern artists might use their own to equal and even exceed the achievements of the ancients. He thus not only deflates

Lavater's Graecomania and its aesthetic corollary but also sees new possibilities for creating modern art. Such high regard for imagination hardly seems compatible, though, with the empirical kind of fiction that W** favors in "Unterredungen mit dem Pfarrer von ***." To be sure, Wieland defines many levels of Greek ideals, all less elevated than the one noted here. He nevertheless seems to allow modern visual artists greater conceptual liberties than their literary colleagues. Do his thoughts on nature and imagination therefore differ according to artistic medium?

Apparent contradictions between verisimilar writing and idealistic art seem resolved by Wieland's remarks on aesthetic illusion in "Versuch über das deutsche Singspiel." He wrote this third essay in the spirit of Christoph Willibald Gluck, who attempted to reform Italianate opera along the lines of ancient Greek drama. Gluck called for simplicity of expression and the unity of text and music, criteria established by his opera *Alceste* (1767). Wieland welcomes such reform, and his statements on German *Singspiele*—musical dramas with spoken dialogue, like Mozart's *Entführung aus dem Serail* (1782)—can be considered part of his literary aesthetics. After all, arguments for and against opera and novels were largely interchangeable in his day.[118] Gottsched dismissed opera as sheer nonsense, for example, an attitude that Wieland tries to change. He corrects the mistaken notion that opera seria is a kind of fairy tale, saying that its subjects do not need to be drawn from the realm of the marvelous. Like Bodmer, however, he recommends using the marvelous for aesthetic effect. The stories of Greek heroes seem foreign in *Singspiele*, he explains, and they excite "ein Gefühl des *Wunderbaren*" (26:264) that allows a modern audience to overlook the improbable fact that such heroes sing rather than speak on stage. Far from merely incredible, then, the marvelous can paradoxically help prevent the collapse of verisimilitude. Wieland himself tried to achieve such effects in collaboration with the composer Anton Schweitzer (1735–87). Following Gluck, he wrote the text for a *Singspiel* titled *Alceste*, which Schweitzer set to music and which was first performed at Weimar in 1773. Their effort, though short-lived and rather inconsequential, was widely acclaimed.[119] "Briefe an einen Freund über das deutsche Singspiel Alceste" (1773–74), in which he explains his deviations from Euripides, prompted Goethe's satiric *Götter, Helden und Wieland* (1774), moreover, but both authors sought to raise the *Singspiel* to a higher literary level.[120] Such links between music and literature confirm the appropriateness of "Versuch über das deutsche Singspiel" as a key to Wieland's novels.

Its significance for reading them lies in its stress on aesthetic illusion. Opera charms its listeners with pleasant *Täuschungen*, Wieland observes, illusions produced by musical and dramatic imitation. Such enchantment and the art that induces it are explained in the aesthetic contract that he describes when noting how authors, actors, and their audiences cooperate: "Jede Schauspielart setzt einen gewissen *bedingten Vertrag* des Dichters und Schauspielers mit den Zuschauern voraus. Die letztern gestehen jenen zu, daß sie sich, in so fern man ihnen nur wahre Natur . . . darstellen werde, durch nichts andres, was entweder eine nothwendige Bedingung der theatralischen Vorstellung ist, oder bloß des mehrern Vergnügens der Zuschauer wegen dabey eingeführt worden, in der Täuschung stören lassen wollen, welche jene Darstellung zu bewirken fähig ist" (26:247). Audiences thus accept certain theatrical conventions, submitting to an artistic illusion as long as it seems true to nature. Authors and actors do not expect their art to pass for nature itself, content instead with illusion that moves such audiences at decisive moments: "Wir verlangen nicht von euch, daß ihr poetische, musikalische und dramatische Nachahmung, und ein dadurch entstehendes *Ideal* für die *Natur selbst* halten sollt . . . Wenn wir es in gewissen entscheidenden Augenblicken bis zur Täuschung eurer Fantasie bringen, euer Herz erschüttern, eure Augen mit Thränen erfüllen,—so haben *wir* was wir wollten, und verlangen nichts mehr" (26:248). Authors and actors can thus create temporary illusion, which their audiences, too, recognize as such. What is more, their art can have greater effects than nature itself, according to the terms of Wieland's tacit aesthetic contract: "Das Singspiel setzt . . . einen stillschweigenden Vertrag zwischen der Kunst und dem Zuhörer voraus. Dieser weiß wohl, daß man ihn täuschen wird; aber er will sich täuschen lassen. Jene verlangt nicht für Natur gehalten zu werden; aber sie triumfiert, wenn sie mit ihrem Zauberstab noch größere und schönere Wirkungen hervorbringt als die Natur selbst" (26:260–61). People who listen to *Singspiele* want to be deceived, that is, and Wieland describes illusion induced by contractual catharsis.

Such illusion is an aesthetic state of mind also recommended by other eighteenth-century writers, and some of their remarks help us appreciate its import for reading Wieland's novels as studies of fictionality. To Bodmer and Breitinger, it meant temporary deception of the lower mental faculties, which caused the suppression of critical reflection. Wieland's emphasis on its emotional effect seems more reminiscent of Lessing, however, who once explained how a poet "deceives" an audience to touch and thereby teach it: "Er will uns täuschen, und durch die Täuschung rühren."[121] Discussing the performance of female roles by men as well as the truth and verisimilitude of works of art, moreover, Goethe liked self-conscious aesthetic illusion in the theater.[122] Likewise, Schiller famously urged readers of *Wallenstein* (1800) to thank his muse for openly destroying the kind created there, for an alienation effect—to use Brecht's term—that resulted from rhymed verse and that kept his art from being confused with literal, less serene truth:

> Ja danket ihrs, daß sie das düstre Bild
> Der Wahrheit in das heitre Reich der Kunst
> Hinüberspielt, die Täuschung, die sie schafft,
> Aufrichtig selbst zerstört und ihren Schein
> Der Wahrheit nicht betrüglich unterschiebt,
> Ernst ist das Leben, heiter ist die Kunst.[123]

Wieland's concept of *Täuschung* has psychological, didactic, and theatrical connotations, then, tied to the awareness of literary artifice that figures so often in recent discussions of fictionality. Indeed, the concept of aesthetic illusion has been called a result of thinking about the phenomenon of the fictional and fictive in art, and its mental causes and emotional effects are related in an account of his poetics.[124] Fictionality has also been equated with "aesthetic illusion as a production of senses of the real."[125] "Versuch über das deutsche Singspiel" thus is useful for reading Wieland in terms of fictionality implied by his contemporaries. Like "Unterredungen mit dem Pfarrer von ***" and "Über die Ideale der Griechischen Künstler," it raises an issue that often recurs in his novels, suggesting what they can teach us. Those novels themselves, however, reveal imagination, ideals, and illusion to be issues tied to fictionality considered not only as an aesthetic concept but also as an actual, literary way of life.

Part I. The Early Novels: Imagination

1. *Der Sieg der Natur über die Schwärmerey, oder die Abentheuer des Don Sylvio von Rosalva* (1764)

> *Were it needful, I cou'd put your Lordship in mind of*
> *an Eminent, Learned, and truly Christian Prelate*
> *you once knew, who cou'd have given you a full*
> *account of his Belief in* Fairys. *And this, methinks,*
> *may serve to make appear, how far an antient*
> *Poet's Faith might possibly have been rais'd,*
> *together with his Imagination.*
> —Shaftesbury, *A Letter Concerning Enthusiasm* (1708)

Imagination is the issue tied to fictionality most readily apparent in Wieland's first two novels, *Don Sylvio* and *Agathon*. It figures in the plot, the telling, and the suggested reception of both, a complex role clear from the actions as well as the attitudes of the characters, narrators, and readers who populate each. In part, the two texts share such a strong concern with imagination because Wieland's work on them overlapped. He started to write *Don Sylvio* in early 1763, a few months before signing a contract to publish *Agathon*, which he had begun at least two or three years earlier. He had not yet finished the latter, but his publisher Salomon Geßner had already accepted it, and religious censors in Zurich had seen enough of it to prohibit its scheduled appearance there. He failed to deliver the rest of his manuscript, though, so *Don Sylvio* was published first, in 1764, and not even a tentative version of *Agathon* came out until later, in 1766–67. More important than this coincidence of their composition is the thematic connection between these early novels. Like the essays on comic prose, artistic ideals, and opera in which Wieland discusses it, *Don Sylvio* and *Agathon* show imagination to be an ambiguous attribute, both a curse and a blessing, that turns out to be essential to readers as well as writers of fiction, even in the Enlightenment. The quixotic hero of *Don Sylvio* proves more serious than he seems, confusing life with fairy tales in ways that recall and rekindle historical debates about the marvelous and possible worlds. His vivid imagination also differs in degree, but not in kind, from that needed by Wieland's narrator and fictional readers. Some of the recent theoretical studies noted above, moreover, help clarify the remarks on fictionality made in prior research on his story. The two early novels differ insofar as *Don Sylvio* thus stresses the imagination of readers, while *Agathon* focuses more closely on that of writers, but this shift of emphasis simply indicates how well they augment each other. Taken together, in fact, they present imagination as an issue doubly bound to fictionality.

The plot of *Don Sylvio* is simple and entertaining. Wieland's protagonist is a pubescent Spanish nobleman who reads fairy tales with such a lively imagination that he seems silly and immature. Like Don Quixote, that is, his literary forebear, Don Sylvio overreacts to the everyday world because he experiences it according to fantastic fiction. Indeed, he is weaned on the same romances of chivalry that lead Cervantes's hero astray. He enjoys a childhood described as "romanhaft" (11:16–17), stands to inherit a considerable collection of "Ritterbüchern und Romanen" (11:9), and reaches adolescence guarded by a greedy aunt who tries to inculcate in him the chivalrous virtues praised in such books. Romances do not distract Don Sylvio as much as *Feenmärchen*, though, fairy tales that he secretly reads for amusement. Inspired by their stories of supernatural beings, he one day sets out in search of a blue butterfly but finds instead a small locket containing a pretty young woman's portrait. He mistakes her for a fairy princess in distress and—over the objections of the earthy Pedrillo, his Sancho Panza—decides that he must rescue her. After a series of mishaps and adventures showing how comically his reading conditions his behavior, he and Pedrillo stumble on Donna Felicia, a wealthy young widow who looks like the portrait that Don Sylvio worships, but Don Sylvio cannot understand that she herself is the object of his desire, rather than some marvelous princess. To set him straight, Donna Felicia's brother Don Gabriel tells him the "Geschichte des Prinzen Biribinker," a fairy tale so scurrilous and patently fictitious that it parodies both the *Feenmärchen* dear to Don Sylvio and his readiness to take them at face value. Made to see that those tales as well as his fantasies about them are merely the products of an extravagant imagination, Don Sylvio learns that real life differs from such literature, and after acquiring further polish on a long grand tour, he is able to marry Donna Felicia. *Don Sylvio* thus relates the excesses and ostensible cure of a reader of fiction who seems too gullible for his own good.

Closer reading, however, reveals Don Sylvio's story to be far more complicated than its straightforward plot suggests. To be sure, the cure effected in the end is said to show nature replacing imagination as his epistemological rule. Wieland's narrator writes approvingly of "die Natur, die ihre Rechte nie verliert, und am Ende doch allemahl den Sieg über die Einbildungskraft davon trägt" (12:42), and Don Sylvio himself finally comes to suspect that fancy might be the sole source of the marvelous, "daß die Fantasie vielleicht die einzige und wahre Mutter des *Wunderbaren* sey, welches er bisher, aus Unerfahrenheit, für *einen Theil der Natur selbst* gehalten" (12:306–7). The catalyst in this salutary process is Donna Felicia, whose obvious beauty dispels and displaces all thoughts of less tangible women. Don Sylvio grasps this fact, too, only long after the narrator has made it plain. Near the end of the novel, he finally understands how he feels about Donna Felicia and tells her how she has put out the fire of his fanatical imagination: "Was ich empfinde, seitdem ich Sie sehe, ist unendlich weit von den Schwärmereyen einer erhitzten Fantasie unterschieden. Ihr erster Anblick hat das ganze Feuer meiner Einbildungskraft ausgelöscht" (12: 317). The narrator much earlier gives this same sober summary of what went on in Don Sylvio's mind the first time he saw her: "Seine Einbildungskraft, unfähig etwas vollkommneres zu erstreben als was sich seinen Augen darstellte, wurde nun auf einmahl ihrer vorigen Macht beraubt, und diente zu nichts als den *Sieg der Empfindung* vollkommen zu machen" (12:45). The long delay between their respective insights results in much humorous irony, but the *Empfindung* that conquers Don Sylvio's imagination means "sentiment" as well as "sensation." Don Sylvio grows up to be a man of feeling, that is, one finally moved by socially sanctioned emotion. What is more, Donna Felicia turns out to be descended from the fictional hero Gil Blas. She thus has a literary lineage hinting that Don Sylvio's progress hardly extinguishes an imagination fueled by fiction, but rather refines and tempers it. Arguing only that he learns to be reasonable would therefore vastly oversimplify his story.

The close relationship between Don Sylvio's mature, "real" life and his naive belief in literary fiction has often been noted, and it has suggested that Wieland scorned the rationalistic concept of verisimilitude favored during the Enlightenment and accepted even by his own, more flexible Swiss mentors. *Don Sylvio* has seemed an ironic distortion of that concept, for example, for showing life imitating literature instead of the other way around.[1] Wieland's "soufflé" of fiction and reality has also cast doubt on the moral of his story: "Never . . . was a moral reprobation closer to the wrong-headed course of conduct which it was supposed to be correcting."[2] Wieland drives out the marvelous by dishing up more of the same, that is, an example of how his poetic practice seems at odds with his enlightened psychology.[3] He is similarly said to demonstrate Don Sylvio's confusion of reality and fantasy, yet also to concoct Donna Felicia's literary family tree, thus openly declaring even the "real" setting of *Don Sylvio* to be a literary fiction.[4] Accordingly, the novel is also regarded as an aesthetic-literary construct having its own autonomous, imaginative reality.[5] Indeed, the reality of fiction is said to be its poetological problem, its ironic account of the marvelous to characterize a "Kunstrealität" between the extremes of exaggerated imagination and the everyday world.[6] As McCarthy describes this ironic creation, a "real" world meant to be believed but revealed as fictitious, "The fictional reality (*Romanwirklichkeit*) in *Don Sylvio* is the simultaneous projection of the real and the imaginary in their polarity."[7] The presence of such complexity within the novel itself has also suggested a consciousness of fiction, if only as part of a superficial stylistic game,[8] but Wieland's irony has deeper meaning, given its historical import. It is said to oppose the notion of verisimilitude found in Enlightenment poetics, for example, to parody unpoetic "verisimilitude fanatics," and to defend the marvelous and the fantastic instead.[9] *Don Sylvio* has also seemed to show Wieland liberating himself from Bodmer by legitimating the marvelous.[10] His biographer Friedrich Sengle likewise comments on this rupture, calling Wieland's acknowledgment of the marvelous as subjectively real, albeit objectively chimerical, a sign of "rococo-romanticism."[11] At any rate, the "reality" of Don Sylvio's surroundings is not cut off from fiction, the fictive found in his fairy tales recurs at the end of his story, and he finds himself in the "reality of fiction."[12]

This literary dimension of Don Sylvio's story is especially clear when one observes his dealings with other characters. He is not the only one smitten by fiction, nor is he always as naive as he appears. His aunt is similarly well-read, displaying an "erstaunliche Belesenheit in Kroniken und Ritterbüchern" (11:9), not to mention Prince Biribinker's "hübsche Belesenheit in den Poeten" (12:198). Don Sylvio and Pedrillo often correct each other, moreover, each showing how the other confuses his reading with real life. Paradoxically, for example, Don Sylvio shows that he knows his Cervantes when he scolds Pedrillo for trying to tell him that trees are giants: "Ich glaube, zum Henker! du willst einen Don Quischot aus mir machen, und mich bereden Windmühlen für Riesen anzusehen?" (11:144). He also has sense enough to see that Pedrillo's imagination is spoiled, and he incisively links poetry and puppy love when Pedrillo mistakes Donna Felicia and her maid for fairies: "Du bekommst ja ganz poetische Einfälle! Was die Liebe nicht thut!" (11:280). He fails to see that this diagnosis also holds for himself, though, blinded by his romantic imagination, by "der romanhafte Schwung seiner Einbildungskraft" (11:321). Donna Felicia likewise shows a certain "romanhaften Schwung ihrer Fantasie" (11:234). In fact, her first marriage had been calculated to gain the wherewithal needed to lead a poetic life about as absurd as Don Sylvio's: "Die *Dichter* hatten in ihrem Gehirn ungefähr den nehmlichen Unfug angerichtet, wie die Feenmährchen im Kopf unsers Helden . . . Sie hatte sich den frostigen Armen eines so unpoetischen Liebhabers, als ein Ehemann von siebzig Jahren ist, aus keiner andern Absicht überlassen; als weil die Reichthümer, über welche sie in kurzem zu gebieten hoffte, sie in den Stand setzen würden, alle die angenehmen Entwürfe auszuführen, die sie sich von einer freyen und glücklichen Lebensart, nach den poetischen Begriffen, machte" (11:234). Donna Felicia was once a gold digger, then, who wanted to live according to poetic principles. Even the wife that Don Sylvio takes once he is supposedly cured thus models her life on literary whims, a circumstance confirming the fictionality of his surroundings.

Proof that this fictionality pervading his new world also has historical and theoretical implications lies in Don Sylvio's most direct encounter with Wieland's other characters: the group discussion that follows Don Gabriel's "Geschichte des Prinzen Biribinker." Far from merely making fun of acting as if fairies were real, and thus showing what Don Sylvio does wrong, Don Gabriel's satire also prompts serious debate about the aesthetics of fiction. A female listener who turns out to be Don Sylvio's long-lost sister Jacinte—and who, in the first edition of *Don Sylvio*, admits that she used to think and act like a fictional heroine herself—starts by saying that Don Gabriel intends to discredit her brother's belief in fairies: "Don Sylvio müßte gar zu gläubig seyn, wenn er nicht schon lange gesehen hätte, daß Ihre Absicht ist, die Feen um allen ihren Kredit bey ihm zu bringen" (12:278). Her own life, reminiscent of Richardson's *Pamela*,[13] casts such ideal creatures in a dubious light. Less strictly, her escort, Don Eugenio, replies that fairy tales lie beyond the pale of nature and therefore can be judged only by their own peculiar logic: "Das *Land der Feerey* liegt *außerhalb* der Grenzen der *Natur*, und wird nach seinen eigenen Gesetzen, oder richtiger zu sagen, . . . nach *gar keinen Gesetzen* regiert. Man kann ein Feenmährchen nur nach andern Feenmährchen beurtheilen" (12:278). Don Sylvio himself develops this second, lenient argument. When asked if he thinks the marvelous things mentioned in fairy tales to be both natural and possible, he answers that there must be more to nature than meets the eye: "Ohne Zweifel . . . wenn wir anders nicht den *unendlich kleinen Theil der Natur* den wir vor Augen haben, oder das was wir alle Tage sich zutragen sehen, *zum Maßstabe dessen was der Natur möglich ist machen wollen*" (12:283). This subtle reasoning recalls the claims for possible worlds made by Leibniz and his disciples. As noted above, Breitinger thought that poetry imitates nature not only in the real but also in the possible—in other words, nature not only as it appears in the actual world. Don Sylvio's remarks thus echo ontological defenses of the marvelous as the stuff of novels. Accordingly, even his silly antics seriously pertain to defining the concept of fictionality.

In the debate about "Biribinker," reason appears to carry the day when Don Gabriel announces that tales about spirits such as fairies should be presumed untrue, like everything else not corresponding to the normal course of nature or to human beings' customary experience. His skepticism seems extreme, however, when he tells why the possibility often accorded the marvelous cannot make it more than a chimera until its existence is proven beyond reasonable doubt: "Ob wir gleich allen den Wunderdingen, womit die Geschichtschreiber und die Dichter die Welt angefüllt haben, oder doch dem größten Theil davon eine *bedingte Möglichkeit* einräumen können: so sind sie doch darum nichts desto weniger bloße *Schimären*, so lange nicht bis zur Überzeugung der Vernunft erwiesen werden kann, daß sie wirklich existieren oder existiert haben" (12:287). Apparently ignorant of the concept of verisimilitude, Don Gabriel insists on being told the literal truth here. The phrase "bedingte Möglichkeit," however, recalls a passage about that concept in Gottsched's *Critische Dichtkunst*. Gottsched there defines two kinds of verisimilitude: "unconditional" (*unbedingt*) and "conditional" (*bedingt*). The latter, which he calls "hypothetical," too, can obtain even if the former, strictly speaking, does not.[14] This clause makes theoretical room for the talking animals found in Aesop's fables as well as for the trees that choose a king in a biblical parable (Judg. 9:8–15). While Gottsched rules out *contes des fées* like Don Sylvio's because the marvelous in them lacks allegorical meaning, his strict definition of verisimilitude thus allows some unlikely stories. Don Gabriel's granting the marvelous "bedingte Möglichkeit," then, alludes to fictional beings acceptable even to Gottsched. Not only does Don Eugenio observe that fairy tales have a logic all their own, thereby recalling the special "Logik der Vermuthungen" that Bodmer posited to account for the marvelous; not only does Don Sylvio unknowingly invoke the possible-worlds semantics first proposed by Leibniz; Don Gabriel also uses a term that denotes legitimately stretching the limits of verisimilitude beyond the empirical world. He has the last word on "Biribinker," but he overstates his case by sounding even more hostile to fictionality than Gottsched.

The debate about "Biribinker," then, as some previous studies suggest, is part of Wieland's ironic yet sympathetic commentary on fiction itself, the final chapter of a satirical fairy tale that leaves the genre consisting of other texts like it largely intact and thus hints at a preference for poetry over reason. It also displays considerable imagination. A playful attitude toward fiction was generally admired during the rococo, the irreal objects of fairy tales making that attitude particularly ironic, and the discrepancy between Wieland's frivolous storytelling and the moral lesson that Don Eugenio tries to draw being a witty parody of the usual *"rapport entre les maximes et le conte."*[15] *Don Sylvio* has also been thought to reveal the artifice of fairy tales, since it exposes both the purely poetic character of "Biribinker" and the absurdity of the genre.[16] Similarly, its interruption by the remarks of Don Sylvio's hosts pokes holes in the poetic illusion that it creates.[17] While Wieland thus seems to parody the fantastic and falsely marvelous, "Biribinker" also appears to debunk fairy tales only as Don Sylvio wrongly imagines them, not in general, and actually to express the freedom of poetic imagination.[18] Indeed, "Biribinker" has been called anything but a satire on fairy tales, and though Don Sylvio learns that it is absurd, he is said to possess traits of a poet and to "poeticize" the world.[19] By maintaining a critical distance between reality and fiction, moreover, "Biribinker" is said to keep the dialectic of the Enlightenment alive—to express skepticism about the Enlightenment itself.[20] In sum, the events and ensuing discussion of "Biribinker" expose as well as excuse what one could call its own fictionality. Mocking excessive faith in the marvelous by writing a fairy tale himself, Wieland hardly discredits such products of a poetic imagination. According to Julie von Bondeli, his onetime fiancée, the episode even attested to his own: "Die Episode von Biribinker macht Ihrer zügellosen Imagination Ehre."[21] Despite taking Don Sylvio's credulity ad absurdum, "Biribinker" reinforces such esteem for imagination. Like both the eccentric literacy of Wieland's other characters and their historically resonant debate, then, some prior research on this extravagant tale helps show why imagination and fictionality are so closely connected.

While both the thickening of Wieland's plot and "Geschichte des Prinzen Biribinker" link the concepts of fictionality and imagination, *Don Sylvio* also goes beyond the conclusions cited so far to explain their relationship. Its further ramifications become apparent when one pays closer attention to imagination on three related levels: those of Wieland's main character, his "authorial" narrator, and the readers whom the latter addresses. On the first, explanations given for Don Sylvio's reading habits show at once how wild his imagination is and why it can nonetheless be excused. Those habits are indeed extreme. His aunt likes his eagerness to act according to his reading, "die außerordentliche Begierde, wovon er brannte, den erhabnen Mustern *nachzuahmen,* von deren großen Thaten und Heldentugenden er bis zur Bezauberung entzückt war, und womit er seine Einbildungskraft so vertraut gemacht hatte, daß er sich endlich beredete, es würde ihm nicht mehr Mühe kosten sie *auszuüben,* als er brauchte sich eine *Vorstellung* davon zu machen" (11:12). In this desire to imitate the heroes whom he imagines, Don Sylvio resembles Don Quixote, and Wieland's narrator adds psychological observations accounting for their shared delusions of grandeur. Imagination and the marvelous are false, the narrator writes, but easily confused with feeling, nature, and truth: "Unvermerkt verwebt sich die *Einbildung* mit dem *Gefühl,* das *Wunderbare* mit dem *Natürlichen,* und das *Falsche* mit dem *Wahren*" (11:14). It therefore is understandable that Don Sylvio fails to distinguish merely fictional beings from those found in nature: "Seine Einbildung faßte also die schimärischen Wesen, die ihr die Dichter und Romanschreiber vorstellten, eben so auf, wie seine Sinne die Eindrücke der natürlichen Dinge aufgefaßt hatten" (11:14). Imagination thus takes the place of his senses, moreover, and Don Sylvio mistakes poetic fantasies for the real world: "Solcher Gestalt schob sich die *poetische* und *bezauberte Welt* in seinem Kopf an die Stelle der *wirklichen*" (11:15). Psychologically speaking, then, the narrator is sympathetic, explaining that Don Sylvio performs mental operations parallel to those of his senses, on fictional instead of actual phenomena.

Although Don Sylvio's imagination is presented simply as an instance of general psychological laws, its unusual liveliness in the case of fairy tales shows its specific force, which is quixotic but far from fatal. The narrator remarks that the enthusiasm fueling this imagination results from the same observation of nature that ought to prevent such excesses: "Die *Natur* selbst, deren anhaltende Beobachtung das sicherste *Mittel* gegen die Ausschweifungen der Schwärmerey ist, scheint auf der andern Seite durch die unmittelbaren Eindrücke, die ihr majestätisches Schauspiel auf unsere Seele macht, die *erste Quelle* derselben zu seyn" (11:15). Nature itself is thus the primary source of Don Sylvio's confusion, rather than being a fixed point of mental reference, and its ambiguity helps explain why he believes fairy tales. They, too, make a mixed and powerful impression: "Die Lebhaftigkeit, womit seine Einbildungskraft sich derselben bemächtigte, war außerordentlich: er las nicht, er sah, er hörte, er fühlte. Eine schönere und wundervollere Natur, als die er bisher gekannt hatte, schien sich vor ihm aufzuthun, und die Vermischung des Wunderbaren mit der Einfalt der Natur, welche der Karakter der meisten Spielwerke von dieser Gattung ist, wurde für ihn ein untrügliches Kennzeichen ihrer Wahrheit" (11:21). Far from pejorative, this description of avid reading hints that Don Sylvio is consistent in his own way. Given his circumstances and disposition, in fact, the narrator sees no reason why his hallucinations should not make sense to him, though they seem absurd to us. The narrator displays Don Sylvio for diagnosis, then, rather than simply expose him to ridicule, even when he takes imagination to extremes. Wieland sounds equally sympathetic in remarks on Don Quixote. In 1773, he overlooked the elder don's foolish chivalry, finding him otherwise just as admirable as any actual hero: "Don Quischotte war freilich ein Narr, was den Punkt der irrenden Ritterschaft anbetraf, aber seiner Narrheit ungeachtet, ein so edelmüthiger, frommer, und tugendhafter Mann, als irgend eine wahre Geschichte einen aufzuweisen hat."[22] Wieland added that few books deserve to be read as seriously and repeatedly as Cervantes's novel, and his, too, seems to have a hero whose imaginative folly does not make him frivolous.

With his favorable comments on Don Quixote, Wieland also takes sides in a literary battle waged beyond *Don Sylvio*. Gottsched and Bodmer were enemies in this struggle, and their respective, vastly different opinions of Cervantes's latter-day knight reinforce the theoretical import of Wieland's story. In the same paragraph of his *Critische Dichtkunst* that faults *contes des fées* for utterly lacking verisimilitude, Gottsched dismisses Don Quixote, too, calling him the model of a superstitious simpleton: "Die Welt ist nunmehro viel aufgeklärter, als vor etlichen Jahrhunderten, und nichts ist ein größeres Zeichen der Einfalt, als wenn man, wie ein andrer Don Quixote, alles, was geschieht, zu Zaubereyen machet."[23] Given the enlightenment that Gottsched here respects, a taste for the fiction that Don Sylvio reads so omnivorously seems atavistic. Indeed, Gottsched praises Cervantes for discrediting epics and romances exactly like those that Don Sylvio stands to inherit. Bodmer takes a different tone in the essay "Von dem Charakter des Don Quixote und des Sancho Pansa," part of his *Critische Betrachtungen über die Poetischen Gemählde der Dichter* (1741). Distinguishing *Don Quixote* from earlier romances, he explains that reading it requires seeing things from its protagonist's point of view: "In den Romanzen bezieht das Wahrscheinliche sich unmittelbar auf den Leser . . . ; in Cervantes Roman bezieht dasselbe sich alleine auf Don Quixoten, und es muß von uns so betrachtet werden, wie es ihm vorkömmt; es hat keinen mehrern Grad der Wahrheit nöthig, als was in dem Gesichtspunct des Ritters ein solcher ist."[24] Like the narrator in *Don Sylvio*, Bodmer here relates verisimilitude to a fictional hero's psychology. Don

Quixote is a sophomoric combination of foolishness and wisdom, he explains, and by understanding both human nature and Cervantes's art, readers should judge him marvelous but within acceptable limits of verisimilitude. Don Quixote's logic is strange, but it is consistent, and he finds sufficient reason for the truth of his adventures in his skewed imagination. Bodmer regards Cervantes's don as a psychological case study, then, showing greater insight and tolerance than Gottsched.

By explaining Don Sylvio's reading habits and excusing his behavior in much the same way that Bodmer defends Don Quixote, Wieland's narrator recalls the wider reevaluation of Cervantes's novel that occurred during the eighteenth century. This shift has been linked to Fielding's *David Simple* (1744), which describes Don Quixote as being "at once amiable, ridiculous, and natural," no longer a comic fool but rather a humorous representative of human nature.[25] Bodmer's similar rehabilitation of the don has been linked to Wieland's vision of humanity in *Don Sylvio* and to the conflict between imagination and reason that permeates his other works as well.[26] Given such larger implications, it seems strange that *Don Sylvio* was once considered a superficial imitation of Cervantes's masterpiece.[27] More recent studies argue that Wieland's opposition of fantasy to sentiment differs from Cervantes's antithesis of fantasy and reality, that is, the assertion of such sentiment from the preponderance of actuality, a distinction that matters since it concerns the motivation for illusionistic fictions and their narrative justification, which has seemed to be Wieland's aesthetic task and accomplishment in the novel.[28] The experience of fictional literature in *Don Sylvio* has likewise seemed both a psychological and a poetological problem that makes Wieland's ostensible satire a legitimation of fairy tales and of the fantastic and thus a forerunner of romanticism as well as a work in the style of *Don Quixote*.[29] Regarded as a scion of Don Quixote, then, Don Sylvio has signaled increased tolerance for ignoring the fictionality of what one reads. Indeed, he learns to take his fairy tales with the proverbial grain of salt, but by ending up in a "real" world derived from romances of chivalry, he has simply passed from one sort of fictional realm to another, returning to the relatively realistic kind of place described by Cervantes, too.[30] His maturation thus involves a difference of degree, a distinction between more and less credible genres of fiction. Don Quixote, it has been written, "represents for Wieland the kind of ambiguity in a hero which he himself strives to present. His heroes suffer from differing degrees of quixotic follies but are, nonetheless, good."[31] With his extreme but excusable imagination,

Don Sylvio is ambiguously quixotic indeed, apparently a fool who is more respectable than not.

Don Sylvio associates the concepts of fictionality and imagination not only by making its title character's fantasies seem understandable but also by revealing the attitude that its narrator takes toward reality and writing. In spite of his professed dislike for remarks *ad spectatores*, the narrator constantly comments on his story. He often sounds ironic, as when he explains why modern readers doubt the marvelous. Tongue in cheek, he bemoans the fact that magnifying glasses have made it difficult to believe in invisible spirits: "Seit der Erfindung der Vergrößerungsgläser haben die *unsichtbaren Dinge* ein böses Spiel, und man braucht nur ein *Geist* zu seyn, um alle Mühe von der Welt zu haben, die Leute von seinem Daseyn zu überzeugen" (11:83). This nod to science notwithstanding, he sounds sincere when he adds that there exists a dual reality, "eine zweyfache Art von Wirklichkeit" (11:84). He means that things can be either material or mental—either objective or subjective, that is—and that the latter have equally strong effects and usually motivate humankind, for better and for worse: "So wie es nehmlich, allen *Egoisten* zu Trotz, Dinge giebt die wirklich *außer* uns sind, so giebt es andre die bloß *in unserm Gehirn* existiren. Die erstern sind, wenn wir gleich nicht wissen daß sie sind; die andern sind nur, in so fern wir uns einbilden daß sie seyen. Sie sind *für sich selbst—nichts*; aber sie machen auf denjenigen, der sie für wirklich hält, die nehmlichen Eindrücke, als ob sie *etwas* wären; und ohne daß die Menschen sich deswegen weniger dünken, sind sie die Triebfedern der meisten Handlungen des menschlichen Geschlechts, die Quelle unsrer Glückseligkeit und unsers Elends, unsrer schändlichsten Laster und unsrer glänzendsten Tugenden" (11:85). This ontological insight helps explain Don Sylvio's strong reaction to fairy tales, so it is no surprise that the narrator writes favorably of chivalric romances, too, which he thinks infinitely more useful than tasteless and immoral "*Romans du Jour*" (11:10–11 n. 1). Like the literariness of "real" life in *Don Sylvio*, the narrator recommends one genre of fiction over another here, rejecting fashionable pulp for an older, lesser evil and later defending the subjective validity of "things" such as its fictional referents.

That the narrator respects subjective imagination and literary fiction is also apparent from his statements about his own writing. Comparing *Don Sylvio* and its hero to other fairy tales and theirs, he admits that it, too, is strange and marvelous, but he is serious about its verisimilitude, insisting that his story corresponds to the usual course of nature and relates events that happen all the time, or at least could: "Aber ungeachtet unsre Geschichte so seltsam und wunderbar ist . . . so wird man uns doch nicht vorwerfen können, daß wir unserm Helden jemahls ein Abenteuer aufstoßen lassen, welches nicht vollkommen mit dem ordentlichen Laufe der Natur übereinstimmte, und dergleichen nicht alle Tage sich zu ereignen pflegen oder sich doch ereignen könnten" (12:6). In this sense, Don Sylvio's story is truthful as well as credible, better than narratives by "historians" who misleadingly embellish their reports or add a touch of the marvelous. Indeed, the narrator claims to make it known not for the sake of empty entertainment, but rather for the common good and his readers' well-being of body and soul: "Wir wünschten, daß man von vielen berühmten Geschichtschreibern mit eben so gutem Fuge sagen könnte, daß sie von der betrügerischen Neigung, ihre Gemählde und Karakter zu *verschönern*, oder ihren Begebenheiten einen Firniß vom Wunderbaren zu geben, so entfernt gewesen seyn möchten als wir, die wir uns bey der Bekanntmachung dieser wahrhaften und glaubwürdigen Geschichte nicht etwa . . . eine eitle Belustigung, sondern das gemeine Beste, und die Beförderung der Gesundheit unsrer geliebten Leser an Leib und Gemüthe zum Endzweck vorgesetzt haben" (12:7). The narrator confesses that *Don Sylvio* is made of whole cloth, then, but stresses both its verisimilitude and its therapeutic effect. The novel is made up, in other words, but the marvelous is confined to Don Sylvio's fantasies, which Wieland's narrator rationally explains. Indeed, the latter's asides contain logical reasons for all that Don Sylvio does, thereby demonstrating the sense of Wieland's subtitle, which announces that everything in *Don Sylvio* occurs naturally. A rational romancer, Wieland thus has his cake and eats it, too.

The narrator's remarks on writing and reality also imply a parallel between his own storytelling and Don Sylvio's fantasies. Just as those fantasies are purely subjective yet persuasively real, his story about them is invented but truthful. Broadly speaking, both are fictions. The narrator knows what he is doing, conscious of his art, of course, but he, too, turns out a product of literary imagination. The difference between him and Don Sylvio thus involves their respective senses of fictionality, and is one of degree, not kind. Some previous studies help show why his style and attitude lend *Don Sylvio* this literary depth. The "skilful application of the technique of authorial intrusion used by Cervantes and Sterne" has been called Wieland's most striking achievement in the novel, and this same technique has made the narrator seem its focal point.[32] Indeed, he has been said to dominate its story and be its liveliest character, one who is subjective himself but possesses superior rationality.[33] His subjective, playful treatment of fiction has been called an explicit psychological concern of Wieland's novel, moreover, and such supplemental activity has seemed to detach *Don Sylvio* from a genre of narrative discourse to which it nonetheless belongs.[34] Wolfgang Preisendanz has even noted a dialectic of the narrator's subjectivity and Don Sylvio's, proof that the problem of imagination in the novel extends to all kinds of alternative realities.[35] Footnotes added to the second edition of *Don Sylvio*, which appeared in 1772, reinforce this relationship between Wieland's narrator and title character, for the narrator there displays no mean knowledge of fairy tales himself. His storytelling is also tied to Don Sylvio's visions at the very end of his tale: "Wir haben nunmehr . . . die Geschichte unsers Helden bis zu einem Zeitpunkte fortgeführt, wo sie aufhört *wunderbar* zu seyn, oder, welches eben so viel ist, wo sie in den ordentlichen und allgemeinen Weg der menschlichen Begebenheiten einzuschlagen anfängt, und also aufhört zu den Absichten geschickt zu seyn, welche wir uns in diesem Werke vorgesetzt haben" (12:338). As soon as Don Sylvio's story stops being marvelous, it no longer interests the narrator. In one sense, this is because no error remains to be explained; in another, though, the narrator implies that ordinary events are not worth his while. Like the extensive footnotes, his intentions thus suggest a penchant for fiction parallel to Don Sylvio's.

Those intentions may also be inferred from Wieland's correspondence, which helps show how his novel legitimates imagination. It provided comic relief as well as financial support during difficult years for him, and he often noted that it was meant to make people laugh. He wanted it published because he needed money, describing its origin as a "débauche d'esprit" that took his mind off trouble given him by fellow senators at home in provincial Biberach and by those of its citizens who disliked his having an affair with a local girl.[36] He also expected friends to be surprised that he could write such an entertaining book amid such trying circumstances and told his publishers that heartfelt laughter was its true purpose. Like "Biribinker," it would make the wise as well as the foolish laugh, he thought, though he also hinted at philosophical substance beneath its frivolous surface, at a critique of enthusiasm (*Schwärmerei*) and superstition. He noted that those two states of mind are part of human nature and that each has beneficial effects, but that the extremes of both have always been ridiculed, this being his own intention as well: "Der Scherz und die Ironie sind nebst dem ordentlichen Gebrauch der fünf Sinne immer für das beste Mittel gegen die Ausschweifungen von beiden angesehen worden; und in dieser Intention ist . . . die Geschichte des Don Silvio geschrieben."[37] Wieland also calls Don Sylvio an honest fantast, though, so the laughter recommended by him must have been gentle and not aimed too directly at his hero's sincere reveries. His remarks on enthusiasm recall Locke and Shaftesbury, moreover, who likewise explained its powerful, even noble effects. In an essay that McCarthy links to Shaftesbury's *Letter Concerning Enthusiasm* (1708), a similar "apology against narrow enlighteners," Wieland also distinguished *Enthusiasmus* from *Schwärmerei*.[38] What is more, Don Sylvio's *Schwärmerei* has been said to save him from his spinster aunt, who tries to marry him off to a hideous but well-heeled girl whose uncle would then satisfy the aunt's own desire to be coupled. Without that inspiration, he would be defenseless against her economic and erotic greed.[39] Similarly, his belief in fairy tales has seemed worthwhile for helping him find happiness in true love.[40] For both Don Sylvio and his author, then, such imaginary "debauchery" seems a saving grace.

Wieland's subtle legitimation of fictions and imagination in Don Sylvio's psyche as well as his narrator's storytelling is buttressed by efforts made to ensure that it holds for his readers' responses. Consider such readers' role in the elaborate *Quellenfiktion*, the account of Wieland's bogus source appended to the first edition of the novel but omitted in its second of 1772 and third of 1795, the last published as part of his *Sämmtliche Werke*. As in *Don Quixote*, his narrator claims to edit a manuscript actually written by someone else, here a "Don Ramiro von Z***," then translated and copied before coming into his possession. The narrator knows that this account of his source might sound hard to believe, and he invites readers to doubt his own confidence in it: "Ich muß es dem guten Willen der Leser überlassen, ob sie glauben wollen oder nicht, daß dieses Buch den Don Ramiro von Z*** . . . zum Verfasser habe. Ich meines Orts gestehe, daß ich die spanische Handschrift nicht selbst in Händen gehabt; allein mein Freund, der Herr Uebersetzer, erzählt mir . . . eine so umständliche und wohlzusammen hängende Geschichte der besagten Handschrift und ihrer seltsamen Schicksale, . . . daß ich mir die Mühe nicht geben mag, an der Wahrheit seiner Erzählung zu zweifeln."[41] The truth of his tale thus left up in the air, albeit implied by the seeming coherence of its transmission, the narrator likewise lets his readers themselves decide how they will react to it—with laughter, smiles, scorn, derision, or tears. Nonetheless, he recounts how he, his wife, and their domestic servants all laugh out loud at *Don Sylvio*. Even passersby on the street notice such infectious laughter, which thus seems the response suggested to Wieland's actual readers as well. These humorous and explicit details seem meant to overcome objections that the novel is a satire on religion, a logical implication of Don Sylvio's *Schwärmerei*. One cleric quoted in the *Quellen-*

fiktion condemns it as a godless and dangerous book, but another reverses such censure, remarking that the book is meant to amuse its readers and thereby seconding Wieland's own opinion. Stressing skeptical lightheartedness, his account of the phony source of *Don Sylvio* thus spurs actual readers to enjoy it—as a literary fiction.

That Wieland encourages laughter and allays religious fears so that his fiction might be appreciated as such also seems likely since his letters mention "austere" readers sure to dislike *Don Sylvio* and wise ones whom "Biribinker" did not scandalize. The former would fail to find the novel amusing, it seems, because they lacked the imagination needed to read it properly. Comments later in the novel make plain this shortage and try to relieve its cause. The narrator knows that society would benefit from humorous writings, books that tell the truth with a smile and that he recommends instead of earnest, moralistic ones that simply bore their readers. As in "Unterredungen mit dem Pfarrer von ***," this plea for a little levity involves caricatures modeled on visual art. The narrator does not cite Hogarth here (though Wieland once did so in a letter referring to "Biribinker"),"[42] but in a chapter titled "Ein Gemählde in Ostadischem Geschmack"—an allusion to the Dutch genre painter Adriaen van Ostade (1610–85)—he gives an unflattering, graphic description of Don Sylvio's ghastly fiancée. While listing her misshapen charms, he expressly tries to make his readers imagine her: "Wir wollen einen Versuch wagen, ob wir die Einbildungskraft unsrer Leser in den Stand setzen können, sich einige Vorstellung von ihr zu machen" (11:97). Having compared the effect of the more comely Donna Felicia to the electric current caused by a magnetic field, the narrator likewise urges his readers to take this analogy as far as they like: "Wir überlassen es dem Scharfsinne des geneigten Lesers, die Allegorie so weit zu treiben als er will, oder als sie gehen kann" (12:74). Such encouragement lessens the irony apparent in passages such as the narrator's advice to readers who might reject his sober explanations of Don Sylvio's visions, to fans of the marvelous inclined to trust Don Sylvio himself when he explains what he saw in person. Although the narrator ridicules excessive faith in the marvelous, he leaves even this "allegory" entirely up to his readers. Here, too, they must decide what to make of his story. So often invited just to imagine its humorous scenes and characters, they are repeatedly urged to use their own imagination, and they seem meant to do so wisely but also more liberally than not.

Prior research on readers in and of *Don Sylvio* confirms that both seem meant to play an active role in its interpretation, though most attempts to describe their relationship—the connection of fictional to actual readers—also reveal disagreement. As is clear from its *Quellen-fiktion*, the effect of the novel on fictive readers sets an example for real ones.[43] The effect of this example itself, however, has seemed debatable. According to some, it makes actual readers aware of their own *Schwärmerei*.[44] Like Don Sylvio, that is, such readers should be disillusioned, disenchanted, and become more sober.[45] On this view, the narrator's concern is "the education of his reader to a correct perception of reality," a process that involves developing such readers' reason.[46] To others, this process seems more complex. The narrator has received high marks for being sensitive to different kinds of readers, for example, and for letting them decide for themselves what to believe.[47] Similarly, *Don Sylvio* is said to destroy readers' reasons for naively identifying with literary fiction and to teach them to be more distanced and conscious of their role in constituting it.[48] They are expected at once to recognize the excessive enthusiast in Don Sylvio and to submit to his author's more controlled fantasies, suspending their disbelief and agreeing to play along in his game of fiction.[49] W. Daniel Wilson has made this argument most trenchantly. For him, *Don Sylvio* is a "book about reading, about scepticism and aesthetic illusion, and it forces us to examine our own behaviour as readers."[50] Accordingly, the novel is both a satire of gullible readers who cannot tell fact from fiction and itself too blatantly fictional to be mistaken for satire alone. In this complex sense, Wilson explains that "Wieland's intention . . . was to *train* his readers to read properly," that is, to understand that *Don Sylvio* justifies *Schwärmerei* and the reality of fiction, not in the sense of rationalistic verisimilitude but rather in that of romantic aestheticism.[51] As shown above, Wieland's fictional source and narrator reinforce such training by inspiring readers' imagination. It thus seems no coincidence that Wilson often notes the self-conscious fictiveness of *Don Sylvio*.

One can only speculate about the effect that the novel has had on most of its actual readers, of course, but reactions to its initial publication show why Wieland was so concerned with educating them in the ways of fiction. Even though it met with general approval, few reviewers seem to have fathomed its aesthetic import. The *Göttingsche Anzeigen von Gelehrten Sachen* regretted that it had not appeared forty years earlier, when fairy tales had enjoyed their greatest vogue, and that its author had simply copied Cervantes.[52] Similarly, one Swiss journal lamented that its apt ridicule of fanatics suffered from being mixed with indecent and immodest episodes that no respectable reader could approve, "*les Contes indecens . . . et les Situations plus qu'immodestes qui gatent son ouvrage et qui ne seront approuvés ni des* honnêtes-gens ni de ceux qui respectent les moeurs."[53] Wieland felt that this suggestion of impropriety ignored his satire, but others saw satire everywhere they looked. The *Erlangsche gelehrte Anmerkungen und Nachrichten* called *Don Sylvio* a satire on the female sex, its childish admirers, national governments, and articles of faith, too, wondering why wit so often disparaged religion.[54] Writing in the *Allgemeine deutsche Bibliothek*, Thomas Abbt gave a better appraisal of Wieland's motive for showing how a person could rise to the height of folly: "Der Verfasser . . . scheint auch Philosoph genug zu seyn, um sich in den Un-sinn eines schwachen Kopfes hinein zu denken, damit er ihn nachher vernünftig behandeln könne."[55] None of these reviews, though, hints at the importance of imagination obvious on the several levels of *Don Sylvio* examined here. Not until twenty years later did such a review appear—in *Le cabinet des fées*, a Swiss collection of fairy tales including a French translation of *Don Sylvio*. The novel, it says, shows how such fiction can be enjoyed without misleading one's imagination: "Le ro-man de don Silvio . . . apprend aux jeunes personnes qui lisent ces sortes d'ouvrages, dans quel esprit elles doivent les lire, & comment elles peuvent s'en amuser, sans égarer leur imagination."[56] *Don Sylvio* does indeed seem at least intended to be read in such a sanely imagina-tive spirit.

The issue of fictionality is illuminated, then, by being closely linked to that of imagination, not only in Wieland's ironically intertextual plot and the theoretically informed discussion of "Biribinker," but also in the actions and attitudes attributed to his title character, narrator, and readers. Recognizing this pervasiveness helps one pursue that issue be-yond prior research on *Don Sylvio*. Such research seldom mentions fictionality as such, though a few studies do suggest its significance. It has been noted that even in Wieland's day there could be no doubt about the fictionality of Don Sylvio's fairy tales, that his fellow charac-ters are of one mind about their fictivity, and that recognizing this same fictionality is the key to his disillusionment.[57] The narrator's account of Wieland's bogus source, moreover, is said to thematize the fictionality of both the events reported in *Don Sylvio* and their production.[58] Simi-larly, Donna Felicia's purely literary provenance is said to highlight the fictionality of all that Wieland describes, just as "Biribinker" does, demonstrating the novel to be a product of imagination and thus aes-thetically educating its readers.[59] Pedrillo's speeches are also marked by many humorous slips of the tongue, and such malapropisms have been said to stress "the fictionality of the invented realm" by altering details of Don Sylvio's world of fairy tales.[60] Friction between the two characters' points of view and their differing kinds of imagination thus not only has harmless and comical effects, but also advocates tolerance by showing unavoidable subjectivity and the relativity of judgment.[61] Finally, as noted above, Wilson cites the self-conscious fictiveness of *Don Sylvio*, stressing its "emphasis on its own fictionality" and the "tendency of the novel to point out its own fictiveness" as part of its narrative strategy.[62] Such examples of "fictive extravagance" indicate both the artificiality of such fiction itself and the ambiguity of Wieland's attitude toward illusion, not only in literature but also in life.[63] Previous remarks on fictionality in *Don Sylvio* thus suggest that it involves aesthetic and epistemological principles that apply to Wieland's characters, narrator, readers, and to Wieland himself. The emancipation of fiction in the novel has seemed related to his own needs, in fact, not just to the notion of aesthetic autonomy.[64] Indeed, his first biographer wrote that the novel concerns the Don Quixote that he thought he had been himself.[65]

Some of the theoretical work considered earlier helps put such remarks in an even broader perspective, for many of the issues raised in that work recur in *Don Sylvio*. Given that Wieland does not root out imagination once and for all, but only shows how Don Sylvio takes it to extremes avoided by both his narrator and ideal readers alike, his novel demonstrates the kind of differences between the erroneously fictitious and powerfully fictional, the vaguely imaginary and more concretely fictive, described by Iser and by Luiz Costa Lima. In other words, Wieland draws Kermode's distinction, noted above, between "indulgent mythologies of fancy" and "strict charities of the imagination," thus furnishing evidence of both the basic "dilemma of fiction and reality" and of the history of "antinovels."[66] In fact, from his narrator's fictional source to "Geschichte des Prinzen Biribinker," from Don Sylvio's avid reading to his ironic cure, Wieland delivers what now would be called "metafiction," probing the fictionality of the world along with that of a literary text. One recent theory claims that fictional, projected worlds can be true to only one person's point of view, a thought that might help explain Don Sylvio's subjective bliss.[67] Vaihinger's more comprehensive fictionalism suggests a less solipsistic interpretation, one tied to the locket that Don Sylvio finds. The portrait that it contains proves to be a likeness of Donna Felicia's grandmother, not of Donna Felicia herself. Although this portrait is a variation on a traditional literary motif,[68] it thus also works like Vaihinger's "as-if" fictions, heuristic constructs that do not directly match the actual world but nonetheless serve as pragmatic guides to it. Just as Vaihinger remarks that such fictions do not lose their validity when recognized as such, Don Sylvio attributes his happiness to the portrait, whose true sitter he learns in the end but that he still esteems for leading him to her descendant. In almost the same breath, he values his former belief in fairies, calling them products of imagination that prove beneficent because they inspired him to seek his heart's desire. He turns out to be a literary idealist, then, who openly professes serious fictionalism.

Regarded in current terms of fictionality, the triumph promised in the title of *Don Sylvio—Der Sieg der Natur über die Schwärmerey*—thus sounds ironic indeed. The trouble with Don Sylvio is his hyperactive imagination, which his story cures, but only in the sense of making it more seasoned, a refinement of more than just his simple overreaction to fictional literature. Wieland's problem in the novel has been thought to lie in defining the role, legitimacy, and function of imagination, in fact, and his mimetic account of Don Sylvio's fantastic but productive-synthetic kind has seemed to make the novel come alive.[69] *Don Sylvio* is also said to demonstrate both the productivity and the necessity of imagination, and Wieland's novels are likewise cited as proof that the Enlightenment did not lack imagination, despite rooting it in a moral realism: "The philosophes' attack on fancy was not an attack on imagination but on thought ungrounded in life."[70] One might even argue that *Don Sylvio* defends imagination by grounding fictionality in life. Wieland makes its hero's, its narrator's, and its readers' imagination an issue, treating the theme of figments and fabrication on several levels of his story. Not only does Don Sylvio end up in a fictional world strongly reminiscent of older romances; not only does "Biribinker" raise aesthetic questions that preoccupied Wieland's contemporaries; Don Sylvio's ravings are also presented as psychologically plausible, while the narrator relies on imagination himself, and Wieland's readers seem meant to suspend their disbelief. For these reasons, *Don Sylvio* is a classic study of fictionality. It poses basic questions about the existence, referents, and truth of fictions, textual and otherwise. Such questions are most often put in traditional literary terms, prompted by the fact that fictional characters, settings, and descriptions are made up, but the give and take apparent in the discussion of "Biribinker" also makes their fictionality seem a matter of consensus, something socially accepted rather than ontologically given. In this way, *Don Sylvio* introduces even larger issues of fictionality repeatedly raised—and much more problematically—in Wieland's subsequent novels.

2. *Geschichte des Agathon* (1766–1767)

It is the part of a poet to humour the imagination in its own notions, by mending and perfecting nature where he describes a reality, and by adding greater beauties than are put together in nature where he describes a fiction.
—Addison, "On the Pleasures of the Imagination" (1712)

As in *Don Sylvio*, the issue tied to fictionality most tellingly in *Agathon*, the next novel that Wieland published, is imagination not attuned to actual life. *Agathon* does not examine such imagination from the reader's point of view so humorously embodied in young Don Sylvio, however, but from the writer's so earnestly debated in the essay "Unterredungen mit dem Pfarrer von ***." In this novel, too, Wieland addresses the problem of identifying fictions as such and deciding both what they refer to and how they can be true, but he takes that problem more seriously. Like *Don Sylvio*, *Agathon* has "intertextual" links to other fictional literature that raise this problem indirectly. In the guise of another authorial editor, however, Wieland also poses it expressly, above all in opening remarks on verisimilitude, truth in fiction, and the existence of fictional characters, thereby sketching a theory of fictional "history" modeled on Fielding's *Tom Jones*. In the course of his story proper, he elaborates that theory in asides on his fictional source, on differences between sober *Geschichte* and fantastic *Romane*, and on many pleasures of the imagination enjoyed by both his characters and himself. Loath to accept ethics as prosaic as his style, though, Wieland envisions a didactic end at odds with his means. As a result, he contradicts his own narrative rules and ignores his own advice for writing convincing fiction. Indeed, he eventually recants his theory of *Geschichte* and redefines his initial notion of narrative veracity. The principles of Wieland's narration thus change along with the events that he describes. He, his narrator, and his hero all face the problem of fictionality, a problem broadly defined and then resolved quite differently in each of the three versions of *Agathon*: the first, fragmentary edition of 1766–67; the second, revised one of 1773; and the third, which he completed to open his *Sämmtliche Werke* in 1794. Far from the playful literariness that suffuses *Don Sylvio*, then, the sincere moral development shown in *Agathon* is only gradually acknowledged to be a matter of ethical fictionalism. Since it thus concerns fictionality not only as an attribute of purely literary entities and their narration but also as a property of moral ideals much like Kant's, this second novel stresses both halves of the term *Bildungsroman*.

As the etymology of its title character's name implies, *Agathon* tells the story of a young Greek "good" in the sense of "virtuous." He makes his way in a world that tests his skill at politics, shakes his faith in philosophy, and debunks his constancy in erotic clinches. Banished from ancient Athens by envious political rivals, he is captured by pirates and sold into slavery in Smyrna, where his sophistic master Hippias tries to convert him from his Platonic idealism to hedonistic enjoyment of life. Frustrated by Agathon's steadfastness, Hippias enlists the hetaera Danae to help seduce him. She eventually succeeds, though not without embracing Agathon's Platonism along with his handsome person. Advised of her profession, he soon abandons her, then vainly tries to reform the tyrant Dionysius in Syracuse. Badly disillusioned by such harsh experience, Agathon finally retires to the ideal republic of Tarentum, where Archytas, its sage ruler and his mentor, reveals to him the enlightened wisdom needed both to live virtuously and to govern well. Agathon thus learns to set the very example of virtue and wisdom promised in Wieland's subtitle, a passage taken from Horace's *Epistles*: "Quid *Virtus* et quid *Sapientia* possit / Utile proposuit nobis exemplum." Several subplots complicate this story line, which begins in medias res with Agathon's flight from Athens. Some—his early youth, the tale of his sister Psyche, and the travails of the generous but jilted Danae—emerge in narrative flashbacks, while others—the intrigues at Dionysius's court, for example—simply unfold as Agathon himself goes along. Considerable space is also taken up by debates on the ethical, political, and personal problems that he encounters. Major or minor, all of these episodes are subjected to close scrutiny by Wieland's narrator, who offers a running commentary on the moral lesson meant to be conveyed by his story itself. It has been noted that Wieland plays with well-worn motifs, elements of plot that had become clichés,[1] including devices borrowed from novels of antiquity as well as purple patches meant to parody outmoded romances.[2] At the level of plot, it is said, he corrects or rejects such fictional stereotypes to establish the truth of his own narration.[3] Indeed, one nineteenth-century reviewer wrote that he thereby rebuilt "rude and forgotten fabrics of fiction."[4] The twists and turns of his plot thus suggest theoretical problems raised by writing such literature.

The significance of Wieland's plot for reading *Agathon* as a study of such fiction itself is especially clear from its "intertextual" links to other literary works. One such work is Euripides' tragedy *Ion* (394 B.C.), which Wieland mentions in "Über das Historische im Agathon," a preface added to the second edition of the novel. His protagonist does not resemble the ancient tragedian named Agathon, he writes, despite their shared traits. The actual model for his fictional hero may be found instead in Euripides' title character, an Athenian boy portrayed as the forebear of all Greeks subject to the empire later ruled by his city-state: "Wiewohl nun dieser historische Agathon einige Züge zu dem Karakter des Erdichteten geliehen haben mag, so ist doch gewiß, daß der Verfasser das eigentliche *Modell* zu dem letztern in dem *Ion* des *Euripides* gefunden hat" (1:13). Many specific connections between Wieland's and Euripides' texts show how closely the two young men are related.[5] Like Wieland's, lines spoken by Euripides' chorus express concern like Wieland's with the ethical problem of fairly rewarding good behavior, for example, and both *Agathon* and *Ion* contain numerous references to their heroes' strong but hidden Dionysian traits—among them, their repressed orgiastic beginnings. Discrepancies that distinguish Agathon from Ion shed equally suggestive light on Wieland's storytelling. Despite their similar beginnings—both grow up ignorant of their rightful lineage at the temple of Apollo in Delphi—the two take contrasting routes to manhood, and Ion displays neither the physical and spiritual beauty nor the sensitivity, imagination, and noble enthusiasm that Wieland thinks they have in common. Wieland also rings what seems an Oedipal change on Euripides' story, having Agathon—not his father—lead the Athenians against their rebellious Greek colonies. Both the presence and the marked absence of such parallels thus suggest how the ethical lesson as well as the narrative form of *Agathon* need to be understood in terms of other literature. Its plot frequently turns on Wieland's subtle use of patterns set in related kinds of literary fiction, not only on the empirical definition of verisimilitude given and defended in "Unterredungen mit dem Pfarrer von ***."

Indeed, another *Ion*—Plato's dialogue—comes close to stating the problem of fictionality posed by Wieland's story. This comparison might seem odd, given how Wieland's narrator chides Plato for writing dialogues seeming more forthright than they actually are and for only appearing to be as noble as Archytas, but *Agathon* nonetheless revolves around the issue of whether real life can be lived according to Platonic ideas of virtue, an issue with narrative implications that its similarity to Plato's *Ion* helps explain. Plato's title character is a popular rhapsodist taken to task by Socrates since he, Ion, cannot account for his own success reciting Homer. Socrates calls his gift for doing so divinely irrational, like poetic inspiration itself. No mere rational art or trade, Socrates observes, poetry and its recitation seem more like a magnetic force. Socrates sounds ironic at times, but he is serious about Ion's talent, and he is skeptical of any attempt to explain the narration of fictional literature in terms of experienced facts. With this sympathy for befuddled Ion's plight, Plato reflects on the broad question posed in the telling of *Agathon*: How can narration resulting from poetic imagination be empirically justified? This question is answered differently in each of Wieland's versions, but the parallel with Plato is clear from his initial plot, for Agathon is a rhapsodist like Ion. News of his knack for reciting Homer recurs at decisive moments in his early life. His duties as a slave to Hippias consist of such recitation, and his rhapsodizing helps cause three scenes central to Wieland's ethical scheme: It almost leads to his seduction by a fallen priestess at Delphi, it helps him and his father recognize each other after many years of separation, and it launches his meteoric political career in Athens.[6] That both Ion and Agathon are rhapsodists whose *Schwärmerei* seems the divine right of poets suggests that Wieland wrestles with the same extremes of mundane knowledge and poetic inspiration noted by Plato. This intertextual link, in fact, hints that his story, like Plato's, examines poetic consciousness and aesthetic communication and that such literary issues are intertwined with its moral lesson.

More explicit reasons for reading *Agathon* with regard to such general questions can be found in its comments on the sources and truth of fiction. Those comments make for much narrative static, beginning with its foreword. Wieland's narrator, once again posing as the editor of a manuscript, doubts that readers will credit such a bogus source, and he himself seems no less skeptical of it than solicitous of them: "Der Herausgeber der gegenwärtigen Geschichte siehet so wenig Wahrscheinlichkeit vor sich, das Publikum zu überreden, daß sie in der That aus einer alten Griechischen Handschrift gezogen sey; daß er am besten zu thun glaubt, über diesen Punkt gar nichts zu sagen, und dem Leser zu überlassen, davon zu denken was er will" (1:ix). This ironic concession to readers' reservations presages just as cavalier an attitude toward the fictionality of Wieland's source as the one struck in *Don Sylvio*, where readers are similarly invited to decide for themselves whether to believe that such a document exists. *Wahrscheinlichkeit*, though, is the key word here, for it means not only "likelihood" but also "verisimilitude," and the narrator's further remarks about his dubious source raise serious questions about such general qualities of fiction. The actual existence of manuscripts does not mean much, he adds, since Agathon's story—even if he had really lived and it were written down—would not be worth reading if it told of nothing more important than what usually happens to people: "Gesetzt, daß wirklich einmahl ein Agathon gelebt hätte, daß sich aber von diesem Agathon nichts wichtigers sagen ließe, als was gewöhnlich den Inhalt des Lebenslaufs aller alltäglichern Menschen ausmacht: was würde uns bewegen können, seine Geschichte zu lesen, wenn gleich gerichtlich erwiesen werden könnte, daß sie in den Archiven des alten Athens gefunden worden sey?" (1:ix–x). Not documentary evidence, but the extraordinary importance of the events surrounding Agathon should thus legitimate his story. Wieland here suggests that fiction not be measured by history, starting his novel by alluding to Aristotle's notion that the former is more philosophical for relating "universals" rather than the "particulars" studied by historians.

Although the narrator rejects an unexceptional *Lebenslauf* as the stuff of literary fiction, he embraces the empirical *Lauf der Welt* as the criterion of fictional truth, which he expressly defines as agreement with the normal course of events in the world: "Die Wahrheit, welche von einem Werke, wie dasjenige ist, so wir den Liebhabern hiermit vorlegen, gefodert werden kann, bestehet darin: daß alles mit dem Laufe der Welt übereinstimme" (1:x). He means that characters in novels like *Agathon* must be drawn from nature, rather than arbitrarily invented by their author, and be developed in a way that makes them both general representatives of inner human nature and individuals shaped by specific external circumstances. Observing these rules ensures that events described in such novels could actually have happened, "daß alles so gedichtet sey, daß sich kein hinlänglicher Grund angeben lasse, warum es nicht gerade so, wie es erzählt wird, hätte geschehen können" (1:xi). Wieland's narrator claims that the resulting kind of truth, which he promises to tell, is all that makes books about the human condition useful: "*Diese Wahrheit allein* kann ein Buch, das *den Menschen* schildert, nützlich machen, und diese Wahrheit getrauet sich der Herausgeber den Lesern der Geschichte des Agathon zu versprechen" (1:xi). Paradoxically, the narrator relies on this concept of truth to meet objections to Agathon's sometimes improbable thoughts and deeds, noting that life can be more unlikely than fiction: "Es ist etwas bekanntes, daß im wirklichen Leben oft weit unwahrscheinlichere Dinge begegnen, als der ausschweifendste Kopf zu erdichten sich getrauen würde. Es würde also sehr übereilt seyn, die Wahrheit des Karakters unsers Helden deßwegen in Verdacht zu ziehen, weil es zuweilen *unwahrscheinlich* seyn mag, daß jemand so gedacht oder gehandelt habe wie er" (1:xii). Since one cannot prove that a person in Agathon's position could *not* think or act the way he does, moreover, readers are expected to take the narrator at his word: "So glaubt der Verfasser mit Recht erwarten zu können, daß man ihm auf sein Wort glaube, wenn er zuversichtlich versichert, *daß Agathon wirklich so gedacht oder gehandelt habe*" (1:xiii). *Agathon* sometimes seems strange, in other words, but is always true.

To introduce Agathon as a character out of the ordinary yet true to life is also to make conflicting claims, however, and Wieland's foreword is accordingly fraught with contradictions. Some are apparent in the narrator's attempt to cast his fiction in terms of history. When he explains how Agathon ought to seem true to life in spite of acting improbably at times, he invokes historians such as Plutarch, who cite similar cases: "Zu gutem Glücke finden sich in den beglaubtesten Geschichtschreibern, und schon allein in den *Lebensbeschreibungen des Plutarch*, Beyspiele genug, daß es *möglich* sey, so edel, so tugendhaft, so enthaltsam, oder . . . so seltsam, eigensinnig und albern zu seyn, als es unser Held in einigen Gelegenheiten seines Lebens ist" (1:xiii). Such credible corroboration notwithstanding, the narrator also hints that Agathon is autobiographical, a fact that not only guarantees the truth of his fellow characters, too, but also makes them essentially more "historical" than tales told by some other historians: "Da er selbst gewiß zu seyn wünschte, daß er der Welt keine *Hirngespenster* für Wahrheit verkaufe, so wählte er denjenigen [Karakter], den er am genauesten kennen zu lernen Gelegenheit gehabt hat. Aus diesem Grunde kann er ganz zuverlässig versichern, daß Agathon und die meisten übrigen Personen, welche in seine Geschichte eingeflochten sind, *wirkliche Personen* sind, und daß . . . alles, was das Wesentliche derselben ausmacht, eben so historisch, und vielleicht noch um manchen Grad gewisser sey, als die *neun Musen* des Vaters der Geschichte *Herodot*, oder die Römische Historie des *Livius*, oder die Französische des Jesuiten *Daniel*" (1:xi–xii). While the narrator relies on Plutarch to confirm the existence of figures such as Agathon, he thus also suggests that firsthand knowledge of him is more certain than some nonfictional histories. The point is not only that fiction can be truer than history, however, or that some historians are more believable than others, but that adhering to the empirical course of nature turns out to be a matter of subjective scrutiny. The truth of fiction thus seems something far more personal than the narrator initially implies.

Moral scruples similarly complicate the narrator's seemingly straightforward definition of fictional truth. Like his claim that he describes the character whom he knows best, those scruples show his concern with making fictional characters seem real. He reveals them when preparing readers for Agathon and Hippias. Agathon is not a paragon of virtue, he writes, "kein *Modell* eines *vollkommen tugendhaften Mannes*" (1:xiv), but the world is already filled with didactic books whose heroes think and act too much like moral puppets. Agathon is more like the tragic kind preferred by Aristotle, heroes whose weaknesses make them seem more human. No better in print than in person, he can be recognized as an image of real people: "Damit Agathon das Bild eines *wirklichen* Menschen wäre, in welchem Viele ihr eigenes und Alle die Hauptzüge der menschlichen Natur erkennen möchten, durfte er . . . nicht tugendhafter vorgestellt werden, als er ist" (1:xiv). Explaining Hippias, though, the narrator refuses to set too much stock by such shortcomings of human nature. The eloquent sophist's arguments are not without merit, he concedes, but they should not be mistaken for his—the narrator's—own. Indeed, he brands Hippias's philosophy immoral and irreligious, a rhetorical web that would ruin society if most people could be snared in it, "ein Gewebe von Trugschlüssen . . . , welches die menschliche Gesellschaft zu Grunde richten würde, wenn es moralisch möglich wäre, daß der größere Theil der Menschen darin verwickelt werden könnte" (1:xvii–xviii). That the narrator implicitly rejects this possibility indicates that Hippias represents no more than a moral minority, but he nonetheless speaks for most men and women of the world. This sad fact—that "*der größte Theil derjenigen, welche die sogenannte große Welt ausmachen, wie Hippias denkt, oder doch nach seinen Grundsätzen handelt*" (1:xix)—means that showing the effect of Hippias's principles is consistent with the "moral intentions" of *Agathon*. Standing for much of human society after all, however, Hippias poses a problem. While the truth of *Agathon* is assured by its hero's faults, its narrator admits, but cannot also accept, the larger lack of virtue in the world as a whole.

   Such ethical and narrative vacillation implicit in Wieland's foreword is a sign of similar ambivalence in the novel proper. The fictional source cited but dismissed in the foreword, for example, is repeatedly mentioned in the course of his story, where it not only prompts irony but also betrays unease, mixed feelings toward the fictionality of his tale. Indeed, the narrator clings to that transparently fictional source long after confessing that readers will hardly believe it. Relating one long conversation that Agathon has with himself, he traces his own knowledge of such interior monologues to a diary that Agathon kept, according to the author whose manuscript he claims to edit. The narrator's citing this source and its supposed credibility allows him to keep up the appearance of telling "historical" truth:

Da wir uns zum unverbrüchlichen Gesetze gemacht haben, in dieser Geschichte alles sorgfältig zu vermeiden, was gegen die historische Wahrheit derselben einigen gerechten Verdacht erwecken könnte; so würden wir uns ein Bedenken gemacht haben, das Selbstgespräch, welches wir hier in unsrer Handschrift vor uns finden, mitzutheilen, wenn der Verfasser nicht die Vorsicht gebraucht hätte, uns zu melden: daß seine Erzählung sich in den meisten Umständen auf eine Art von Tagebuch gründe, welches (sichern Anzeigen nach) von der eignen Hand des Agathon sey, und wovon er durch einen Freund zu Krotona eine Abschrift erhalten habe. Dieser Umstand macht begreiflich, wie der Geschichtschreiber wissen konnte, was Agathon bey dieser und andern Gelegenheiten mit sich selbst gesprochen; und schützt uns vor den Einwürfen, die man gegen die Selbstgespräche machen kann, worin die Geschichtschreiber den Poeten so gerne nachzuahmen pflegen, ohne sich, wie sie, auf die Eingebung der Musen berufen zu können.

(1:51)

This swipe at "historians" who wax poetic by reporting characters' inner thoughts without proper documentation appears to be ironic proof of the narrator's own reliability. He does not always cite his source ironically, however, as is clear from how often and earnestly he elsewhere refers to it. It turns up again in the last book of *Agathon*, which opens with a chapter whose title announces how Agathon becomes his own biographer in order to reveal himself to Archytas. Such conspicuous stress on the fictional source is reinforced when the narrator tells how Agathon bares his soul to Archytas in a written confession, "die von Agathon selbst aufgesetzte geheime Geschichte seines Geistes und Herzens, welche nach aller Wahrscheinlichkeit die erste und reinste Quelle ist, woraus die in diesem Werk enthaltenen Nachrichten geschöpft sind" (3:362). Like earlier references to Euripides' *Ion*, the echo of the title of Crébillon's *Égarements du coeur et de l'esprit* audible in this passage hints that the model for that source is a literary fiction, but the narrator is at pains to add how one of Agathon's subsequent dialogues with Archytas survived as an appendix to Agathon's manuscript, and Danae's similar conversations with her mistress Aspasia are likewise said to be written down. The narrator insists on noting documentary evidence, then, apparently reluctant to admit that his story is simply fiction. Not as ironic as he seems, he refuses to give up the pretense that *Agathon* is not invented.

This ambivalence toward the fictionality of the events described in *Agathon* apparent from both contradictions in the foreword and their causes or results in the novel itself has often been overlooked. Most previous studies treat the narrator's citations of the fictional source as a clear case of irony, for example, and though some critics appreciate its aesthetic import, too, his underlying quandary is seldom mentioned. The source is said to be a mere fiction that unmasks itself as such, though it also establishes trust between the narrator and his readers.[7] In other words, its own fictionality is ironically conceded while pure factuality is rejected, which makes the narration of *Agathon* transparent and thematic.[8] According to Gabriel, the narrator's citing this source is ironic through and through.[9] His ironic quotations of it are also said to make truth seem relative and to reveal the world to be one of mere appearance.[10] Retaining the ostensible fiction of editing a manuscript throughout the novel, moreover, allows the narrator to distance himself from his story and to discuss it.[11] That fictional source has likewise seemed not only to comment ironically on the authentication of the novel but also to create a "ruptured fiction" that allows the narrator to distance himself at will from both the objects that he describes and their description itself.[12] It is also said to legitimate fiction, however, insofar as it makes aesthetic closure possible without neglecting the narrator's realistic cast of mind.[13] As Friedrich Beißner remarks, Wieland's attention to that source reveals his sense of narrative order as well as his concern with the verisimilitude of his tale.[14] Indeed, it is said that the *Quellenfiktion* not only shows *Agathon* to be fictitious, but destroys its illusion of literal truth in order that readers recognize its general validity and hypothetical nature.[15] The fictional source of the novel is routinely regarded as part and parcel of Wieland's ironic commentary, then, but it also betrays his sincere concern with narrative verisimilitude and truth, and it thus seems more than just an ironic gag. The foreword to *Agathon* has similarly been said to make an ironic issue of fiction and to establish a new concept of it,[16] but the narrator's ambivalence toward fictionality itself still needs to be explained.

Reasons for his mixed feelings are suggested by "Über das Historische im Agathon," which defines the relationship of Wieland's fiction to history. As in the foreword, his goal of moral utility is linked to the likeness that his fictional characters and events bear to actual ones, but he expressly connects this similarity to imagination, a theme more fully developed in the novel itself. The narrator notes that *Agathon* resembles Xenophon's *Cyropaedia* less than Fielding's *Tom Jones* since Xenophon described the Persian ruler Cyrus as he ideally should have been instead of how he actually was. Wary of all writers whose characters thus embody pure wisdom and virtue, the narrator declares his intention to describe Agathon as he would have been, according to the laws of human nature, had he actually lived in the circumstances assigned him. This sober technique is meant to make *Agathon* a "history" rather than just a product of imagination: "Aus diesem Gesichtspunkte hoffet der Verfasser von den Kennern der menschlichen Natur das Zeugniß zu erhalten, daß sein Buch (ob es gleich in einem andern Sinne unter die Werke der Einbildungskraft gehört) des *Nahmens einer Geschichte* nicht unwürdig sey" (1:5). The narrator does not deny that his story often deviates from the historical record, but he insists that its fiction agrees with its basis in fact. The historical models for his characters did not all live at the same time, for example, but he claims to have made them seem neither better nor worse than they really were, thereby limiting fiction to fleshing out details of actual events: "Man hat der Erdichtung nicht mehr verstattet, als die historischen Begebenheiten näher zu *bestimmen* und völliger *auszumahlen*, indem man diejenigen Umstände und Ereignisse hinzu dichtete, welche am geschicktesten schienen, sowohl die Hauptperson der Geschichte, als den bekannten Karakter der vorbennanten *historischen* Personen in das *beste Licht* zu stellen" (1:21). Adding that such restricted use of fiction is also the best way to achieve the overriding moral purpose of *Agathon*, the narrator both limits and discounts the role of imagination in writing such "historical" literature.

The narrator likewise constrains imagination when he distinguishes his kind of history (*Geschichte*) from mere romances (*Romane*). Like his fictional source, this distinction is cited throughout *Agathon*, where it reveals contradictions in his initial concept of fiction. While his long preambles define *Geschichte* as fiction faithful to the everyday course of the world, fiction ironically shown to be invented but still limited to elaborating on history, the novel itself unfolds along narrative fault lines caused by tension between his empirical method and his ethical ideals. Such lines emerge even as the narrator reinforces his disdain for purely fictional *Romane*. He describes Agathon's chastity as strange but true in a chapter whose title leaves no doubt that it might seem invented (*erdichtet*), and he later states his own narrative obligations sternly: "Unsre Pflicht ist zu *erzählen*, nicht zu *dichten*" (3:231). With this circumspection and scorn for poetic license, the narrator sets himself apart from "Romanendichter," romancers whose shamelessly fantastic style and overt moralizing contradict the natural and impartial writing of "Geschichtschreiber," historians who truthfully record objects and explain events according to natural laws of cause and effect. The senses seldom obey the heart as completely as some

"Romanschreiber" assume, he explains, and feigning such heroic constancy makes their writing easier than the more reliable accounts given by "Geschichtschreiber": "Wie groß ist in diesem Stücke der Vortheil eines Romanendichters vor demjenigen, welcher sich anheischig gemacht hat, ohne Vorurtheil oder Parteylichkeit, mit Verläugnung des Ruhms, den er vielleicht durch Verschönerung seiner Karakter und durch Erhebung des Natürlichen ins Wunderbare sich hätte erwerben können, der Natur und Wahrheit in gewissenhafter Aufrichtigkeit durchaus getreu zu bleiben!" (1:251). The narrator draws this distinction to excuse describing Danae's temptation of Agathon, and he here respects writing that tells such hard truths, skeptical of fiction that glosses over them by relying on the marvelous instead.

   Such skepticism also informs the narrator's further remarks on how *Geschichte* differs from *Romane*, but he implies that these extremes are not always dissimilar. A mere romancer has an easier time winning the approval of moralistic readers, he notes, especially when such a writer is taken with the products of his exalted imagination, "verliebt in die schönen Geschöpfe seiner erhitzten Einbildungskraft" (1:253). Readers suffer, however, when fiction affects them too strongly. Having conversed at length instead of first fleeing their kidnappers, Agathon and Psyche regret that they waste time "nach dem Beyspiel der Liebhaber in Romanen" (1:49), and Hippias cannot comprehend why Agathon later remains devoted to Danae "mit romanhafter Treue" (2:175). Romantic in this sense of acting like some fictional lover, Agathon is just as quixotic as Don Sylvio. By contrast, the narrator professes "historical" fidelity for sticking to the unflattering facts of Agathon's story: "Wir werden mit der bisher beobachteten historischen Treue fortfahren seine Geschichte zu erzählen, und versichern ein-für allemahl, daß wir nichts dafür können, wenn er nicht allemahl so handelt, wie wir vielleicht selbst hätten wünschen mögen, daß er gehandelt hätte" (2:217–18). Here the narrator uses such empiricism as an excuse to describe Agathon as less than ideal. Moreover, as in the foreword, he elsewhere claims that life can seem stranger than fiction, history even less likely than *Romane*, since connections between things are often imperceptible: "Daher scheint es zu kommen, daß die Geschichte zuweilen viel seltsamere Begebenheiten erzählt, als ein Romanschreiber zu dichten wagen dürfte" (1:28–29). The narrator thus justifies singular characters and events, blurring his sharp distinction between normal *Geschichte* and outlandish *Romane*. His hope that his audience will read Agathon's story less cursorily than "einen efemerischen Roman" (2:198) therefore recalls similar criticism of *"Romans du Jour"* (11:12–13 n. 1) by the narrator of *Don Sylvio*, who openly prefers chivalric romances instead. The history attempted in *Agathon* is likewise one kind of fiction recommended over another, from which it differs only in degree and not in kind.

That *Geschichte* and *Romane* seem more closely related than their apparent difference allows can be explained by noting that Wieland cites the former term in accordance with eighteenth-century usage. He once wrote that poets should not care how a historical event actually happened, only how it would have had to happen in order to be pleasant, entertaining, or touching.[17] Praising more credible writers, though, he called truth arrived at through one's senses "historical": "Die Wahrheit, zu deren Erkenntnis man . . . durch die Sinnen gelangt, ist die historische Wahrheit."[18] This kind of truth was considered "pragmatic" in novels as well as historiography. One of Wieland's favorite authors, the Greek satirist Lucian, liked Thucydides for writing history without rhetorical or poetic embellishments.[19] The historiography of Wieland's day was not so much historical as pragmatic in this sense—concerned with describing, discussing, and improving human nature—and its style and substance were suited to novels like *Agathon*.[20] Both types of writing belonged to the epic genre, and both showed psychological causality that obviated traditional criticisms of fiction.[21] In *Agathon*, then, Wieland uses "history" in the sense of a hypothetical fiction,[22] one that describes probable and typical events, taking the term to mean "not . . . that the events he relates happened *once*, but that they *might* happen at any time."[23] While *Agathon* suggests a poetics opposed to the idea of possible worlds, and though Wieland's preference for historians over romancers seems to refute his Swiss mentors' aesthetics,[24] it thus seems wrong to equate *Geschichte* with "antinovel."[25] Wieland's use of historical facts makes such judgments seem hasty. He has been said to exemplify the attitude toward history taken by the Enlightenment, clothing his psychological accounts of human beings in historical costume without altering their invariable moral nature.[26] In *Agathon*, such general affinities between antiquity and the eighteenth century are offset by aesthetic distance that demonstrates the utopian character of its story.[27] In his ancient setting, for example, Wieland can define sexual politics differently than in a contemporary one.[28] Proper names that he uses do not refer to specific historical figures, moreover, but do have general associations for his readers, an example of how historical facticity authenticates the fictionality of *Agathon*.[29] Like many of his contemporaries, he thus approaches *Geschichte* much as Aristotle did poetry.

The narrator's sincere ambivalence toward the fictionality of his story reflects the ambiguity of the term *Geschichte*, then, which can

mean either nonfictional "history" or a made-up "story." More re-
vealing, however, are remarks about imagination made by Agathon,
Danae, Hippias, and the narrator himself, which show his complex
similarity to these three main characters. Such remarks show Agathon
to be a self-conscious Don Sylvio. He, too, has an imagination fueled
since his early youth and downright *romanhaft*, as Hippias tells him:
"Die Einsamkeit deiner ersten Jugend und die morgenländischen
Schwärmereyen . . . haben deiner Fantasie einen romanhaften Schwung
gegeben" (1:95). Far more reflectively than Don Sylvio, however,
Agathon analyzes his own penchant for the marvelous, sharing his
psychological insight into notions of ideal beauty: "So viel ich unsre
Seele kenne, däucht mich, daß sich in einer jeden, die zu einem merk-
lichen Grade von Entwicklung gelangt, nach und nach ein gewisses
idealisches Schöne bilde, welches . . . unsern Geschmack und unsre sitt-
lichen Urtheile bestimmt, und *das allgemeine Modell* abgiebt, wonach
unsre Einbildungskraft die besondern Bilder dessen, was wir groß,
schön und vortrefflich nennen, zu entwerfen scheint" (2:7–8). Agathon
knows that such heady idealism derives from mere sense impression,
but he also observes that it can nonetheless make human beings hap-
pier than can any other state of mind. This assessment of how imagina-
tion works includes its ability to open up new worlds like those that
Don Sylvio and Don Eugenio cite in defense of fairy tales. As Agathon
says to Danae, "So seltsam es klingt, so gewiß ist es doch, daß *die Kräfte
der Einbildung* dasjenige weit übersteigen, was die Natur unsern Sinnen
darstellt . . . kurz, sie erschafft eine *neue Natur*, und versetzt uns in der
That in fremde Welten, welche nach ganz andern Gesetzen als die uns-
rige regiert werden" (2:16–17). His attraction to her helps him discover
the natural source of this apparent magic, however, this *"scheinbare
Magie* der Einbildungskraft" (2:17), and he wants to enjoy for real the
ideal perfection that he could, for so long, only imagine. By the time he
becomes Danae's live-in lover, Agathon thus speaks of imagination as
wisely as the newlywed Don Sylvio.

Discussing Danae herself, the narrator reinforces both Agathon's re-
semblance to Don Sylvio and the importance of imagination for relat-
ing Agathon's affair with her. Danae is able to cure Agathon's enthusi-
asm for the same reason given to explain the healing of frustrated
imagination at the end of *Don Sylvio*: "weil er bey ihr alles dasjenige ge-
funden, wovon er sich vorher nur in der höchsten Begeisterung seiner
Einbildungskraft einige unvollkommene Schattenbegriffe habe machen
können; und weil es natürlich sey, daß die *Einbildungskraft* zu wirken
aufhöre, so bald der Seele nichts mehr zu thun übrig sey, als *anzu-
schauen* und zu *genießen*" (2:144). Despite putting such an abrupt end

to his fantasies, the strong impression that Danae makes on Agathon comes from the capacity of imagination to substitute the ideal for the real. This mental process is described more precisely here than in *Don Sylvio*: "War nicht dieses zauberische Licht, welches seine Einbildungskraft gewohnt war über alles was mit seinen Ideen übereinstimmte auszubreiten; war nicht diese unvermerkte *Unterschiebung* des *Idealen* an die Stelle des *Wirklichen* die wahre Ursache, warum Danae einen so außerordentlichen Eindruck auf sein Herz machte?" (2:222). Imagination and the real seem similarly related when the narrator writes that Agathon is better able to reflect on escaping Danae's realm of the senses because he was really there, whereas the narrator would first have to imagine it, "da er sich *wirklich* in dem Falle befand, in welchen wir uns erst durch Hülfe der Einbildungskraft setzen müßten" (2:200). As in the explanations given for Agathon's idealism, imagination serves a higher purpose here, however, where reality is ascribed to fictional circumstances that the narrator claims he can only imagine. Ironic as this claim may be, it underscores the fact that telling Agathon's story takes considerable imagination. Indeed, it suggests that imagination alone can provide access to Wieland's fictional world. Like Agathon, the narrator thus seems to indulge necessarily in what Danae thinks suggestive "Vergnügungen der *Einbildungskraft*" (2:151), pleasures of the imagination that transcend the real.

Such pleasures and their poetic character are resisted by Hippias, who opposes them in favor of a more sensual hedonism, but imagination nonetheless interests him. His house is surrounded by gardens so elaborate, for example, that they are similar to fanciful landscapes imagined by poets, "diesen Spielen einer dichterischen und mahlerischen Fantasie, welche man erstaunt ist außerhalb seiner Einbildung zu sehen" (1:80–81). Hippias helps account for this circumstance when he calls his sophistry the art of controlling other people's imagination, "die Kunst über die *Einbildungskraft* der Menschen zu herrschen" (1:142). Not only does he cultivate imagination both on his property and in his lucrative philosophical business, though; he also analyzes its effect on Agathon (now called Kallias, a name that conveys how Hippias prefers beauty to goodness), who he thinks possesses such a charming, poetic quality to a degree extreme in real life: "Dein Übel, lieber Kallias, entspringt von einer Einbildungskraft, welche dir ihre Geschöpfe in einem überirdischen Glanze zeigt, der dein Herz verblendet, und ein falsches Licht über das, was wirklich ist, ausbreitet; von einer *dichterischen Einbildungskraft*, die sich beschäftiget schönere Schönheiten und angenehmere Vergnügen zu erfinden als die Natur hat; einer Einbildungskraft, ohne welche weder *Homere*, noch *Alkamene*,

noch *Polygnote* wären; welche gemacht ist unsre Ergetzungen zu ver-
schönern, *aber nicht die Führerin unsers Lebens zu seyn"* (1:111–12). Criti-
cal of the supernatural pleasures that it affords, Hippias here limits
"poetic imagination" to literary and visual artists, finding it too mis-
leading in life. When he adds that such pleasures either recall or
heighten sensual ones, he echoes Joseph Addison's "On the Pleasures
of the Imagination" (1712). Addison traces all aesthetic pleasures to the
sense of sight, though he also observes that one can never see anything
that measures up to one's highest ideas. He mentions describing gar-
dens more perfect than those found in nature, moreover, as an example
of how poets should humor imagination. Indirectly, the sense as well as
the setting of Hippias's skeptical lecture thus suggest Addison's more
receptive view of imagination and its ideal, literary pleasures.

The narrator regards imagination much as Hippias does, citing the
extraordinary pleasures that it affords as well as the errors of judgment
that too much of it can cause. While he explains Platonic love in terms
of such dubious pleasures, though, he also encourages readers of
Agathon to enjoy them, revealing his dilemma as a narrator of fiction
who questions the same mental capacity needed to appreciate it. He
confirms Hippias's diagnosis of Agathon in a chapter whose title an-
nounces that imagination can be extremely dangerous. A vivid imagi-
nation not only enables its possessor to feel pleasures and delights un-
known to other mortals, he writes, but also leads to excesses and pain
stronger than virtue and wisdom, the very qualities that, according to
Wieland's subtitle, are supposed to be exemplified in *Agathon*:

> Wenn eine lebhafte Einbildungskraft ihrem Besitzer eine unend-
> liche Menge von Vergnügen gewährt, die den übrigen Sterblichen
> versagt sind; wenn ihr zauberischer Einfluß alles Schöne in seinen
> Augen verschönert, und ihn da in Entzückung setzt, wo andre
> kaum empfinden; wenn sie in glücklichen Stunden ihm diese Welt
> zu einem Paradiese macht, und in traurigen seine Seele von der
> Scene seines Kummers hinweg zieht, und in bessere Welten ver-
> setzt, welche durch die vergrößernden Schatten einer vollkomm-
> nen Wonne seinen Schmerz bezaubern: so müssen wir auf der
> andern Seite gestehen, daß sie nicht weniger eine Quelle von
> Irrthümern, Ausschweifungen und Qualen für ihn ist, wovon er,
> selbst mit Hülfe der Weisheit und mit der feurigsten Liebe zur Tu-
> gend, sich nicht eher los machen kann, bis er (auf welche Art es
> nun seyn mag) dazu gekommen ist, die allzu große Lebhaftigkeit
> derselben zu mäßigen.

(1:197–98)

Thus weighing the pros and cons of a lively imagination and, in the end, favoring moderation, the narrator reinforces Wieland's own remarks on curing enthusiasm like Don Sylvio's. Not only does he here discount pleasures of the imagination no less exclusive than those cited by Addison, though; he also qualifies better worlds that could be compared to the possible ones suggested by Leibniz. Such close links between Agathon's psychology and the aesthetics of fiction seem particularly clear when the narrator invites his readers to imagine Danae's country estate. He leaves its details to their imagination, which he prods by referring them to a similar scene in Torquato Tasso's *Gerusalemme liberata* (1575): "Wir widerstehen der Versuchung eine Beschreibung von diesem Landgute zu machen, um dem Leser das Vergnügen zu lassen, sich dasselbe so wohl angelegt, so prächtig und so angenehm vorzustellen als er selbst will. Alles was wir davon sagen wollen ist, daß diejenigen, deren Einbildungskraft einiger Unterstützung nöthig hat, den sechzehnten Gesang des *befreyten Jerusalems* lesen müßten, um sich eine Vorstellung von dem Orte zu machen" (1:226). Some pleasures of the imagination are here expressly reserved for readers of *Agathon* itself. Nonetheless, the narrator reveals the natural causes of the similar pleasure felt in a state of Platonic love, an attraction that he traces to imagination: "Die *Quelle* der *Liebe* . . . ist *das Anschauen eines Gegenstandes, der unsre Einbildungkraft bezaubert*" (1:232). Analyzing Agathon's life, the narrator thus explains as well as seems bound to deflate many pleasures of the imagination much like the ones provided by Wieland's fictional literature.

When compared to Wieland's three main characters, then, his narrator seems torn between indicting and indulging in pleasures of the imagination. As skeptical as Hippias, and as self-conscious as Agathon, he nonetheless seems as suggestive as Danae, who seduces Agathon by appealing to his imagination, not just to his senses. The narrator's psychological lesson accordingly is at odds with the mental means by which he and his readers enter his fictional world. This ambivalence is further compounded in remarks on imagination made by as well as about Wieland himself, by early reviewers of *Agathon*, and in some previous studies of the novel, but its import has not been fully appreciated. In the 1760s, Wieland was said to have found Agathon too imaginative to be a complete philosopher, yet he himself seemed guided wholly by his own imagination.[30] Moreover, he was later hailed for moving "the world of imagination at his will" in *Agathon*,[31] though its first reviewers routinely argued that there were two sides to his story. While they admired the imagination needed to write it, a poetic quality that they thought he possessed in abundance, they faulted its frank

morality, which hardly seemed suitable for inexperienced readers.[32] As
Isaak Iselin put it, "Überhaupt möchte man fast sagen, daß um ein nütz-
liches Muster . . . den Menschen darzustellen die Form eines Romans
die unbequemste und die gefährlichste sey."[33] More recently, *Agathon*
has been said to disallow Wieland's imaginative fabulating as well as to
show his insistence on the existence of imagination as a psychological
principle indifferent or even hostile to reason.[34] Wieland's imagination
has also seemed to fall short of his psychological knowledge, though
his notion of *Einbildungskraft* has been likened to Roman Ingarden's
phenomenological concept of poets' production as well as readers'
concretization of fictional worlds in literary texts.[35] Imagination has
also seemed the motive for Agathon's idealism, Hippias's pleasures,
and the writing of the former's autobiography,[36] its scope said to in-
clude entire *Weltanschauungen*, which Wieland presents by putting it
to narrative use.[37] Most tellingly, Monika Schrader has argued that
Agathon tries to integrate a new aesthetics of illusion into an old con-
cept of mimesis and thus turns on competition between poetic and
mimetic qualities of imagination.[38] Schrader remarks that this issue of
imagination causes tension both at the level of Wieland's plot and at
that of his narration, since the interdependence of imagination and
reflection characteristic of his narrative form may also be found in his
constellation of characters. Whereas his narrator relates imitation and
illusion by means of irony, she writes, Agathon is unable to rise above
a "disjunction of fantasy and experience."[39] As shown above, though,
the narrator's irony hardly keeps him from feeling mixed about the fic-
tionality of his story.

   The narrator not only betrays ambivalence, and thus contradictions
in Wieland's concept of fiction, however, but also tries to resolve them.
Nowhere are his efforts more revealing than at the end of *Agathon*. In
all three of its versions, Agathon's story turns out the same, but each
shows a decidedly different attitude toward the fictionality that charac-
terizes not only its literary medium but also its moral message.
Agathon always finds final refuge in Tarentum, but the narrator frames
this happy ending differently each time. The last book of the first edi-
tion begins with a long "Apologie des griechischen Autors," in which
the narrator denies responsibility for the neat denouement about to oc-
cur, assigning it instead to the Greek author whose manuscript he os-
tensibly only edits. The problem is that Agathon's disillusionment does
not warrant such a rosy outcome. He has grown older and wiser, but
only at the expense of ideals like those embodied by Archytas. The nar-
rator expressly links this ethical dilemma to the rules for writing fiction
set forth in the foreword:

Bis hieher scheint die Geschichte unsers Helden, wenigstens in den hauptsächlichsten Stücken, dem ordentlichen Lauf der Natur, und den strengesten Gesetzen der Wahrscheinlichkeit so gemäß zu sein, daß wir keinen Grund sehen, an der Wahrheit derselben zu zweifeln. Aber in diesem eilften Buch, wir müssen es gestehen, scheint der Autor aus dieser unsrer Welt, welche, unparteiisch von der Sache zu reden, zu allen Zeiten nichts bessers als eine Werkel-Tags-Welt . . . gewesen ist, ein wenig in das Land der Ideen, der Wunder, der Begebenheiten, welche gerade so ausfallen, wie man sie hätte wünschen können, und um alles auf einmal zu sagen, in das Land der schönen Seelen, und der utopischen Republiken verirret zu sein.[40]

The narrator here thinks that the utopian conclusion of *Agathon* flatly contradicts the principles of verisimilitude and empirical accuracy that assure the truth of fictional *Geschichte*. He adds, however, that it seems cruel when sympathetic fictional characters meet a tragic end, especially since authors can easily spare their readers the pain caused by such products of a melancholy, misanthropic imagination. Indeed, he excuses the highly unlikely set of circumstances surrounding the final reward of Agathon's virtue: "Wie soll sich ein armer Autor helfen, der (alles wohl überlegt) nur ein einziges Mittel vor sich sieht, aus der Sache zu kommen, und dieses ein gewagtes? Man hilft sich wie man kann, und wenn es auch durch einen Sprung aus dem Fenster sein sollte."[41] The narrator leaves no doubt that he dislikes the end of *Agathon*, though, since it is not supposed to be a novel, "da dieses Buch, in so fern der Herausgeber Teil daran hat, kein Roman ist, noch einer sein soll."[42] His apology is thus made for the patently fictional character of Wieland's conclusion. By turns critical, lenient, and distanced, the narrator remains skeptical of indulging imagination, especially to wrap up a story whose hero seems to outgrow it.

That Wieland tried to resolve this contradiction between the stern style and the happy ending of *Agathon* is clear from emendations made in its second edition, most notably the addition of Danae's autobiographical "Geheime Geschichte der Danae." She tells this story of her life to Agathon in Tarentum, where she happens to turn up long after he leaves her to run off and play philosopher-king in Syracuse. At the level of plot, their reunion is inconsequential, leading merely to vows of friendship, not to marriage. Judged by its narrative form, however, her account of her life fundamentally alters the acceptance of fiction in *Agathon*. That account, too, is *Geschichte* insofar as it relates a plausible, "pragmatic" series of events. As autobiography, though, it is held to a different standard of truth. The narrator reverses himself when he assesses the credibility of such first-person narratives. In an earlier episode, he notes that Danae fails to follow his own rules for writing "history" when she gives Agathon a selective version of her former life: "Dieß ist gewiß, daß Danae in der Erzählung ihrer Geschichte mehr die *Gesetzen des Schönen und Anständigen,* als die Pflichten einer genauen *historischen Treue,* zu ihrem Augenmerke genommen" (2:166). Agathon himself is hardly more candid, and the narrator rejects all autobiographers as egoistic "Geschichtschreiber ihres eignen werthen Selbsts" (2:167). He soon accepts Danae's story after all, however, siding with her against her many detractors: "Sie sah natürlicher Weise ihre Aufführung, ihre Schwachheiten, ihre Fehltritte selbst, in einem mildern, und (lasset uns die Wahrheit sagen) in einem *wahrern* Licht als die Welt" (2:178). This statement does not seem ironic, and the narrator has a similar change of heart just before Danae begins her "private history." He is still skeptical of autobiography, but authors like her, who at least *want* to tell the truth, now seem believable enough: "Aber uns däucht, man kann mit dem Grade von Glaubwürdigkeit zufrieden seyn, der daher entspringt, wenn der Erzähler seiner eignen Geschichte die Wahrheit sagen *will*" (3:245). Here, narrative truth seems sufficiently guaranteed by an autobiographical author's sincere intentions.

This difference between the first and second versions of *Agathon,* between the criteria of credibility applied in "Apologie des griechischen Autors" and in "Geheime Geschichte der Danae," signals increasing comfort with the fact of fictionality.[43] In part, this shift occurs because *Agathon* itself is autobiographical. Wieland did not hide this fact, often drawing comparisons between himself and his hero that leave no doubt about their similarity. He explained, for example, "Ich schildere darin mich selbst, wie ich in den Umständen Agathons gewesen zu seyn mir einbilde."[44] To be sure, this similarity is complex, and the irony so plain at the end of the first edition has struck many scholars as anything but an artistic flaw. It has been noted that the fictional source mediates between Wieland's own life and Agathon's autobiography and that Wieland uses the antique setting of his novel to treat its autobiographical problematic objectively.[45] He also toned down his references to himself in the second edition and has been said to tell the inner truth of pragmatic autobiography, which can be found in fiction and nonfiction alike.[46] It is also argued both that the open-ended structure of the novel conveys dissatisfaction with Agathon's status quo as well as its utopian alternative in Tarentum and that Wieland deftly uses the fiction of being merely an editor to distance himself from his forced conclusion.[47] The openness of the conclusion, which exposes his resolution as a fiction, has been thought to confirm the modernity of *Agathon,* moreover, and the first version has been praised for thereby conveying the honest truth of an unfinished fragment.[48] The "Apologie des griechischen Autors" introduces a utopia, then, but one narrated ironically, with clear indications of its fictionality.[49] As Walter Erhart argues, the fictionality of the ending is ironic yet necessary in the ethical scheme of *Agathon*, a novel that shows poetic justice stripped of its metaphysical import thanks to the admission of its fictionality.[50] Equally significant, though, is Franz Stanzel's insight that the fictionality of first-person narrators was recognized earlier than that of their third-person counterparts.[51] Knowing this insight helps us see that by accepting Danae's autobiography as true, the narrator recognizes fictionality as being characteristic of a credible literary mode.

In addition to being related to Wieland's own biography, the narrator's shift from mostly ironic to more sincere remarks about the truth of fiction like *Agathon* occurs because the moral lesson of the novel implies such acceptance of fictionality in broad terms. Accepting literary fiction as such, in other words, is much like subscribing to the ethical ideals embodied by Archytas. This parallel emerges clearly in the third edition of the novel, which adds an account of his philosophy, the eminent "Lebensweisheit des Archytas." In conversations with Agathon, Archytas disdains the empiricism practiced so cynically by Hippias, arguing that reason should not be subject to the senses, a circumstance that only degrades the human intellect. The inner world that he prefers is less illusory: "Doch laß es auch seyn, daß in der *sichtbaren Welt* das Meiste für uns *Täuschung*, alles nur *Erscheinung* ist . . . : liegt nicht in unserm *innern Sinn* eine *unsichtbare Welt* in uns selbst aufgedeckt, deren Grenzen noch kein Sterblicher erflogen hat?" (3:381–82). Such rejection of visible phenomena in favor of an ideal world that is more than mere appearance, and therefore the site of lasting truth, not only sets Agathon straight after his many ethical lapses. It also transcends the limits of fiction defined as mundane *Geschichte*. The ideal world that Archytas posits does have practical consequences for governing Tarentum, but it is not bound by the empirical constraints imposed in the narrator's initial concept of fictional prose. The third version of *Agathon* thus exposes a flaw inherent in that concept all along: Adhering consistently to the workaday world, as the narrator plans, would make him, in literature, what Hippias is in life, a cynic whose system proves the folly of high moral ideals. As Samuel Johnson once summed up this problem of narrating fiction meant to edify, "knowledge of the world will be found much more frequently to make men cunning than good."[52] To avoid thus undermining his own didactic purpose, the narrator accepts the fictionality of Agathon's story along with that of Archytas's ideals. Broadly speaking, Wieland's message and his means are both fictions, a fact that makes them seem well suited to each other in the end.

Wieland does not make seeing this fundamental connection easy, but it is clear when he describes what Agathon learns from Archytas. The language chosen to convey Agathon's new knowledge reverses the terms that define fictional truth in the foreword. Those terms first resurface when the narrator remarks that Agathon will not be as idealistic when reforming Dionysius as he had been when earlier run out of Athens: "Er hatte . . . diesen Unterschied der *Menschen* um uns her, von dem was *der Mensch an sich* ist und seyn soll, bereits zu gut kennen gelernt, um seinen Plan auf *Platonische Ideen* zu gründen" (3:54). Here the narrator still presumes moral strictures consistent with his plans for writing concrete *Geschichte*. Agathon later sees something ideal in Archytas, though, an urge that the narrator explains with surprising nonchalance: "Die Ursache ist ganz einfach: weil dieses Idealische nicht in seinem Gehirne, sondern in dem Gegenstande selbst lag" (3:188). Archytas here represents precisely the kind of ideal that the narrator initially shuns by writing like Fielding, not Richardson. To be sure, Archytas himself later warns against the penchant for the marvelous encouraged by mystical poets, and he tells Agathon not to take ancient fables literally, "auch die ehrwürdigsten Fabeln des Alterthums für—Fabeln zu halten" (3:411). He thus encourages being more conscious of fictional literature, though, not simply reviling it, and Agathon soon takes a grand tour that confirms Archytas's idealism by reversing the relative merit of the terms used to define *Geschichte*. The way people *should be* is now more edifying than how they *are*: "Seine Beobachtungen vollendeten, was der Umgang mit Archytas und anhaltendes Nachdenken über seine eigenen Erfahrungen angefangen hatten: sie überzeugten ihn, daß die Menschen, im Durchschnitte genommen, überall so *sind* wie *Hippias* sie schilderte, wiewohl sie so seyn *sollten*, wie *Archytas* durch sein Beyspiel lehrte" (3:419). This ultimate lesson could not be conveyed by unflinching *Geschichte*, and the ethics that Archytas teaches by precept as well as example thus suggest greater respect for narrative fictionality in novels such as *Agathon*.

Seeing how the fictionality of Agathon's story dovetails with that of Archytas's ideals helps reevaluate the ending of the third version, the relationship between that final version and the first, and the role of fictionality in *Agathon* as a whole. Agathon's sudden salvation in Tarentum has often seemed unconvincing. It is said to be as bombastic as an operatic finale, so artificial and unsuited to Wieland's own imagination as not to be worth considering.[53] It has likewise been called an ironic and impossibly utopian fiction, one that does not blur the line between fiction and reality as decisively as Borges's *Ficciones*.[54] It has also been called no more than a heuristic construct, however, and Archytas's wisdom has seemed to represent an ideal that could be realized only in the future, to set a utopian example whose hypothetical quality the narrator makes plain.[55] Scholars similarly differ on the issue of whether the third version improves on the first. It has been argued, for example, that Archytas's wisdom unfortunately persuades Agathon not to attempt the social change logically required by the rest of Wieland's novel.[56] Wilson notes, however, that Wieland tried to meet Horatian demands for artistic unity in the third version, even though the narrator rejects such classical aesthetic precepts in the first.[57] While the end of the third version displays Wieland's attempt to overcome tension between the real and the ideal, moreover, this contradiction left over from the first is said to be one that he could not resolve.[58] Erhart argues that the various versions of *Agathon* do not try to solve this problem but rather examine narrative possibilities that preserve the difference between the constructs of fiction and the contingency of life. Both the first and the third, he says, contain a "metareflection" on the legitimacy of literature in general.[59] Such insights by others involve fictionality, too. In addition to comments made on that concept in connection with Wieland's fictional source and the "Apologie des griechischen Autors"—comments noted above—Klaus-Detlef Müller writes that the fictivity characteristic of utopian Tarentum informs the "historical" passages of *Agathon* as well, and Horst Thomé observes that Wieland's admission of the fictionality of his utopian ending is not unique, since *Don Sylvio* and *Diogenes* similarly thematize it.[60] The general notion persists, though, that Agathon is naive when he acts according to "fictions" such as gratitude, generosity, and pity.[61] Reasons for relating his ethics and story to the concept of fictionality can thus be found in a few previous studies, but such reasons have not been given as a cogent, coherent interpretation.

Any such reading needs to note that the view of fictionality taken in *Agathon* resembles Vaihinger's, whose comprehensive fictionalism—as cited above in the introduction—considers ethical ideals a kind of fiction, a logical construct that serves a practical purpose, even though its fictivity is known. Kant, of course, posited three such heuristic principles: the soul as substantial and permanent, the world as a causally related totality, and God as absolute perfection—three "transcendental Ideas" put to "immanent" or "regulative" use, even though no objects correspond to them. The neo-Kantian Vaihinger, with his Nietzschean nominalism, thinks Kant's insights through to purely pragmatic conclusions in his philosophy of the "as-if," and *Agathon* combines their complementary arguments. Like Kant, through Archytas, it defines rational postulates that make Agathon's moral knowledge possible. Like Vaihinger, it also regards such postulates as fictions, an angle implied by the explicit fictionality of its story. The ethical lesson of the novel loses none of its force for thus being conceptually bracketed by its narrative form. Indeed, their relationship proves *Agathon* to be serious fiction—serious about the fictionality that pervades both its message and its medium. To interpret the novel this way is to clarify Wieland's connections to Kant and its similarity to Kant's epistemology. Kant's ideas of enlightenment and humanity have been called a major theme of Wieland's novels, but Kantian philosophy has also seemed utterly foreign to Wieland.[62] He was familiar with that philosophy thanks to his son-in-law Karl Leonhard Reinhold, who expounded it in letters published in Wieland's *Teutscher Merkur* in 1786–87, and he expressly criticized Kant, though only after Fichte, who seemed to take Kant's ideas to extremes, succeeded Reinhold as professor of philosophy in Jena.[63] Moreover, he was pleasantly surprised to find that he had carried the seeds of a Kantian kind of philosophy within him when first writing *Agathon*, and the Danish poet Jens Baggesen considered the end of the novel proof that Wieland was "Kant in der Poesie."[64] While some scholars equate Archytas's moral philosophy with Kant's, arguing that Agathon demonstrates Kant's concepts of the ego,[65] others discern no more than a general similarity, observing that Kant himself opposed showing ideals such as Archytas realized in novels.[66] Moreover, although Tarentum has seemed a "regulative idea" in Kant's sense, Wieland is said to have favored Archytas's Kantian ethics only briefly, and though there are close parallels between Wieland's and Kant's moral assumptions, the empirical narration attempted in *Agathon* has seemed to rule out accepting Kant's pragmatic, "as-if" fictions.[67] Accordingly, it has been argued that Kant's philosophy, not literature like Wieland's novels, conceived of the productive functions of imagination as such.[68] Adducing Vaihinger's *neo*-Kantian fictionalism resolves such disputes and avoids such conclusions by helping present the concept of fictionality as characteristic of Agathon's ideals and his story alike.

To argue that ethical and aesthetic aspects of fictionality make each other more credible in the course of *Agathon* is also to rethink its status as a *Bildungsroman*. Overlooking the Kantian concept of fictionality inherent in it might lead one to conclude that Wieland's story is deeply flawed, that its moral lesson is not commensurate with its narrative form. One might judge it solely by the rules explained in the foreword, thinking that it devalued fictionality in ways consistent with the sobering drift of most *Bildungsromane*. After all, the narrator there defines a kind of writing—*Geschichte*—that seems well suited to describe *Bildung*, such maturation often being construed as an idealistic young man's compromise with the outside world. By the end of the final version of the novel, however, both the narrator's style and his message change. Neither he nor Agathon remains within the empirical limits set at the beginning of their respective ventures: writing true *Geschichte* and undergoing moral refinement. Each shows more imagination than at first thought proper, and both therefore turn out quite differently than intended. Agathon initially seems meant to foreswear imagination in much the same way that the narrator already has, but the ethical lesson that he ultimately learns from Archytas reinforces ideals seldom found in real life. Agathon's hard knocks have disproved the narrator's claim that regarding people as they really are will further morality by furnishing useful examples. The scheming Hippias seems anything but an anomaly, virtuous people like Archytas turn out to be exceptions, and Agathon's own dalliance with Danae seems to reflect poorly on the moral potential of humankind. Nonetheless, Archytas's idealism prevails, and the narrator takes an accordingly different tone in defense of its fictionality. If one failed to note this coincidence, *Agathon* might seem to reflect an attitude toward moral ideals almost as cynical as Hippias's. The novel might also seem to show its own hero outgrowing imagination not unlike the kind needed to read his story as more than an empty gesture. Its narration and ethical lesson might seem mutually exclusive, its irony and idealism utterly incompatible, its story no more than an impressive failure.[69]

Such skeptical arguments are indeed often found in studies of *Agathon* as a case of fictional *Bildung*. Its story is sometimes thought to contradict that concept, and remarks more receptive to the way in which fictionality informs its literary as well as its moral lesson are rare. In part, this circumstance results from dim views of Agathon's development itself, according to which he, at best, ends up back where he started. His goal is said to be a return to his initial beliefs, purged of emotional excess and purified by reason.[70] This circularity also appears to prove his lack of development, though, and *Agathon* has seemed not to be a *Bildungsroman* at all, largely because it progresses from certain knowledge to an unsolved problem, not vice-versa.[71] Both such skepticism and a more generous assessment of Agathon's *Bildung* can be found in the work of Jürgen Jacobs, who has written widely on that genre. Jacobs notes that the utopia needed to save Agathon's morality contradicts basic principles of the *Bildungsroman*, which should instead describe productively coping with disappointment in real life.[72] He does not deny that *Agathon* shows a moral aporia typical of the genre, however, and the apparent contradiction that he cites seems resolved by his later remark that Agathon does undergo *Bildung*, as long as one does not define that term too narrowly.[73] Others have found that the explicit narration of the novel educates its readers, occasionally beyond the level attained by Agathon himself.[74] Beddow even praises Wieland for aptly perceiving that "prose fiction was uniquely fitted to explore the full reality of human nature, because it was capable of conveying at one and the same time both imaginative aspirations and empirical reality, thus occupying a mediating position between purely imaginative art and purely factual history."[75] Wieland helps "reveal truths about human nature through reflections on fictional plausibility," Beddow adds, thus confirming and clarifying Martin Swales's conclusion that *Agathon* is "a novel which makes traditional novel fiction (and its attendant expectations) explicitly thematic and challenges them."[76] As argued here, such favorable judgments are further reinforced by noting the ever greater respect for fictionality shown in the successive versions of *Agathon*.

Wieland's second novel, then, teaches a fundamental lesson about the concept of fictionality. Its plot, its foreword, its kind of fictional "history," its passages on imagination, and its various endings all give reasons for defining that concept broadly, for they tie his general concern with moral examples to specific questions of literary genres. At the level of plot, Wieland debunks literary conventions and forges "intertextual" links to Euripides and Plato, inviting interpretation of *Agathon* as a study in the writing of fiction itself. His definition of verisimilitude as distinct from actual fact yet true to both the way of the world and human nature, moreover, revises strictly rationalistic concepts of literary mimesis to establish a more refined, Aristotelian art of fiction. His autobiographical and moral motives seem at odds with his intention to write accurate *Geschichte*, however, and tension between his high ideals and sober style becomes increasingly apparent in the course of the novel proper. His narrator's mixed feelings about his fictional source show that his attitude toward fictionality is not always ironic, and ambivalence about pleasures of the imagination like those described by Addison betrays that narrator's affinity to his three main characters. The three versions of *Agathon* accordingly reach different conclusions, suggesting a gradual acceptance of its fictionality, a characteristic shared by its story and its ethical ideals. Such high ideals themselves are products of the human imagination and likewise require a leap of faith in fictionality. To argue that Wieland's ethical lesson and its narrative vehicle are thus related by their common fictionality is to apply that concept in the broad sense of Vaihinger's neo-Kantian fictionalism. If *Agathon* is a *Bildungsroman*, then, it both depicts and provides an aesthetic education that pertains to actual life as well as fictional literature. Indeed, as a "self-conscious" novel, it defines its ethical lesson as a useful fiction, thereby showing greater respect for the genre of the novel itself. The concept of fictionality should therefore no longer be neglected in studies stressing its psychological, sexual, political, religious, or intellectual import.[77] Wieland's broad acceptance of fictional*ism* might well seem abrupt, moreover, if one considers *Agathon* in isolation, but he examines fictional*ity* in his other novels as well, most of which he wrote between publishing the first and final versions of *Agathon*. To understand how he got from starting *Don Sylvio* to finishing *Agathon*—from modifying Cervantes to accepting Kantian "fictions"—one thus needs to consider those several other novels, too.

Part II. The Middle Novels: Ideals

3. Sokrates Mainomenos, oder die Dialogen des Diogenes von Sinope (1770)

Hegesias having asked him to lend him of his writings, Diogenes said, "You are a simpleton, Hegesias; you do not choose painted figs instead of real ones; and yet you pass over the true training and would apply yourself to written rules."
—Diogenes Laertius, *Lives of the Eminent Philosophers* (A.D. 200–250)

Imagination remains an important theme in all the novels that Wieland wrote in addition to *Agathon* and *Don Sylvio*, but it is subsumed there by the two other issues related to the concept of fictionality in his essays: ideals and illusion. His concern with cultural and artistic ideals like those defined in "Über die Ideale der Griechischen Künstler" is especially strong in his four middle novels, beginning with *Sokrates Mainomenos oder die Dialogen des Diogenes von Sinope* (1770). Like the other three—*Der goldne Spiegel* (1772), *Danischmend* (1775), and *Die Abderiten* (1781)—*Diogenes* links such ideals to utopian notions of social reform, both describing those notions with the vocabulary of visual art and conveying how persuasively literary fiction can present them. Wieland there refers to the art of painting in numerous ways, for example, that circumvent the irony characteristic of his writing, thus suggesting considerable sympathy for Rousseau, whose life and opinions partly resemble those of his odd protagonist. Moreover, the irony apparent in Wieland's wry account of his fictional source is compounded by that character's being a writer himself, and painting is shown to be a luxury that leads to injustice, but many scenes and descriptions pertaining to that sister art—a parallel drawn in reviews of *Diogenes* as well—betray sincere respect for Rousseauean possible worlds. The other middle novels similarly attempt to overcome the impasse so obvious at the end of the first version of *Agathon*, where Wieland's mundane style proves unsuited to his lofty lesson. *Agathon* and *Don Sylvio*, too, contain remarks on painting and sculpture, thereby relating images to imagination in ways reminiscent of essays by Bodmer and Breitinger.[1] In the four middle novels, though, such scattered remarks become more systematic. Indeed, Wieland there reflects on writing as well as reading fictional literature in terms of visual art, which he invokes not only to explain his own narration but also to guide and correct his readers' responses. As such "self-conscious" statements about their origin and effects, his middle novels anticipate—and sometimes surpass—more recent treatments of the concept of fictionality.

Diogenes links that concept to Rousseauistic ideals in a hodgepodge of anecdotes, soliloquies, daydreams, tales, and treatises assembled to restore the reputation of the Cynic philosopher Diogenes of Sinope (c. 412–323 B.C.). These biographical bits and pieces are related in the first person by the title character, who concludes them with a "Republik" not unlike Plato's. As Wieland explains in yet another extensive foreword, again pretending to be the editor of an ancient manuscript, Diogenes' detractors were wrong to malign him. Plato labeled him "Socrates gone mad," for example, for exaggerating the principle that a wise man should be as free as possible from material wants. Diogenes' extreme asceticism and self-sufficiency, however, reflected his spiritual opposition to what he thought the corrupting influence of luxury, pleasure, and desire. Although he actually wrote a *Republic* attacking convention, moreover, he also declared himself a citizen of the world. He has been dismissed as a glutton who often misbehaved, but Diogenes Laertius describes him more dispassionately, and both Arrian and Lucian give favorable and sometimes glowing accounts of his life and teachings.[2] Wieland relies on these last two authors for philological support, but he also cites two modern authorities, Johann Jakob Brucker and Christoph August Heumann, who likewise held Diogenes in high esteem. In thus making Diogenes' cynicism seem harmless, Wieland belongs to a modern tradition including works such as *Diogenes Cynicus Redivivus* (1638), a school play by the Czech humanist Jan Amos Comenius, and *Diogène fabuliste*, a one-act comedy in verse by L. H. Dancourt, first performed in Paris in 1782.[3] Wieland's title character has been called distinctly rococo,[4] in fact, and he himself admits that he has made the scurrilous Cynic seem ideal, "ein ziemlich *idealischer* Diogenes" (13, Vorbericht: 23–24). As a result, his Diogenes appears to be quirky yet decent, a well-meaning and thoughtful critic of much human folly: "Dieser ist zwar ein *Sonderling,* aber ein so gutherziger, frohsinniger und . . . so vernünftiger Sonderling als es jemahls einen gegeben haben mag" (13, Vorbericht: 29–30).

Thus idealizing Diogenes meant much more to Wieland than simply rehabilitating the notorious Cynic, however, for he thereby addresses the controversial life and works of Rousseau as well. In his foreword, he notes that Rousseau, too, acquired an undeservedly poor reputation merely by seeming eccentric and defying accepted moral conventions: "Man müßte wenig Kenntniß der Welt haben, wenn man nicht wüßte, daß etliche wenige Züge von Sonderbarkeit und Abweichung von den gewöhnlichen Formen des sittlichen Betragens hinlänglich sind, den vortrefflichsten Mann in ein falsches Licht zu stellen. Wir haben an dem berühmten Hans Jakob Rousseau von Genf (einem Manne, der vielleicht im Grunde nicht halb so sonderbar ist als er scheint) ein Beyspiel, welches diesen Satz ungemein erläutert" (13, Vorbericht: 22–23). By defending Diogenes, Wieland thus seems to offer an apology for Rousseau as well. Indeed, he takes this tactic of comparing the two philosophers a step further by having Diogenes share Rousseau's social philosophy. Diogenes speaks of a social contract, natural law, and the distribution of wealth as if he has read Rousseau's seminal works on these subjects. He explains, for example, how one wealthy young Corinthian's private revenues actually accrue from the state, since they are the result of a long-standing social contract: "Sie sind dein Eigenthum, es ist wahr; aber nur kraft des Vertrags, welcher zwischen den Stiftern der Republik getroffen wurde, da sie die erste Güthertheilung vornahmen" (13:103). Diogenes alludes to Rousseau more directly when he likewise cites *der gesellschaftliche Vertrag und die daher fließenden bürgerlichen Gesetze* (13:104), a social contract and civil laws binding thanks to the explicit or tacit agreement on which he says society rests. He himself likes living beyond the pale of such jurisdiction, obeying only natural law—"nach dem Gesetze der Natur" (13:103)—but this circumstance will be universal, he explains, once the state withers and dies: "So bald der Staat ein Ende hat, fängt der Stand der Natur wieder an, alles fällt in die ursprüngliche Gleichheit zurück" (13:108). Diogenes' interlocutor probably does not learn this lesson, but its sources certainly lie in Rousseau's *Discours sur l'origine et les fondements de l'inégalité parmi les hommes* (1754) and *Du contrat social* (1762). Indeed, like these two works, *Diogenes* has been called required reading for the Illuminati in prerevolutionary France.[5]

Nonetheless, Diogenes does not sound very sympathetic to Rousseau's argument that progress in the arts and sciences corrupts primitive virtue, and he derides the idea of the noble savage. In fact, his satiric "Republik des Diogenes" describes a utopia where primal innocence is shown to be so much wishful thinking and where returning to nature is exposed as an unworkable dream. Intended as a happy land where "alles natürlich zugehen soll" (13:178)—the same phrase that serves as the subtitle of *Don Sylvio*—Diogenes' republic is no less ironic a fiction. Indeed, Diogenes imagines it as "eine Republik nach meiner Fantasie" (13:125), a place that he expressly posits with the help of a magic wand and that can later be saved from corrupt Europeans only by disappearing, which is what he ultimately has it do, intending it as no more than a mere chimera. Wieland thus mocks pipe dreams offered not only by Rousseau but also by Plato, whose own *Republic* is the explicit butt of Diogenes' scorn. Diogenes criticizes Plato's ideal state as a republic, "die aus *lauter Ideen* zusammen gesetzt ist, und lauter Ideen zum Endzweck hat!" (13:177–78). This opposition to airy abstractions shows Diogenes' larger anti-Platonism, but he is hardly hostile to social ideals as such, as is clear from his attitude toward art. Although he has no use for overrefined and decadent art, he bans painters and sculptors from his republic only reluctantly, approving of the arts and sciences as long as they restore corrupt civilization to its natural simplicity. He even hails certain pictures and portraits as masterpieces showing ideal beauties that elevate the mind to concepts of sublime perfection. Such faith in intellectual beauty, in fact, is what moves Diogenes to write his "Republik," a task that he undertakes after seeing Alexander the Great set out to change the world for real. As he informs that young king, "*Du hast* . . . *den Entwurf von einem allgemeinen Reiche gemacht, und gehst hin ihn auszuführen!—Ich sehe dich von der hohen Schönheit deiner Idee begeistert*" (13:155). Beneath his ironic crust, Diogenes thus seems to admire grand designs for reforming society after all, though he has doubts about putting ideals like Rousseau's into practice.

This reluctance to think like Rousseau is not surprising, given the reservations expressed in two essays that Wieland wrote about the Swiss philosopher, both of them published the same year as *Diogenes*. In those essays, Wieland professes respect for Rousseau, and he implicitly likens him to Diogenes, but he also disagrees with Rousseau's conclusions, especially the idea that the original state of mankind was one of blissful ignorance and splendid isolation. In "Betrachtungen über J. J. Rousseaus ursprünglichen Zustand des Menschen" (1770), Wieland calls Rousseau strange yet sincere, a Cynic whose imagination leads him to hypotheses that would seem ironic coming from anyone else. Specifically, Wieland argues that human beings were never cut off from each other and that nature itself helps civilize them, "daß die Menschen aller Wahrscheinlichkeit nach *von Anfang an in Gesellschaft lebten*—und von allen Seiten mit *natürlichen* Mitteln umgeben sind, die ihnen die Entwicklung ihrer Anlagen *erleichtern* helfen" (14:142). Similarly, in "Über die von J. J. Rousseau vorgeschlagenen Versuche den wahren Stand der Natur des Menschen zu entdecken" (1770), he adds that the highest perfection or refinement of human life is just as natural as the simplicity praised by Rousseau. Rousseau also figures in other writings by Wieland, but his influence is strongest in *Diogenes*, for which the significance of such remarks is still debated. The novel has been considered an echo of Wieland's earlier Rousseauistic leanings, for example, while Diogenes' satirical judgment of Rousseau has seemed one-sided, and Wieland's polemic against him misplaced, not least due to the idealistic method, applied in Wieland's essays as well, of divorcing Rousseau's writings from his personal life.[6] *Diogenes* has also been called a gentle parody of Rousseau, one that discredits his radical ideas of social reform by means of poetic fictions that take ad absurdum plans for realizing them.[7] Given Diogenes' weakness for ideals instilled by art, though, and Wieland's implicit defense of fictionality in his earlier novels, such claims need to be examined more closely.

The role of fictions in *Diogenes* is tied to its fictional source, which is cited in a clearly ironic *Quellenfiktion*. The "editor" writes that he has loosely translated a manuscript that he discovered in an abbey where it was simply gathering dust. This origin has been called a fiction aimed at clerical ignorance,[8] and it prompts mock worries about his convincingness, as well as many admissions and reminders that his story is made up. For example, the editor fears that his account of finding a sympathetic librarian in the abbey will seem so extraordinary as to make all else he tells suspicious, and a footnote to only the third page of the text proper reveals a playful lack of concern with historical accuracy: "Wir können es keinem Kenner der Griechischen Sitten und Gebräuche in den Zeiten des Diogenes verdenken, wenn er an der Ächtheit dieser Stelle zweifelt. Freylich ist es nicht die einzige in diesem Werke, die zu einem solchen Zweifel Anlaß giebt—Aber desto schlimmer! werden die Kenner sagen" (13:5 n. 1). Not even pretending to write accurate *Geschichte* here, the editor later regrets that a lacuna mars the manuscript, thereby underscoring the fictionality of its location: Diogenes' "Republik." The author of that manuscript claims to have translated it from Arabic into Latin, moreover, so the editor guesses that Moors brought it from Baghdad to Salamanca, accounting for the transmission of its Greek original by a circuitous route that combines the antique and the Spanish varieties of fictional sources found in *Agathon* and *Don Sylvio*. This conclusion reinforces its fictionality when the editor tells how he identified his manuscript by imagining this mere possibility of its source to be real:

Und nun brauchte ich nichts weiter als von den Regeln der Verwandlung des Möglichen ins Wirkliche einen kleinen Gebrauch zu machen, um mir einzubilden, daß diese Dialogen ohne Zweifel unter den Griechischen Handschriften gewesen seyen, welche der berühmte *Kalif Al-Mamon* zu Bagdad mit großen Kosten zusammen suchen und ins Arabische übersetzen ließ.

(13, Vorbericht: 14)

Diogenes himself takes this same logical leap when he enacts his dislike of abstract ideas. Appalled that an Athenian crowd should let itself be swindled by a sham metaphysician, he goads it by similarly discoursing on the man in the moon. This spoof on philosophical certainty starts with feigned hesitation about which comes first, the real or the possible:

> Aufrichtig zu reden . . . so seh' ich mich doch in keiner geringen Verlegenheit, ob ich von der *Wirklichkeit* des Mannes im Mond, oder von seiner *Möglichkeit* zuerst reden soll. Denn damit er *wirklich* seyn könne, muß er *möglich* seyn, und damit er *möglich* seyn könne, muß er *wirklich seyn.* Hier liegt der Knoten!

(13:133–34)

Diogenes cuts this logical knot simply by assuming that the man in the moon exists, a solution narratively important because the editor gives it, too. The editor's text, that is, and Diogenes' example of a metaphysical mirage share the quality of being a deliberate fiction. The editor repeatedly cites the fictional source ironically, then, and irony seems to pervade Diogenes' plans as well.

Together with satire and skepticism, irony is accordingly the concept that crops up most often in research on *Diogenes*. The novel is said to be complex in ways that both display Wieland's socially critical intentions and determine how binding his fiction is on its readers, questions often closely linked to its fictional character. Scholars cite Diogenes' skepticism toward idealistic plans for social reform, call his skeptical irony the defining trait of Wieland's social criticism, and note that the fictional conversations in the novel are meant to be taken as satire on its readers' own times.[9] It has even been argued that Wieland satirically encourages hatred for the evils of capitalism.[10] Less dogmatic critics discern a "dual perspective" that accounts for Diogenes' skepticism and irony as well as his idyllic dreams of a simple life, or they see a "double refraction" in Wieland's ironic connection to his ironic protagonist, asserting that the substance of Wieland's moral message is not diluted by the fictionality of its playful, open narrative form.[11] The most detailed analysis of Wieland's irony in *Diogenes*, by Hans-Joachim Mähl, ties it to conscious reflection on the hypothetic character of all utopias such as Diogenes' "Republik." This narrative awareness not only casts doubt on the truth of such utopian fiction but also calls for reflecting on its nature and narration. Wieland's irony, that is, shows the conditions of the possibility of utopia as well as of utopian narration being reflected in such fiction itself.[12] Mähl doubts that eighteenth-century readers appreciated this irony toward both the form and the content of Wieland's fiction, posing the same kind of question about its validity earlier raised in another study that stresses the role of readers in making sense of *Diogenes*, a role supposedly assigned them by Wieland's ironic style.[13]

Wieland himself likewise suggests that satire and irony best describe both his intentions in *Diogenes* and most readers' reactions to it. In his correspondence, he explains his similarity to Diogenes, his blithe inspiration, and the modernity of his satire, which many readers misunderstood. He told Sophie von La Roche that his own philosophy resembled that of Diogenes, for example, and though he disliked the cynicism of Wilhelm Heinse, who he thought paid too little heed to propriety, a few months spent at the stuffy court in Weimar later moved Wieland to prefer a tub or barrel like the one in which the frugal Diogenes lived.[14] In Erfurt, where he wrote *Diogenes* during his stint as a professor of philosophy, he called it a work conceived in a capricious spirit and written on a philosophical whim like that of Laurence Sterne's Yorick, a frivolous "baggatelle" consisting of several "bons morceaux" and some "jolies vignettes."[15] While he also distinguished himself from his fictional character, denying responsibility for Diogenes' use of an unnamed dirty word, he called Diogenes' "Republik" his own best effort (a high opinion that he hardly tempered later in life), adding that its satire, like that of the episode about the man in the moon, was aimed at targets other than those explicitly named in it but was often lost on his muddle-headed readers: "A mon avis, elle est mon chef-d'oeuvre. La plupart des lecteurs sont des têtes—comme des têtes de choux, surtout parmi le *peuple savant*. Tous ces gens-là admirent la harangue sur l'homme de la lune;—comme une satyre contre les *anciens Sophistes*, et la république de Diogène comme une belle satyre contre les républiques à la Platon. Et ce sont des personnages, qui se croyent biens fins avec cette découverte là."[16] Objections raised by such benighted readers did not ruffle Wieland, though, who dismissed them by quoting an ancient Greek inscription rendered into German as "Sie sagen von mir was sie wollen; mögen sie doch! was kümmerts mich?"[17] This same inscription is pondered in his "Gedanken über eine alte Aufschrift" (1772), an essay defending misperceived geniuses like Diogenes. Wieland there warns that writers should not always welcome popularity, since many an admiring reader misses their irony: "Bey genauerer Nachfrage zeigt sich, daß es eine *Ironie* war, die er *für Ernst* nahm" (13:239).

The issue of Wieland's own ironic intentions is complicated, however, for Diogenes himself is shown to be a writer, one whose apparent independence has struck some critics as a more or less appealing ideal. He encounters problems writing at the outset of Wieland's story, which begins with his search for something on which to scribble. Lacking metal or stone, and refusing to write in the sand, he decides to inscribe the walls of his tub. Later, his patron Xeniades gives him a costly writing tablet, which he is supposed to fill and return. Both of these surfaces have been assigned narrative meaning. Klaus Bäppler argues that Diogenes' writing on his tub—in effect, on his own four walls—demonstrates his intention to describe and interpret himself, an introspective focus similarly cited by Peter Michelsen, who notes that such writing is not an attempt to communicate with the outside world.[18] By contrast, Diogenes' use of the writing tablet does seem such an attempt, one made by an oddball like Sterne's Yorick, a character repeatedly mentioned in discussions of Wieland's debt to the English humorist.[19] Bäppler observes that anything written on such a tablet can be erased, a fact that he thinks releases Diogenes from binding narrative structures, and he explains that Diogenes' reluctance to right any actual wrongs shows the impotence of socially concerned intellectuals.[20] This parallel between Diogenes' writing and his social influence has been drawn most sharply by Wilson. Diogenes' use of the expensive writing tablet is an exception to his strict avoidance of luxury, so it belies his philosophy and compromises his independence. Wilson relates the attendant failure of a would-be social critic to Wieland's own frustrated ambitions in Erfurt, reading *Diogenes* as a comment on ideals of political patronage: "The novel is not only a work of social criticism, it is a probing examination of the *origins* of social criticism, a metacritique of the preconditions of a free and critical existence for the intellectual."[21] In this complex sense, though he also notes their differences, Wilson confirms earlier claims that Diogenes was a model for Wieland or an idealized self-portrait.[22]

The most revealing clue to Wieland's and Diogenes' roles as social critics, however, lies less in what either reveals about the profession of writing than in their remarks on the related art of painting. As noted above, visual art in *Diogenes* is both a source of the decadence censured by Rousseau and a vehicle for ideals sincerely embraced by Diogenes. This apparent discrepancy of visual voluptuousness and intellectual beauty is actually a sign of Wieland's attempt to overcome the irony that he, his fictional editor, and Diogenes all demonstrate in their respective writing. Irony seems an inescapable part of their literary prose, which cannot transcend its own fictionality. In painting, though, a more receptive attitude toward the social ideals described in *Diogenes* seems possible. This difference may be due to the semiotic contrast between "arbitrary" signs of language and "natural" ones of visual art, a distinction that had only recently been developed in Lessing's *Laokoön* (1766). It can be traced more directly to works by Wieland's mentors in Zurich, however, especially to Bodmer's *Critische Betrachtungen über die poetischen Gemählde der Dichter* (1741) and Breitinger's *Critische Abhandlung von der Natur den Absichten und dem Gebrauche der Gleichnisse* (1740). These works analyze the effect of poetry on its readers, describing similes, metaphors, and rhetorical figures as poetic "Gemählde" or "Bilder," and Wieland likewise relates visual images and literary imagination. In a note to *Diogenes* in his *Ausgabe letzter Hand*, for example, he explains that the location of his Latin manuscript can no longer be found: "Zur Steuer der Wahrheit können wir nicht verhalten, daß seit den 25 Jahren, da alles hier gesagte historische Wahrheit war, . . . die Gestalt der Sachen sich so mächtig geändert hat, daß es dem *inquisitivsten Reisenden* unmöglich seyn würde, das ehmahlige Urbild von dem hier aufgestellten Gemählde ausfündig zu machen" (13, Vorbericht: 4 n. 1). Wieland uses similar terms in "Gedanken über eine alte Aufschrift," urging his readers to see people in a proper light, their true colors, and the right perspective—not "in einem *falschen Licht*, und mit andern als ihren *eigenen Farben*" (13:225). As in his essay on Greek artists, these terms suggest models and matters of perception not confined to the imitation of nature.

Reading *Diogenes* aware of the imaginative vision thus suggested by Wieland's talk of art demonstrates that irony is not his last word on ideals like Rousseau's. The novel includes several episodes that mention painting and sculpture, revealing such visual art to be a rhetorical means of making Wieland's story seem more than ironic satire. Most of those episodes involve an evil character named Chärea, a wealthy collector of art who ignores the human suffering caused by indulging in such an expensive habit. Diogenes rails against the social inequality that he thinks enables visual artists to thrive when he describes one of Chärea's paintings. It depicts what he calls "ein recht poetischer Ort," a pastoral landscape that enthuses even him, "de[n] unpoetische[n] Diogenes" (13:33). Thus linking painting to poetry, he expresses his feelings at the sight of such an idyllic scene, exclaiming that it is "ein liebliches Gemählde" (13:33), a painting that he wishes his own readers could see illustrated (*ausgemahlt*) as vividly as he imagines it. Only after letting his female readers know that his imagination can be extremely erotic does he admit that his written description is no more than a copy of an actual painting. He thus deflates what seems a purely imaginary ideal, and he goes on to rebuke Chärea for having paid too much for the painting and simply driven up the price of frivolous art instead of spending his money to relieve poor people's misfortune. Such combined aesthetic and social criticism is less severe, however, when Diogenes meets one of Chärea's tenant farmers, who laments that his cruel master refuses to ransom his kidnapped daughter. Diogenes does not know whether the farmer is really the missing girl's father until the old man's account of her removes all doubts. Here, too, Diogenes calls such a description a painting: "Ich erkannte den Vater in der Wärme des Gemähldes" (13:37). Despite cursing the painters whose art, thanks to Chärea, causes the farmer's distress, Diogenes is deeply moved by this touching "Gemählde."[23] It elicits a sincere, ethically sound response from him, so his dim view of painting does not mean that such art cannot sometimes be put to good use. Expressed in words, at least, its effects seem socially justified.

Another, related scene similarly shows visual images cited for rhetorical effect. Diogenes not only responds sincerely to verbal "paintings," but also makes effective use of them himself. Chärea complains that he does not feel like defending his old friend Lamon, who has been wrongly accused of embezzling public funds. Lamon's wife once begged his help, but instead of aiding her, Chärea says he only saw the artistic potential of her awkward position: "Die Scene war rührend; ich hätte funfzig Minen um einen guten Mahler gegeben, der mir auf der Stelle ein Gemählde daraus gemacht hätte" (13:26). Shocked by such callousness, Diogenes asks how Chärea could possibly have had such thoughts, but Chärea simply replies that a painting of Lamon's wife would have been well worth the money. When Diogenes then chides him for propositioning her, Chärea answers that he is in no mood for moralizing and wants to go visit a looser woman instead. He invites Diogenes to accompany him, once again linking lasciviousness to painting: "Willst du mit mir zur *Thryallis* gehen?—Mein Mahler nimmt das Modell zu einer Venus Kallipyga von ihr.—Es wird ein treffliches Stück werden!" (13:28). Rather than tag along, Diogenes publicly speaks up for Lamon, whose release he succeeds in winning. The rhetoric that he uses is inspired by Chärea, though, whose scene of the weeping wife and her sons is the climax of Diogenes' speech to Lamon's judges. As Diogenes later reports, "Ich sprach mit aller der Wärme, die mir die Idee der schönen Frau und der zwey lieblichen Kinder mitgetheilt hatte . . . Ich vollendete meinen Sieg mit dem Gemählde der schönen Frau, und der zwey kleinen Jungen, die ich zu ihren Füßen hinwarf und für ihren ehrlichen Vater bitten ließ" (13:31). This example of justice served proves the power of *verbal* art. According to Wilson, Diogenes is an "*artist* in words," whose saving of Lamon's wife and children shows the "proper, *critical* and moral use of art," art produced to achieve virtuous social ends, that is, instead of being consumed as soft pornography.[24] Given how Bodmer and Breitinger relate visual art to figurative language—and thus to their possible-worlds semantics as well—such scenes should also be understood as comments on the fictionality of both the referents suggested by literary prose and the moral idealism preached in *Agathon.*

Further scenes in *Diogenes* pertaining to painting and sculpture reveal that such art is indeed a key to Wieland's literary as well as moral fictions. Those scenes show how Diogenes learns to resist the erotic effects of art like Chärea's, a lesson neatly tied to Diogenes' own narration insofar as it concerns spiritual beauty. One kind of person who could use Chärea's help, he explains, is the innocent woman who must pose for certain painters' libidinous portraits, "die unschuldige Schönheit, welche du von der Schmach, einem *Parrhasius* zum Modell seiner leichtfertigen Täfelchen zu dienen . . . befreyen könntest" (13:41). As a young man, Diogenes once made a fool of himself when tempted by a woman looking at such a painting, "eine *Leda* von *Parrhasius*" (13:18). Later in life, when he saves a beautiful lady from drowning, however, Diogenes can face such temptation with equanimity: "Aber ein Mann von funfzig Jahren, der seit mehr als zwanzig von Salat, Bohnen und Wasser lebt, darf eine jede schöne Statue ansehen, sie mag nun aus den Händen eines *Alkamenes* oder der *Natur selbst* gekommen seyn" (13:71). He also takes revenge on a woman who has slandered him, despite both her picturesque young slave, "der einem Mahler die Idee zum schönsten *Bacchus* gegeben hätte" (13:81), and her own ever more picturesque appearance, her increasingly "*mahlerischeres* Ansehen" (13:83). Diogenes even likens his own writing to visual art when he falls in love with Laidion, a woman whose checkered past includes modeling for a sculptor. He gets carried away when he tells how he and Laidion first met, apologizing to his readers and calling his description of her a copy of a beloved original: "Aber in der That, ich bitte euch um Verzeihung; ich vergesse, daß ich dieses Nachbild eines Originals, an dessen kleinste Züge ich mich mit Vergnügen erinnere, nicht für mich selbst mache" (13:45). The young Laidion is so attractive to Diogenes because her beauty is more than merely physical. Indeed, she is a "beautiful soul," a concept that assumes, for him, almost Rousseauean artlessness: "Wie? es sollte also nicht auch *schöne Seelen* geben, wie es *schöne Gesichter* giebt, die der Kunst nichts schuldig, und gerade *darum* nur *desto schöner* sind?" (13:42). An ideal like the "belle âme" possessed by Rousseau's Julie d'Étanges in *La Nouvelle Héloïse* (1761) thus seems central to Diogenes' art of verbal depiction.

That such art did not go unnoticed in Wieland's day may be gleaned from the initial reception of *Diogenes*. Reviewers often praised Wieland's style as verbal painting, calling his prose "picturesque" (*mahlerisch*) and his scenes "paintings" (*Gemählde*). The *Allgemeine deutsche Bibliothek* gave the novel an often mixed but ultimately favorable review, recommending its "mahlerische Schönheiten" in general and one chapter in particular as "das feinste satyrische Gemählde."[25] The reviewer observed that tasteful readers would distinguish Wieland's indecent ambiguities from his "anständigen Gemählden," commending him for making Diogenes' thoughts seem so charming: "Wir bewundern den Dichter, welcher den Gedanken des Philosophen mit so vielen mahlerischen und sittlichen Reizen ausgezieret hat."[26] The *Erlangsche gelehrte Anmerkungen und Nachrichten* similarly used the vocabulary of painting to describe his Diogenes: "Herr Wieland mahlt uns ihn als den liebenswürdigsten Weltweisen, der nur jemals gelebt hat."[27] Even Goethe compared Wieland's writing to painting. In a letter thanking Wieland's publisher Philipp Erasmus Reich for a copy of *Diogenes*, Goethe expressed mixed feelings, "die . . . Wieland so süsse mahlen kann."[28] To some extent, this common thread running through reviews of *Diogenes* may be due to a failure to distinguish writing from painting on semiotic grounds. As noted above, Lessing's *Laokoön* had only recently appeared. Wieland himself, however, the student of Bodmer and Breitinger, seems unlikely to have simply confused these sister arts. He would not publish his essay on the ideals of Greek artists for another seven years, but *Diogenes* already associates social ideals with their art, which Wieland considered related to literary imagination. As a result, the novel is fraught with tension between ironic writing conspicuously done on all of its several levels—that of Wieland, the editor, and Diogenes himself—and visual art conceived as a more immediate means of narration, one that can convey social ideals more sincerely. Despite its ironic commentary, that is, *Diogenes* introduces idealistic concepts in scenes about painting, an art presented as more persuasive than hyperconscious literature.

Although it describes a Cynic, then, *Diogenes* is anything but a cynical novel. Wieland's remark that Rousseau's ideas would sound ironic coming from anyone else only seems to set the tone of his story, where Diogenes stands for the Swiss philosopher, representing him more subtly than its irony implies. One wonders if Wieland knew of Frederick the Great's strikingly similar comparison of Rousseau and Diogenes, which the monarch made in a letter that recalls Wieland's monastic *Quellenfiktion*: "Ich glaube, daß Rousseau seinen Beruf verfehlt hat; er war ohne Zweifel geboren, ein großer Klosterbruder zu werden . . .

aber jetzt wird man ihn nur als einen sonderbaren Philosophen anse-
hen, der nach zweitausend Jahren die Sekte des Diogenes erneuert."[29]
In any case, Wieland himself describes Diogenes as an eccentric crank
in his poem *Musarion* (1768), where the famous Cynic connotes thread-
bare clothes and an unkempt appearance. As Musarion asks the down-
and-out Fanias, "wozu die Außenseite / von einem *Diogen?*" (9:23).
Kleanth, the disgraced Stoic of the poem, moreover, sheepishly steals
away, "vielleicht in eine *Tonne*" (9:101), into a tub like the one that
housed Diogenes, and Musarion alludes to this same odd dwelling
when she chides moralists who make a virtue of forgoing things that
they cannot have in the first place. To her, Diogenes represents this phi-
losophy of frustration:

> "Was, meinst du, bildete der *Mann im Faß* sich ein,
> Der, groß genug Monarchen zu verachten,
> Von Filipps Sohn nichts bat, als freyen Sonnenschein?"
>
> (9:95)

She soon adds that Fanias should not dismiss all castles in the air that
are constructed this way, however, reminding him that Platonic com-
pensation for earthly pleasures is serious dreaming—and not only for
its idealistic creator:

> "Ein Schlag mit seinem Zauberstab
> Heißt Welten um uns her bey Tausenden entstehen;
> Sind's gleich nur Welten aus Ideen,
> So baut man sie so herrlich als man will;
> Und steht einmahl das Rad der äußern Sinne still,
> Wer sagt uns, daß wir nicht im Traume wirklich sehen?
> Ein Traum, der uns zum Gast der Götter macht—"
>
> (9:96)

Musarion here refers to the same kind of magic wand that Diogenes
wields when narrating his "Republik," and it, too, seems justified by
this eloquent defense of fictional worlds. At any rate, Diogenes' sincere
relation of social ideals in writing conceived, described, and under-
stood as painting implies that fictionality is a characteristic conveyable
by visual as well as verbal representation. This implication not only an-
ticipates the "unified account of fictionality" noted above, in contrast
to other, stricter definitions; it also is developed, and with clearer nar-
rative consequences, in Wieland's other middle novels.

4. Der goldne Spiegel, oder die Könige von Scheschian (1772)

J'ai vû et parcouru Usong, mais je ne l'ai pas lû;
raison pourquoi? c'est que je me suis endormi à la
7me page.
—Wieland, in a letter to Sophie von La Roche,
on Albrecht von Haller's *Usong* (1771)

As in *Diogenes*, social ideals like Rousseau's are the subject of the other novel that Wieland wrote in Erfurt, *Der goldne Spiegel, oder die Könige von Scheschian* (1772). Here, too, such ideals seem presented ironically in a highly "self-conscious" narrative frame but related sincerely in scenes and terms tied to visual art. The explicit narration and verbal "painting" of *Der goldne Spiegel*, however, reveal how Wieland tried to go beyond Diogenes' skepticism, beyond adding a purely utopian "Republik" to Diogenes' story as an afterthought, that is, as an ideal that could be envisioned but never realized. Wieland now develops such ironic idealism more fully, discussing not only its general import but also its specific implementation. His "true history" is set somewhere in Asia and traces the weal and woe of a fictional line of kings, whose most distinguished member finally embodies the ideal of enlightened despotism. Wieland also tells how well literary fiction instills such ideals, both in the course of this "history" itself and in remarks by characters who read it in his frame story, which takes place sometime later and recalls *Arabian Nights*. Further remarks are added in footnotes, ostensibly by translators said to have rendered the manuscript recounting that history from the language of Hindustan into Chinese, Latin, and German. With his usual tongue-in-cheek citations of such a fictional source, Wieland poses serious questions about the fictionality of literary media as well as social morality, questions that recur on all levels of his novel. His story proper, narrative frame, and footnotes all show or discuss both the use and the abuse of imagination, for example, while his depiction of utopian social ideals and of debates about their usefulness suggests not only good government but also the best way to translate fiction into action. He conveys that applying concepts learned from novels is not easy, but such pragmatic concern with the objects and effects of narrative fiction understood to be neither pure fantasy nor merely personal satire is what *Der goldne Spiegel* literally reflects.

The title of *Der goldne Spiegel* indicates this broad concern with the issue of fictionality, but it does so indirectly, holding a mirror up to life not in the sense of the literary reflection often noted in studies of nineteenth-century realism but rather in that of *Fürstenspiegel* like Xenophon's *Cyropaedia*, works that describe and try to inculcate qualities of an ideal leader, often glossing over unpleasant historical facts. Wieland had attempted such a work once before, his *Cyrus* (1759), in which he announces didactic aims characteristic of the genre:

> Und Ihr, höret mich, Freunde der unentheiligten Musen
> Und der Tugend, vor andern *Ihr künftigen Herrscher der Völker*,
> Deren jugendlich Herz die Gewalt der Wahrheit noch fühlet:
> Hört mich, und lernt von *Cyrus* die wahre Größe der Helden!
> (16:7–8)

Der goldne Spiegel is similarly didactic in intent, tacitly addressed to Joseph II in Vienna, though it secured Wieland the job of tutor to Karl August in Weimar. Just as Xenophon's *Cyropaedia* is said to be the archetypal *Fürstenspiegel*, in fact, *Der goldne Spiegel* has been called the high point of the genre, one that typically cloaks its social criticism in the costume of oriental lands like Wieland's "Scheschian."[1] Walter Benjamin notes, though, that Wieland's novel differs from its predecessors by subordinating its plot to the lively conversation that takes place in its frame story, a narrative technique also praised for striking a perfect balance between a satire and a utopia.[2] This technique has similarly been hailed as an acceptance of the challenge posed by all *Staatsromane*, hailed for relating the reception of the genre, that is; but not all scholars judge it so favorably, saying that it either relativizes the *Staatsroman* or criticizes the genre by taking its inherent aporia to extremes.[3] This difference of opinion may be due to the fact that the genre itself was long taboo or that even present-day theory cannot make much of *Fürstenspiegel*.[4] At any rate, the generic questions posed by *Der goldne Spiegel* lend themselves to answers framed in terms of fictionality that apply to visual as well as verbal representation.

Such terms are implicit in Wieland's dedicatory preface, where the education of an imperial reader is related to the language of visual art and the logic of Wieland's fictional source. This "Zueignungsschrift" is attributed to the Chinese translator, who knows that simply addressing royal listeners, as Wieland does in his *Cyrus*, is not the same as actually getting them to live up to heroic ideals. The translator regrets that good intentions are difficult to carry out, even for his patron: "Wie glücklich müßten Sie selbst seyn, Bester der Könige, wenn es gleich leicht wäre, ein Volk glücklich *zu wünschen*, und es glücklich *zu machen*! wenn Sie, wie der König des Himmels, nur *wollen* dürften, um zu *vollbringen*, nur *sprechen*, um Ihre Gedanken in Werke verwandelt zu sehen!" (6:vii–viii). This gap between proposing and disposing is faced by rulers and writers alike. The former can learn from the annals of human history, one reads, including the checkered past of the kings of Scheschian, which the latter relay in "mirrors" described in terms of visual art, mirrors "worin sich die natürlichen Folgen der Weisheit und der Thorheit in einem . . . starken Lichte, mit . . . deutlichen Zügen und mit . . . warmen Farben darstellen" (6:xviii–xix). Such strong, clear, and vivid accounts are necessary because virtue and vice as well as truth and deceit are often indistinguishable, "tragen einerley Farbe" (6:xi), that is, especially when tinged by scheming courtiers. Indeed, verbal "mirrors" must clear away "den falsch gefärbten Duft . . . womit sie die wahre Farbe der Gegenstände überzogen haben" (6:xiv). This literally colorful language recalls the rhetorical use of visual art in *Diogenes*, where Wieland describes social ideals as poetic images, the figurative *Bilder* recommended by Bodmer and Breitinger. What is more, the dedication ends with the news that the text to come is a translation and with a footnote in which the Latin translator apologizes for a lacuna in his Chinese manuscript, further reminders that *Der goldne Spiegel* is a tall, if useful, tale. From the outset, then, Wieland's gilded *Fürstenspiegel* is presented as a matter of persuasive fiction.

That this matter will not be easy is clear from the introduction to the novel, which follows its dedication and displays strong ambivalence toward the concept of fictionality. Wieland there establishes the narrative frame within which the history of Scheschian serves as a royal civics lesson. He begins by tracing the ancestry of the sultan meant to learn that lesson, one Schach Gebal, the fifth in a line of rulers whose most notable trait is their extreme reaction to fairy tales. Their patriarch, Schach Riar, is the despot entertained by Scheherezade in *Arabian Nights*, and though one knows little about his son, Schach Lolo, his grandson Schach Baham follows his example and turns out to be an uncontrollable fan of fairy tales, a great "Liebhaber von Mährchen" (6:5). Schach Baham's tutor teaches him that the ancients draped their wisdom in such tales, and he is as full of folksy sayings as Sancho Panza. His son Schach Dolka, however, is so sick of hearing fairy tales that he, like Plato, bans poets from his republic, "ein erklärter *Feind* von allem, was einem Mährchen gleich sah" (6:7). Schach Gebal is equally averse to such fiction, but he seems susceptible to more refined musing. He has no patience with *Arabian Nights*, so opposed to such tales that one cannot tell them in his presence. For him, stories have to be less dubious, more reliable, and not the least bit marvelous: "Er erklärte sich, daß er keine Erzählungen wolle, wofern sie nicht, ohne darum weniger unterhaltend zu seyn, *sittlich* und *anständig* wären: auch verlangte er, daß sie *wahr* und *aus beglaubten Urkunden* gezogen seyn, und (was er für eine wesentliche Eigenschaft der Glaubwürdigkeit hielt) daß sie *nichts Wunderbares* enthalten sollten; denn davon war er jederzeit ein erklärter Feind gewesen" (6:29). These moral, epistemological, and aesthetic criteria, which were applied by eighteenth-century readers as well, link Schach Gebal to larger issues of fictionality. Indeed, he likes to discuss the best of all possible ways to set his finances straight and would take offense at troubles started by the man in the moon, qualities that tie him to Leibniz's possible-worlds semantics and to the episode in *Diogenes* that mocks metaphysics in the same language of the possible and the real used to describe Wieland's fictional source there.

Mixed feelings about fictions are related to the spurious source of *Der goldne Spiegel*, too, both in Wieland's introduction and in research about the multiple narrative levels of the novel. The introduction explains that Danischmend, court philosopher to Schach Gebal, and Nurmahal, the latter's concubine, read the history of Scheschian aloud to put their master to sleep. The German translator adds, though, that his Chinese colleague provided only excerpts of the original manuscript containing this unusual cure for insomnia. He also leaves readers free to doubt the Chinese translator's claim that Schach Gebal's interruptions and interjections are authentic, though he finds them plausible and hardly thinks it fair to expect them to be as witty and entertaining as Schach Baham's. Wieland thus ironically makes his frame story sound credible, inviting readers to take one fictional figure as the measure of another. Research on the structure and significance of *Der goldne Spiegel* similarly notes the ironic yet plausible force of Wieland's narration. By combining various levels of fiction—his history and its frame—he is said to show the difference between an idea and reality, ironically diffusing his political lessons.[5] This strategy has also been called a reflection on the relationship between utopia and reality, a narrative game that demonstrates the difference between rational and empirical concepts of mimesis.[6] As Peter Uwe Hohendahl expresses it, Wieland recognized the formal problematic of the utopian novel and found an appropriate solution. By thematizing the difference between reality and fiction in fiction itself, Hohendahl explains, Wieland can describe a utopia and simultaneously maintain the verisimilitude of his story.[7] More recently, scholars have found Wieland's story of an ideal king a reasonable and respectable fiction meant to be matched by reality, relating such remarks to its "fictional transmission."[8] According to some, that fictional narrative makes a theoretical legitimation of royal authority unnecessary, though others argue that theoretical politics alone result from thus realizing Wieland's ideals only in a fictive realm.[9] Finally, Scheschian has seemed true precisely because it is fictive and thus corresponds to general laws of human nature.[10] Like his own introduction, such remarks reveal conflicting views of fictionality itself.

The process of describing and presenting utopian notions to readers, moreover, also links the feelings about fictionality expressed in Wieland's introduction to the events of his novel proper. Those events occur on two narrative levels, the fictional kings of Scheschian being closely related to the characters in the frame story. Each generation of those kings shows a different attitude toward ideals and imagination, topics also explored in Nurmahal and Danischmend's interspersed discussions with Schach Gebal. In this way, Wieland makes notions of social reform parallel the reception of fictional literature, urging the acceptance of fictionality in both. This structural strategy emerges as soon as Nurmahal starts to read the early history of Scheschian. Unified by a neighboring king who rules it as an absolute monarch, that imaginary land enjoys increasing comforts and amenities under the reign of Queen Lili, who refines its customs by following the path onto which she is led by "eine wollüstige Einbildungskraft" (6:73). Such indulgence of her imagination worries some of her subjects, who think that it will lead to sloth and decadent daydreaming, but wise elders dismiss this danger, noting that the progress of man is a product of nature, which works via imagination, "indem sie durch die Bedürfnisse seine Einbildungskraft und durch die Einbildungskraft seine Leidenschaften spielen macht" (6:71–72). Wieland similarly attributes civilization to nature itself in his essays taking issue with Rousseau, but Schach Gebal is hardly disposed to think so highly of imagination. He likes neither fairies nor satires, and he falls asleep whenever Wieland's "history" seems either too much like a fairy tale or too moralistic and critical of the divine right or dissolute habits of kings like himself. Nurmahal observes that most nations trace their origins to prehistorical legends, a reliance on narrative fictions reinforced when Wieland tells his readers that Nurmahal does not always strictly adhere to the text she reads, either deleting episodes or adding her own reflections or altering the author's tone, so that one never knows whose narrative voice one hears. This circumstance is said to be unimportant, though, and readers are assumed able to judge it for themselves. Thus reminded that Wieland's source is purely fictional, such readers should not agree with Schach Gebal when he chides Danischmend for being well versed in fairy tales.

A generation later, Lili's son Azor affords another example of Wieland's subtle link between narrative fiction and the corruption criticized by Rousseau. Poetically inclined, Azor is a weak king. He quickly learns to appreciate "die Schönheiten der Dichtung" (6:157), and though his own accomplishments in this art amount to no more than a taste for rhetorical flourishes, his poetry helps him become the patron of starving poets, and he entertains romantic notions—"romantische Begriffe" (6:159)—about the value of his crown. This fan of the marvelous—"Freund des Wunderbaren" (6:201)—is controlled by Alabanda, a consort who has him build expensive fairy castles, fueled by her inexhaustible imagination and helped by some poetically minded courtiers. Like Lili, Alabanda achieves such success thanks to her inventive fancy, also called a "voluptuous imagination." Schach Gebal likewise seems ready to learn from marvelous fiction, apparently overcoming his initial skepticism, but he fails to act on his urge to emulate the princes who Danischmend says fulfilled the duties of a king. Such princes worked for the common good, Danischmend explains, by striving to match an intellectual ideal: "Sie strebten hierin nach Erreichung eines gewissen *Ideals*, welches sie sich in ihrem Geiste entworfen hatten" (6:162). Schach Gebal desires a catalogue of such kings, a sign of interest as well as doubt. A story about his youth reveals that willing chambermaids loosed his own imagination at an early age, and now a similar nymph arouses it and keeps him preoccupied for days. Such susceptibility to mental images explains why Schach Gebal plans to inspect his domains and promises to tear down some of his palaces for the sake of his subjects, two projects described in Danischmend's story. He never carries out either project, though, so his imagination seems malleable only in the voluptuous sense of Lili's and Alabanda's. Content that he is generous in thought, if not in deed, Schach Gebal here confirms Danischmend's fear that good impressions made on sultans by wise advisors are quickly erased. At this stage, Schach Gebal himself thus exemplifies the cultured indolence that results from an imagination like Azor's.

The religious strife that marks Azor's reign affords a similar parallel between the events of Wieland's "history" and their narrative frame. Like the influence of Alabanda and Schach Gebal's harem, this strife involves manipulating imagination, a tactic also used by Danischmend to improve the dubious sultan, though Danischmend himself takes comfort in flights of fancy. The king who first conquers Scheschian knows that monarchs have no power over their subjects' imagination, so he does not try to change their religion. Trouble starts when contentious clerics oppose his tolerance by picking a fight about the color of the ape that they worship. The resulting satire on religious schisms criticizes the power of priests such as the Jesuits, but it also pertains to the aesthetics of literary fiction. Rumors spread by priests sound plausible, for example, largely due to commoners' penchant for the marvelous, and such rumors also seem believable because they are embellished with made-up details. Danischmend similarly insists that his story is credible, a concern raised by Schach Gebal's objection that defending the freedom of reason, wit, and imagination—even though such freedom can be abused, as in this religious case—is fine when talking about utopias filled with ideal people, but not when a particular, real-life state is at issue. Danischmend demurs, admitting that the actual history of most nations is depressing, but explaining a way out of the resulting dilemma in the same terms of visual art, fictional worlds, and abstract ideals that also occur in Wieland's essays:

> Für einen Menschen, der an den Schicksalen seiner Gattung wahren Antheil nimmt, ist es Pein, bey diesen ekelhaften und grauenvollen Gemählden zu verweilen. Das Herz des Menschenfreundes schauert vor ihnen zurück. Ängstlich sieht er sich nach Scenen von Unschuld und Ruhe, nach den Hütten der Weisen und Tugendhaften, nach Menschen, die dieses Nahmens würdig sind, um; und wenn er in den Jahrbüchern des menschlichen Geschlechtes nicht findet, was ihn befriedigen kann, flüchtet er lieber in erdichtete Welten, zu schönen Ideen, welche, so wenig auch ihr Urbild unter dem Monde zu suchen seyn mag, immer Wirklichkeit genug *für sein Herz* haben, weil sie ihn . . . in einen angenehmen *Traum von Glückseligkeit* versetzen.
>
> (6:296–99)

Such an uplifting escape from the same annals of humankind earlier cited as the source of edifying examples for kings, here cast in language that Wieland so often uses to discuss the general issue of fictionality, firmly links the message and the medium of *Der goldne Spiegel*. Like his religious satire, the narrative philanthropy of Wieland's mouthpiece Danischmend makes fictions seem problematic but potent.

Just how difficult it can be to control imagination fired by such fictions is clear from the damage done by Azor's son Isfandiar and the reaction that the latter elicits from Schach Gebal. Here, too, social ideals and their narration are related via visual art. Isfandiar is taught that virtue is arbitrary, not an obligation, and he keeps his subjects from knowing that he and they are bound by a social contract. Such crimes are compounded by the art that Rousseau thought caused them. Like Chärea, Isfandiar spends huge sums on paintings and other morally suspect pastimes. To him, moreover, the best painter is a man who treats frivolous subjects erotically, and the best singer a woman who seductively evokes suggestive images in her listeners' fancy. Isfandiar is aided and abetted by Eblis, a priest who ruthlessly exploits his people's hopes and fears but who is killed after he miscalculates the power of imagination. He fails to understand that the force of religion depends on popular beliefs, and his decision to spread news of rebels' punishment has the opposite of its desired deterrent effect on the Scheschians' imagination. A better advisor would have been the author Kador, who derides caricatures of humankind in a manner much like Danischmend's. Schach Gebal does not want a satire on sultans, and Danischmend denies ever intending one, but the latter's irony is clear. Still, he rejects Eblis's ugly images of the people, "seine häßlichen Gemählde von der Bösartigkeit des Volkes" (7:50), and his own opinion of human nature betrays what he calls the rosy color of his fancy. Schach Gebal uses a similar vocabulary to praise Danischmend's own vision: "Wie du mahlst, Danischmend! . . . und wehe dem Sklaven, dem ich die Sorge für meine Unterthanen anvertraut habe, in dessen Bezirk ein Urbild deiner verfluchten Mahlerey gefunden würde!" (7:49). Schach Gebal is so impressed, in fact, that he orders Danischmend himself to investigate the need for reform in Scheschian. Like Eblis, Danischmend thus learns that steering others' imagination can have unintended effects.

Danischmend's thanks for the job of having to practice what he preaches are left to the imagination of Wieland's readers, a gambit like the one that Danischmend himself uses when telling the story of Tifan, the king who succeeds Isfandiar and rescues Scheschian. Tifan is not only taught Rousseauean social ideals by a mentor better than Isfandiar's Eblis; he also embraces, embodies, and enacts them. Unaware of his lineage, he is raised in rural isolation by a man named Dschengis, who imparts to him sublime ideas of civil society, the human race, nature, the universe, and its creator, ideas that Dschengis says are the measure of ethical perfection. Such concepts are not the whims of philosophical hermits, he explains, a claim that sets his lessons apart from those of the odd Diogenes. Dschengis also outlines concepts resembling the rights of man, and he has already filled Tifan's head with tales of innocent customs, stories of a poetic golden age that are refined when love fuels Tifan's urge for fantastic new ideas and that take a religious turn as soon as Dschengis teaches him about the ideas of an infinite spirit and divinity. Like Agathon, however, Tifan soon learns that everything is other than it should be, unlike beautiful ideas of innocent people and golden ages. Like Agathon, moreover, he also learns the difference between how people ideally should be and how they really are. Danischmend suggests how ethics and narrative fiction nonetheless combine in this education when he calls Tifan's desire to do good romantic, "etwas Romanhaftes," but nonetheless the passion of great souls and the source of beautiful ideas. Tifan himself seems such an ideal when Danischmend hails his "*stille Größe*" (7:187) and "*edle Einfalt*" (7:243), terms connoting the ideal calm of Winckelmann's ancient Greeks.[11] Tifan has also been likened to Rousseau's Émile, an example of education meant to counter Rousseau's own cultural skepticism. Wieland ostensibly turns this example into a "fiction of a plebeian king" that is impracticable but ontologically true.[12]

What most distinguishes Tifan, however, is the effect that his life and works have on Schach Gebal. Like Schach Gebal, Tifan is a nephew of the king who came before him, and he sets an example that Wieland's sultan appreciates, even though it seems suited only to novels, and that therefore shows how closely the social content of *Der goldne Spiegel* parallels its narrative form. At first, Schach Gebal doubts Dschengis's report that Tifan neither looked nor acted better than his rustic neighbors, and he threatens to punish the poets and romancers who would make him believe such things. He soon grows curious, however, approving and envious of Tifan as well as impatient to hear more of Danischmend's story, even though his skepticism of fictionality persists: "Bisher klang der größte Theil deiner Erzählung so ziemlich wie eine Geschichte *aus dieser Welt* . . . Aber ich hasse alles, was einem Mährchen ähnlich sieht, Danischmend!" (7:169). This allusion to the Leibnizian definition of novels as histories set in other worlds becomes more explicit when Schach Gebal's liking for Tifan leads him to wish he could emulate such a fictional character: "Es ist wahr, man merkt je länger je mehr, daß er nur der fantasierte Held eines politischen Romans ist. Aber, beym Bart des Profeten! man kann sich nicht erwehren zu wünschen, daß man dreyßig Jahre jünger seyn möchte, um eine so schöne Fantasie wahr zu machen!" (7:174). Schach Gebal remains critical of fairy tales, but he is not too proud to learn from Tifan's example, especially when Tifan brings mischievous clerics to heel. To be sure, the sultan's requests for copies of Tifan's correspondence and book of rights and responsibilities all lead nowhere, and his desire for a book containing Tifan's maxims is not too serious, since he only plans to put it next to his pillow. Such gentle reminders of Wieland's fictional source no longer seem ironic, however, when Schach Gebal decrees that Danischmend is free to fill lacunae in his fictional manuscript: "Schon wieder eine Lücke! . . . Ich erkläre hiermit, daß ich dieser Lücken äußerst überdrüssig bin . . . Wenn eine Lücke in deinen Handschriften ist, so magst du sie ergänzen wie du kannst" (7:290).

This striking, if grudging and gradual, acceptance of Danischmend's story at the same time that Schach Gebal learns to like Tifan confirms that fictionality informs both the literary medium and the social message of *Der goldne Spiegel*. It does not resolve, however, the closely related problem of actually realizing ideals thus conveyed in novels. That this problem bothers Schach Gebal seems clear from his contradictory interjections. Despite his desire to emulate Tifan, he objects that the young king's economic policy is possible only in an ideal state, yet he also wants Tifan's portrait painted, expressing his admiration in the same language of visual art that denotes such ideals in *Diogenes*: "Ich muß schlechterdings sein Bildniß haben. Ich will es in allen ersinnlichen Größen und Stellungen mahlen lassen" (7:266). Danischmend has gone to great lengths to evoke such enthusiasm, making clear that Tifan represents more than a passing fancy: "Mein Herz sagt mir, daß die *Idee* eines solchen Fürsten, die ich in diesem Augenblick, wie durch eine Art von Eingebung, auf einmahl in meiner Seele fand, kein Hirngespenst ist" (7:140). Danischmend admits that Tifan's story seems to come from another world, but this hint of fictional semantics occurs in the same breath as an emphatic plea for its normative force: "*Tifan ist kein Geschöpf der Fantasie*: es liegt dem ganzen Menschengeschlechte daran, daß er keines sey" (7:170). Schach Gebal himself finally comes around to this way of thinking, but he botches things when he appoints Danischmend prime minister. Reluctantly, the idealistic philosopher battles the evil priests whom Schach Gebal wants to be more pliable, a wish expressed in terms that take Tifan's lesson too literally: "Du hast das Recept, wie man sie machen kann; warum sollte in Indostan nicht möglich seyn was in Scheschian möglich war" (7:286). This equation proves too simple. Not only does Schach Gebal probably never read his philosopher's plan for reforming corrupt priests; his clergy also brings about Danischmend's downfall, finally managing to have him banished in disgrace. In episodes added in Wieland's *Ausgabe letzter Hand* (partly because he had switched publishers),[13] Tifan's kingdom, too, declines, further evidence that putting ideals into practice is difficult.

The effect of fictions is a subject that Wieland raises, though, not only by having his "history" and frame story treat it on parallel levels, but also by explicitly commenting on it in footnotes, an episode, and a foreword that show how to avoid Schach Gebal's mistakes. Most of Wieland's footnotes suggest that *Der goldne Spiegel* is fiction, attributed as they are to its Chinese, Latin, or German "translator," who all find fault with their source, show off their learning, and humorously interrupt the narrative flow of the novel. Other notes are anonymous and often offer defenses of fictional literature and pleas for the efficacy of ideals. When Danischmend describes fictional worlds as a refuge from the horrors of history, a note warns not to exaggerate his penchant for romances and fairy tales but hardly dismisses everything that takes the form of fiction: "So gewiß indessen der hohe Werth der Geschichtskunde ist, so ist doch nicht zu läugnen, daß die gerümpfte Nase, womit gewisse Geschichtsforscher auf alles, was die *Form* der *Erdichtung* hat, herab sehen Unbilligkeit und lächerliche Pedanterey ist . . . und empfindsame Seelen werden . . . sich nur allzu oft genöthigt fühlen, mit dem weisen Danischmend in die möglichen Welten der Dichter zu fliehen" (6:298 n. 28). A second note implies this same preference for the possible worlds of poetry over history when it tells how Tifan's story lacks historical truth, as does a third admitting that lone individuals are unlikely to change the real world but defending such quixotic quests: "Und gleichwohl ist nichts wahrscheinlicher, als daß *ein Dutzend Don Quichotten*, die sich mit einander verständen, und . . . auf *die Feinde des menschlichen Geschlechtes* mit eben dem *Muthe*, mit welchem der Held von Mancha seine schimärischen Gegner bekämpfte, (nur freylich mit einem gesundern Kopfe als der seinige war) los gingen,— die Gestalt unsrer sublunarischen Welt binnen einem Menschenalter mächtig ins Bessere verändern würden" (7:152 n. 1). Here citing Cervantes to justify Tifan's social agenda, Wieland argues for action inspired by improbable literary fiction no less urgently than he does in a fourth footnote, one addressed to royal readers of his novel: "Sollt' es möglich seyn, das unter allen *künftigen* Regenten . . . auch nur Einer wäre, der, nachdem er diesen *Tifan* kennen gelernt, den Gedanken ertragen könnte, einen solchen Karakter ein bloßes Ideal bleiben zu lassen?" (7:201 n. 1).

In answer to this rhetorical question about the effect of his own fiction, Wieland does not oversimplify its suggestive force, expressing caution also encountered in studies of *Der goldne Spiegel*. A further footnote concedes that Tifan's rules and regulations would not work in all circumstances, especially since actual states are not ideal: "In einem *idealen Staate* kann man alles einrichten wie man will; in einem wirklichen ist der größte Monarch nicht allezeit noch in allen Stücken Herr über *die Umstände*" (7:246 n. 1). Some scholars have voiced similar reservations, relating such awareness of political necessity to the narrative form and the normative value of Wieland's story. The emphatic connection of fiction and social ideals, both in Danischmend's outbursts and in Wieland's footnotes, has been thought to betray fading hopes for royal enlightenment, a pessimism put bluntly by W. H. Bruford, who observes with regard to the rulers of Weimar: "It is hard to believe that [*Der goldne Spiegel*] can ever have been of the slightest practical value to Anna Amalia or anyone else."[14] Paradoxically, such judgments often seem to result from praise for Wieland's narrative ventriloquism. The "polyphonic chorus of narrative voices" in his novel sometimes makes all that it says seem merely relative, nothing more than a game played with hypotheses.[15] Similarly, the novel has been dismissed as a nonbinding conversation, and the force of its lessons has seemed dubious or limited, its satire mixed with skepticism about the effect of literature, and its narrative validity problematic.[16] Its ironic reflection on the possibility of the utopia that it describes has accordingly been reduced to a subjective "utopian emphasis," but the function of Wieland's utopia has also been called an "encouragement effect" that complements concrete plans for reform with an aesthetic, imaginative vision.[17] The most utopian episode in *Der goldne Spiegel* confirms that this latter explanation makes more sense when considering Wieland's social ideals in general.

That episode describes Rousseauean children of nature—"Kinder der Natur"—happy inhabitants of a remote mountain valley much like Diogenes' isolated island. In the language of visual art so often used by Diogenes, too, the episode makes its own depiction of such an ideal explicit, and it also occasions a spirited debate about the effect of all fiction like it. With this narrative intermezzo—which serves a purpose similar to that of "Geschichte des Prinzen Biribinker" in *Don Sylvio*— Wieland demonstrates the usefulness of *Der goldne Spiegel* as a whole. The episode is cast as fiction from the very start, recalling *Don Sylvio* when Danischmend assures Schach Gebal, "daß alles so natürlich darin zugehen soll, als man es nur wünschen kann" (6:75). When Schach Gebal objects that the beginning of the episode sounds like a fairy tale and threatens to have Danischmend whipped, an echo of *Diogenes* is audible as Danischmend admits that his source is a Greek poet who embellished the truth to make his paintings, "seine Gemählde" (6:84), more interesting. The concepts of fictionality and visual art are likewise associated in the idyllic community itself, where the wise Psammis and his followers have returned to nature from corrupt modern life. The principles informing their code of conduct are embodied in three marble images, which are said to be symbols of love, innocence, and pleasure—"*Sinnbilder* der *Liebe*, der *Unschuld*, und der *Freude*" (6:104–5). Inhabitants of Psammis's ashram are required to observe nature and fill their imagination with ideas of beauty, and they are taught to see their own image in all human beings. Social ideals and visual art are also closely connected in the general impression left by Psammis and his brood: "Alles zusammen machte *ein lebendiges Gemähldte, dessen Anblick die Güte der Moral des weisen Psammis besser bewies, als die scharfsinnigsten Vernunftgründe hätten thun können*" (6:124). As in *Diogenes*, the art of painting is cited here to convey social ideals more directly than reason could. In fact, the ethics underlying Wieland's utopia are demonstrated here in a literary tableau vivant.

This explicit depiction of Wieland's "Kinder der Natur" is followed by an equally deliberate debate about the effect of such utopias. Awareness of fictionality plays an important part there, as it does in the telling of those children's tale by an emir who strays into their valley. The emir possesses the same knowledge of fairy tales that marks Danischmend, and at first he assumes that what he sees is some kind of magic. Like Don Sylvio, moreover, the emir thinks himself pursued by magicians and fairies. Later, he returns to his own country, where he becomes such a dour moralist that he forbids all sensual pleasures, including those of the imagination, "Vergnügungen der Einbildungskraft" (6:126) like those indulged in *Agathon*. The emir thus goes from one extreme to another, overreacting to his stay in a utopia by later rooting out every kind of fantasy. A similar reaction occurs in the ensuing debate between Danischmend and Schach Gebal's imam, who doubts that peoples like the "Kinder der Natur" exist, and, if they do, says that news of them should be suppressed because such depictions (*Schilderungen*) of ideal people only lead to laziness among the working classes. Danischmend refutes this attack, calling Psammis's ethics a matter of valid principles, not fictions: "*Die Grundsätze des weisen Psammis . . . sind keine Erdichtungen*" (6:131). He explains how people might wish they lived in such utopian worlds but would soon tire of merely dreaming about them and instead do what they could to change their own. When Schach Gebal objects that the "Kinder der Natur" amount to a fairy tale and notes that Psammis's laws would not work in a large nation, Danischmend admits that any plan to render luxury harmless in such nations would be a chimera, but this hint of Diogenes' chimerical "Republik" does not keep him from insisting that his story still affords a few basic maxims useful in such situations. As usual, Schach Gebal likes such fantasies and does nothing to make them law, but Wieland's lesson seems clear: Read for the ethical principles informing their ideals, utopian narratives can afford practical pleasures of the imagination.

It is curious how often this seemingly obvious lesson was lost on scholars who described the ideals of *Der goldne Spiegel* in the nineteenth and early twentieth centuries. The "Kinder der Natur" had been assessed more astutely in one of the initial reviews of the novel, and subsequent studies discussing those ideals likewise mention it favorably. In between, however, the episode often prompted dismissiveness, scorn, and disgust. While some praised the idealism of *Der goldne Spiegel* as high-minded, others found the "Kinder der Natur" a polemic aimed at Rousseau by a good but less than original hack, someone whose sober realism betrayed the contradictory views of a tendentious, spineless philistine. Such contradictions in Wieland's views were traced to his ostensibly "soft" and unstable character.[18] Even Bernhard Seuffert's otherwise incisive remarks on Wieland's ideals, describing Tifan as a model for Joseph II, dismiss the "Kinder der Natur" as a hedonistic fantasy.[19] Joseph von Eichendorff's history of the German novel in the eighteenth century contains the most damning criticism, lambasting the pursuit of happiness shown in the episode as proof of Wieland's irreligious sensuality. All would agree, Eichendorff huffed, that such prosaic contentedness, which is perfectly happy with the fleshpots of Egypt and earthly "plunder" and displays no longing for the promised land, was certainly not Christian.[20] A more tolerant assessment had appeared in a review of *Der goldne Spiegel* written by Johann Heinrich Merck in 1772 for the *Frankfurter gelehrte Anzeigen*. Merck questioned Wieland's style, not Psammis's morality, grateful for the latter, with which he wholeheartedly agreed.[21] Merck also marveled at Wieland's belief in authors' influence, a topic raised by Wilson, too, who argues that *Der goldne Spiegel* is less about political ideals than an ideal of patronage that preserves intellectuals' independence.[22] Others claim that the "Kinder der Natur" represent a personal ideal, not a political one, or that such ideals have only "orientational meaning."[23]

Wieland himself left no doubt about the effects that he wanted *Der goldne Spiegel* to have. Writing as its editor, he even explains how and why it should have them, making clear that they depend on accepting its fictionality. In his foreword to the third part of the novel, omitted in its revision for the *Ausgabe letzter Hand*, he describes two methods of teaching readers practical philosophy. The first works deductively, citing general observations, theories, and proofs a priori. The second works inductively, by giving examples. Both have their pros and cons. The first is conceptually clearer and more thorough, but it also seems dry and unpleasant to most people, who therefore seldom read or understand treatises written according to it. The concepts that such works convey, moreover, are seldom apprehended or applied correctly. The second affords a more intuitive kind of knowledge, one that is more entertaining and has more emotional effects: "Wir *fühlen* das *Wahre*, wir *lieben* das *Schöne* und *Gute*, wir *verabscheuen* das *Unrecht*, das *Laster*, wir *beten* die *Tugend* an."[24] This second method thus furthers truth, beauty, and virtue, but it also leads to misunderstanding, since readers seek the original model (*Urbild*) for any well-drawn fictional character among their own acquaintances. Such identifications are an unavoidable abuse of that method, Wieland adds, "wiewohl ein Mißbrauch, der auf Seiten des Schriftstellers unmöglich anders vermieden werden kann, als wenn er auf den edelsten Teil seines Amtes Verzicht tun wollte."[25] In other words, Wieland not only finds fiction more moving than discursive prose but also regards creating fictional characters as an author's highest calling. Some authors do write personal satires, he concedes, but most ordinarily intend only to show the results of thinking and acting like their fictional models (*Modelle*) or to make their readers respond appropriately to virtue, merit, weakness, and evil. Wieland does not give his own reasons for writing fiction rather than history in the strict sense of the word here, but in a separate advertisement for his novel he reveals that authors of fiction should not miss their chance to be even more "pragmatic" than actual historians.[26]

Such an explicit defense of the ethical force of fiction—indeed, of fictionality itself as an author's most effective means of bringing about moral improvement—spells out the literary lesson implicitly taught over the entire course of *Der goldne Spiegel*. The novel encourages skeptical readers like Schach Gebal to accept the useful fictionality of stories like Danischmend's, that is, to accept that literary fiction can be something other than either the pure fantasy indulged in fairy tales or the personal attacks thinly veiled in satire. Wieland thereby tries to instill social ideals that themselves should be understood as symbolic, useful fictions. To argue that fictionality is thus the definitive feature of Wieland's narration and social ideals alike is not to deny that his novel is satirical in its ironic attacks on kingly corruption and despotic inertia. Despite later recalling it as a "sweet dream" that he had wished to realize, he himself doubted that he could have written *Der goldne Spiegel* after living in Weimar, which was hardly as ideal as Scheschian.[27] As earlier letters to, from, and about his patrons in Vienna and Weimar reveal, however, his hopes of fashioning a young prince according to those ideals were high indeed. Wieland often called himself or compared himself to Danischmend, and even Karl August wished that Wieland would accept Anna Amalia's invitation to come to Weimar as such a sage, "als Philosoph, u. Leib Danischmende."[28] Wieland's faith in the ideals shown in *Der goldne Spiegel*, in fact, went so far that he supposed certain tribes in Africa and the inhabitants of Tahiti still to be unspoiled "Kinder der Natur."[29] He expressed his delight at this thought to Johann Ludwig Wilhelm Gleim, and though he knew that German peasants were too oppressed ever to be turned into such happy children, he gave Gleim permission to try edifying less unfortunate segments of the rural population with the corresponding episode in his novel.[30] Even though he warned that the episode would need to be emended for this purpose, Wieland thus had enough faith in his social ideals that he both assumed they were realized in other parts of the world and agreed they might be adopted even in Europe. For all the hesitation that he expresses in *Der goldne Spiegel* about the effect of fictions on society, he thus seems to have meant what he wrote in a letter to Sophie von La Roche: "Und dann ist am Ende doch gewiß, daß durch solche Bücher wirklich gutes in der Welt gestiftet wird, so unmerklich es auch ist."[31] That is, imperceptible as it may be, such books do some good, a claim investigated by his showing the incremental, limited effects of fictions throughout *Der goldne Spiegel* itself. With its suggestion of workable ideals, the novel thus combines the extremes of empirical and ideal fiction noted above, in the first and third versions of *Agathon*.

5. Geschichte des Philosophen Danischmende (1775)

The Descriptions *are singular, the* Comparisons
very quaint, the Narration *various, yet of one*
colour: The purity and chastity of Diction *so*
preserved, that in the places most suspicious, not
the words *but only the* images *have been censured.*
—Pope, *The Dunciad* (1728)

The same pragmatic idealism so clearly and cleverly tied to the issue of fictionality in *Diogenes* and *Der goldne Spiegel* is also the most pressing concern of Wieland's *Geschichte des Philosophen Danischmende* (1775). He published this novel serially, in eleven monthly installments of *Der teutsche Merkur*, and later expanded it for his *Ausgabe letzter Hand*. It too discusses utopian social ideals and imagination that is linked to literary fiction, reinforcing the connections between Rousseauean "Kinder der Natur" and Wieland's narration forged in his first two middle novels. It also develops those connections beyond the artful irony of *Diogenes* and the frustrated didacticism of *Der goldne Spiegel*. The rhetorical use of visual images is even more explicit in it than in *Diogenes*, for example, and it shows effects of manipulating imagination even stronger than those felt by Schach Gebal in *Der goldne Spiegel*. The risk of misconstruing such images and abusing imagination has increased as well, though, and consequences of the misuse that Wieland thought readers make of a novel when they fail to grasp its fictionality are accordingly clearer. *Danischmend*, that is, hints at how fictions can be a balm for readers' imagination and a boon to society, but it also shows how manipulating imagination is socially ambiguous, something done for better or worse, for good as well as evil ends. To illustrate this point, the novel relates imagination to the joy of fathering children, the horror of suffering rape, and the intricacy of ensuring sexual loyalty. Wieland's selective use of his literary and artistic sources in such episodes seems manipulative itself, but his narrator directly addresses readers to clarify such matters arising between authors of literary fiction and their audience. Subsequently subtitled *Ein Anhang zur Geschichte von Scheschian*, *Danischmend* is indeed a sequel to *Der goldne Spiegel*, then, thanks not only to its social theme and title character but also to the ways in which both are related to its author's broad concept of fictionality. The social significance of the novel emerges over the course of its plot, which develops events described in the frame story of *Der goldne Spiegel*. *Danischmend* tells of a paradise lost and regained, showing how a utopia like those dismissed as chimerical in *Diogenes* and depicted for the sake of abstract maxims in *Der goldne Spiegel* can not only exist but also survive the moral corruption caused by modern civilization. After being deposed by the sly clerics of Indostan, Danischmend asks Schach Gebal to let him found a small colony of happy human beings. The dubious sultan derides such plans as fairy tales, Wieland's general term for implausible fiction, but he agrees to finance them, if only to see whether Danischmend, whose reforms seem unworkable in populous Indostan, has better luck with a small band of rough but unspoiled "Söhne und Töchter der Natur" (8:12). These "children" are like the ones posited in *Diogenes* and *Der goldne Spiegel*, and Danischmend retires to raise them in "Jemal," an aptly named never-never land somewhere in the mountains separating Kashmir from Tibet. Strictly speaking, any geographical location would indicate that Danischmend's community is not u-topian at all, and his concerns do seem more limited than his grand design for Tifan. He marries Perisadeh, herself a simple "daughter of nature," but is driven by his desire for *"häusliche Glückseligkeit"* (8:19–20), domestic bliss that he recommends as the best guarantee of civil and social order. He enjoys such bliss only until the arrival of a "Kalender," one of three mendicant and mendacious friars who briefly appear in *Der goldne Spiegel*. This Kalender, Alhafi, insists that his monastic order resembles that of the ancient Greek Cynics, thus suggesting that he is similar to Diogenes. His schemes, however, are not as speculative as Diogenes' "Republik." Although he defines a Kalender as a "son of nature," he also introduces manufacturing that destroys innocence and virtue in Jemal by cultivating its inhabitants' taste for refinement and luxury. Danischmend is driven away by the Kalender, but he later returns to revive the simple virtues of his spoiled "children," restoring a state of nature in a novel that thus seems Wieland's most sympathetic comment on Rousseauean social ideals.

Like *Agathon* as well as Wieland's other middle novels, *Danischmend* conveys its social message in a narrative form that shares certain qualities of fictionality with the ideals that it describes. Here too Wieland's narration itself therefore reveals much about its subject and vice versa. Prior research has suggested such reciprocity by citing structural parallels in *Danischmend* and *Der goldne Spiegel*, above all their liberal use of footnotes by various hands, which is more extreme in the later novel and there implies a perspectivism far more radical in its epistemological and aesthetic consequences. Both have been called prime examples of an "open" narrative form able to integrate elements of all kinds.[1] Such disparate elements include the humorous footnotes to *Danischmend*, which are attributed to a host of historical and fictional figures, among them Pliny, Epictetus, Hume, Tristram Shandy, "P. Oncefalus," and "M. Skriblerus," to name but a few. Wieland borrowed this strategy from Pope's *Dunciad* (1728), and it has met with shifting critical favor. Jean Paul found the "Notenprose zu seinem 'Danischmend'" proof that Wieland's novels were a poor imitation of Sterne, but the notes have also been cited to praise his learning and literary skill.[2] Herman Meyer regards them as part of Wieland's "playing with the fictive," a game blurring the limits of literary fictivity and part of Wieland's larger, ideological perspectivism.[3] *Danischmend* has similarly been said to show reality splintered into a plethora of perspectives, its multiperspectival notes to make Wieland's satire seem relative for being tied to subjective points of view.[4] Truth lies somewhere in the middle of his competing commentaries, that is, as something construed by readers rather than an authorial narrator.[5] His narrator has struck scholars not only as whimsical and imaginative, however, but also as sincere about Danischmend's sentimental ideal of an idyllic, natural life à la Rousseau.[6] As in *Diogenes*, irony and idealism thus sound thoroughly mixed in the narrative voices of *Danischmend*. Wieland's storytelling and his social criticism accordingly seem at odds here too, bound only by complex and significant tension.

As in *Der goldne Speigel*, however, Wieland here relates his social message and his literary medium in a series of episodes about imagination. *Danischmend* does not retain all of his earlier frame story, in which Schach Gebal learns to like narrative fiction along with the ideal of an enlightened despot; instead, it describes more immediate effects of manipulating mental images. Such effects seem obvious in a conversation about conceiving children. "Kinder der Natur" are not the only children mentioned in the novel—Danischmend's own figure in it, too. The circumstances of their conception are discussed at length, an echo of *Tristram Shandy* that involves imagination and that Wieland associates with such literary fiction. Danischmend explains that his children turn out so well because he knows when his imagination is conducive to making babies. He means that one's imagination should not be colored by petty irritations, an issue that Wieland's narrator raises as well when he cites medical benefits of properly impressing people's hearts and minds. Such concern with the imagination of others is literally cast in terms of color. The narrator regards "eine *rosenfarbne* oder *himmelblaue Fantasie*" (8:33) as essential to success in human affairs, advocating rosy notions like Danischmend's in *Der goldne Spiegel*. A reader objects that siring children does not depend entirely on "die Farbe der Einbildung" (8:34), but the narrator replies that doing so is risky if a man is distracted by cares "die . . . seine Fantasie mit Kapuzinerbraun austapezieren" (8:35). The narrator also lists a whole palette of colors suited to various states of mind, giving a prescription for psychosomatic ills that includes the two most famous examples of "metafiction": "Wie viele körperliche Übel zeugt, nährt und verschlimmert eine kranke Fantasie! Wie oft würde eine rührende Musik, eine scherzhafte Erzählung, eine Scene aus dem *Shakspeare*, ein Kapitel aus dem *Don Quichotte* oder *Tristram Shandy*, das gestörte Gleichgewicht in unsrer Maschine eher wieder herstellen . . . als irgend ein Recept im *Neuverbesserten Dispensatorium*!" (8:32). Danischmend's healthy home life thus seems closely linked to the aesthetics of Cervantes's and Sterne's "self-conscious" novels.

Danischmend does not always describe a vivid imagination as beneficial. It also shows how tinkering with imagination can do serious psychological and social damage. This danger is clear in an episode about three fakirs, ascetics like the Kalender, who cause trouble with religious trinkets that they bring to Jemal. The Kalender once dealt in such amulets and talismans, which he calls "herrliche Arzneyen für eine kranke Fantasie; Dinge, die an sich *nichts* sind, aber *durch den Glauben, den man an sie hat*, zuweilen wunderthätig wirken" (8:80). Like the narrator, the Kalender here refers to imagination in medical terms, but he turns superstition into a wonder drug. The fakirs play on such irrational belief by distributing pendants shaped like a lingam, the phallic symbol of the Hindu god Shiva. Women in Jemal wear these pendants, and neither they nor their husbands see any harm in them until one of the fakirs, pretending to be Shiva, forces himself on a guileless wife. She screams, her husband discovers them, and he cuts off the culprit's actual lingam, but the symbolic kind have sown seeds that Danischmend tells the Kalender are not so easily rooted out: "Glaubst du, die Lingams, weil wir sie mit großem Pomp und allgemeinem Beyfall verbrannt haben, seyen auch in der Einbildungskraft unsrer Weiber und Töchter im Rauch aufgegangen? Sey versichert, sie leben und weben, glänzen und funkeln dort noch immer, und vielleicht mehr als jemahls" (8:199). Although no physical rape occurs, the Jemalites' imagination is no longer unsullied and chaste, a fact convincing Danischmend that other fakirs will succeed where the first three failed: "Unsre Fantasie wengistens wird bald mit ihnen unter der Decke spielen, und die

Folgen werden am Ende die nehmlichen seyn. Für eine verdorbene Fantasie ist alles Lingam" (8:200). Indeed, the women have fallen so far in their husbands' estimation (*Einbildung*), that Danischmend would preserve his people's way of life in large part to calm their imagination—"ihrer Einbildung wieder einen festen Ruhepunkt zu geben" (8:211). Important in the development of their own religion as well, the effects of imagination in Jemal thus seem ambiguous.

Such ambiguity recurs in a third episode about sex, in which the manipulation of imagination is most deliberate but also does the most good. Driven out of Jemal, Danischmend returns to Dehli thirteen years after relating his long "fairy tale" about the kings of Scheschian. He and Nurmahal teach Schach Gebal a lesson again, but just as Danischmend now finds happiness at home, the lesson is personal rather than political. The episode, which Wieland added in his *Ausgabe letzter Hand*, turns on Aruja, the beautiful young wife of a merchant named Sadik. Schach Gebal desires Aruja and enlists Danischmend to offer the aging Sadik money in return for relinquishing her. The sultan knows that Danischmend can imagine his plight, telling how he is smitten by his mental image of her: "Eine Einbildungskraft wie die deinige, Danischmend, bedarf . . . keiner umständlichern Schilderung des Gemüthszustandes, worin die schöne Aruja mich zurück ließ . . . mit jedem Morgen steht Aruja's Bild frischer, wärmer und glänzender vor meinen Augen" (8:385–86). Danischmend does such an odious errand unwillingly, expresses relief when the couple refuses to part, and reports that Aruja is driven by the notion (*Einbildung*) that only she can make Sadik happy. When Danischmend's failure to woo her only fuels the sultan's lust, this emphasis on images and imagination is even stronger. The title of Chapter 49 announces a means of curing sultans of such fantastic passions. At first, Nurmahal shrugs off Schach Gebal's urge for Aruja as a passing fancy, "nur eine von den Fantasien . . . deren ihm schon manche eben so leicht vergangen als gekommen waren" (8:446). She soon feels threatened, though, and she tries to obscure his image of Aruja by putting a more immediate one in its place: "Sie mußte nehmlich dem *Bilde* der schönen Aruja, welches allen diesen Unfug in der Fantasie Sr. Hoheit anrichtete . . . eine andere Schönheit entgegen stellen, die durch den gegenwärtigen Eindruck, den sie unversehens auf den Sultan machen würde, das Bild der abwesenden Geliebten zu verdunkeln fähig wäre" (8:448). A slave girl serves this seductive purpose, diverting Schach Gebal until he forgets Aruja.

Nurmahal's maneuvering is cited to prove how easily kings can be controlled by those who exploit their weaknesses, but it seems an equally revealing comment on the power of literary fiction, since its source contains no such substitution of one image for another and tells a story subtly tied to the aesthetic concerns raised in *Der goldne Spiegel*. That source is "Histoire de la belle Arouja," a Persian tale describing a fictional sultan no less smitten than Schach Gebal but better able to master his passions and much less inclined to commit an injustice. Twenty years after first seeing and then forgoing Arouja, moreover, he cannot get her out of his mind: "Je suis sans cesse occupé de son image."[7] Nurmahal's manipulation of Schach Gebal's imagination to make Aruja disappear thus seems all the more deliberate, a twist that Wieland added after reading fiction much like the fairy tales that the same sultan detests in *Der goldne Spiegel*. What is more, the first-person narrator of "Histoire de la belle Aruja" is Sultan Lolo, a fictional figure also found in Wieland's "Schach Lolo" (1778). This "morgen-ländische Erzählung," an oriental tale, sharply criticizes the divine right of kings and tells of revenge by a spurned advisor like Danisch-mend. Schach Lolo is the sole ancestor of Schach Gebal noted but not described in *Der goldne Spiegel*. Here, wise Duban heals him with a tal-isman like those used by the fakirs and the Kalender, a stick that works simply by making the lazy monarch exercise. The ungrateful Lolo later beheads Duban, who gets revenge by having given the sultan a book that kills him when he licks his finger to turn its poisoned pages. Cursed as a "königliche[s] Vieh" (10:323) and a "*nickende Pagode*" (10:350), Schach Lolo thus not only embodies all that is bad about ab-solute rulers, but also reads a book that fatally changes his life, thereby reinforcing the literary aspect of Aruja's story. Nurmahal influences Schach Gebal because his image of Aruja fades faster than Sultan Lolo's impression of her namesake, both this sultan and the "belle Arouja" be-ing characters in the kind of fiction that Schach Gebal rejects. If Schach Gebal were more receptive to such fiction, he might know and follow the example set by that cautious sultan, instead of being countered and duped as easily as his far less fortunate ancestor Schach Lolo.

The ambiguity of imagination shown in *Danischmend* has to do not only with handsome children, cult rape, and despotic desire, however; it also figures in a debate about other social behavior. Like Agathon and Hippias, Danischmend and the Kalender disagree about human nature and idealistic attempts to improve it. The Kalender has no truck with the fictional and utopian, not the kind of man to lie around dreaming "von Feenschlössern und Schlaraffenländern und goldnen Zeiten und schönen Seelen" (8:99). Instead, he exclaims, judging hu-man nature depends on knowing facts. Danischmend is less skepti-cal, arguing that such facts are often a matter of perspective, actually more hypothetical than not: "*Fakta* sind alles, was man daraus machen will . . . : aus jedem neuen Augenpunkte scheinen sie etwas anders; und in zehn Fällen gegen Einen ist das vermeinte Faktum, worauf man mit großer Zuversicht seine Meinung gestützt hatte, im Grund eine bloße Hypothese" (8:103). Meyer reads this passage as proof of Danischmend's idealistic perspectivism, but the notion of perspective also recalls the visual arts and images so important in Wieland's other middle novels. Here too such images are related to social ideals and to the general concept of fictionality. The Kalender claims that wise men do not try to help humanity until they are sure that their wishes can be carried out. By contrast, enthusiasts might try to enact their ideas but soon settle for mere contemplation. Their idea of virtue is such a fantastic concept of moral beauty that it could never work in the real world, he explains, citing the same "Lauf der Welt" that measures the truth of fiction in *Agathon* and *Don Sylvio*. In response, Danischmend defends such *"Enthusiasten der Tugend"* (8:124), enthusiasts whom he thinks justified even if they do no more than envision such moral and aesthetic ideals and thereby assure the endurance of the most precious possession of humanity.[8] In this debate alluding to fairy tales and the truth of fiction, imaginative "virtuosi" thus seem impractical but important in the terms of visual art and figurative language that connote fictionality in Wieland's previous novels.

Such terms are also used in several episodes that explicitly mention visual art and literally illustrate the social message of *Danischmend*. Danischmend's sons and daughters are a pleasure to behold, unlike caricatures and grotesques—"Karikaturen und Grotesken . . . wie man sie alle Werkeltage in Menge sieht" (8:28)—and Alhafi becomes a Kalender after a friend "paints" a very pretty picture of the order and its vows: "Er mahlte mir die Pflichten desselben sehr leicht und angenehm vor" (8:92). Listing Aruja's charms, moreover, Schach Gebal omits many small details and brush strokes, "eine Menge kleiner Züge und Pinselstriche" (8:380), and one of the Jemalites comes to Dehli and tells Danischmend what has happened back home, narrating what seems a painting true to life, a "Gemähldе nach dem Leben" (8:421). The best example of how such images convey ideals is a *"Familienstück"* (8:129), a genre painting actually acted out, which Danischmend shows the Kalender to settle their argument about human nature. Far from merely describing his ideal family values, Danischmend also displays them. He and the Kalender hide near a cottage in Jemal, where they observe a young couple getting engaged, a scene that the narrator calls "eine so schöne Gruppe, als jemahls von einem Mahler in Athen, Paris oder Peking gezeichnet, gemahlt oder gesudelt worden seyn mag"

(8:130). This "painting" turns out to be just that, an artistic image translated into words. In one of Wieland's footnotes, an engraver bets that the author of *Danischmend* has stolen it from the French painter Jean Baptiste Greuze (1725–1805): "Ich wollte gleich alles wetten, daß der Autor dieß Gemählde dem *Greuze* abgestohlen hat" (8:130 n. 1). As Meyer has found, the scene does more or less match an actual painting by Greuze, *L'accordée du village* (1761).[9] The expert who opines in a further footnote, though, notes that the narrator omits one of the bride's sisters, which he thinks is an attempt to conceal such theft: "Der leibhafte *Greuze!*—Aber warum hat man die andre Schwester weggelassen, die hinter des alten Vaters Stuhl hervor guckt, und den Bräutigam und ihre glückliche Schwester mit so neidischen Augen anklotzt, daß man ihr gleich ein paar Ohrfeigen geben möchte?—Vermuthlich hoffte man durch solche Weglassungen den Diebstahl desto eher zu verbergen?" (8:131 n. 2). Wieland thus not only borrows but also alters the visual art most graphically expressing the domestic goodness that Danischmend embraces as his highest social ideal.

This suggestive use of visual art is even more selective than the noted "expert" says, for the missing sister is not the only change that Wieland's narrator makes. Greuze's scene does not take place in the open air on a beautiful summer morning, as the narrator reports. Instead, it is set inside a house that hardly looks like the happy abode described by the narrator. Moving the engagement outdoors, into a rosy bower, he makes it seem more idyllic. Even more striking is the absence of the money bag that Greuze places in the hands of the fiancé. Presumably containing a dowry, this bag makes lucre a motive in an encounter that Danischmend wants to prove the virtue of human nature. Conspicuously absent too is a somber figure, apparently the fiancé's father, who humorlessly holds a sheaf of papers in his hand. Like his son's awkward grip on the money bag, his own firm hold on what seems a marriage contract makes human nature seem a good deal less spontaneous and unselfish than Danischmend thinks. Indeed, such changes show the ideal of human nature represented in this episode to be even prettier than an already sentimental picture. What is more, the effects of the scene are powerful but ambiguous. Even the Kalender admits that the image is moving: "Ich muß gestehen, . . . was wir da gesehen haben, macht kein gleichgültiges Gemählde" (8:136). His cynicism keeps him from being as carried away as Danischmend, though, and his sexual lust for the bride is not at all what the philosopher means to make him feel. The overt strategy of this scene appears to backfire, then, moving the Kalender, but in an unintended way. Even though mundane details given by Greuze are removed, the effect of such images seems as slippery here as it is in the episode about the fakirs' symbolic lingams. Danischmend still likens those images to painting, however, when he explains why he cannot finish telling how badly off the people in this scene would be in a land where rajas and sultans oppressed them: "Ich kann das abscheuliche Gemähilde nicht vollenden" (8:140–41). Despite its demonstrated moral ambiguity, the art of painting thus remains closely associated with that of verbal narration.

The narration of *Danischmend* itself is often shown to be as selective as its only partial account of Greuze's painting. Its narrator makes his authorial presence felt throughout the novel, addressing readers to whom he explains his deliberateness. Most of these exchanges concern the Kalender. After the Kalender's first encounter with Danischmend, the narrator remarks that he has forgotten to tell his readers anything about this strange figure: "Ich habe einen Fehler begangen, lieber Leser, den ich erst jetzt gewahr werde. Da bring' ich einen *Kalender* auf die Scene, laß' ihn reden und disputieren, und habe nicht gesagt, wann und wie und warum und von wannen er kam, und wer er ist, und was er will" (8:48). Perhaps Wieland simply could not think of a better way to correct a mistake made in an earlier chapter of a novel published in monthly installments, but his narrator claims that concealing it would alter the plan of *Danischmend,* and there is indeed more to this conspicuous confession. Trying to tell a lady reader how the Kalender looks, the narrator regrets that he lacks the help of a painter or an engraver: "Es wird schwer seyn, Madam, Ihnen ohne Hülfe eines Mahlers oder Kupferstechers einen anschauenden Begriff davon zu geben, wie ein Kalender . . . aussieht" (8:51). This citation of visual art in connection with verbal description occurs in a passage prodding the reader's imagination when the narrator adds that she can picture the Kalender by mentally removing the beard that a monk or a hermit would wear: "Schneiden Sie diesem Kapuziner oder Waldbruder seinen . . . Bart . . . ab,—oder befehlen vielmehr Ihrer Fantasie es für Sie zu thun" (8:51).[10] Such emphasis on activating readers' imagination is mixed with equally clear signs of the narrator's arbitrariness. In a chapter titled "Ein Dialog zwischen dem Leser und dem Autor" (8:66), the narrator tells a fictional reader that he could make his story about the Kalender much longer and that the reader would still be obliged to read it, but he later makes a point of omitting further details. Readers expressly told to use their own imagination are thus shown to be at the mercy of the narrator's.

Such lopsided dealing in literary detail makes *Danischmend* itself seem much like the ideal of family life shown in the narrator's selective view of *L'accordée du village,* and even like Nurmahal's scheme to take

Schach Gebal's mind off Aruja, attempts to manipulate images and imagination. The narrator's frank exchanges with fictional readers, however, reveal his own manipulation as such. He also takes pains to remove such readers' doubts about the "inner truth" of his story. Some might wonder why Danischmend tolerates the evil Kalender, he expects, a circumstance that he explains by citing the Kalender's seeming kindness to Danischmend's children. *Danischmend* thus includes proof that its fiction is psychologically plausible. Children figure in the foreword to the novel as well, a brief introduction ironically called "Keine Vorrede." Like the long accounts of fictional sources in Wieland's other novels, this short opening statement pertains to the fictionality of his characters. Its author mentions children when writing that he cannot help readers who need a foreword to make sense of his sultans and clerics: "Schaffe mir Kinder, oder ich sterbe, sagte Rahel zu Jakob ihrem Manne. *Bin ich denn Gott*? antwortete der Erzvater.—Dieß ist gerade der Fall eines ehrlichen Autors, den unverständige Leser zwingen wollen, *ihnen Verstand zu geben*" (8:4). This denial that Wieland's characters have satiric connotations is disingenuous, but it is also a reminder that narrative fiction is lost on readers who lack imagination as vivid as Danischmend's when he begets his brood. Recalling that the notes to *Danischmend* are modeled on Pope's *Dunciad*, one might argue that no author can manipulate dullards. Whereas "Keine Vorrede" is ironic, moreover, there really are no notes in the nineteen chapters of the novel that Wieland added to its original thirty-one in his *Ausgabe letzter Hand*. His story of how Jemal lost but then regained its Rousseauean virtue thus seems a case of faith in utopian social ideals that forbids interrupting readers' concentration. Wieland's narrator, foreword, and discontinuation of his footnotes thus all show his own manipulation of readers in *Danischmend* to be explicit, limited, and benign.

Danischmend makes literary fiction seem manipulative, then, no less ambiguous than the libidinous imagination and idealistic images so closely related to it throughout the novel, but much less likely to be abusive in its ends. Both the ambiguity and the potential for abuse of such fiction seem greater than in Wieland's previous novels because his description here of a successful social utopia assumes stronger faith in fictionality, a quality common to his narration as well as his social ideals. In this respect, *Danischmend* anticipates the third version of *Agathon*. Danischmend is sadder and wiser than in *Der goldne Spiegel*, moreover, but happier too, in the end, when his dream of dwelling among "Kinder der Natur" comes true. This difference between the two novels is apparent in the more immediate use made of visual art to convey social ideals in *Danischmend*. The emir who stumbles on such children in *Der goldne Spiegel* later writes that he once saw wise Psam-mis's laws embodied in a *"lebendiges Gemählde"* (6:124), but Danisch-mend and the Kalender regard such a tableau vivant themselves. As noted above, Wieland alters this visual source of his story, omitting details included by Greuze that make human nature seem less ideal than Danischmend thinks. Wieland similarly alters one of his literary sources, improving Danischmend himself even more remarkably. In "Histoire de la belle Arouja," Danischmend is not an avuncular family man, but a brutal seducer, one of the several lechers whom Arouja approaches for help. Compared to this namesake, Wieland's philosopher cuts a far better figure, resembling Wieland's idealized Diogenes. Perhaps such improvement is due to Danischmend's being a poet at heart, a thinker who prefers fairy tales and romances. Wieland's so-called "Handbuch" of 1774 contains notes for a future novel about Danisch-mend, notes describing the philosopher's love of poetry, his career as an author writing prose as well as verse, and his study of metaphysics and morality in *Arabian Nights*. Such literary tastes seem the result of his penchant for reading frivolous fiction: "Il ne lit que de romans, et de livres frivoles."[11] Although hardly frivolous, Wieland's novel named for this sympathetic character is steeped in the ethos of fiction itself, further reinforcing comparisons that its author elsewhere draws between the expressly fictive and the vaguely imaginary, between narrative and other kinds of fictionality.

6. *Die Abderiten* (1781)

Das Kunstwerk kann den Menschen so an sich
ziehen, daß eben diese Leidenschaft die andern
Kräfte und Neigungen aus der Faßung bringt,
und so wird die Wuth des Geschmacks, wie
jede andre Wuth, Fallstrick.
—Herder, "Ursachen des gesunknen Geschmacks bei den
verschiednen Völkern, da er geblühet" (1775)

Like Wieland's first three middle novels, his fourth and last, *Die Ab-deriten* (1781), raises the issue of fictionality by relating social ideals to artistic imagination. It too examines social life apparently corrupted by refinement in the arts, citing visual arts to tie such Rousseauean notions to the fictional nature of its own story. Whereas Wieland presents a Rousseauean utopia as a patently unattainable ideal in *Diogenes,* a distant pedagogical goal in *Der goldne Spiegel,* and a dream privately fulfilled in *Danischmend,* however, he treats its ostensible opposite, a distinctly *dys*topian city, with humorous satire in *Die Abderiten.* Like *Danischmend,* most of *Die Abderiten* first appeared serially in *Der teutsche Merkur,* beginning in 1774, and it too reveals how duping imagination can disrupt communal life but still be relatively harmless in Wieland's storytelling. Indeed, *Die Abderiten* shows none of the ironic cynicism, impractical plans, and disappointed hopes that mark his earlier middle novels. Instead, it often discusses artistic taste and aesthetic beauty, matters that it connects to the kind of comical figures described by Fielding and depicted by Hogarth. Wieland thereby links the fictionality of verbal and visual art to give a singular lesson in reading satirical literature. Episodes about the theater reinforce that lesson, urging the acceptance of aesthetic illusion also described, as noted above, in his "Versuch über das deutsche Singspiel." His silly title characters help show how this same lesson holds for reading *Die Abderiten* itself. As social and political animals, they are ridiculous, and Wieland pokes fun at their poor taste in plays, too, but their simple submission to theatrical illusion when they finally see a compelling performance also makes them seem aesthetic "Kinder der Natur," an audience whose receptive example readers of fiction would do well to follow. Rousseau's social contract thus becomes an aesthetic one in this novel concerned with the kind of illusion created by literary fiction.

This metamorphosis of the social agenda apparent in Wieland's other middle novels takes different forms in the five books of *Die Abderiten*. All five show why Abdera deserves its ancient reputation for harboring dense inhabitants. In Book 1, the Abderites meet the philosopher Democritus, himself a native of Abdera, but one who has traveled for many years and therefore returns to his hometown far wiser than his fellow citizens. He is more respected there than Diogenes in Corinth, but his studies in natural science are similarly misunderstood. In Book 2, a greedy relative goes so far as to doubt Democritus's sanity and try to have him declared incompetent. This scheme to disinherit him involves summoning Hippocrates, but the eminent doctor proves to be just as enlightened a cosmopolite as Democritus, so he pronounces the Abderites themselves sick in the head. In Book 3, the Abderites encounter a third Greek luminary, Euripides, whose tragedy *Andromeda* is performed twice—once by local hams who leave no doubt that the Abderites' national theater is absurd, and then by Euripides' own troupe, which shows them how powerful such plays can be when properly done. Book 4, "Der Prozeß um des Esels Schatten," spoofs a litigious society. Venal lawyers twist facts and bend rules, slow-witted judges stall the wheels of justice, and dubious friends of both parties bribe and bully the mob—all to settle the meaningless question of whether a man who rents an ass to ride can also sit in its shadow. Book 5 is a similar farce about religious superstition, which forces the Abderites to abandon their city when they can think of no better way to keep from being overrun by frogs sacred to their patron goddess. In part, these five books of *Die Abderiten* are products of Wieland's own experience as an author writing for the German national theater in Mannheim, as a senator in his hometown of Biberach, and as a professor at the Catholic university in Erfurt, but their rough treatment of science, medicine, art, law, and theology has also been called a parody of the academic canon.[1] At any rate, the legendary ship of fools seems to have landed smack in Wieland's Abdera.

Much prior research on *Die Abderiten* stresses its urban setting, conflicts that distance Democritus from his compatriots, and how Wieland transforms history into fiction. Called the first comprehensive account of urban life in eighteenth-century German fiction, the novel has also been said to describe a civic community turned upside-down.[2] Similarly, it has been hailed as the first German novel about mass society, though the mass of Abderites has seemed to embody all that bourgeois thinkers such as Democritus feared and disliked.[3] When writing *Die Abderiten*, however, Wieland no longer seems to have wanted to change the world, and cosmopolites like Democritus have often been called an

enlightened ideal.[4] Moreover, Democritus's troubles as a creative indi-
vidual living in backward Abdera appear similar to Wieland's own in
Biberach, and his relations with the Abderites have seemed like Wie-
land's with humankind at large.[5] Just as Wieland and his apparent hero
in *Die Abderiten* thus show complex concern with the role of the intel-
lectual in society, a role played by Diogenes and Danischmend as well,
Wieland's innovative use of Greek history reveals the artistic quality of
his fiction. It has been argued that the novel reflects his realistic con-
ception of the ancient Greeks, whose folly and foibles seem more im-
portant than his allusions to the eighteenth century.[6] While Wieland
does seem to have flirted only briefly or intermittently with the idealis-
tic notion of the Greeks entertained by Winckelmann, his novel has
also been said to be only loosely connected to the historical Abdera.[7]
Indeed, he has seemed to offer a playful fiction of historicity, the fiction
of having a historian for a narrator, and authorial truth that is itself a
fiction.[8] In fact, his narrator has been thought to mix up reality and
imagination no less than the Abderites, albeit consciously, and *Die Ab-
deriten* has seemed ample proof of Wieland's own inexhaustible imagi-
nation.[9] Finally, the novel has also been said to take an ironic attitude
toward its fictionality.[10] Narrative features of the novel thus sug-
gest that it, like his others, explores the issue of fictionality on multiple
levels.

What distinguishes the "self-conscious" fiction of *Die Abderiten* from
that of Wieland's other novels is its specific satirical edge. Just *how*
specific such satire is, however, remains as crucial a question in recent
research on the novel as it was in Wieland's day. At issue is the way in
which any satirical novel refers directly or obliquely to people alive
and events current at the time of its writing, the extent to which its tar-
gets can seem particular individuals as well as universal types. Some
argue that Wieland's satire is aimed at his own contemporaries. *Die Ab-
deriten* opened the genre of German novelistic satire in the Enlighten-
ment, it is said, a genre including clear references to reality and even
concrete instructions meant to inspire its initial readers.[11] The novel is
not a timeless story of foolishness, it has been claimed, but one with
clear parallels as well as more abstract links to German bourgeois soci-
ety in the eighteenth century.[12] As models of human error still being
committed, Wieland's Abderites have similarly been thought to show
sociopolitical faults of early, bourgeois capitalism.[13] By contrast, those
characters have also often been understood more generally, as standing
for more than just Wieland's fellow Germans. Instead of bourgeois so-
cial order, one scholar remarks, general laws of group behavior are
Wieland's subject in the novel.[14] Abdera is a paradigm, not a cipher,

that is, a fictional city unlike any actually existing in Germany around 1770.[15] Respect for the fictionality of Wieland's novel is likewise clear in Matthecka's claim that it conveys a higher reality than the one given in empirical experience.[16] Wieland's satire is directed against a type, Matthecka argues, an opinion elsewhere shared to the extreme of finding readers who see in the Abderites no more than Wieland's neighbors as stupid as those fictional buffoons themselves.[17] Such emphasis on the generality of Wieland's satire reinforces a view taken by the preeminent German satirist prior to him, Gottlieb Wilhelm Rabener, who wrote in 1751 that ridicule like his own was not meant personally: "Ein Schriftsteller verspottet die Lächerlichen, ohne darauf zu denken, ob diese oder jene unter die Lächerlichen gehören."[18]

Rabener relates animosity toward satire to an ignorance of irony and a lack of taste, two shortcomings shared by Wieland's Abderites, whose significance for reading satirical fiction itself also emerges in the foreword to his novel. Often taking an ironic attitude among them, Democritus tells his compatriots tales that he does not believe. Whatever he says ironically, however, they take literally. The foreword, though, hints that such apparently poor judgment is not always as bad as it seems. Readers who want to convince themselves that the events and characteristics cited in Wieland's story are true, his narrator writes, can consult the articles on Abdera and Democritus in Pierre Bayle's *Dictionnaire historique et critique* (1697), which will show that the Abderites are not true in the sense of Lucian's fantastic *True History*, but rather in that of fidelity to nature, which outweighs all other sources. Such narrative adherence to nature is said to make *Die Abderiten* neither more nor less than what all history books should be if they would distinguish themselves from mere legends and fairy tales. The truth that Wieland tells may indeed be learned by actually reading Bayle and Lucian. In Gottsched's translation, Bayle's *Dictionnaire* recounts how the Abderites suffered from erratic imagination, above all in their heated reaction to a performance of Euripides' *Andromeda*: "Weil ihre Einbildungskraft von dem Trauerspiele ganz eingenommen war, so stellte ihnen die Phantasie, welche durch das Fieber erregt wurde, nichts anders, als die Andromeda, den Perseus, die Medusa, und was darauf folgt, vor; und erweckte die Bilder von diesen Gegenständen, und das Vergnügen der Vorstellung dergestalt, daß sie sich nicht halten konnten . . . Verse herzusagen, und zu agiren."[19] The source of this incident is Lucian's treatise on how to write history—which Wieland later translated—but Lucian has more in mind when he mentions the Abderites' "fever" than a unique case of imagination run wild. He thereby mocks historians who take rhetorical liberties, but he hardly disparages poetic enthusiasm. He even notes that historians would not be crazy at all if they, too, were fascinated by good poetry.[20] In Lucian's original context, then, the Abderites' histrionics do not seem simply demented.

Defending the Abderites' extreme response to Euripides and connecting them to the truth of Wieland's fiction, however, require attention to their general fondness for art. Their drollery after seeing *Andromeda* is only one instance of a mania for the muses that seems outrageous but raises serious aesthetic questions. Numerous episodes in *Die Abderiten* concern this same artistic urge, which is tied to literary fiction from the very outset of their story. The origins of Abdera lie "in der fabelhaften Heldenzeit" (19:3), its narrator remarks, a phrase suggesting fabulation noted again when he relates the Abderites' genealogy. Their forebears were Athenians who settled in Ionia, a place called the seat of modern fiction: "Die *Milesischen Fabeln* (die Vorbilder unsrer *Novellen* und Romane) erkennen Ionien für ihr Vaterland" (19:8). At first, such proof that the muses favored the Abderites' ancestors seems refuted by the Abderites themselves. They fancy themselves enthusiastic connoisseurs—"feine Kenner und schwärmerische Liebhaber der Künste" (19:12) and "Enthusiasten der schönen Künste" (19:17)—but their folly often concerns fine art and belies such appellations. A fountain that they commission from a famous sculptor proves useless because they lack enough water to make it work, for example, and they acquire a statue of Venus by Praxiteles but put it on a pedestal so high that the goddess is all but invisible. Such arts thrive at the same time that the Abderites flee their sacred frogs, but this hint that Rousseau was right to link refinement and decline needs to be understood in connection with the issue of fictionality. Imagination gets the better of the Abderites' reason as soon as they leave Ionia, so much so that it makes them the laughing stock of Greece. Theirs is so lively, in fact, that their logic seems to derive from hearing fairy tales as children. They also find Democritus's experiments marvelous (*wunderbar*), and they ask him what marvelous things he saw abroad. Democritus answers that he had no time for the marvelous and that he observes nature instead of indulging his imagination, as metaphysicians and poets would. On his trips and in his science, he thus applies the same criterion noted to assure the truth of literary fiction in Wieland's foreword.

The Abderites' significance for reading fiction lies not only in their penchant for imagination and the marvelous, a trait that they share with Don Sylvio, but also in their remarks on artistic taste and beauty. The narrator raises the issue of taste when he explains that the Abderites lack it, despite their remarkable passion for the arts. This lack of taste keeps their city from being a second Athens, a fictional fact especially clear in the case of music. In Abdera, the best singer has always been chosen "Nomofylax"—guardian of the laws, that is—and there is no separation of art and state. Ethics, politics, theology, cosmology, and medicine are all founded on musical principles there, but the Abderites do not deserve the respect accorded the similarly speculative Orpheus, Pythagoras, and Plato. Instead of feeling moved by music, they prefer pretty but meaningless sounds, which the narrator thinks consistent with their general lack of taste: "Diese Widersinnigkeit erstreckte sich über alle Gegenstände des Geschmacks; oder, richtiger zu reden, mit aller ihrer Schwärmerey für die Künste hatten die Abderiten gar keinen Geschmack; und es ahndete ihnen nicht einmahl, daß das Schöne aus einem höhern Grunde schön sey, als *weil es ihnen so beliebte*" (19:22–23). This belief that beauty is more than a matter of arbitrary whim applies not only to outward appearance but also to inner goodness, the two being combined in the notion of *kalokagathia*, a Socratic concept best realized by cultivating taste: "Die Bildung des Geschmacks, d. i. eines feinen, richtigen und *gelehrten Gefühls alles Schönen*, ist die beste Grundlage zu jener berühmten *Sokratischen Kalokagathie* oder *innerlichen Schönheit und Güte der Seele*, welche den liebenswürdigen, edelmüthigen, wohlthätigen und glücklichen Menschen macht" (19:16). Wieland was qualified to make such sweeping claims, having edited Bodmer and Breitinger's *Sammlung der Zürcherischen Streitschriften zur Verbesserung des deutschen Geschmacks* (1753), a volume of polemical pieces on the topic of taste that the two Swiss critics aimed at Gottsched and his disciples as part of their larger feud with him about figurative language and literary mimesis.

   The importance of narrative fiction is likewise implicit when the Abderites defend their taste for beauty. They scoff at Democritus's news that people in Ethiopia find each other attractive, and they laugh at his story of an Ethiopian woman whose beauty he says caused no less strife than Helen's. That black could be beautiful strikes the Abderites as ludicrous, even though Democritus explains that the light-skinned people who seem most beautiful to them do so only because they resemble them most closely. One Abderite argues that Ethiopians must have no concept of beauty, but Democritus answers that since the Ethiopian Helen was desired by everyone, she must have matched their common ideal, the "*Idee von Schönheit* . . . die jeder in seiner Einbildung fand" (19:47). Ethiopians agreed that the woman was beautiful, though Greeks might find her ugly, he adds, and both might well be right. The Abderites howl at this hint of relativism, which they exaggerate ad absurdum: "Und *wenn*—und *wenn* ein Wahnwitziger Pferdeäpfel für Pfirschen äße?" (19:57). Their daring Democritus to "crack open" such hypothetical horse apples, which they "serve up" but he can barely "get down" or "swallow," wittily underscores the sense of this scene as a lesson in taste. Its wider import lies in its similarity to statements by three of Wieland's contemporaries. Friedrich Justus Riedel, Wieland's friend and colleague in Erfurt, argued that concepts of beauty are relative in his *Theorie der schönen Künste und Wissenschaften* (1767), a thought that he elsewhere suggested Wieland demonstrate by describing a beautiful black woman,[21] and such relativism has been praised as a kind of perspectivism constituting the poetic structure of *Die Abderiten.*[22] The narrator's show of ignorance about the Ethiopian woman and her relationship to Democritus, moreover, recalls similar disingenuousness in *Tristram Shandy.*[23] Finally, like Democritus, Addison noted how concepts of beauty could differ: "Every different Species of sensible Creatures has its different Notions of Beauty, and . . . each of them is most affected with the Beauties of its own kind."[24] Addison makes this remark in "On the Pleasures of Imagination," mentioned above in connection with *Agathon.* Wieland's disputation on beauty thus raises aesthetic questions subtly related to "metafiction" and literary imagination.

Wieland answers those questions by referring to visual art, technical terms of which he uses to explain his satirical intentions in *Die Abderiten.* In the episode just discussed, he refers to Hogarth, though for reasons different than those that move him to defend the English artist in "Unterredungen mit dem Pfarrer von ***." In that essay, published shortly after the early books of *Die Abderiten,* his mouthpiece W** calls Hogarth's caricatures accurate depictions of all-too-human human nature. Here, realizing that the Abderites cannot comprehend the concept of black beauty, Democritus simply laughs out loud. They soon join him, most laughing so hard that some cannot help publicly urinating. The ensuing chaos, the narrator remarks, causes a scene worthy of Hogarth's stylus: "Alles dieß zusammen machte eine Scene, die des Griffels eines *Hogarth* würdig gewesen wäre, wenn es damahls schon einen Hogarth gegeben hätte" (19:61). This mention of Hogarth hardly seems coincidental, since his *Analysis of Beauty* (1753) addresses the same problem of fluctuating taste posed by the Abderites' debate with Democritus.[25] Hogarth often likened his drawing to writing, moreover, and opposed the established hierarchy of genres in both media. The Abderites' antics here show Wieland's similarly generic concern, since their seeming so worthy of being drawn by Hogarth is best explained by way of Fielding, who shared Hogarth's high opinion of low genres in both verbal and visual art. As noted above, Fielding distinguishes "comic" prose, which he confines to imitating the ridiculous in nature, from "burlesque" writing, which shows what is monstrous and unnatural.[26] Comic prose seems like comic painting, he notes, while burlesque writing resembles painters' *caricatura*. Although he accordingly holds comic authors strictly accountable to nature, Fielding goes on to warn that his novel *Joseph Andrews* should not be misunderstood. Worried that some readers will link its fictional characters to particular, real people, he explains that it mocks an entire species, not individuals. Defining his fiction in terms of painting, then, Fielding foresees snags in its reception by readers who take comic prose too literally.

Wieland, too, refers to specific kinds of painting to help explain fiction that he expects readers will misunderstand. Like Fielding, moreover, he does so to stress that he ridicules *kinds* of people rather than individuals, showing the same concern with human folly in general that Rabener regarded as appropriate to satire. "To prevent . . . malicious applications," as Fielding put this concern in *Joseph Andrews*, "I declare here once and for all, I describe not Men, but Manners; not an Individual but a Species."[27] Related remarks occur in "Der Schlüssel zur Abderitengeschichte," the key that Wieland appended to *Die Abderiten* in 1781, ostensibly for readers seeking its double, hidden meaning. That key, however, reveals neither the real identity of its fictional characters, nor the sort of allegorical meaning that learned commentators commonly find in epic poems, as later came to be expected of all satirical novels, "als ob ein jedes Buch, das einem *satirischen Roman* ähnlich sieht, mit einem versteckten Sinn begabt sey; und also einen *Schlüssel* nöthig habe" (20:295). Posing as the editor of the Abderites' story, Wieland instead quotes its author, who tells how he gave his fantasy free rein, describing those old fools as imaginatively as he could so that no one would mistake his writing for satire referring to other people. Readers' responses, though, proved him wrong: "Der Erfolg bewies, daß ich unschuldiger Weise *Abbildungen* gemacht hatte, da ich nur *Fantasien* zu mahlen glaubte . . . und wo man sie [*Die Abderiten*] las, da wollte man die *Originale* zu den darin vorkommenden Bildern gesehen haben" (20:300). Speaking in such terms of visual art again, the author also recounts how he controlled his imagination to avoid inventing further caricatures. Wieland was certainly not this innocent of alluding to his contemporaries—he confessed that Mannheim, Biberach, Nuremberg, and Weimar all inspired Abdera—and many of them actually did refuse to believe that the Abderites were fictional.[28] Rather than explain his novel as a roman à clef, moreover, a label that he felt slighted his creativity, his *Schlüssel* seems to parody the baroque "keys" that it describes.[29] It thus seems written in the spirit of his mentor Bodmer, who dismissed such devices as unnecessary: "Der einzige Schlüssel eines moralischen Werkes, das gewisse Namen gebrauchet, das Laster oder das Lobenswürdige damit zu belegen, ist der lasterhafte oder der ehrliche Mensch, weil dieser das einzige Original ist, nach welchem seine Charakteren geschildert sind . . . Die Personen . . . bestehen nur in der Einbildung, in während er Zeit das Laster oder die Tugend . . . ganz real ist."[30]

This advocacy of characters understood to be fictional, though they embody real vices or virtues, also occurs in remarks on *Die Abderiten* that Wieland printed in *Der teutsche Merkur* along with initial installments of the novel but did not include in his subsequent *Schlüssel*. Like Fielding, he addresses this matter of fictional prose by distinguishing various kinds of painting. His specific concern is that his fictional history should not be mistaken for personal satire, which he expresses by comparing authors to painters who produce ideals, portraits, or grotesques: "Ein Maler kann Ideale, Bildnisse, oder Grotesken machen, je nachdem es ihm gefällt; aber Ideale und Grotesken sind keine Bildnisse; und wenn es sich zutrifft, daß sie jemanden ähnlich sehen, so hat vermutlich Natur oder Zufall die Schuld daran."[31] Wieland here raises an issue of decorum: portraits should always seem like their sitters, while ideals and grotesques seldom do. Thanks to this distinction, he has been numbered among eighteenth-century theoreticians of the grotesque.[32] He also observes, however, that it is difficult to exaggerate beyond recognition what one depicts, especially in caricatures: "Es ist schwer, sich in Gedanken zu einem Grade von Schönheit zu erheben, der das schönste in der Natur merklich übertreffe; aber vielleicht ganz unmöglich, eine Karrikatur zu erfinden, die keinem Geschöpfe Gottes ähnlich sehe."[33] Wieland thus presents his fiction as caricature, a kind of art unavoidably similar to life. Indeed, he explains how readers everywhere admired the Abderites' striking likeness to living persons, "die treffende Ähnlichkeit meiner Gemälde."[34] He denies responsibility for such similarities, though, claiming that he unwittingly "painted" portraits when putting his idea of the Abderite character into a series of fictional events, "ein[e] Reihe von erdichteten Begebenheiten."[35] This talent for making abstract thoughts and ideals seem concrete, for individualizing "allgemein[e] Charaktere oder Ideale," is even noted to be the mark of a true poet, though it often results in unintentional likenesses.[36] Just as in his *Schlüssel*, then, Wieland here reinforces the fact that his Abderites are fictional characters.

The importance of fictionality for reading *Die Abderiten* is similarly expressed in terms of visual art throughout it. Like Wieland's other middle novels, it often links painting to narration and the perception of ideals. As in his remarks on grotesques and caricatures, however, Wieland's vocabulary is also more precise here. Female Abderites have such a vivid imagination that they swoon upon hearing Democritus's description of Ethiopia, a kind of verbal "painting" that he therefore resolves to tone down: "In seinem Herzen beschloß er, künftig seine Gemählde nur mit Einer Farbe zu mahlen" (19:42). The Abderites themselves associate painting and ideals when they assume that Ethiopians have no taste in beauty: "Was das für ein dummes Volk seyn muß! Haben sie denn keine Mahler, die ihnen den Apollo, den Bacchus, die Göttin der Liebe und die Grazien mahlen?" (19:43). Beyond using "Gemählde" and "mahlen" to indicate the force of imagination and ideals, Wieland also employs the expression "helldunkel"—German for chiaroscuro. It first occurs when Democritus mocks Abderite moralists for wanting the world to be like Cockaigne, an imaginary land of idleness and luxury that he considers impossibly utopian. One Abderite insists that he spell out this comparison with "das Mährchen vom *Schlaraffenlande*" (19:109), which the philosopher regrets: "Sie lieben eine starke Beleuchtung . . . Aber zu viel Licht ist zum Sehen eben so unbequem als zu wenig. *Helldunkel* ist . . . gerade so viel Licht, als man braucht, um in solchen Dingen weder zu viel noch zu wenig zu sehen" (19:110–11). The analogy that Democritus draws should thus be "seen" in merely general terms. Although he admits taking details of his description from a Greek comedy, he denies intending it as personal satire. Wieland does not always cite chiaroscuro in contexts so literary or so benign. One of the shady lawyers in Abdera, for example, makes a fortune by using this same technique to tell half-truths: "Er steifte sich auf lauter *unläugbare Fakta*: aber seine Stärke lag in der *Zusammensetzung* und im *Helldunkeln*" (19:197). As a narrative means to a rhetorical end, then, chiaroscuro seems morally ambiguous.

In further remarks on *Die Abderiten* made in *Der teutsche Merkur*, Wieland himself alludes to the term "helldunkel," however, to explain why the novel needs to be read as a work of fiction. Like the shady lawyer's speeches, it is composed of falsehood and truth, a mixture that remains pleasing and useful as long as its readers are not too particular: "Die Geschichte der Abderiten ist eine Dichtung—wie alles andre Dichtwerk—eine Komposition von Wahrheit und Lüge, von Licht und Schatten. Wer sie als Komposition betrachtet, kann Freude daran haben. Dem, der sie als einen kleinen Taschenspiegel, bloß zu seinem eignen Gebrauch, führen will, kann sie zuweilen Dienste tun. Aber wer sie als einen Reflexionsspiegel brauchen will, mag sich in Acht nehmen!"[37] In other words, Wieland's art is not a direct reflection of life but rather a combination of narrative light and shadow, of clear as well as obscure references to reality. The targets of his satire in *Die Abderiten* accordingly seem as imaginary as Tifan, the enforcer of his social ideals in *Der goldne Spiegel*. Both novels certainly pertain to his contemporaries, but neither mirrors them in naive *Widerspiegelung*. Given this significance, the concept of chiaroscuro explains what might otherwise seem merely an ironic comment by Wieland on his satire: "Sollte aber jemand auf die Gedanken kommen, daß diese Abderiten wohl eine Art von Satyre auf kleine Republiken sein könnten; so lassen wir ihm unverhalten, daß es wenigstens des Verfassers Meinung nicht gewesen, eine Satyre zu schreiben; es wäre dann, daß man diesem Wort eine Bedeutung geben wollte, vermöge welcher jede Geschichte zur Satyre würde."[38] Just because his story corresponds to life, it should not be taken as *personal* satire, that is, satire referring only to particular, real people. Wieland later expressed this same thought in another remark on *Die Abderiten*, again comparing poets to painters: "Wehe dem Dichter, dessen Gemälde niemanden gleich sehen!"[39] Since a technical term borrowed from painting, chiaroscuro, thus suggests the attitude that Wieland thought appropriate not only to writing but also to reading his fiction, visual art seems the true key to *Die Abderiten*.

Die Abderiten not only mentions visual art as prominently and as suggestively as Wieland's other middle novels; it also includes revealing remarks on aesthetic illusion, the overriding issue of fictionality raised in his later ones. Wieland makes those remarks in scenes about the theater, which he relates to both the Abderites' debate about taste and his essay on the *Singspiel*. Democritus speaks of the theater in Book 1, where he insists that the rules governing works of art can never be arbitrary. He explains that a poet must know both human nature, which should be the model (*Modell*) for dramatic characters, and the ways to touch the hearts of an audience. He adds that moving an audience is not enough, however, apparently reversing his stand on the relativity of taste. Whereas earlier he argued that black, too, could seem beautiful, now he claims that music made on the Gold Coast is not excellent just because it pleases the natives there. Indeed, he objects to making art either arbitrary or a matter of popular sentiment: "Eigendünkel? Das ist es eben, was ich aus den Künsten der Musen verbannt sehen möchte . . . Aber das Gefühl eines ganzen Volkes, wenn es kein *gelehrtes* Gefühl ist, kann und muß in unzähligen Fällen betrüglich seyn" (19:82). Democritus here recommends aesthetic education that applies to narrative fiction as well, since he also observes that children are moved by even the most ridiculous fairy tale. Convincing proof of the need to cultivate taste comes in Book 3, which tells how the Abderites encourage their local playwrights at the expense of good taste and how plays written elsewhere seem better suited, "*ihren Geschmack zu bilden*" (19:256), but how taste also assumes a natural ability that no amount of cultivation can ever replace and that Abderites simply seem to lack. In short, everything tastes good to them—"Ihnen schmeckte *Alles*" (19:257). Still, they know that some things taste better than others, and they can be strangely moved by the truly beautiful, an indication that they are not wholly without taste, "nicht . . . *ohne allen Geschmack*" (19:262). Book 3 thus poses anew questions of aesthetic taste only apparently settled in Book 1.

The Abderites' own behavior in the theater hardly seems the answer to such aesthetic questions, but they prove far less silly an audience than they appear to be. Their own nonsensical production of Euripides' *Andromeda* admittedly attests to their poor taste. Bad casting, worse staging, and an awful performance do not prevent them from being swept off their feet and proud of all the havoc that they have wrought. This dubious success is the work of their Nomofylax, whose taste is confined to his own compositions and who goes to laughable lengths in order to make Euripides' play create the illusion of life, "um die *Illusion* vollkommner zu machen" (19:290). The Abderites' strong reaction to such illusion, though, soon turns out to be their saving grace. At their botched performance of *Andromeda*, Euripides himself happens to be in the audience. They fail to recognize him, and when he introduces himself, they insist on comparing him to a bust that bears his name. This encounter has been linked to Wieland's sojourns in Mannheim, but it also shows how badly the Abderites muddle nature and art.[40] Their preference for art proves to be a virtue, however, when Euripides stages *Andromeda* a second time, with his own actors under his own direction. The Abderites are amazed by his professionally painted sets and could swear that the scenes in his story really are as they appear. Affecting music, acting, and declamation likewise create a degree of illusion new to the Abderites, "einen Grad von Täuschung . . . wie sie noch in keinem Schauspiel erfahren hatten" (19:351). The narrator explains that the Abderites' susceptibility to such illusion is not a failing and does not cast doubt on their reason. Indeed, he adds that they are human, too, all the more so, in fact, the more that they allow themselves to be deceived by such "Täuschungen der Kunst" (19:353). Not only the narrator, but also the author whose story he edits is fond of the Abderites for indulging this urge, "sich von den Künsten der Einbildungskraft und der Nachahmung täuschen zu lassen" (19:353). Wieland thus takes Lucian's hint that the Abderites were not necessarily crazy when it came to poetic mimesis.

Wieland's narrator even regrets that refined and enlightened audiences are not as ready to submit to aesthetic illusion, citing the Abderites as an example for them to follow. To be sure, Euripides' performance leaves them moonstruck, and they fall into outrageous paroxysms, but such theatrical lunacy seems preferable to its opposite, the petty rejection of all aesthetic illusion: "In der That haben Dichter, Tonkünstler, Mahler, einem aufgeklärten und verfeinerten Publikum gegen über, schlimmes Spiel . . . Anstatt sich zur Illusion zu bequemen, wo die Vernichtung des Zaubers zu nichts dienen kann als uns eines Vergnügens zu berauben, setzt man ich weiß nicht welche kindische Ehre darein, den Filosofen zur Unzeit zu machen" (19:353–54). This censure of pseudo-enlightened skepticism is more than a request not to spoil the fun of an evening at the theater, for it also helps discern the objects of Wieland's satire. Whatever other resemblances his readers bear to the Abderites—similarities sure to be embarrassing, his narrator hints—they would do well to be as enchanted by the muses, even if dramatic artists themselves are not always sublime: "Unser eignes Gewissen mag uns sagen, ob und in wie fern wir in andern Dingen mehr oder weniger Thracier und Abderiten sind: aber wenn wirs in diesem einzigen Punkte wären, so möcht' es nur desto besser für uns— und freylich auch für den größten Theil unsrer poetischen Sackpfeifer, seyn" (19:356). Wieland's satire thus stops short of mocking a weakness for aesthetic illusion. Indeed, the otherwise stupid Abderites' surprising degree of cultivation was once thought to be a flaw of his novel, but their response to works of art has seemed to transcend their nonsense, and their enthusiasm for the theater has been said to make them far more than mere philistines.[41] The narrator also notes that poets must work hard and well to create and maintain aesthetic illusion, but Wieland's emphasis is squarely on the Abderites themselves. By recommending their receptiveness to such illusion, Book 3 shows the late eighteenth-century shift from making rules of art toward analyzing responses to it, a shift from arbitrating taste to the philosophy of aesthetics.

Further remarks in Book 3 reveal that the Abderites' example also holds for reading *Die Abderiten* itself. Wieland's readers, too, seem meant to accept aesthetic illusion. Just as the curtain is about to go up on *Andromeda*, the narrator requests that they join the audience: "Die Schauspielstunde ist inzwischen herbeygekommen, und wir versetzen uns also ohne weiters in das Amfitheater dieser preiswürdigen Republik, wo der geneigte Leser nach Gefallen . . . Platz zu nehmen belieben wird" (19:279). Readers are here invited, albeit tongue-in-cheek, to imagine the ensuing scenes *about* Euripides' play as vividly as the Abderites see two performances *of* it. Acceptance of Wieland's own aesthetic illusion is encouraged again when the narrator explains Euripides' presence in Abdera. Such unexpected appearances are common on stage, he writes, but must be accounted for when they occur in the orchestra: "So gewohnt man dergleichen unvermutheter Erscheinungen *auf dem Theater* ist: so begreifen wir doch wohl, daß es eine andre Bewandtniß hat, wenn sich eine solche Erscheinung im *Parterre* ereignet; und es ist solchen Falls *der Majestät der Geschichte* gemäß, den Leser zu verständigen, wie es damit zugegangen sey" (19:311–12). Here explaining a fictional event to make it seem plausible, Wieland helps readers accept illusion also associated with plays. These exchanges recall another at the outset of his novel. When readers seem impatient, the narrator responds that they should not allow themselves to be distracted: "Wer mit Vergnügen und Nutzen lesen will, muß gerade sonst nichts andres zu thun noch zu denken haben" (19:6). This request for undivided attention is a condition, in fact, that the narrator thinks should govern his dealings with his readers: "Geduld! günstige Leser, Geduld, bis wir, eh' ich weiter forterzähle, über unsre Bedingungen einig sind" (19:5). Given that readers are asked to put themselves in the Abderites' place in Book 3 and to accept aesthetic illusion like that induced in the theater, such conditions seem part of the contract—the *"bedingte[r] Vertrag"* (26:247) or *"stillschweigende[r] Vertrag"* (26:260)—honored by art and its audience in Wieland's essay on the *Singspiel*.

As models for readers of fiction, then, the Abderites seem parties to an aesthetic contract that supersedes the social one noted time and again in Wieland's other middle novels. Indeed, they replace the idyllic "Kinder der Natur" repeatedly cited in *Diogenes, Der goldne Spiegel*, and *Danischmend* to answer Rousseau's speculation about the moral course of society. To be sure, readers entering Abdera must abandon all hope of finding a social utopia. Wieland's narrator writes that the Abderites are foolish, however, not evil, that their good nature gives them the patience to deal with Democritus, and that they are so absurdly stupid as to seem sublime. They thus come off far better here than in Sterne's *Sentimental Journey* (1768), where Abdera is smeared as "the vilest and most profligate town in all Thrace."[42] They even recall the utopian "Kinder der Natur." Like both Psammis and Danischmend, the Abderites forbid travel that might make one of them wiser than the rest. Some of their plays seem "eine Art von lebendigen Abderitischen *Familiengemählden*" (19:270), moreover, a term reminiscent of the *"lebendiges Gemählde"* (6:124) of Psammis surrounded by his children and the enactment of Greuze's *L'accordée du village* in an equally ideal tableau vivant. The only noble savages mentioned in *Die Abderiten*, though, are *aesthetic* "Kinder der Natur." Remarking that the arts have always seemed most moving to peoples still uncivilized, the narrator tells how the Abderites' fellow Thracians once succumbed to Orpheus because they listened to his songs like *"bloße Naturmenschen"* (19:355). In Wieland's "Schlüssel," moreover, archaic Greeks seem best able to appreciate the elements of fiction in Homeric poems, "das *Wahre* unter der Hülle des *Wunderbaren,* und das *Nützliche* . . . vereinbart mit dem Schönen und Angenehmen" (20:292). Thus shifting the emphasis of Wieland's ideal "Kinder der Natur" from society to aesthetics and epic fiction, *Die Abderiten* is indeed a *"Beytrag zur Geschichte des menschlichen Verstandes"* (19, Vorbericht: 5), a title nearly—and not coincidentally— identical to that of Wieland's collected essays on Rousseau, *Beyträge zur geheimen Geschichte des menschlichen Verstandes und Herzens* (1770).

   To argue that the Abderites' behavior in Book 3 casts them as aesthetic "Kinder der Natur," an ideal to be emulated by actual readers of Wieland's satire, is to regard them more kindly than previous scholars have. Book 3 has been said to treat the aesthetics of drama and the theory as well as practice of opera, and Wieland's satire on theater in Germany has seemed to reflect his own experience of it there, just as Euripides' performance of *Andromeda* conforms to Wieland's concept of the *Singspiel.*[43] At best, though, the Abderites have seemed a "negative ideal," an antidote to the Graecomania inspired by Winckelmann.[44] Satire often works precisely by means of such pathetic contrasts, however, by showing how reality falls short of ideals, so one can rightly consider the Abderites' artistic urge germane to reading *Die Abderiten* itself. Their role for reading fiction is seldom mentioned favorably. Wieland's authorial narrator has been said to manipulate readers into the ironic "fictional field" of the novel, but insofar as the fictional ones whom he addresses resemble literal-minded Abderites themselves, they have not seemed models for their real counterparts.[45] Similarly, the Abderites have seemed too gullible to set an example for actual readers of fiction.[46] Nonetheless, the novel is said to teach its audience how to read satiric literature, a lesson closely tied to understanding its own satire as more than merely personal.[47] In the last two books of *Die Abderiten,* moreover, its readers seem meant to use their own judgment, without Democritus, Hippocrates, Euripides, or the narrator to tell them what to think.[48] Given the evidence presented here, the Abderites themselves seem to teach such readers best. By advocating aesthetic illusion and hinting that the Abderites are an ideal audience for his story, that is, Wieland suggests that readers should be more, not less, like them. Although he makes fun of their *"Schauspielfieber"* (19:368), a malady that apparently also afflicts his fellow Germans, he does not simply expose the Abderites to ridicule. Like Don Sylvio, those silly Greeks display imagination and a taste for the marvelous that have gone awry but should not be eradicated. On the contrary, Wieland himself refines that taste in *Die Abderiten* for the sake of reading its satire properly—in other words, as fiction.

Wieland's subtle lesson in the aesthetics of fictionality is less obvious in the second part of his novel, which comprises Books 4 and 5, "Der Prozeß um des Esels Schatten" and "Die Frösche der Latona." Both show his satire at full strength but without the hints about how to read it given by precept as well as example in Book 3. Their relatively direct narration assumes, however, that his readers now need no further such instruction. At the beginning of Book 4, the narrator remarks that the Abderites' making a mountain out of a molehill will not surprise readers who have come to know them from the foregoing chapters. What is more, he regrets that the manuscripts of their lawyers' speeches are lost but explains that the excerpts cited by him have a "Duft der Abderitheit" (20:128), a literal air of probability proving his story genuine, "ein innerliches Argument, das am Ende doch immer das beste zu seyn scheint, das für das Werk irgend eines Sterblichen, er sey nun ein *Ossian* oder ein *Abderitischer Feigenredner*, sich geben läßt!" (20:128). This stress on the internal logic of fiction is especially strong since it mentions not only fictional characters such as the Abderites' sycophantic lawyers but also Ossian, the made-up author of James Macpherson's *Fragments of Ancient Poetry* (1760). "Der Prozeß um des Esels Schatten" thus not only treats the motif of the shadow in a comic tradition that includes an adaptation of Wieland by Friedrich Dürrenmatt, nor are its psychological insights confined to social behavior, its literary significance to allusions to Jonathan Swift and Friedrich Gottlob Klopstock.[49] "Die Frösche der Latona" is similarly suggestive. It shows how imagination informs religion no less than aesthetics, it doubts the likelihood of myths that defy the *"Lauf der Natur"* (20:246), and it ends with the hope that the Abderites' story will last until their antics seem like "Geschichten aus einem andern Planeten" (20:288). *Die Abderiten* includes so much advice on how to read its satire mindful of fictionality, in fact, that it already recalls such a phrase, Breitinger's definition of literary fiction as a history or tale from another, possible world.

Throughout *Die Abderiten*, then, Wieland displays aesthetic concern with the fictionality of his satire, combining insights into imagination like those shown in *Don Sylvio*, analogies with visual art drawn in Fielding's *Joseph Andrews*, and further reflection on the social ideals inspired by Rousseau in his other middle novels. Its subtitle—*Eine sehr wahrscheinliche Geschichte*—thus seems more than just an ironic comment on narration that claims to be true. *Wahrscheinlich* here ought to be taken not in the sense of "probable" but rather in that of "verisimilar," an indication that *Die Abderiten* should be read as fiction, not—at least not only—as an attack on Wieland's contemporaries. As fictional characters, that is, the Abderites should be understood to exist in their own, imaginary right. As implied by the full title of Bodmer and Breitinger's essay on imagination, moreover—*Vom Einfluß und Gebrauche der Einbildungskraft zur Ausbesserung des Geschmacks* (1727)—the cultivation of taste in *Die Abderiten* is related to the defense of fiction in *Don Sylvio*. Wieland's narrator remarks that the Abderites lack taste but know what they like, that they affect "ohne den mindesten Geschmack eine ungeheure Leidenschaft für die Künste" (19:70), but as Fielding explains in *Joseph Andrews*, "Affectation doth not imply an absolute Negation of those Qualities which are affected."[50] Indeed, when it comes to accepting the aesthetic illusion created by plays, *Singspiele*, and literary fiction, the Abderites seem a chosen people. Like *Don Sylvio*, *Die Abderiten* also affords comic relief from more earnest writing on a subject closely tied to fictionality, here the social ideals that Wieland debates in his other middle novels. His satire in *Die Abderiten*, in fact, is simply the logical obverse of the idealism manifested in *Diogenes*, *Der goldne Spiegel*, and *Danischmend*. The import of such shifts of focus, too, is best explained by Fielding, who wrote that "it may not be always so easy for a serious Poet to meet with the Great and the Admirable; but Life every where furnishes an accurate Observer with the Ridiculous."[51] In this sense, and thanks in no small part to its treatment of fictionality as a trait of artworks other than novels, *Die Abderiten* seems consummate comic fiction.

Part III. The Late Novels: Illusion

7. Geheime Geschichte des Philosophen Peregrinus Proteus (1791)

Seine Phantasie glich einem neugierigen Wanderer,
der die einladenden baumbestandenen Nebenpfade
der geraden Hauptstraße vorzieht, seine
Geschichten umspannten in kühnem Wurf den
Erdkreis, und im Moment, da er sie erfand, warf er
das Netz seiner Imagination weiter aus, über die
Ränder der Welt hinaus.
—Michael Kleeberg, *Proteus der Pilger* (1993)

The issues of imagination and ideals raised in Wieland's essays as well as in his early and middle novels remain important in his late ones— *Peregrinus Proteus* (1791), *Agathodämon* (1799), and *Aristipp* (1800–02)— but they are regarded there along with the concept of illusion, the *Täuschung* considered both in his "Versuch über das deutsche Singspiel" and in *Die Abderiten.* The late novels show how such illusion concerns not only aesthetic enjoyment like the Abderites', moreover, but also the epistemological and ontological problems posed in *Agathon* and *Don Sylvio.* Those problems pervade the plots as well as narration of all three, which explore how closely *i*llusion and *de*lusion are related in their characters' attempts to lead either spiritual lives inspired by early Christianity or the examined kind famously favored by Socrates. Wieland thereby draws parallels between life and fictional literature that demonstrate as well as help resolve ambiguities inherent in the illusion created by his own novels, not least in the idealistic, Kantian acceptance of fictionality apparent at the end of the third version of *Agathon.* The *Täuschung* thus studied in *Peregrinus Proteus*, which first appeared in *Der teutsche Merkur* in late 1788 and early 1789, is so severe as to be fatal, but it is explained, defended, and justified in ways that recall the sense and structure of Wieland's earlier novels. Here too both the marvelous found in literary fiction and the visual images conveyed by painting and sculpture reveal the power of a vivid imagination and high ideals. Wieland's title character succumbs to theatrical illusion even more completely than the Abderites, moreover, so much so that such illusion seems "romantic," a term with historical links to the genre of the *Roman.* Illusion also informs Peregrinus's belief in Gnostic

135

Christianity and his conversion to Cynicism, both of which are related to Lavater's dubious science of physiognomy. Like Lavater's body language, Peregrinus learns, figurative language too can be extremely misleading, an insight that connects his story to its complex narration by Peregrinus himself, his interlocutor Lucian, Lucian's sources, and Wieland's narrator. *Peregrinus Proteus* thereby indicates how Wieland's late novels continue to probe the complex, larger realm of fictionality.

The novel is mostly a story told by Peregrinus to Lucian when they meet in Elysium sixteen centuries after their deaths. The historical Lucian died sometime after A.D. 180, and the historical Peregrinus set himself on fire at the Olympic games of A.D. 165, an act recorded in Lucian's "Passing of Peregrinus" (c. A.D. 169). Wieland translated this work as part of his *Lucians von Samosatas Sämmtliche Werke* (1788), and his novel begins with an excerpt from it, which shows Lucian doubting claims that Peregrinus was wise and divine, dismissing him instead as a vainglorious fool. Wieland then adds a dialogue between his fictional characters that is modeled on Lucian's *Dialogues of the Dead.*[1] That dialogue constitutes an autobiography of Peregrinus, an apology punctuated by Lucian's occasional comments. Peregrinus rejects slander reported in Lucian's treatise, but Lucian replies that he meant no harm and agrees to hear Peregrinus set the record straight. Peregrinus does so by recounting the main events of his life, which result from his erratic imagination and his pursuit of spiritual happiness. Such eudaemonism is so otherworldly that he fails to foresee how his attraction to young people in Parium as well as Athens can be construed as sexual, a mistake that he repeats when he travels to Smyrna and seeks the philosopher Apollonius of Tyana, whose supposed daughter Dioklea and her Roman mistress Mamilia Quintilla seduce him by posing as a priestess and the goddess she serves. Similar problems arise when Peregrinus is swindled out of his fortune by two mysterious men named Kerinthus and Hegesias, who preach Christianity to achieve secret political aims. Peregrinus's stint as a Cynic in Rome proves equally futile, for he is seduced there by its emperor's daughter Faustina, a lapse that demonstrates how badly he can still be deceived. Reflecting on these repeated *Täuschungen*, Peregrinus confesses his folly but consoles himself with having convinced Lucian that though he was an enthusiast, he was at least an honest one: *"Peregrinus Proteus* steht nun, als ein *Schwärmer*, wenn du willst, aber wenigstens als ein *ehrlicher* Schwärmer vor dir da" (28:219).

This admission of forthright *Schwärmerei* develops a theme found in Wieland's earlier novels, and its significance emerges from its similar connections to their settings, characters, plots, and narrative forms.

Much like Don Sylvio, Peregrinus misinterprets sense impressions because he has a lively imagination, a poetic cast of mind that Mamilia Quintilla shares with him as surely as Donna Felicia does with Don Sylvio: "Ihre Fantasie hatte, wie die meinige, in früher Jugend einen gewissen dichterischen Schwung bekommen" (27:187). In retrospect, Peregrinus dismisses Dioklea's rituals as so much *"Feerey"* (27:138), but when she visits the prison where he is held for professing his Christian beliefs, she makes his cell seem like a "Zimmer eines Feenpalasts" (28:48). Indeed, Peregrinus and Lucian debate the right to deride *Schwärmerei*, invoking the same test of ridicule applied in *Don Sylvio*. With his poetic streak, Peregrinus also resembles Agathon. He too, moreover, recites poetry like a professional rhapsodist and meets an important mentor in Smyrna. His attempt to improve Roman morals recalls Agathon's similar effort in Syracuse, and a friend warns him that an idyllic Christian family he once met could not possibly live up to his ideals for long and that he would have to escape it by taking "einen Sprung aus dem Fenster" (28:128), the same kind of leap that the fictional Greek author of *Agathon* is said to take when his story fails to turn out well. Peregrinus similarly longs to get away from pagan "Kind[er] der Finsternis" (28:6) and to live among Christian "Kinder des Lichts" (28:7), who seem just as utopian as the "Kinder der Natur" posited in *Diogenes, Der goldne Spiegel,* and *Danischmend.* Finally, like Schach Gebal, Lucian takes increasing interest in the story that he hears, a willing and grateful listener curious about its details and convinced that it justifies Peregrinus. These many thematic and formal links to Wieland's earlier novels suggest that *Peregrinus Proteus* takes up business left unfinished there, returning to the multifarious problem of fictionality.

This suggestion is clearest in the case of illusion. Here such *Täuschung* goes beyond the purely aesthetic kind that the Abderites experience in the theater. It is so important that *täuschen* is the first word of the novel proper, which conveys Peregrinus's surprise at seeing Lucian again: "Täuschen mich meine Augen, oder ist es wirklich mein alter Gönner *Lucian von Samosata,* den ich nach so langer Zeit wiedersehe?" (27:29). This question is legitimate, since Peregrinus later recalls his irrational tendency, "immer auf eine oder andere Art zu schwärmen und getäuscht zu werden" (27:219). Actually, others deceived him less than he deceived himself, as Dioklea explains when describing his love for Mamilia Quintilla, whom he imagined to be a kind of Venus: "Sie täuscht dich! oder vielmehr du täuschest dich selbst mit einer Art von *fantasierter Liebe"* (27:159). Lucian too finds him highly prone to self-deception, a diagnosis that Peregrinus accepts with the help of hindsight: "Ach! was mich täuschte, war immer *in mir selbst!*" (28:54). Illusion is not as simple, however, as such skepticism implies. Peregrinus calls Lucian its foe, a "Feind aller Täuschungskünste" (28:98), but Lucian notes that even sworn "Gegner aller Täuschungen" (27:164) would envy Peregrinus's imagination. Apprised of his erotic fulfillment, Lucian goes so far as to find delusion worthwhile: "Täuschung oder nicht! welcher König . . . ja welcher Weise in der Welt hätte sich nicht um diesen Preis täuschen lassen wollen!" (27:239). When he hears how Peregrinus was tricked by sham evangelists, Lucian again values deception: "Armer—oder vielmehr *nicht* armer, reicher, an süßen Täuschungen reicher Peregrin!" (28:54). Dioklea explains the "ganze Kette von Täuschungen" (28, Inhalt: 7) that misled Peregrinus, moreover, and says that it is always better to know the truth, "auch dann, wenn sie uns der schmeichelhaftesten Täuschungen beraubt" (28:77), but she describes nature itself as the source of fantasies that, guided by reason, are a boon to humanity: "Täuscht sie etwa nicht uns alle durch Fantasie und Leidenschaften? und sind, dieser Täuschung ungeachtet, Fantasie und Leidenschaften, von Vernunft geleitet, nicht unentbehrliche Springfedern des menschlichen Lebens?" (28:79). Although it causes him so much trouble, *Täuschung* thus rightly seems Peregrinus's reason for living.

Täuschung proves so important throughout Peregrinus's life because it determines the way he thinks. For him, it is not just an accidental state of mind, but an unavoidable part of perceiving truth. He notes the difficulty of telling truth from mere appearances when he calls his weakness for *Täuschung* unwitting and unintentional: "Ich bin getäuscht *worden*, und habe andere getäuscht; aber *jenes* immer unwissend, *dieses* immer ohne Vorsatz: ich gestehe beides offenherzig; aber am Ende ist es doch nur Gerechtigkeit, wenn ich sage, daß ich zu beiden fast immer durch *Anscheinungen* verleitet wurde, die so lebhaft auf mich wirkten daß ich sie für *Wahrheit* hielt" (28:100). Peregrinus's feelings are equally strong when he describes sensing sights and sounds during daydreams so vivid that "das, was wir . . . *erfahren*, es uns vielleicht durch unser ganzes Leben unmöglich macht, dem Gedanken Raum zu geben, daß es Täuschung gewesen seyn könnte" (27:127–28). Such powerful experiences seem less subjective when Peregrinus insists that something in nature really corresponds to Gnostic concepts, just as Juno corresponds to the cloud that the mythological king Ixion mistakes for her. Skeptics like Lucian knew that such mystical concepts are *Täuschungen*, he recalls, but dreamers like himself saw much more in them: "*Wir Ixionen* . . . glaubten in der Wolke *die Göttin*, deren Gestalt sie uns vorspiegelte, *selbst* zu umfassen, und fühlten uns selig, nicht nur, weil wir *nicht wußten*, daß wir getäuscht wurden, und also unser *Genuß* (so lange die Täuschung dauerte) *wirklich* war; sondern auch, weil die *Ähnlichkeit der Wolke mit der Göttin etwas wirkliches*, und also der *Gegenstand*, der uns in diese Entzückungen setzte, mehr als ein bloßes Hirngespenst war" (28:14). Peregrinus here resembles Agathon, who similarly perceives something ideal in Archytas. What is more, Dioklea persuades Peregrinus that his *Täuschung* by Kerinthus concerned only the apparent form of Christianity, not its actual truth—"daß diese Täuschung nicht in der Sache selbst, sondern bloß in den Formen, oder vielmehr in den *Hüllen* liege, worin die Wahrheit sich zeigen müsse" (28:81). Peregrinus proves so susceptible to *Täuschung*, then, not only because he thinks it true and trusts his own instincts but also because he believes that it neither diminishes his happiness nor discredits truth itself.

Peregrinus's *Täuschung* is thus an epistemological problem posed in terms like those spelled out in *Don Sylvio* and *Agathon* and more or less explicit in Wieland's subsequent novels as well. Research on *Peregrinus Proteus* has sometimes stressed its allusions to people, politics, and other fiction of Wieland's day, occasionally asking whether this *Roman* about illusion can be called "romantic." Peregrinus has been compared to Franz Anton Mesmer, Alexander Cagliostro, Lavater, and Rousseau— contemporaries whose psychic excesses Wieland exposed in his *Teutscher Merkur*.[2] Parallels with Lavater are drawn especially often (Wieland later confessed having intended them),[3] not least because Wieland's narrator claims to write "zu dem unschuldigen Zweck, *Menschenkunde und Menschenliebe zu befördern*" (27, Vorrede: 6), an echo of the title of Lavater's *Physiognomische Fragmente zur Beförderung der Menschenkenntniß und Menschenliebe*. Sengle thinks that Wieland softens harsh judgments passed on Lavater, but others find him critical or refer to the Swiss pastor when calling Peregrinus the butt of Wieland's satire.[4] Some prefer to see Peregrinus as politically relevant, tying his personal striving to the emancipation desired by bourgeois secret societies during the French Revolution.[5] The dim view of those societies taken in his tale has seemed a "quotation" of Schiller's "Der Geisterseher" (1787), one revealing how indirectly Wieland's novel represents reality, and his similarity to the hero of *Don Quixote*—Lucian, though not above criticism himself,[6] dubs him an "irrende[r] Ritter der cynischen Tugend" (28:153)—has seemed proof that his moral heroism is romantic (*romanhaft*) in a prosaic world.[7] The main phases of Peregrinus's life have even been likened to the major kinds of novels written in the Enlightenment.[8] It has also been noted that Wieland links the word "romantic" to literary imagination, not always negatively in *Peregrinus Proteus*, where references to Dionysian cults likewise help mark him as a forerunner of romanticism.[9] While the novel has struck some as pre-romantic in its sympathy for illusion and its dialogic form, however, others argue that Wieland was still ambivalent about Peregrinus's *Schwärmerei* and that romanticism only later regarded such fantasies as objectively real.[10] The extent to which this *Roman* is romantic thus seems debatable.

Closer consideration of Wieland's narration in *Peregrinus Proteus* has suggested how the illusion that he describes is related to the fact that the novel itself is fiction. Most scholars agree that the subjectivity apparent in the narrative frame, a conversation between characters whose knowledge is limited, makes it difficult to define or distinguish truth, though they differ in their readiness to accept the concomitant illusion in life as well as art. Matthecka compares Peregrinus's and Lucian's subjective views with the narrative voice of Wieland's earlier novels, taking the relativity of their respective judgments as a sign of Wieland's growing skepticism.[11] Jan-Dirk Müller writes that all the episodes in *Peregrinus Proteus* have to do with illusion and disillusion, adding that subjectivity is not regarded primarily as a source of error in the novel but that the notion of *Täuschung* makes sense only if illusion is measured against the real. Like Lucian, moreover, readers can consciously enjoy the artful illusion created by Peregrinus's story.[12] McCarthy argues that the structure and style of the novel, which he regards as "a vindication of the sincere fantast," correspond to Peregrinus's epistemology. Imagination is implicitly necessary to the cognition of truth there, he explains, which shows how closely fantasy and reality are related.[13] Peregrinus's initial critique of Lucian's storytelling has also been said to indicate that Wieland's own narration is pure fiction, removing any illusion of adhering to historical fact.[14] Similarly, Michael Voges contrasts the *Täuschung* connected to secret societies in the novel—Hegesias and Kerinthus stand for such *Geheimbünde*—with the transparency of Wieland's narrative frame, the latter a literary fiction plainly revealed as such.[15] Voges thus examines the artificial character of Wieland's fiction together with the reality of Peregrinus's illusions, a reality that he thinks adds a new dimension to the novel.[16] Given the complexity of *Täuschung* noted above, further study of it along such narratological lines is needed.

Wieland mentions illusion together with literary fiction from the moment that Peregrinus starts to look back on his life. His *Schwärmerei*, like Don Sylvio's, is a product of his boyhood bookishness, which he recalls in terms of imagination and the marvelous, and which connects his quixotic career to Bodmer and Breitinger's semantics. He explains his belief in spirits by citing Plato's *Symposium*, where Diotima defines love as a daemon that appeared to him "durch eine sonderbare Art von Täuschung" (27:68). Such illusion reflects his earlier reading too. He was naturally receptive to sense impressions, he notes, and blessed with an extremely vivid imagination, talents tapped when his literary schooling began with Homer, who "unbeschreiblich auf meine Imaginazion wirkte; vornehmlich alles Wunderbare" (27:55). He eagerly devoured such fiction in his grandfather's library, which included all kinds of marvelous stories, legends of gods and heroes, ghost tales, "Milesian fables," and the like. This grandfather was a dreamer, but he read about the marvelous merely for amusement, while his grandson took it seriously: "Ihm war das Wunderbare nichts als eine Puppe, womit seine immer kindisch bleibende Seele spielte; bey mir wurde es der Gegenstand der ganzen Energie meines Wesens. Was bey ihm Träumerey und Mährchen war, füllte mein Gemüth mit schwellenden Ahndungen und helldunkeln Gefühlen großer Realitäten, deren schwärmerische Verfolgung meine Gedanken Tag und Nacht beschäftigte" (27:62–63). Lucian sums up the confusion caused by such keen reading when he implies that Peregrinus is like Don Quixote: "Dein Großvater las die Geschichte der Abenteurer zum Zeitvertreib, und *Du* machtest alle mögliche Anstalten selbst auf Abenteuer auszuziehen" (27:63). Recounting a dangerous liaison with his cousin Kallippe, Peregrinus too speaks of acting like a fictional character, explaining that he never expected to be "der unglückliche Held dieses Mährchens" (27:71), the hero of a lascivious tale told by one of Lucian's sources. Lucian observes that experience should teach one to be more careful, but Peregrinus objects that what *has* happened is no guide to what *might*, distinguishing "was *meistens* geschieht" from "was *möglich* ist" (27:76).

In addition to thus tracing Peregrinus's *Täuschung* to a weakness for possible-worlds semantics induced by fictional literature, Wieland frequently associates it with the visual arts. As in his middle novels, such art connotes ideals, but the effect of painting is not strong enough for Peregrinus, who is aesthetically entranced by sculpture instead. In Smyrna, he asks to see a bust of Apollonius, an echo of the Abderites' encounter with Euripides, and this need for images of his ideals proves serious indeed. It derives from his belief that eudaemonism means seeing and enjoying increasing degrees of beauty, which he discovers thanks to Dioklea, whose scheme to seduce him defies common sense but strikes him as plausible: "Meine Einbildung war von früher Jugend an mit allen Arten des Wunderbaren vertraut, und was im gemeinen Laufe der Dinge wunderbar heißt, war, nach meiner Vorstellungsart, in dem höhern Kreise, zu welchem Dioklea gehörte, natürlich" (27: 138). Such stress on the marvelous lends special weight to a painting instrumental in Peregrinus's seduction, "ein wunderschönes Gemählde" (27:138–39) of Venus and Adonis, which preoccupies him for hours since it seems to augur well for his meeting with Venus Urania, the goddess whose servant Dioklea pretends to be. The painted Venus falls short of his ideal, however, because she does not have the full effect that he expects to feel when he meets the goddess herself. Dioklea teaches him greater respect for such images, which she calls monuments of former theophanies, and Peregrinus soon mistakes a statue of Venus for the actual goddess, an example of the force of aesthetic illusion. "In der That war es doch wohl Täuschung" (27:151), he recalls, but Dioklea mentions that it might have been "bloße Täuschung" (27:155) only so that she can further manipulate him. As she later reveals, the sculpture was modeled on Mamilia Quintilla, whom Peregrinus therefore thinks a goddess when he meets her—another "abgezielte Täuschung" (27:217). Craving the marvelous, then, Peregrinus overreacts to aesthetic illusion induced by a piece of sculpture.

Wieland discusses illusion not only by citing such paintings and sculptures but also by referring to visual art metaphorically. Peregrinus's mental images are presented as *Bilder*, his seduction and conversion are cast in terms of chiaroscuro, and such terms are tied to the effect of verbal narration. He envisions Kallippe's *Bild* and searches for Apollonius, "dessen Bild keine Zeit aus meinem Gedächtniß auslöschen kann" (27:122). He returns from seeing Mamilia Quintilla's sculpture "mit einem neuen Bilde in meiner Seele" (27:152), moreover, and says of Kerinthus, "sein Bild folgte mir" (27:256). Mamilia Quintilla, Dioklea, and Kerinthus mislead Peregrinus by making such images seem *helldunkel*. The first appears "in einer helldunkeln Wolke" (27:162), the second puts her charms "in das vorteilhafteste *Licht* oder *Helldunkel*" (27:208), and the third keeps Peregrinus's reason cloaked "in dem gehörigen *Helldunkel*" (28:10). While *helldunkel* suggests Peregrinus's dim awareness of the world,[17] such terms borrowed from painting are related to verbal narration when Lucian notes that Peregrinus is unable to give him an idea of the true colors of invisible objects, an inability that Peregrinus finds frustrating: "Immer bleibt zwischen deiner Vorstellung, mein lieber Lucian, und dem was damahls in *meiner* Seele gegenwärtiges Gefühl und Anschauen war, der Unterschied, wie zwischen einem gemahlten Feuer und einem wirklichen" (27:339). Verbal and visual art are related yet again when Peregrinus talks about his idyllic Christian family. He fondly recalls its "Bild in meiner Seele" (28:103), praising the mother as an artist's model for the Virgin Mary: "Ein Mahler oder Bildner hätte, um die Mutter des Gottgesandten darzustellen, kein vollkommneres Modell finden können" (27:298). He himself, however, cannot paint a convincing verbal picture of the family for his friend Dionysius: "Ich bot also alle meine Mahlerkunst auf, ihm eine Abschilderung von [m]einer Familie . . . zu machen: aber ich trug meine Farben so dick auf, daß mein Gemählde gerade das Gegentheil dessen, was ich beabsichtigte, bey ihm wirken mußte" (28:118). Indeed, Dionysius says that such colorful rhetoric is a trick played by a wizard in Peregrinus's breast: "Die Farben, womit er dir die Seligkeit vormahlt, die im Schooße der vermeintlichen Engel . . . deiner warten soll, sind *Zauberfarben*; das Licht, worin du diese guten Menschen siehst, ist *Zauberlicht*" (28:127). Here too a kind of "painting" fails to tell the whole story.

Peregrinus succumbs to the *Täuschung* common to verbal and visual art most completely when it is presented as theatrical. Like the Abderites, he loses his head when he sees good acting, a momentary lapse that has lasting consequences. He does not attend an actual play, but Dioklea and Mamilia Quintilla put on erotic performances for him that literally leave nothing to be desired. Mamilia's villa is built for such dramatic purposes, a place "wo alles zu jedem Schauspiel, jeder Theaterveränderung, die zu ihrer Absicht nöthig seyn konnten, aufs sinnreichste eingerichtet und vorbereitet war" (27:188). The morning after she takes the place of her statue and first embraces him, Peregrinus accordingly finds himself "in einem großen Parterre" (27:191), a rococo garden where he gazes upon Mamilia Quintilla as she demonstratively bathes in the nude. She soon tires of this role, though, and they consummate their relationship, an act that delights but also disillusions Peregrinus, who finally understands the farcical part he has played, "der Held einer lächerlichen Posse" (27:202). He uses this same vocabulary when he tells Lucian "noch einige Scenen meines *Lebens-Mimus*" (27:210), and Dioklea drops her pretensions to priestliness as if they were a theatrical costume "mit der Gleichgültigkeit einer Schauspielerin, die ihre Theaterkleidung von sich wirft" (27:211), proof that Peregrinus had been no more than the plaything of a merry widow and an aging actress, "einer—alternden Griechischen Schauspielerin" (27: 189). He failed to foresee this sobering "Entwicklung des Lustspiels" (27:189), and even later his shame is mixed with fond memories of such a pleasant illusion: "Ich schämte mich . . . eine Theatergöttin für Venus Urania genommen zu haben, und erinnerte mich doch mit Entzücken der Augenblicke, wo mich diese Täuschung zum glücklichsten aller Sterblichen machte" (27:223). Indeed, when Mamilia Quintilla stages a bacchanal, he is publicly caught in the act of having sex with her, a humiliating conclusion to "dieses ächte Satyrspiel" (27:244). As is clear from his choice of such words, Peregrinus takes theatrical illusion to even greater extremes than the Abderites, unable or unwilling to tell life from art.[18]

In the same erotic scenes that Peregrinus explains by likening them to theater, Wieland often uses the expression "romantic," connecting illusion to concepts of fantasy and the marvelous that confirm its literary import. For all her rational plotting to seduce Peregrinus, Mamilia Quintilla seems romantic in this sense. He himself describes her as a young widow who decides to enjoy her husband's fortune "nach einem eigenen romantischen, aber . . . nicht übel ausgedachten Plane" (27:186), a wealthy Roman lady, "deren Einbildung auf einen so romantischen Lebensgenuß gestimmt war" (27:188). Her desire to play the part of Venus Urania attests to her "Hang zu romantischen Einfällen" (27:232), moreover, a romantic inclination that lends Peregrinus what Dioklea calls "allen möglichen Reiz der Neuheit und des Wunderbaren" (27:212–13). Bodmer and Breitinger similarly linked the new and the marvelous in their aesthetics of literary fiction, which may well account for the poetic cast—the "dichterischen Schwung" (27:187)—of Mamilia Quintilla's imagination. To be sure, she leaves Peregrinus for a new object of her "launenvolle Fantasie" (27:226), letting Dioklea have him, like all her other men, "so bald ihr die Fantasie zu ihnen vergangen wäre" (27:232). She seduces Peregrinus so easily, however, that she is tempted to see in him more than a mortal, he recalls, and just as he thinks that she embodies an ideal of beauty, she wants to make her charms come close to a certain ideal perfection. Like Peregrinus, Mamilia Quintilla thus seems to have an imagination that is more than merely whimsical. She does not doubt the effect of putting him in a romantic spot where the marvelous serves her ends, of the "bloße Versetzung in einen so romantischen, mit lauter schönen Gegenständen angefüllten Ort, verbunden mit dem Scheine des *Wunderbaren*, den alles von sich werfen sollte" (27:214–15). Peregrinus adds that this romantic landscape pales beside the sight of Mamilia bathing, which he calls "ein ganz anderes Schauspiel" (27:195). In this seductive setting, then, "romantic" connotes illusion closely tied to the marvelous and to poetic imagination.

Peregrinus's *Täuschung* also pervades his religion. His imagination and ideals predispose him to believe in miracles and the men who perform them, but such faith is shown to be ambiguous, often abused though apparently justified in the case of Jesus. Lucian notes that miracles attributed to the early Christians must have appealed to Peregrinus's imagination, and Peregrinus himself explains his attraction to their sect by citing his moral enthusiasm, which he says subjected him to new "Illusionen der Einbildung und des Herzens" (27:324) but also brought him closer to human perfection. These illusions result from his urge to forget old fantasies and to live according to his ideals of harmony and beauty, "ohne Furcht vor Täuschung und Reue" (27:324). Kerinthus exploits this aversion to illusion, telling Peregrinus that he has been deceived long enough: "Du bist lange genug getäuscht worden, Peregrin!" (27:260). Hegesias similarly dupes Peregrinus by calling his zeal to convert to Christianity a "Täuschung deines noch nicht ganz überwältigten Selbst" (27:329). A proselyte whose own fear of illusion is thus used to fool him, Peregrinus has not lost his sense of the marvelous. He calls Kerinthus a "Wunderbares Wesen" (27:260) and defends his own credulity by finding a weakness for illusion necessary to the success of such miracle workers: "Wie wollten die Wundermänner auch zurechte kommen, wenn es nicht solche gutwillige, jeder Täuschung immer selbst entgegen kommende Seelen in der Welt gäbe?" (27:277). Lucian is less generous, claiming that such figures either deliberately deceive their followers or unwittingly deceive themselves as well. As Kerinthus's agent, Peregrinus acts in the second way, respected by believers "deren größter Theil sich eben so treuherzig von mir täuschen ließ als ich selbst getäuscht war" (28:30). Jesus, however, seems to behave in the first. Dionysius describes Jesus as an enthusiast in the best sense of the word, one who did not deceive himself about the marvelous means that he used to achieve his moral end. Is Peregrinus therefore right, at the height of his *Schwärmerei*, to consider Jesus the ideal of humanity? Is Wieland arguing that morally motivated *Täuschung* can be condoned and called religion?

Maintaining religious illusions for the sake of humane ideals is an issue treated thoroughly in *Agathodämon*. *Peregrinus Proteus* simply raises it before Peregrinus succumbs to other *Täuschungen*. When he embraces Cynicism, he sees his prior illusions for what they are, but does so only as a prelude to worse ones yet to come. While he is in prison for spreading the Christian gospel, Dioklea appears and identifies herself as Kerinthus's sister, revealing the political motives behind her brother's religious order. She has already explained the elaborate pains taken to create the "beneidenswürdige Täuschungen" (28:68) that Peregrinus enjoyed while living with Mamilia Quintilla, and when she exposes Kerinthus's similar machinations, he exclaims, "*O so war auch dies alles Täuschung!*" (28:52). Worried that Dioklea too might be deceiving him, he soon runs away. Perhaps he is suspicious because she says that their reunion is "ganz natürlich zugegangen" (28:74), an echo of *Don Sylvio* that hardly encourages faith in facticity. In any case, he thus escapes "die Täuschung, die mir eine Wolke statt der Juno in die Arme gespielt hatte" (28:84), a modern Ixion no longer in love with a mirage. Peregrinus is nonetheless still idealistic, going off in search of the philosopher Agathobulus, whom Dionysius describes as a model Cynic, and doing all he can to live up to such an ideal. He falls short of it in Rome, however, thirty years older than when first seduced by Mamilia Quintilla but still sensual enough to make a fool of himself by desiring Faustina and thereby betraying his asceticism. Misanthropic because he has so often been deceived, Peregrinus is now sure that he always will be, and he becomes a bitter recluse. A few students seek him out, but only because they entertain "die täuschende Hoffnung, durch den Unterricht eines weisen Mannes selbst weise zu werden" (28:209), and his own best hope seems suicide, the only way out of a world that he regards as "dieses verhaßte Land der Täuschungen" (28:215). Although his religious illusions might be morally justified, then, and though he was satisfied while deceived by Mamilia Quintilla, *Täuschung* makes Peregrinus cynical to the point of self-destruction.

Peregrinus's flings with Christianity and Cynicism both show illusion at work on another level as well—that of physiognomy. If *Peregrinus Proteus* is critical of Lavater, it might also be expected to criticize his association of facial features with moral character. Faces are indeed important in the novel, where they sometimes correspond to morals but often seem misleading. Peregrinus recalls being blessed with "einer glücklichen Gestalt und Gesichtsbildung" (27:55), and he is struck by Dioklea's similarity to Apollonius, "es sey nun daß es Täuschung oder Wahrheit war" (27:131). Such traits speak truly when they draw him to his friend Dionysius: "Die Heiterkeit und anscheinende Ruhe, die sich in der Fysionomie dieses Dionysius ausdrückte, zog mich eben so stark zu ihm, als ihn ich weiß nicht was in der meinigen hinwieder anzuziehen und zu interessieren schien" (28:23). Peregrinus is saved by a Cyprian merchant, moreover, whom he once lent money "auf die bloße Bürgschaft seiner Fysionomie" (28:144), trusting the face of a man who proved true to his word: "Glücklicher Weise mußte es sich fügen, daß die Fysionomie des Cypriers die Wahrheit gesagt hatte" (28:144). Peregrinus never suspects foul play from pretty Faustina, however, "unter deren so lieblich lächelnden Gesichtzügen ich keine Schalkheit ahndete" (28:176), and Hegesias is likewise more dangerous than he looks. Peregrinus remembers trusting him at first sight: "Es war etwas in der Fysionomie dieses Mannes, das mir Vertrauen einflößte" (27:291). Even after Hegesias starts to mislead him, Peregrinus cannot distrust a man, "der . . . ein so sprechendes Zeugniß seiner Redlichkeit in seinem Gesichte trug" (27:292). He even believes stories about Jesus' miracles solely "auf das Wort und die ehrliche Miene meines Freundes Hegesias" (27:326). He also says that his cynicism had "eine ziemlich *chri-*

stianische Miene" (28:133), and he never doubted his religious calling, which Kernithus once seemed to see written all over his face: "Hatte nicht der *Unbekannte das Zeichen meiner Erwählung* auf meiner Stirne gesehen?" (27:318–19). Peregrinus's faith in physiognomy thus seems part of his all-around *Täuschung.*

Parallels with Lavater lie less in Peregrinus's analysis of faces, however, than in his animosity toward language. Like Lavater, he pays attention to facial features because spoken and written words seem poor means of communication. He too desires a more transparent medium of human expression and divine significance, and his habit of feeling ineffably moved makes him receptive to music and dance as well as to Gnosticism. His sensations seem beyond words when he tries to tell Lucian how he felt at the foot of Mamilia Quintilla's statue: "Doch ich will nicht versuchen, unbeschreibliche Empfindungen, oder Täuschungen, wenn du willst, beschreiben zu wollen" (27:151). Similarly, he cannot say what it was like to see Mamilia Quintilla herself: "Du wirst mir gern glauben, daß mein Gefühl bey dieser Erscheinung—möchte sie nun Täuschung oder Wahrheit seyn—alle Beschreibung zu Schanden machen würde" (27:182). In both cases, ineffability is tied to illusion, as it is when Peregrinus has the feeling that he is experiencing a daemonic *unio mystica,* "ein Gefühl, unter welchem (wie viel Täuschung auch dabey seyn mag) alle menschliche Sprache einsinkt" (28:11). Such illusion seems avoided when Dioklea performs a pantomime for him, speaking to him "in einer allgemein verständlichen, unmittelbar zur Empfindung und Einbildungskraft redenden Sprache" (27:238), and he is similarly moved by both the antiphonal chant of a Christian congregation and the singing of his Christian family. The language that affects him most, though, is that of Gnosticism. Kerinthus speaks convincingly of supernatural powers, and he promises to tell him the secrets hidden in Gnostic images. As Peregrinus tells Lucian in turn, Gnostic theosophy expresses philosophical concepts in symbols, imbuing empty words with unknown beings and forces. He repeatedly translates such symbolic terms "aus der räthselhaften Bildersprache unsrer Sekte in die gewöhnliche Menschensprache" (28:8), assuring Lucian that they made sense: "Alle diese pompösen Bilder waren keine Worte ohne Sinn" (28:9). Indeed, he sincerely believed that they were more than just illusions like the cloud that Ixion mistook for Juno. Peregrinus's problem with *Täuschung* thus includes such language too. Far from merely unable to describe religious experience,[19] that is, Wieland is interested in semiotic questions of language here.

Mindful of Lavater, one might say that Peregrinus takes Gnostic concepts and language at face value. He describes them both in terms of physiognomy, believing in them as strongly and taking them as literally as an overeager reader of fiction. Lucian notes the "mien" of Gnosticism when he scorns its philosophy, "die sich die Miene giebt, das *unergründliche Geheimniß der Natur* ausfündig gemacht zu haben" (28:13). Even more reminiscent of physiognomy are occurrences of the terms *Schatten, Schattenriß,* and *Schattenbild,* which all mean "silhouette" in Lavater's *Fragmente.* Kerinthus promises to initiate Peregrinus into *"Mysterien,* wovon jene zu *Eleusis* nur täuschende Schatten sind" (27:265), and Peregrinus recounts a sermon in which Kerinthus claimed that words to describe his eschatological vision failed him, though he exhausted the resources of language to trace "einen matten Schattenriß davon" (27:282). Verbal language here, like a silhouette, can give only a vague idea of what it represents. Lavater relied heavily on silhouettes, however, which could be drawn with the help of mechanical instruments and thus showed their sitters' profiles accurately. Peregrinus too places great faith in such *Schattenbilder* when he insists on the reality of objects that one can only imagine: "Immerhin mögen also die Bestrebungen der wärmsten Einbildungskraft, sich zum wirklichen Anschauen dieser unerreichbaren Gegenstände zu erheben, vergeblich seyn: so sind doch diese Gegenstände selbst wirklich; so besitzt doch die menschliche Seele das Vermögen sich eine Art von *Schattenbildern* von ihnen zu machen" (28:15). This plea for the existence of ideal objects, then, alludes not only to the shadows cast in Plato's famous cave but also to Lavater's silhouettes. Such objects are related to fiction as well when Dioklea tells Peregrinus that he took Gnosticsm and its symbols too literally: "Die erhabnen Offenbarungen der unsichtbaren Welt, . . . die du . . . im *buchstäblichen Verstande* genommen hast, scheinen mir weder mehr noch weniger als die unschuldigste *Poesie;* entweder bildliche Einkleidungen großer Wahrheiten . . . oder Versinnlichung edler Zwecke" (28:78). Peregrinus thus fails to grasp the fictionality of concepts conveyed in figurative, "physiognomic" language.

If Peregrinus's *Täuschung* consists of such verbal, visual, theatrical, religious, philosophical, and physiognomic confusion so often and so closely tied to the issue of fictionality, how are readers to approach Wieland's novel itself? Should they suspend their disbelief but therefore risk repeating Peregrinus's mistakes, which start with avid reading? Should they avoid all *Täuschung* but thereby violate the aesthetic contract explained in "Versuch über das deutsche Singspiel" and exemplified in *Die Abderiten*? In other words, how are Peregrinus's fatal illusions related to the effect that Wieland thought his fiction should have? To answer such questions, one needs to regard the multiple levels of Wieland's narration, which show marked ambivalence toward its fictionality but also leave little doubt that Peregrinus's susceptibility to illusion is a weakness that readers of his story would do well to indulge, albeit with greater caution than he. That narration is the sum of tales told by Peregrinus, Lucian, a source cited in Lucian's "Passing of Peregrinus," and the narrator of *Peregrinus Proteus*, whose remarks are confined to a foreword added to the novel when it appeared as a book in 1791 and whose tone resembles the one that Wieland takes in two related works—"Eine Lustreise ins Elysium" (1787) and "Ueber die Glaubwürdigkeit Lucians in seinen Nachrichten vom Peregrinus" (1788). Each of these narrative voices expresses a different attitude toward imagination, the marvelous, and literary fiction, and only by considering their combination can one fully understand how Wieland treats the topic of fictionality here. Examined in this way, in fact, the concept of *Täuschung* connects its plot to problems of fictionality posed by its own narrative form. *Peregrinus Proteus* too might thus be called "metafiction."

The foreword to the novel shows both the narrator's sympathy with its hapless hero and a playful attitude toward imagination, the exact opposite of Peregrinus's *Schwärmerei*. The narrator rejects Lucian's "Passing of Peregrinus," but his irony about his own omniscience recalls Lucian's skepticism. In "Ueber die Glaubwürdigkeit Lucians in seinen Nachrichten vom Peregrinus," moreover, Wieland defends Lucian against the charge of calumny. The narrator recalls Lucian's portrait of Peregrinus as a foolish, half-crazed charlatan, wondering whether Lucian was sufficiently impartial and doubting that Peregrinus could have been both a deceitful fraud and an enthusiastic fantast. This moral puzzle, he observes, remains insoluble for readers who want to be fair to a man no longer around to defend himself. His own respect for Peregrinus seems diminished, though, when he explains overhearing the two dead men in Elysium, a feat that he claims to perform by means of a dubious psychic ability, "einer kleinen Naturgabe . . . die ich (ohne Ruhm zu melden) mit dem berühmten Geisterseher *Swedenborg* gemein habe, und vermöge deren mein Geist zu gewissen Zeiten sich in die Gesellschaft verstorbener Menschen versetzen, und, nach Belieben, ihre Unterredungen mit einander ungesehen behorchen, oder auch wohl, wenn sie dazu geneigt sind, sich selbst in Gespräche mit ihnen einlassen kann" (27, Vorrede: 5–6). In this variant of Wieland's usual *Quellenfiktion*, the narrator ridicules visionaries like Peregrinus. He also professes to use his own spiritualistic gift only for pleasant distraction, not to found a new religion or hasten the millennium, schemes that Peregrinus supports as a tool of Gnosticism. By contrast, the narrator regards Lucian as a good friend. Wieland too likes Lucian, whom he assumes meant to tell the truth about Peregrinus and whose story he thinks credible, if incomplete. Hardly "eine verläumderische Erdichtung," he argues, it plausibly explains Peregrinus's death, which is "ein *innerer* Beweis ihrer Wahrheit." [20] Lucian thus meets some of Wieland's own criteria for writing fiction true to life. Psychological likelihood and internal coherence, in fact, are primary characteristics of *Peregrinus Proteus* too.

Despite intending to clear Peregrinus's name, both Wieland and his narrator thus sound closer to Lucian when discussing products of literary imagination. The narrative case is not always so clear. In the introduction to *Peregrinus Proteus*, and in the novel proper as well, Lucian is shown to use imagination more earnestly than he allows, and Peregrinus seems anything but an advocate of the marvelous, talking of narrative truth and verisimilitude instead. The two regard imagination together with *Schwärmerei*, and Lucian recalls scorning the latter, while Peregrinus replies that their very presence in Elysium now proves him wrong. Lucian agrees but adds that only "das hitzige Fieber in einem hohen Grade" (27:31) could have made him imagine that they would ever meet there. This high fever recalls the Abderites' *Schauspielfieber*, likewise a symptom of vivid imagination. Peregrinus also says that Lucian's writings certainly show no lack of imagination, but Lucian explains that he used his imagination only in jest, "daß ich die Imaginazion nie anders als zum *Spielen* gebrauchte" (27:32). He also objects to people who use their own more seriously, prophets and dreamers whom he thinks dangerous fools. Lucian himself nonetheless significantly embellishes the main source cited in "The Passing of Peregrinus," an unnamed speaker who sharply criticizes its title character. Lucian explains that this speaker was not made up, "kein Geschöpf von meiner Erfindung" (27:44), but that his oracle unfavorable to Peregrinus was, being "eine Verschönerung von meiner eigenen Erfindung" (27:46). Peregrinus censures such inventive half-truths, a fault that he finds common to other writers too: "Man kann, denke ich, immer darauf rechnen, daß Schriftsteller, denen es mehr um Beyfall als um strenge Wahrheit zu tun ist, sich eben kein Gewissen daraus machen werden, der Komposizion zu Liebe manchen Eingriff in die Rechte der letztern zu thun" (27:46). Peregrinus promises to tell Lucian the truth, moreover, and he excuses the anonymous speaker's poetic embellishments: "Übrigens sind diese Verzierungen . . . zu gewöhnlich, als daß man dem Ungenannten ein großes Verbrechen daraus machen könnte, sie, vielleicht ohne historischen Grund, der bloßen Wahrscheinlichkeit zu Ehren hinzu gedichtet zu haben" (27:92). Here it is Peregrinus who seems closer to Wieland's idea of credible literary fiction.

Not only do Lucian and Peregrinus show a complex attitude toward concocting fiction; Lucian's admission that Peregrinus was right to imagine places such as Elysium also makes the narrator's initial irony about traveling there ring hollow. Lucian is soon persuaded by Peregrinus's story, moreover, and the narrator never reappears. His significance seems clear from "Eine Lustreise ins Elysium," however, where a similar narrator mocks his own gift for reaching Elysium but then also betrays sincere faith in at least some fiction. As in *Peregrinus Proteus*, this second narrator possesses a gift that enables his spirit to roam beyond his body. He explains this psychic talent not only by citing the mystic Emanuel Swedenborg but also by referring to *Arabian Nights* and to fairy tales, which he ironically claims are as credible as they are well-known. Lavater seems chided too when the narrator adds that this rare gift furthers "die . . . *allgemeine Menschenliebe*" (28:237) and when souls in Elysium have familiar physiognomies. The narrator's skeptical opinion of fiction changes, though, when he mentions Homer. He apologizes for writing a prologue that tries the patience of readers used to Homer's style of starting in medias res, he expects that finding the philosophers' stone and fountain of youth in Germany would unleash "eine ganze *Ilias* von Verwirrung und Unheil" (28:232), and he invokes "*Vater Homer*" (28:256) to prove his point that monarchy is the best form of government. In matters of literary form, metaphors, and politics, then, this narrator relies on Homer, the same poet who initially inspires Peregrinus. He also relies on Lucian. As Wieland's mouthpiece, he explains that he wanted to visit Elysium after translating Lucian's *Dialogues of the Dead*, and he does not know what to do there until he meets "den Lucianischen *Menippus*" (28:243). Such references to Lucian's writings also occur in *Peregrinus Proteus*, where Peregrinus tells Lucian that Dionysius recommended "das Ideal, das du in deinem *Cyniker* aufgestellt hast" (28:132) and that a certain Cejonius described Rome "mit den Worten deines *Nigrinus*" (28:158). In the foreword to the novel, moreover, Lucian himself is identified only as "*Lucian der Dialogenmacher*" (27, Vorrede: 8), a name that likewise stresses his own narration of literary fictions. Indirectly, the ironic narrator of *Peregrinus Proteus* thus shows sincere respect for characters, concepts, places, and authors associated with such fictions.

Knowing how to read *Peregrinus Proteus*, then, is not simply a matter of finding its narration more like Lucian's skepticism or Peregrinus's *Schwärmerei*. With his subtle comments on that narration itself, Wieland recommends an attitude toward fictionality more balanced than such extremes. In other words, one needs to know how the *Täuschung* recurring throughout Peregrinus's life also pertains to reading Wieland's literature. This narrative knowledge involves some unexpected twists and turns. Enthusiastic Peregrinus criticizes skeptical Lucian for writing about him in ways inconsistent with verisimilitude and truth, and the narrator of Wieland's novel feels sympathetic but dubious about Peregrinus, while the similar narrator of "Eine Lustreise ins Elysium" ends up relying on the same poet, Homer, whose stories set Peregrinus on the road to suicide. This ambivalence audible in Wieland's narrative voices makes sense when compared to his plot, which shows his hero repeatedly taking aesthetic illusion too far. First, the taste for the marvelous that Peregrinus acquires as an avid reader of fiction exaggerates the possible-worlds semantics connecting Wieland to some current theories of fictionality. Second, the erotic traps set by Dioklea and Mamilia Quintilla are sprung by Peregrinus's overreaction to painting and sculpture and reveal him to be a Pygmalion misled by his own mental images. Third, his seduction succeeds because he submits to theatrical illusion even more completely than the Abderites. Citing Wieland's allusions to physiognomy helps explain Peregrinus's similar submission to Gnosticism, given his interest in faces and his impatience with verbal language. He takes the abstract terms of Gnosticism literally, misconstruing figures of speech that are as suggestive but also as imprecise as Lavater's silhouettes. Peregrinus never knows that *Täuschung* can be temporarily induced by art without directly affecting life, despite all its seriousness. Readers shown the ambivalence toward fictionality apparent in Wieland's several narrative voices are better able to draw such distinctions and thus to see how aesthetic illusion is a state of mind appropriate to perceiving Wieland's novel itself. Thanks to such highly "self-conscious" suggestions about its own fictionality, which are often made with regard to other arts, *Peregrinus Proteus* certainly does seem a romantic *Roman*.

8. *Agathodämon* (1799)

Über den Schein läßt sich viel, vom reinen Daseyn
wenig sagen. Als ich mein Buch über Johannes
vollendet hatte, fühlte ich mich am Anfange, legte
die Feder nieder und sagte: "ich bin kein Mahler."
—Herder, "Von Gottes Sohn" (1797)

Wieland links epistemological, ontological, and aesthetic qualities of *Täuschung* even more closely in his second late novel, *Agathodämon* (1799). He does so by treating such illusion not as the pathological symptom of one man's *Schwärmerei*, as in *Peregrinus Proteus*, but as a practical means of mass, enlightened pedagogy. Because most people neither think nor act according to reason, he hints, benignly deceiving them by appealing to their superstition is an acceptable way of making them behave. In the course of his plot, both popular fantasies and religious beliefs turn out to be useful fictions, much like a Kantian "as-if." Wieland's title character, the neo-Pythagorean philosopher Apollonius of Tyana, admits private doubts about such public *Täuschung*, however, wondering whether its ethical ends justify this dubious means. Scholars likewise debate the sense of *Täuschung* in *Agathodämon*, asking whether the novel, in theme as well as form, transcends the Enlightenment and displays a kind of romanticism. This question is best answered by considering Wieland's story in broad terms of fictionality. Apollonius explains belief in daemons, for example, by discussing imagination and the existence of possible worlds. Verbal and visual art, he adds, meet the human need to imagine such supernatural beings, but both also hypostatize their referents, thereby distorting abstract concepts by making them seem concrete. Music, however, is shown to avoid this semiotic fault, deeply moving its audience while representing cosmic harmony less deceptively. Wieland's polyphonic narration similarly avoids simplistically reifying its referent. Credulous peasants and one of Apollonius's biographers believe in the marvelous too strongly to get their facts about him straight, but Apollonius himself and his servant seem reliable sources of information that Wieland's main narrator, Hegesias, uses to tell the philosopher's true story. Other, actual biographers have compared him to Jesus, whom Apollonius greatly admires, though he does not credit the evangelists' news of miracles and foresees that Christianity will corrupt Jesus' teaching, not

153

least because the faithful will take its symbolic language literally. In the end, Wieland discourages such literalistic reading by describing and demystifying Apollonius instead of Jesus, the actual hero of *Agathodämon*. He thus discounts and transcends an aesthetic illusion created by his own novel, a narrative twist that anticipates romantic irony.

Reaching these conclusions about *Täuschung* in *Agathodämon* requires starting with its subject, its narrative frame, and its plot. Apollonius of Tyana flourished around A.D. 100, and his few extant works include a biography of Pythagoras. His own biographers Damis of Nineveh and Flavius Philostratus portray him as a wise prophet and devout wonder-worker, and pagan apologists such as the Neoplatonic philosopher Porphyry often hailed him as a "Hellenistic Christ."[1] Wieland describes him favorably too, as the title *Agathodämon* implies, since it means "good spirit." After spending most of his life trying to reverse the moral decline of the Roman Empire by reviving popular belief in pagan gods, Wieland's fictional Apollonius has retired to the mountains of Crete. Hegesias happens upon him there and hears the story of that life from both Apollonius himself and his servant Kymon. Both call Damis's biography wildly inaccurate, and Hegesias spends three days listening to their own, sober account of the philosopher's *vita*, later writing it down in letters addressed to a friend, Timagenes. As a young man, Apollonius was inspired by an ideal of human nature informed by reason, not imagination or religious belief. He founded a Pythagorean society to help people live up to this ideal, but the paralysis of their reason caused by their weakness for religious enthusiasm persuaded him to exploit their superstitions first. Some prejudices and errors are beneficial, he found, and should not be exposed until a new order is firmly in place. This attempt to improve public morals via people's urge to believe in the marvelous and the supernatural made a strong impression, since Apollonius often performed apparent miracles. His society also took political action by helping assassinate the despotic emperor Domitian, but he agrees that belief in a spirit that animates and governs the world is the only way to tame the passions of simple people and lighten the load of the educated. Accordingly, he praises Jesus for having taught a *"praktische Theosofie"* (32:466) that expresses the supreme ideal of moral goodness and human perfection. Like Kant, Apollonius thus accepts the existence of God as a useful idea, the kind of ethical postulate that Vaihinger called "fictions." Wieland also likened this view of religion to Fichte's as well as his own.[2]

Presented in this way, Apollonius and his story recall Wieland's earlier novels, especially *Peregrinus Proteus*. He himself traces superstition to people's belief that their dreams are real, an explanation of the

"*Glauben* an *übernatürliche Dinge*, oder, so zu sagen, an eine *zweyfache* Natur" (32:193) that resembles similar ones given in *Don Sylvio*. He also notes that trying to realize utopian dreams does much harm, an echo of the ironic "Republik" concluding *Diogenes*, and his manipulation of religious beliefs reminds one of the history of Scheschian in *Der goldne Spiegel*, the evil fakirs in *Danischmend*, and Latona's sacred frogs in *Die Abderiten*. Like Archytas, moreover, Apollonius never indulges his imagination, and he was such a handsome boy that painters and sculptors may have pursued him, as they do Agathon. His good looks also raise the issue of physiognomy, which is so revealing in *Peregrinus Proteus*. Like Peregrinus, he recalls having "eine vorzüglich glückliche Gestalt und Gesichtsbildung" (32:62), and he strikes Cretan goatherds as "ein langer hagerer Greis von einer Ehrfurcht gebietenden Gesichtsbildung" (32:12). Hegesias likewise admires his "majestätische Gesichtsbildung und ehrwürdige Gestalt" (32:284), and Apollonius agrees that most people bear resemblances to animals, which one could almost always see, "vorausgesetzt daß er auch alle bekannten Arten von Luft- Land- und Wasserthieren fysionomisch studiert hätte" (32:317). Appearances are deceptive in *Agathodämon*, though, which also develops the theme of *Täuschung*. The Orphic order that Apollonius takes as his model has two kinds of members: *Schwärmer* who deceive themselves as much they do others, and superiors who do not delude themselves about their irrational methods. The first are unsuspecting collaborators like Peregrinus, and the second are mystagogues such as Theofranor, "ein großer Meister in der Täuschungskunst" (32:89), who, like Dioklea, argues that nature itself furnishes many salutary illusions. The *Täuschung* thus essential to Apollonius's scheme also pertains to his narrative, which he tries to relate without it, telling Hegesias, "Denn für dich . . . soll hier keine Täuschung seyn" (32:40). An audience of one, Hegesias is in the same position as Lucian, then, while Apollonius assumes Peregrinus's narrative role. Indeed, *Agathodämon* seems the inverse of *Peregrinus Proteus*. It too regards *Täuschung*, but from a superior point of view.

The attitude that Apollonius himself takes toward *Täuschung* is clear from how he discovers and dismisses but then nonetheless deploys it. Pondering the existence of God, the young Apollonius soon learned that imagination produces strange illusions: "Ich überließ mich der Einbildungskraft, und erkannte gar bald ihre magischen Täuschungen" (32:472). If people used their reason to its full extent, he argues, they would not need such illusions, which also result from religious belief at odds with their own inner instincts: "Der Mensch, über welchen die Vernunft so viel Macht hat als ihr zukommt, wozu sollte er die Täuschungen der Einbildungskraft und eines Glaubens, der seinem innern Gefühle Gewalt anthut, vonnöthen haben?" (32:52). Theofranor, however, taught Apollonius that "Täuschung ihrer Sinne und Einbildungskraft" (32:87) is an indispensable aid to making people observe religion and obey the law, as long as sensual impulses still outweigh their reason. He did not doubt that early Greek religious and political figures were right to fool their followers by using such "heilsame Täuschungen" (32:88), and Apollonius came to consider "diese Art von wohlthätiger Täuschung" (32:246) innocent and necessary to his own plan. No one wishing to cure the moral infirmities of mankind can make the least impression on the lower classes, he thinks, "ohne ähnliche Behelfe und Täuschungen" (32:252). To the gullible goatherds who are his only neighbors, for example, his reputation as a beneficent daemon is such a harmless illusion, "eine Täuschung, die ihnen unschädlich ist" (32:42). Restoring such simple people's faith in pagan religion, moreover, which has so badly deteriorated that it appears about to collapse, seems an end that justifies the means of his secret society, whose few superiors regarded such belief as the only way to preserve civil order, the welfare of the human race, and hope for a better future. As Apollonius puts it, "Gestehe, Hegesias, daß ein *solcher* Zweck auch täuschende Mittel, sobald sie tauglich sind, rechtmäßig macht!" (32:84). Although he saw through it and found it unworthy of rational human beings, then, Apollonius gladly used *Täuschung* to educate the rest.

He also doubts his justification of such deliberate *Täuschung*, however, which he liked to induce in a way that later revealed what it was, though he does not wholly oppose deceptive fantasies and even finds at least one illusion pleasant. In retrospect, he knows that his moral cause was noble, but he questions his means as well as his own later justification of illusions. In practice, he favored illusions that were only temporary. To help poor peasants farm more rationally, for example, he couched his simple advice to clear and drain their fields in terms of a holy oracle, a trick that the brightest of them subsequently understood. This was a *Täuschung* containing its own antidote, lasting only until it had its desired effect, a "*Täuschung* . . . , die, so zu sagen, *ihr Gegengift bey sich führt*, weil sie in eben dem Augenblicke, da sie ihre abgezielte Wirkung gethan hat, als Täuschung *erkannt* wird. Sie fällt dann, wie die Schale von einer reifen Frucht, von selbst ab, und die Wahrheit, deren Hülle sie war, bleibt allein zurück" (32:130). Thus using illusions to convey abstract truths is easy, Apollonius adds, because most people are afflicted with a strong urge to *be* deceived, "mit einer . . . großen Anlage und Neigung sich täuschen *zu lassen*" (32:316). He thinks it remarkable, for example, how readily most deceive themselves to conceive of the infinite. To imagine the future lasting longer than the past, he explains, just because one can logically posit an endless series is "eine bloße und ziemlich grobe Täuschung" (32:329). When he says that life after death is probable, however, he sees no harm in letting one's imagination probe the future. At the age of ninety-six, he also notes how well Kymon's family cares for him, doing everything possible, "um mich in die angenehme Täuschung zu setzen, als ob mein Leben im Elysium schon angegangen sey" (32:41). Far from staging *Täuschung* in ways that he neither doubts nor reveals, Apollonius thus explains why people are so prone to it, especially when they envision the afterlife. He does not dismiss the solace that such notions afford them, and he even expects such a future life for himself soon, one anticipated by a present, pleasant illusion.

Like Apollonius, scholars studying *Agathodämon* express mixed feelings about the concept of *Täuschung*. They debate the extent to which Wieland approves of it, regarding the novel as more or less in agreement with the Enlightenment. Martini considers *Täuschung* a pedagogical tactic that frees people's humanity by using the fetters of their imagination, while Hans Würzner thinks it politically meaningful, since Apollonius seems to oppose Jacobinic abuse of political beliefs.[3] Thomé calls Apollonius's psychology of illusions a radically empirical critique of religion, noting both that imagination seems the source of metaphysical as well as erotic illusions and that the ethical potential of Christianity makes it an illusion elevated above all others.[4] Karl Heinz Ihlenburg contends that *Täuschung* is a theme linking the various sections of *Agathodämon*, the structure of which he thinks closely connected to its justification. Wieland reveals that Apollonius has renounced *Täuschung* only after Hegesias hears the story of his life, for example, which therefore takes on the character of a new illusion.[5] Jan-Dirk Müller writes that Apollonius's reforms fail because they rest on *Täuschung* and that Wieland's critique of religious illusions includes their rise in Hegesias.[6] Voges replies that *Täuschung* is indispensable to Wieland's novel, being its object as well as its means, and that Hegesias's literary initiation—his introduction to the utopian nature of its setting—legitimates such illusion.[7] In 1780, the Berlin Academy of Sciences similarly asked whether illusion could be expedient among the lower classes, a question about the Enlightenment that Wieland has seemed to answer in *Agathodämon*.[8] The novel appears to agree with Lessing's *Erziehung des Menschengeschlechts* (1780), where religion is said to anticipate the course of reason, revealing the same things sooner, and Apollonius has been dubbed a hero of the Enlightenment, though his philosophy does not seem satisfied with it.[9] While Voges insists that *Agathodämon* is the didactic kind of art prescribed by the Enlightenment, moreover, Thomé argues that it thematizes the rational limits of the Enlightenment and resembles the "new mythology" called for by the early romantics.[10] Considering how *Täuschung* can be reconciled with reason thus involves both the content and the form of *Agathodämon*.

Formal and thematic concerns similarly coincide in studies treating the fictional nature of Wieland's narration. The many perspectives shown in its dialogues and letters seem mirrors that put his story into innovative relief, and the fact that it is fiction has seemed appropriate to his larger purpose. Martini finds that Wieland's achievement lies in putting common knowledge into a dialogic, multiperspectival form that combines opposing points of view and lends Apollonius depth.[11] Beißner regards this dialogic style as a new way of conveying the mediateness of Wieland's storytelling, and Sengle thinks that the many resulting "refractions" afford epic distance.[12] Since Hegesias transcribes his conversations in letters, *Agathodämon* is an epistolary novel too, whence Wolfgang Albrecht calls it a bold, successful experiment.[13] Thoughts of fictionality thus suggested by its form also seem suited to its subject matter. Both the poetic guise of a novel, Johanna Mellinger argues, and the religious issue of early Christianity have less to do with reason than imagination.[14] Thomé notes the social and anthropological import that *Agathodämon* has as fiction and that transcends its antiquarianism, while Albrecht finds it proof that Wieland's concept of poetry encouraged his spirit of humanity.[15] Matthecka adds that its narrative frame is Wieland's first unironic fictive reality, and Jan-Dirk Müller regards the allegorical structure of the novel as a metaphor for the utopian reality experienced by Hegesias.[16] Voges likewise stresses Hegesias's initiation into a realm of utopian knowledge shown as a "transparent" or "reflexive" fictional medium making social and political criticism itself utopian, itself a "romanhafte Reflexion."[17] As Voges puts it, *Agathodämon* fashions the reflexive utopia of the late Enlightenment, as a novel.[18] This transparency of Wieland's literary method is also said to lend legitimacy and dignity to aesthetically mediated knowledge.[19] It thus seems logical to pursue the issue of fictionality, beyond the kinds of parallels cited so far, by linking his stress on *Täuschung* to the concept of aesthetic illusion.

The aspect of fictionality most prominent in *Agathodämon* first takes shape in Apollonius's remarks on belief in daemons, the same belief that causes Peregrinus's frequent *Täuschung*. He attributes such belief to most people's habit of imagining supernatural beings only in human form, but his similar critique of fanciful utopias seems tempered by his sympathy for better, possible worlds. Unlike the Cretan goatherds who dub him "der *Agathodämon*" (32:14), Hegesias doubts that daemons exist, and Apollonius agrees: "Es hat—für die Menschen wenigstens— nie andere Dämonen gegeben als *Menschen*" (32:22). Apollonius traces the idea of daemons to two conflicting causes, people's instinctual urge to transcend the visible world and their inability to exceed the limits of human imagination. The result is an illusion, "ein mehr oder weniger täuschendes Bild" (32:24), one hiding the fact that daemons are simply idealized human beings. Hegesias asks whether this inability means that daemons exist only in the human imagination, and he sums up Apollonius's opinion that they have "*keine* andere Existenz . . . als die sie durch die Gesänge der Dichter, den Meißel der Bildhauer, und den Glauben des Volks erhalten" (32:32). Apollonius similarly associates superstition and poetry when he says that the human habit of always imagining a better world leads to the utopias of poets and philoso- phers, "diese lieblichen Träume der Dichter und Filosofen von einem goldnen Weltalter, von Götter- und Heldenzeiten, von Unschuldswel- ten, Atlantiden und Platonischen Republiken, womit die Menschen sich von jeher so gern haben einwiegen lassen" (32:25). Such sweet dreams seem more than soporific, however, when Apollonius explains the human urge to transform the empirical world into imaginary ones. This urge strikes him as solipsistic, but he also says that the empirical world is not the real one, calling it "die Welt der Erscheinungen und Täuschungen, welche man sich irriger Weise als die *wirkliche* vorzu- stellen gewohnt ist" (32:24). Sounding like Peregrinus here, Apollonius seems privy to another, better world. His remarks on the human form and imaginary existence of daemons, in fact, are ambiguous too.

That Apollonius accepts the existence of possible, fictional worlds is plain when he later returns to the theme of the supernatural. He repeats that there is more to the world than meets the eye, defining nature broadly enough to account for places described in poems while betray- ing quixotic faith in the results of his own politics. Kymon notes that belief in the supernatural is, paradoxically, part of human nature. This insight helps explain how, in *Don Sylvio*, "alles Wunderbare natürlich zugeht," for it hints that there is nothing unusual about Don Sylvio's psyche. In this sense, the existence of the marvelous is natural, an opin- ion that Apollonius shares when he explains so-called supernatural things as either products of human imagination, and therefore natural in a way, or part of some higher order, and therefore only apparently supernatural, since they simply lie beyond the scope of the world that people perceive with their senses, which should not be mistaken for nature itself. Strictly speaking, then, nothing is supernatural, "oder die *Natur* müßte nicht *Alles was ist, war,* und *seyn wird,* umfassen" (32:183).

With this loose idea of nature, Apollonius sounds much like Bodmer and Breitinger stretching the limits of poetic mimesis. He admits that nature includes chaos as described by ancient Greek poets, and he asks credulous wedding guests if they have ever seen another poetic place, the fruit trees hanging over Tantalus in Hades: "Habt ihr, fuhr er zu den Gästen fort, jemahls den *Garten des Tantalus* gesehen?—Sie antworteten: Ja, *im Homer*; denn in den Tartarus sind wir nie hinab gestiegen.—So wißt ihr, versetzte Apollonius, daß dieser Garten *ist* und *nicht ist*" (32:155). Apollonius thus suggests that this location exists, if only in a poem, not in the actual world. He blurs this boundary, however, when voicing his hopes for future emperors. If Trajan's successors follow Nerva's good example, he argues, a golden age awaits the world. Although highly skeptical of just such utopias, Apollonius thinks that he has made one possible. Thus wishing that his own poetic kind of dream would come true, he acts according to Wieland's observation, made in 1774, that he was a philosophical Don Quixote.[20]

Despite his sympathy for some poetic, possible worlds, Apollonius faults art that describes or depicts the gods, as skeptical of verbal and visual images as he is of daemons. Anthropomorphic concepts of supernatural beings, he thinks, are found not only in superstition but also in poetry and fine art, which likewise traffic in *Täuschung*. He says that daemons are human beings ennobled by popular belief that priests, poets, and artists support. Poets and artists too imagine such spirits in human bodies. Indeed, neither can help making the gods seem human, even if they remove the physical imperfections of their models: "Zwar kann und soll der Dichter und der bildende Künstler, um uns *würdige* Göttergestalten zu zeigen, die Menschen, die er zu Modellen zu nehmen genöthigt ist, von allen der Einzelnheit anklebenden Mängeln befreyen; kann und soll sie in ihrer *reinsten Schönheit* denken, . . . aber nichts desto weniger werden seine Götter, sobald er sie *erscheinen* läßt, zu dem was sie in seiner eigenen Einbildung zu seyn genöthigt sind, zu *Menschen*" (32:28). While artists are thus constrained by their imagination, their work takes on a life of its own in the eye of its beholder. Even if Jupiter actually appeared in all the majesty bestowed on him by Homer and Phidias, Apollonius says, one could not distinguish him from their images: "Was hättest du da gesehen, als ein Bild, das dir Dichter und Mahler oft genug vorgemahlt haben, um es deiner Einbildungskraft einzuprägen?" (32:33). With these arguments about the structure of understanding and the experience of phenomena, Apollonius sounds like Kant defining the limits of human knowledge. Kymon seems less critical when he compares Apollonius's remarkable memory to a large, well-ordered picture gallery, but he also observes that many people found Apollonius's miracles as natural as sculptors' busts, and Apollonius's account of such magic as "täuschend[e] Künste" (32:190) recalls his remark that Zeuxis's statue of a centaur joins the animal and spiritual halves of human nature only in an artistic, optical illusion. Even if one believes that possible worlds exist, then, how can one not think artists' images of their inhabitants deceptive?

Apollonius makes several further remarks on verbal and visual art that suggest an answer to this aesthetic question. In addition to decrying the *Täuschung* common to them, he also distinguishes poets from sculptors on moral and semiotic grounds. He criticizes poets for making the gods seem morally dubious, a fault that he finds less serious in the case of sculptors. The latter do all that they can to present the gods as decent and even sublime, he explains, whereas the former undermine Greek religion, an unjustifiable sin: "Unläugbar haben die *Letztern* sich *am wenigsten* an den Göttern versündiget. Denn was ihre Kunst vermag, haben sie gethan, uns *anständige* und sogar *erhabene* Vorstellungen von denselben zu gewöhnen: da hingegen *Homer* und seine Familie gegen den Vorwurf, daß sie sogar die *großen* Götter, an welche die öffentliche Verehrung der Hellenen vorzüglich gerichtet ist, als Muster der unsittlichsten Handlungen aufgestellt, vielleicht mit den rohen Sitten seiner Zeit zu entschuldigen, aber nie zu rechtfertigen ist" (32:188–89). Despite this condemnation of poets, Apollonius attributes the decline of religion less to them than to sculptors. Poetry makes the gods seem human, but it still leaves some room for imagination, he argues, unlike the art of Phidias, Alkamenes, Scopas, and Praxiteles. In fact, the gods have come to seem identical with the particular images assigned them by such sculptors: "Denn obschon auch die Dichter den Göttern eine Menschen-ähnliche Gestalt zu geben genöthigt waren, so behielt doch die Einbildungskraft by ihren Darstellungen noch einige *Freyheit*; da sie hingegen durch die genau bestimmten Götterbilder unsrer Künstler gefesselt wurde, und daher mit der Zeit ganz natürlich erfolgen mußte, daß der Gott oder die Göttin mit ihrem Marmorbilde, so zu sagen, Ein Ding wurde, und, indem man sich die Götter nie anders als unter diesen bestimmten Formen dachte, unvermerkt die Bilder selbst an die Stelle derselben traten" (32:210–11). Indeed, Apollonius thinks that moral order has collapsed since the Greek gods seem no more than statues. For reasons at once moral and aesthetic, then, an art avoiding such hypostatization—one even more abstract than poetry, perhaps, so that it might give imagination even freer rein—would better indicate what lies beyond the empirical world.

Wieland describes such an art in *Agathodämon*: music. Apollonius is not a neo-Pythagorean for nothing, admiring moral consonance similar to Pythagoras's "harmony of the spheres," and the powerful effect of songs sung for Hegesias shows how well such harmony suggests possible worlds. Recalling his decision to be like Pythagoras, Apollonius tells how he mortified his flesh, arguing that one lives up to human nature more truly, the more one's body resembles a lute used to make a musician's spiritual harmonies audible, "je mehr der Körper einer rein gestimmten Laute gleicht, die dem Tonkünstler bloß *dazu* dient, die melodischen Harmonien, *die er in sich selbst spielt*, hörbar zu machen" (32:76). He admits that sensual pleasure, refined by reason, might lead to no little moral perfection and inner harmony, and he sounds skeptical when Hegesias says that it is sometimes necessary to believe that our fate is benign, that "jeder einzelne Mißklang sich im Ganzen in die reinste Harmonie auflöse" (32:50). Doubting such theodicean notions, Apollonius wonders whether the thought that present dissonances will be resolved in a harmony that humans do not hear can have much effect, "ob der Gedanke, 'die Mißklänge, die jetzt mein Ohr zerreißen, werden in eine Harmonie, *die ich nicht höre*, aufgelöst,'—ob dieser Gedanke, so lange mein Ohr gepeinigt wird, eine sonderliche Wirkung thun kann?" (32:51). The effect that songs have on Hegesias, however, is as strong as it is spiritual. After Apollonius, talking like Kant, tells him that one can never know what daemons themselves are like, one's knowledge of them being limited by the structure of the human mind, Hegesias hears a voice singing, "eine liebliche Singstimme . . . , deren reine Silbertöne, von dem schönsten Echo vervielfältigt, meine ganze Aufmerksamkeit nach dem Ort, woher sie zu kommen schienen, hinzog" (32:38–39). This hint that music can help one know a reality higher than that of phenomena is later reinforced when Kymon's wife and daughter sing a Pindaric ode, a performance that makes Hegesias feel disembodied and transported to the heavenly dwelling of the immortals, moved by the "Macht des Gesanges über das menschliche Herz" (32:215). The power of music here thus seems an epistemological matter.

Apollonius explains such strong effects of music on the evening of the second day that Hegesias spends with him. They both hear another song suggesting other worlds, one that does so distinctly yet also less deceptively than the art of painting. Apollonius likes to collect himself at the end of every day by listening to soothing music, and Hegesias feels uplifted, as he had before, but he also observes that this new song is polyphonic, a formal feature that heightens its psychological effect. Apollonius calls it a *"Psychagogikon"* (32:373), in fact, and Hegesias confesses that he has never heard "eine so seltsame Art von dissonierender Harmonie" (32:369). He feels deeply affected by such harmony, moreover, as if he were carried off to a better world on the wings of song: "Mein ganzes Wesen schien sich nach und nach in Harmonie aufzulösen, und mir war zuletzt, als ob alle diese lieblichen Töne zu lauter ätherischen Geistern würden, die mich in ihre Mitte nähmen, und auf ihren weit verbreiteten mächtigen Flügeln in eine andere bessere Welt empor trügen" (32:372). This feeling is so otherworldly because music avoids the fault that visual art commits by seeming too concrete. At first, Apollonius explains the effect of the song, a canon, by comparing acoustic intervals other than octaves to demitints, intermediate shades of color in paintings: "Diese Grund- und Mitteltöne bringen in einem vielstimmigen oder mit Instrumenten begleiteten Gesang ungefähr eben dieselbe Wirkung hervor, wie die Mitteltinten in einem Gemählde" (32:368). He soon adds, however, that music gives a clearer idea of cosmic harmony than light, colors, and chiaroscuro. Indeed, he knows no way to convey a better sense of the more rational order and intellectual life that he expects to find when he dies: "Ich kenne nichts, was einer mit zarten Sinnen und erhöhter Einbildungskraft begabten Seele einen anschaulichern Begriff und weniger täuschende Vorgefühle von einer vollkommnern Ordnung der Dinge und einem geistigern Leben geben könnte, als diese Art von Musik, die du eben gehört hast" (32:373–74). Music too stimulates the imagination, then, but it does so with a minimum of *Täuschung*.

The Pythagorean polyphony that Apollonius likes to hear also makes words superfluous, a semiotic consequence significant for Wieland's narration. Hegesias writes that words cannot describe the effect of the canon, and Apollonius prefers to do without them. Music is a more immediate, intellectual language, he argues, one that speaks for itself instead of referring to something else: "*Ich* bedarf bey einer Musik, wie die heutige, keiner Worte, die mir ihren Sinn erst erklären und sie gleichsam in meine Sprache übersetzen müßten; ich bedarf nicht nur der Worte nicht dazu, sondern sie stören mich sogar im reinen Genuß derselben, indem sie den freyen Flug meiner durch sie leichter beflügelten Seele hemmen, und meine Aufmerksamkeit zerstreuen, und von dem, was mir die Musen in ihrer eigenen geistigen Sprache unmittelbar mittheilen, durch Vergleichung der Worte mit dem, was sie ausdrücken sollen, abziehen" (32:374–75). Just as he also objects to poetry that describes the gods in all-too-human form, Apollonius here resists translating the meaning of music into words that must be compared to their referents. In both cases, he opposes reifying concepts that cannot be reduced to sensory experience and that he thinks should remain abstract. Moreover, as soon as Hegesias retires, Kymon and his family sing the song again, but so softly that Hegesias cannot hear the words, which convinces him that Apollonius is right, "daß eine Musik, wie diese, uns in ihrer eigenen, unsrer Seele gleichsam angebornen Sprache, anrede, und keiner Übersetzung in eine willkührliche kalte Zeichensprache bedürfe, um von ihr verstanden zu werden" (32:376). Unlike cold and arbitrary verbal language, then, music is the innate language of the human soul itself. If he did not know who was singing, Hegesias adds, he would believe that their voices came from another world, the invisible one that he soon enters in his dreams. With this suggestive force, but without the explicitness that devalues both sculpture and poetry, music solves the problem of how to represent the supernatural. Although it dismisses with words, it therefore also affords a semiotic model for the narration of *Agathodämon*.

One cannot narrate a novel without using words, of course, but *Agathodämon* is nonetheless strikingly like the music that moves Hegesias. It too is polyphonic, comprising several narrative voices with a strong combined effect, and those voices speak at increasingly abstract levels, thereby leaving its referent aptly implicit and invisible. Like music, in fact, the narration of the novel is an art best explained as only indirectly representing the supernatural. The goatherds who live near Apollonius and think him a daemon, for example, are also the least reliable narrators. Their readiness to believe fantastic tales recalls Bodmer and Breitinger's definition of the marvelous, but Apollonius discredits such gullibility, distinguishing actual people from fictional characters. Hegesias says that the goatherds' favorite subject is marvelous stories, "wunderbare Geschichten" (32:9–10), and that no one in the world is as inclined as such Cretans to tell and believe incredible tales, "unglaubliche Dinge zu erzählen und zu glauben" (32:10). The goatherds talk of such things as if they had actually seen them, but Hegesias questions their narrative veracity, citing the same concept of *Täuschung* crucial to Apollonius's plan for reviving popular religion: "Ob nicht etwa der erste Erzähler zuweilen ohne seine Schuld sich selbst getäuscht haben, oder von anderen getäuscht worden seyn könnte?" (32:11). After Apollonius has explained such simple people's belief in daemons, Hegesias also understands how they make the merely unusual seem marvelous, "wie diese guten Leute, in ihrer abergläubischen Einfalt, *ungewöhnliche* Erscheinungen zu *wunderbaren* zu erheben wissen" (32:39). Bodmer and Breitinger similarly explain the marvelous as the extreme form of the new, but Apollonius is skeptical, calling faith in magic and its "Zaubermährchen" (32:93) proof of the power of imagination over common sense. Not so easily deceived, he resists one woman with a reputation for seducing men as successfully as Homer's Circe, and sees through another who tries to frighten him by appearing as Hecate, "wie sie von den Dichtern geschildert wird" (32:103). Avoiding confusion of fact and fiction, Apollonius thus dispels the kind of *Täuschung* that fools the goatherds who describe him to Hegesias.

The goatherds are not the only narrators who misrepresent Apollonius because they believe in the marvelous. Damis of Nineveh, his biographer, is shown to be equally liable to credit the supernatural and distort the facts of Apollonius's life. Damis's love for the marvelous seems an imaginative foible, though, that cannot obscure the grain of truth present in his unlikely stories. Hegesias, Kymon, and Apollonius all read and dismiss his biography. Kymon is especially harsh, calling it a fantastic "Mischma[s]ch von Milesischen Mährchen und Landfahrerlügen" (32:219) and a "Wundergeschichte" more far-fetched than "alles, was in dieser Art je gefabelt worden ist" (32:220). This strong dislike of narrative fabulation is compounded by Kymon's ironic compliment that Damis was a master at turning commonplace events into old wives' tales, "ein wahrer Meister in der Kunst, eine ziemlich alltägliche Begebenheit in—ein Ammenmährchen zu verwandeln" (32:156). When Apollonius interjects that Damis certainly possessed a felicitous imagination, Kymon concedes that he has done no more than all "Liebhaber des Wunderbaren" (32:167), fans of the marvelous who mislead their readers not because they are liars but because their imagination gets the better of them—"nicht, weil sie *uns* vorsetzlich belügen wollen, sondern weil sie im Erzählen von ihrer Liebe zum Wunderbaren in eine so lebhafte Begeisterung gesetzt werden, daß sie das, was sie mit ihren Augen sahen, von dem, was ihre erhitzte Fantasie hinzu thut, selbst nicht mehr zu unterscheiden vermögen" (32:167). Thus unable to distinguish fact from fantasy because he is so inclined to believe in miracles, Damis is a tool, like Peregrinus, that Apollonius uses to sway the even more credulous masses. Like the Abderites, however, Damis is always ready to let others laugh at his folly, and his stories of wonders worked by Apollonius are not without at least some basis in fact, as Kymon notes: "Aber allen Mährchen, wie ungereimt sie seyn mögen, liegt immer etwas Wahres zum Grunde" (32:313). Strange but true in this sense, Damis's writing seems the work of a narrator too superstitious for his own good but useful for furthering that of others.

While tales told by Cretan goatherds as well as Damis sound dubious because both think the marvelous directly at work in the world, Kymon and Apollonius seem more reliable narrators. Kymon knows that Apollonius's apparent miracles result from manipulating the imagination of the masses, and Apollonius calls his own narration as accurate as possible, admitting that it might nonetheless contain unintended *Täuschung*. Unlike Damis, Kymon seems a credible witness of the many wonders that Apollonius supposedly worked, which he explains by revealing how most can be attributed simply to power over people's imagination. Apollonius's seeming ability to raise the dead can be explained this way, though news of such episodes usually spreads in the "Gestalt eines Mährchens" (32:149). Apollonius himself explains events like his disappearance from Rome at the time of Domitian's death more rationally than Damis's "Wundermährchen" (32:300), taking care to cast his story in a more credible narrative form. It is truthful for being told in the first person rather than the third, he says to Hegesias, since the former does not exceed the limits of his self-knowledge: "Hätte ich mich verbindlich gemacht, dir von mir selbst wie von einer *dritten* Person zu reden, so könntest du ein billiges Mißtrauen in meine Wahrhaftigkeit setzen; denn noch nie hat ein Mensch sich selbst gesehen, wie er einen andern sieht. Aber ich versprach dir nur was ich halten kann, mich dir darzustellen *wie ich mich selbst sehe*" (32:59). He might deceive himself from this subjective point of view, but Apollonius finds this possibility part of being only human: "Hat die Eigenliebe demungeachtet geheime Täuschungen, die ich selbst nicht gewahr werden kann, und die einem unbefangenen fremden Auge vielleicht nicht entgehen, so laß mir die Entschuldigung zu gute kommen, daß ich mich zwar für keinen *gewöhnlichen* Menschen, aber . . . *nur für einen Menschen* gebe" (32:60). Apollonius thus sounds honest about not being an omniscient narrator. He seems as fallible as Damis when he adds that he can deceive Hegesias only by deceiving himself, but his general sobriety makes his story appear judicious.

At the four levels of Wieland's narration noted so far, the story of Apollonius's life seems more reliable, the less its authors represent him as a superhuman being. Hegesias seems caught in the middle of these several levels, at first regarding him in a mood to believe in the marvelous, but later required to tell that story truly, without *Täuschung*. He also describes his writing by using terms borrowed from visual art that help decipher the narration of *Agathodämon* as a whole. He is skeptical of the goatherds but eager to meet Apollonius after hearing their fairy-tale account of him, their "mährchenhafte Erzählung . . . von diesem vermeinten Genius" (32:17). Apollonius appears just as they describe him, moreover, convincing Hegesias that imagination works in mysterious ways: "Es ist ein wunderlich Ding um unsre Einbildungskraft" (32:19). His imagination jogged by tall tales, that is, Hegesias too is tempted to see more in Apollonius than a human being. He is so curious to know who Apollonius is, in fact, that he almost blurts out this penchant for the marvelous, nearly crying, *"Welch ein wunderbares We-sen bist du?"* (32:43–44). Apollonius nonetheless picks Hegesias to tell his story more truly than writers who he knows will do nothing but damage by falsifying it or falling victim to such psychological *Täu-schung*: "Meine wahre Geschichte könnte der Welt vielleicht nützlich werden: verfälscht oder in ein täuschendes Licht gestellt, kann sie nicht anders als Schaden thun" (32:45). In his first letter, Hegesias likewise tells Timagenes that a carefully written narration suits his subject bet-ter than a rambling conversation, which would miss many a trait of such a remarkable man, "manchen nicht gleichgültigen Zug an dem Bilde dieses merkwürdigen Menschen" (32:8). This allusion to a visual image is even clearer when Hegesias warns that his writing conveys no more than a pale outline of the colorful figure that Apollonius cut for him: "Was du hier empfängst, wird doch weiter nichts als ein leicht gefärbter Umriß des lebendigen Bildes seyn, welches Agathodämon selbst mit enkaustischen Farben meinem Herzen einbrannte" (32:8). Since Apollonius himself finds all such visual art semiotically crude compared to music, however, Hegesias's narration seems flawed from the start after all.

This ambiguity is only apparent, though, when regarded from the final level of Wieland's narration. No one there writes or speaks so ex-plicitly, and Apollonius turns out not to be the hero of *Agathodämon*. In-stead, he himself admits falling short of Jesus, having only seemed what Jesus actually was. Images suggested by Hegesias's writing can therefore rightly help portray Apollonius, but Wieland hints at the less tangible life of Jesus in narration modeled on the more abstract art of music. To reach this conclusion, one needs to recall the parallel tradi-tionally drawn between the lives of these spiritual leaders and to note its relevance in previous studies of *Agathodämon*. The two were com-pared not only by pagan apologists, as noted above, but also by more modern authors. Hierocles, a Roman governor in Egypt under Diocle-tian, claimed that Apollonius was greater than Jesus, whereas Eusebius of Caesarea (c. 263–339?), a Greek church historian, chided both Hiero-cles and Philostratus, arguing that Apollonius, far from being equal to Jesus, was simply a charlatan.[21] In 1793, Johann Balthasar Lüderwald likewise took Hierocles to task, favoring religion based on reason in-stead of superstition, but finding Apollonius utterly unworthy of com-parison with Jesus.[22] This conclusion is far more extreme than the one encouraged in *Agathodämon*, and Mellinger claims that Wieland did not use Lüderwald's treatise, though she considers Jesus the hero of the novel.[23] Ihlenburg counters that Apollonius is its main character, while Martini interprets him as a great man whose ceding to Jesus makes the latter seem even greater.[24] (In less scholarly terms, this same parallel has also been drawn between Wieland and Goethe.)[25] Sengle argues that the novel was occasioned by Johann Gottfried Herder's "Vom Erlöser der Menschen" (1796) and "Von Gottes Sohn" (1797), a claim rejected by Beißner, who regards an earlier Latin translation of Ralph Cudworth's *The True Intellectual System of the Universe* (1678) as the source of Wieland's sympathetic account of Apollonius.[26] In any case, *Agathodämon* has also been said to express Herder's ideal of humanity since Wieland too thought that Christian ethics surpassed those of antiquity.[27] All of these issues, though, involve Wieland's narrative technique.

That technique can be explained by observing just how Wieland's Apollonius compares himself to Jesus. He does so in terms of *Täuschung*. Apollonius raises the issue of deceptive appearances when he finds the similarity between himself and Jesus so remarkable that even he was briefly deceived (*getäuscht*) by it but also concedes that Jesus was a contemporary, "der das *war*, was *ich schien*" (32:345). His own seeming piety and apparent miracles amounted to deliberate deception, "*absichtliche* Täuschung" (32:387), Apollonius admits, while Jesus did not want to deceive anyone, and could have done so only by deceiving himself first: "Er *wollte nicht täuschen*, und wurde jemand durch ihn getäuscht, so war ers selbst vorher" (32:386). This possibility of self-deceptive proselytizing recalls Peregrinus's dubious *Schwärmerei*, however, and Hegesias asks whether Jesus was really so innocent, whether he did not at least tolerate deceptions staged by his supporters: "Aber sollte dein Held wirklich von allen täuschenden Mitteln zu seinem, wenn du willst, edeln und wohlthätigen Zweck so frey gewesen seyn, wie du annimmst, oder sich nicht wenigstens durch ein leidendes Verhalten zu den Täuschungen bequemt haben, die von seinen Freunden ihm zu Liebe veranstaltet wurden?" (32:400–401). Apollonius finds nothing wrong with such a performance (*Veranstaltung*) if it fans the nearly extinguished flame of human morality. When Jesus died, for example, his disciples despaired, believing not that he had intentionally deceived them, but that he had deceived himself: "Sie glaubten zwar nicht, daß er sie vorsetzlich habe täuschen wollen; aber sie glaubten, er habe sich selbst getäuscht" (32:415). After the Resurrection, though, they were sure that their belief in him was not deceptive: "Sie waren nun gewiß, daß ihr Glaube an ihn sie nicht täuschen könne" (32:421). Jesus' superiority to Apollonius might thus seem to rest on the power of positive thinking, but Apollonius also notes how much he differs from other, Greek sages: "Der Jüdische Weise scheint neben den unsrigen ein Mann aus einer andern Welt zu seyn" (32:386).

By means of *Täuschung* more earnest than a mere didactic trick, Jesus would be the perfect hero of fiction defined as a story set in other, possible worlds. Apollonius highlights such literary potential when he foresees how Jesus' fame will spread, making remarks on narrative credibility, poetic images, and figurative language. Christianity sets itself apart from pagan *Täuschung*, he explains, but like the language of Gnosticism that misleads Peregrinus, its verbal and visual signs will be taken too literally. Apollonius says that early Christianity needed to appear to achieve what pagan polytheism had tried to bring about "durch eitle *Täuschungen*" (32:431). Jesus' sense of purpose assuredly enabled him to perform much that was marvelous, he adds, but rumor and biographers doubtless distorted such acts as badly as his, Apollonius's, own deeds were skewed. Indeed, Apollonius thinks the Christian gospels so incredible that they often seem more like fairy tales than solid, reliable evidence: "Überhaupt fehlt diesen Erzählungen, wiewohl ihnen nicht alle Glaubwürdigkeit abzusprechen ist, doch sehr viel von dem, was von einer zuverlässigen Urkunde gefordert wird, und dem Schreiber einer wahren Geschichte das Zutrauen der Leser erwirbt. Sie sind im gemeinsten Mährchenton erzählt, mit Widersprüchen und unglaublichen, zum Theil schlechterdings unmöglichen Wunderdingen angefüllt" (32:383). These narrative criteria are the same ones that Wieland establishes for novels in *Agathon*. Apollonius also traces Jesus' success to Jewish prophets who embellished their predictions about the Messiah with poetic language, "mit den prächtigsten und reitzendsten Farben der Dichtkunst" (32:411). Christians too will either invent new words or invest old ones with new meanings, he adds, their language already consisting of many curious figures of speech, "eine Menge sonderbarer *figürlicher Redensarten*" (32:436). Christianity will lead to a new daemonism, moreover, as soon as images of its saints seem talismans corresponding to invisible archetypes in heaven. Such verbal and visual signs quickly become more powerful than the ideas that they denote: "In kurzem wirken die *bloßen Zeichen* derselben, Worte oder symbolische Bilder, in welche jeder so viel selbstbeliebige Bedeutung legen kann als er will, stärker als die Ideen selbst" (32:426). Apollonius thus foresees that faith in Jesus and his sincere illusions will degenerate into mere idolatry as Christianity and the language of its dubious Gospels undergo semiotic corruption.

As "self-conscious" fiction, *Agathodämon* not only relates but also avoids such hypostatization, narrated in a way that does not reify its hero, and thus develops Wieland's earlier treatments of *Täuschung*. It tells the story of Apollonius only as a prelude to the even more remarkable one of Jesus, whom it neither describes nor depicts, however, in verbal or visual images like those shown to abet superstition and idolatry. Such indirect narration resembles poetry, painting, and sculpture less than music, an art better suited to represent the supernatural, which it does not make seem misleadingly concrete. This semiotic significance of music has not been noted in previous studies of the novel. Music has seemed a symbol of the social concord enjoyed by Apollonius and Kymon's family, and one of Apollonius's speeches has been compared to an Orphic hymn, but the fact that the historical Democritus and Archytas, models for main characters in two of Wieland's other novels, thought highly of Pythagorean harmony is a better clue to the narration of *Agathodämon*.[28] Drawing such generic parallels to other arts, Wieland also defines the illusion that his novel induces as *Täuschung* containing its own antidote, like the educational kind preferred by Apollonius. He creates a fictional character, Apollonius, who gradually takes shape but then admits to falling short of an even greater, more remote ideal: Jesus. While his secular message is still largely consistent with the moral theory of the Enlightenment, then, Wieland's new attitude toward the fictionality of his narration prefigures the kind of aesthetic reflection known as romantic irony. That attitude develops the notion of *Täuschung* defined as aesthetic illusion in his essay on the *Singspiel*, recommended despite being taken to extremes in *Die Abderiten*, and revealed as suspect if indulged too sincerely in *Peregrinus Proteus*. It also examines fictionality in the art of music, thereby extending current theoretical limits to that concept. Precisely by *not* telling the whole story of *Agathodämon*, Wieland thus suggestively links its subject matter to its narration. When told that Jesus was thought to have ascended to heaven on a cloud, Hegesias balks: "In einer *Ode* laß' ich das gelten; aber prosaisch von der Sache zu reden,—" (32:418). In *Agathodämon*, Wieland overcomes this objection, narrating the poetic in prose, the metaphysical in supreme "metafiction."

9. Aristipp und einige seiner Zeitgenossen (1800–1802)

Bücher wie "Aristipp," die gleichzeitig eben so reinlich das Stahlskelett der Trägerkonstruktion zeigen, wie die "Fülle" menschlicher und geistiger Ereignisse bewältigen, gehören in allen Literaturen zu den größten Seltenheiten, und sollten von jeder Schriftstellergeneration immer wieder studiert werden.
—Arno Schmidt, *Berechnungen I* (1955)

Illusion is also the issue tied to fictionality most important in the last of Wieland's three late novels, *Aristipp und einige seiner Zeitgenossen* (1800–2). Named for the philosopher Aristippus of Cyrene, a student of Socrates who first proposed the doctrine of hedonism, the novel deals less with daemonism or didactic *Täuschung*, however, than with the aesthetic pleasure afforded by fine art. By analyzing such art while casting Socrates as a secular saint, it shifts the emphasis placed on music and Jesus in *Agathodämon*, and by discussing aesthetic pleasures so strong as to be fatal, it further regards the kind of delusions that lead to Peregrinus's death. Its title character enjoys *Täuschung* consciously and in moderation, but its heroine, the hetaera Lais, takes such illusion to greater lengths. This difference of degree not only raises the questions about imagination and ideals posed in Wieland's earlier novels, but also helps settle scholarly arguments about the literary character and quality of *Aristipp*, which has often seemed little more than a long gloss on the history of philosophy. Its import is clear from Aristippus's opening remarks on poetry and sculpture, not least because he often links such verbal and visual arts, likening the prose of Xenophon's *Anabasis*, for example, to Polyclitus's statuesque canon of physical beauty. The effect of visual art is shown in scenes reminiscent of the Abderites' craze for theater and Peregrinus's passion for statues, moreover, while that of verbal art is studied in letters about Aristophanes' *Clouds*, a comedy said to abet Socrates' execution, and about two Platonic dialogues: *Phaedo*, which drives one of its first readers to suicide, and *Symposium*, which helps explain Lais's demise. Aristippus similarly judges Plato's *Republic* according to its effect as a work of fiction, regarding its

171

Socrates as a character whose narrative physiognomy is tied to Plato's notion of literary mimesis. Although Wieland openly declares his own sympathy for fiction only in notes and glossaries, as the "editor" of *Aristipp*, he thus subtly examines the illusion that it induces. Indeed, the issue of illusion unifies his sprawling text, the difference between Aristippus and Lais playing itself out in ways that make this final novel the height of his "self-conscious" fiction.

As in Wieland's earlier novels, the events shown in *Aristipp* seem meaningful because its main characters perceive and present them differently. Its story line is tortuous, tracing personal liaisons among contemporaries of Aristippus. Like him, most are modeled on historical figures who flourished in the late fifth and early fourth centuries B.C., and they move easily in the philosophical, literary, and artistic circles of Athens in the thirty years following the Peloponnesian War. Writing letters to each other as they come and go from that defeated city to other regions of Greece and the Mediterranean, they all give vivid accounts of its cultural life. They exchange thoughts on Socrates, for example, who is their mentor right up to the moment of his death and whose personality is one focal point of the novel. Another is the erotic and intellectual charm that Lais holds for Aristippus, at least when these two pen pals are not otherwise occupied with their respective senses of cosmopolitan independence. A third focus is the work of painters and sculptors such as Parrhasius, Scopas, and Timanthes, who appear in the novel both to explain their intentions and to discuss the effect of their art, thereby recalling Wieland's essay on the ideals of Greek artists. A fourth is Plato, acknowledged to be Socrates' most famous student, whose abstract idealism distorts his master's more tangible teachings. Wieland locates these four axes of what little action there is in *Aristipp* against a background of social and political unrest, and the letters sent to and from Aristippus include digressions on the relative merits of democracy, oligarchy, and tyranny—the forms of government prevailing in Athens, Cyrene, and Syracuse, respectively. Aristippus avoids politics, however, preferring aesthetic pleasure instead, which he takes in everything from the Olympic games to history written by Xenophon and plays by Aristophanes. Indeed, his strong interests in Socrates, Lais, visual art, and Plato are all linked by the concept of aesthetic illusion and its application in life as well as literature. Accordingly, *Aristipp* provides insights into the *Täuschung* considered in some of Wieland's essays and other novels too.

It does so partly by employing characters, themes, and commentary also found in those other novels. Like *Agathodämon*, *Aristipp* is an epistolary novel about a philosopher, and Aristippus is less important than Socrates, whom he, sounding just like Apollonius singing the praises of Jesus, hails as the purest moral embodiment of humanity ever seen, "die reinste *sittliche Gestalt*, in welcher die *Humanität* je der Welt persönlich im wirklichen Leben sichtbar geworden ist" (33:63). Such a concern with the appearance of an ideal in real life is characteristic of Aristippus, who does not believe in popular religion but thinks it useful for maintaining order among the masses and, taking this position further than Apollonius, claims that one needs to assume the existence of the divine if one is not to succumb to solipsism. What is more, he meets a Pythagorean who observes how people have to imagine divinity in a human form and how poetry produces vague images that the art of sculpture must make more concrete. Other remarks on the psychological force of visual art recall *Peregrinus Proteus* and *Don Sylvio*. Like Mamilia Quintilla, Lais poses nearly nude for a statue of Venus, and when Aristippus sees her undressed, she warns him that Ixion did not do well to boast of thus spying Juno, while, like Don Sylvio, one of her young admirers fancies that she has been turned into that statue by some evil magician. Litigious Athenians' "Proceßfieber" (33:55) echoes *Die Abderiten*, as does Aristippus's taste for comedy that avoids personal satire, and Diogenes of Sinope appears in *Aristipp* too, where Plato's utopia and its model citizens are regarded even more skeptically than in *Diogenes*. Such parallels seem clearest in the case of *Agathon*. The historical Agathon hosted the dinner described in Plato's *Symposium*, and Lais's final lover poses as a reader of poems, the same job held by Wieland's fictional hero. Moreover, Lais is Aristippus's neighbor on Aegina, just as Danae lives next to Agathon in Tarentum, and one of her protégées is called Chariklea, the name that Danae takes there. Aristippus even learns oratory from Hippias, with whom he visits the tyrant Dionysius, and admires the Sophist's knowledge of the real world, "der *wirklichen* Menschen . . . und des Laufs der Welt, nicht wie wir ihn alle gern hätten, sondern wie er ist" (33:277–78). Like Wieland's other novels, then, *Aristipp* involves several kinds of fictions and delusions, thereby addressing the topic of fictionality on a broad scale.

Aristippus seems strangely disposed to literary fiction, displaying considerable ambivalence toward *Täuschung*. Skeptical of imagination, he encourages certain illusions while remaining committed to understanding them. Hippias derides myths about gods and heroes as mere phantasms and consigns them to the amusing but unscientific "*Gebiet der Dichter*" (34:44); Diagoras of Melos, another philosopher whom

Apollonius meets, likewise shuns the marvelous, explaining how he once listened to such tales but did not believe them and tried to discover their natural causes, "d. i. woher wohl die dabey vorwaltende Täuschung gekommen" (34:336). Aristippus similarly ignores his imagination, aware that it almost always leads him astray, and he dismisses idealistic abstraction as illusory, but he hardly objects to *Täuschung*. He likes seeing happy crowds of people, for example, which make him feel philanthropic for no good reason: "Denn da wiege ich mich unvermerkt in die süße Täuschung ein, sie alle für gut und wohlwollend zu halten" (33:133). He also believes in looking on the bright side of life: "An diese sollten wir uns dann, wenn wir weise wären, fest halten, ohne spitzfindig nachzugrübeln, wie viel davon etwa bloß Täuschung seyn möchte" (34:23). This preference for pleasant *Täuschung* is equally strong when Aristippus wants to feel useful, longing for "die angenehme Selbsttäuschung, daß ich der Welt zu etwas nütze sey" (35:26), but he also wants to understand such illusion and self-deception. When he thinks that he has seen the ghost of Lais, his friend Kleonidas explains how his reason drew a false conclusion, "dessen Täuschung sie keine Zeit hatte wahrzunehmen" (34:251), and in a letter to Plato's nephew Speusippus, Aristippus himself strikes such a clear-headed balance, writing that *Täuschung* can be pleasant and even beneficial but that one always needs to be aware of its limits, too: "Es giebt, wie du weißt, angenehme und sogar wohlthätige Täuschungen; aber es ist immer gut, in allen menschlichen Dingen . . . *klar* zu sehen; zu wissen, *wann*, *wo*, und *wie* wir getäuscht werden, und auf keine Art von Täuschung mehr Werth zu legen als billig ist" (36:285). Unlike Hippias and Diagoras, Aristippus thus welcomes *Täuschung*, albeit with an underlying caveat.

If Aristippus seems likelier to accept the realm of literary fiction than philosophers who reject it together with *Täuschung*, Lais takes such a penchant for illusions too far. She entertains them just as self-consciously and with equal self-control, but she eventually succumbs to self-deception, acting like a literary character come to life. An intellectually emancipated woman, she turns the battle of the sexes into one of wits, convinced that her own happiness when pleasing men is a passing *Täuschung*, one seldom recognized as such: "Aber daß beides, das Glück das ich gebe, und was ich dagegen zu empfangen scheine, im Grunde bloße Täuschung ist, davon sind die Wenigen, mit denen ich bisher den Versuch gemacht habe, so gut überzeugt als ich selbst" (35:246). Antipater, the son of Kleonidas, adds that her having no illusions about love sets Lais apart from other beautiful women: "Die Täuschungen, wodurch die Eitelkeit, Unschuld, oder Schwäche eines schönen Weibes sich selbst über das, was die Männer Liebe nennen, verblenden kann, hat vermuthlich bey ihr nie Statt gefunden" (35:289). Aristippus similarly predicts that Arasambes, Lais's Persian lover, will suffer when he learns that he can never induce in her the same illusion that he mistakes for real passion, but Aristippus also observes that Lais's amusing herself with Arasambes' wealth is a costly self-deception, and Learchus, a fellow citizen of Lais in Corinth, notes how willfully she deceives herself in her ultimate infatuation with a Thessalian wastrel: "Sie sieht zu hell, um nicht zu sehen, daß sie ihr ganzes Glück in eine bloße Täuschung setzt; aber sie *will* getäuscht seyn, und so *ist* sie es denn auch *wirklich*" (35:348). After Lais disappears, never to be seen or heard from again, Aristippus agrees that she combined remarkable judgment with a boundless capacity to deceive herself, "eine . . . unerschöpfliche Gabe sich selbst zu täuschen" (36:29). Far from merely coquettish or deliberately frigid,[1] a free spirit modeled on Julie von Bondeli, Sophie von La Roche, and Sophie Brentano,[2] or one whose story reflects Wieland's larger concept of women but seems to have little to do with the rest of his novel,[3] Lais thus embodies the precariousness of *Täuschung*.

Lais's rise and fall seem particularly instructive for relating such illusion to the issue of fictionality. She has high ideals and a vivid imagination, and she lives out her fantasies and then loves against her will in ways that prove the truth of poetry. Like the title character of Wieland's *Musarion*, she is a kind of philosopher herself, inspired by an unattainable moral ideal of womanhood. The same rich imagination that produces this ideal also causes her downfall, however. Not only can she well imagine Socrates' last hours without having witnessed them; tired of Arasambes, she also longs for her old surroundings, which appear transformed in the "*Medeen-Kessel* der Fantasie" (34:211). Artists and performers at Arasambes' court amuse her for a time by enacting the extravagant products of her imagination, "die Kinder meiner üppigen Fantasie" (34:223), she explains, but Aristippus knows that her natural indolence stymies its force. Kleonidas says that she has acquired the bad habit of satisfying her every whim, "jede Fantasie, die ihr zu Kopfe steigt" (34:256), and Aristippus asks for patience with her fertile imagination, while Learchus calls her running off with the Thessalian ne'er-do-well another of her fantastic caprices. Lais's imagination thus results in her self-deceptive fling, which is also related to literary fiction. She insists that she will never behave like Euripides' Phaedra nor throw herself from a cliff, like Sappho, refusing to believe poets who say that love defies reason. She admires Xenophon's *Cyropaedia* as a work of fiction, however, and is scared by the passion that seizes its

Araspes, a merely imaginary man whose effect on her perplexes Aristippus: "Sollte denn das Beyspiel eines Araspes, der . . . außer der Einbildungskraft des Dichters der Cyropädie nirgends existiert hat, von so schwerem Gewichte seyn, daß es eine so weise, ihrer selbst so mächtige, und durch eine Erfahrenheit von zwanzig Jahren zum ruhigsten Selbstvertrauen so sehr berechtigte Frau . . . furchtsam machen müßte?" (35:279). Fictional characters are also suggestive when Lais moves to Thessaly, the cradle of many Greek myths, and lives in Pharsala, "diesem dichterischen Lande" (35:216), for when she is deserted there, Aristippus sadly reflects on the drama of her life, sure that she fell as nobly as Euripides' Polyxena. He too thus links her fateful *Täuschung* to a fictional character.

Previous studies of *Aristipp* show why regarding such effects of fiction is part of grasping its full significance. The reception of the novel has been checkered, not least because some read it primarily as history, social criticism, or pop philosophy rather than as a novel. Wieland himself called it one of his best and most important works, but Schiller preferred not to think of it as an aesthetic composition, and its ideals as well as its main characters left him cold.[4] Heinrich Pröhle likewise admits that its artistic form is weak and faults it for lacking a clearly defined theme, while Sengle brands it a long-winded cross between learning and fiction, a largely unedifying encounter with the elderly Wieland.[5] Armin Sinnwell, however, raises the possibility that *Aristipp* is an orderly, systematic composition.[6] Such judgments often mirror their own authors' views on the mix of fiction and history in *Aristipp*. To Pröhle, Wieland's adherence to the few facts known about the actual Aristippus makes it seem less like a novel than his similar works, whereas his frequent departures from the historical record convince Sinnwell that it is not a dry collection of facts, but a radical attempt to translate epistemological and aesthetic premises into art.[7] According to Helmut Kind, Wieland's historical interests are stronger in *Aristipp* than in his other novels and its parallels to his own times weaker, while Knuth Mewes finds its names of actual persons and places less important than their associations with the eighteenth century.[8] Mewes adds that *Aristipp* is less a novel than a vehicle for philosophy, a position like that of Thomas Höhle, who similarly links Socrates' execution to the French Revolution and Aristippus's politics to constitutional reforms in the Helvetic Republic, and who observes that Aristippus's commentary on Plato's *Republic* no longer resembles a novel, at least not as the genre had previously been known.[9] Precisely because its poetic nature has been neglected,[10] paying closer attention to its treatment of fictionality seems crucial to assessing the quality and coherence of *Aristipp*.

The need for such a new approach is similarly clear from studies that discuss its narration, especially when they interpret the novel as a fictional conversation in the style of Plato's dialogues. Since Aristippus remarks on that style, *Aristipp* is said to define its own narrative form, revealing its implicit poetics along with Wieland's stance toward Kant and the romantics, a stance toward illusion best described by comparing verbal and visual art. Consisting of letters written and answered by a host of characters and thus reminiscent of the myriad footnotes to *Danischmend*, the novel has a narrative form praised as subjective and multiperspectival, one in which contiguity and contemporaneity seem more appropriate than a single plot line.[11] Aristippus's criticism of Plato is said to spell out the principles of Wieland's own dialogic style, moreover, a style defined in ways that help us judge the artistic quality of his late novels.[12] Such criticism reflects a realistic concept of the novel, that is, while modifying the model provided by Plato's *Republic* is said to create the form of Wieland's fictional reality.[13] Letters cannot be equated with loose talk, Mewes adds, though the principle of Wieland's narration is universal communication.[14] Thomé finds that narration utopian, a kind of fictional dialogue ideally preserving the discourse of the Enlightenment on a level far removed from practical political constraints,[15] and Klaus Manger discerns a comprehensive poetics of conversation in *Aristipp*, distinguishing levels of fictionality — fictional letters from stories that they contain, for example — and applying its critique of Plato's *Republic* to German romantics' political fictions.[16] While Matthecka argues that the form of the novel conveys subjective idealism and a phenomenology like Kant's, in fact, its critique of Plato has often seemed aimed at Kant, Fichte, or philosophy in general.[17] Wieland tries to show that such thinkers' systems are fictions (*Dichtung*), says Sengle, to whom *Aristipp* conveys "illusionism" more conscious than the early romantics' aesthetic abandon.[18] Whether illusion is more rewarding than reason in the novel has been debatable,[19] but *Täuschung* is also occasioned by the paintings described there and presumably viewed as actively as the novel is meant to be read.[20] Aristippus's frequent remarks on such visual art would thus seem a clue to the role of fictionality in his story.

Fictionality, illusion, and the visual arts are indeed related from the outset of *Aristipp*. In its initial letters, Aristippus compares his own prosaic cast of mind to the imagination of poets, scorns the illusion of heroism produced by the Olympic games, and hails the more aesthetic kind that he feels in the presence of sculpture. He starts by describing his trip from Cyrene to Athens, having seen neither tritons, which populate the sea, according to poets like Kleonidas, nor mermaids, a fact that proves the difference between the two friends, "den großen Unterschied, den die Götter zwischen euch Dichtern und uns andern prosaischen Menschen machen, zu meiner nicht geringen Demüthigung" (33:5). His envy of poets seems genuine here, since he adds that Kleonidas's visions would delight him, even if he could not see beyond the surface himself. Passive appreciation of poetic spectacles also marks Aristippus's attitude toward the Olympic games, which he initially views as grand, gruesome drama that appears to prove the truth of poets' tales of heroic deeds, "die Erzählungen der Dichter von den unglaublichsten Thaten der Göttersöhne" (33:25). He is soon saddened and repulsed by such sham tragedy, though, which creates an illusion of myth that could not last: "Aber die Täuschung war von kurzer Dauer" (33:26). Aristippus senses a more enduring kind of illusion when he sees another sight in Olympia: Phidias's statue of Jupiter. It too fills him with a strange feeling of awe, one that he says surpasses even poets' imagination and that he attributes to its titanic, colossal proportions. Large and small may be deceptive (*täuschende*) concepts, he adds, but he gladly lets himself be fooled by them. Although he is keen to explain the effect of Phidias's statue, then, Aristippus enjoys the illusion necessary to such art, as he indicates when noting how a balustrade keeps Phidias's audience from coming too close: "Denn bey einem Kunstwerke, wo am Ende doch alles auf eine gewisse Magie, und also auf *Täuschung* hinausläuft, muß man die Zuschauer nicht gar zu nahe kommen und zu gelehrt werden lassen" (33:45). A prosaic connoisseur willingly charmed by art, Aristippus seeks aesthetic illusion.

Phidias's Jupiter is just one of many examples of visual art cited in *Aristipp*. Others show how such art also informs its setting, its debates on aesthetic matters, and its accounts of Wieland's characters, especially Lais. Aristippus collects art, and his story is set in post-Periclean Athens, which he calls the temple of the Muses, seat of taste, and home of the fine arts. He also holds forth on a painting by Parrhasius called *Demos*, which shows a crowd of Athenians leaving some public assembly. Aristippus thinks that this group portrait is a good historical painting but that it fails to show the universal idea of *demos*, a goal impossible in Parrhasius's art. Lais disagrees, replying that allegory was not the painter's intention, and Parrhasius himself confirms that *Demos* is not allegorical, though characteristic of the citizens of Athens. In a note, Wieland tells how some scholars find this painting similar to

Raphael's *School of Athens*, a parallel that Manger remarks when he stresses the perspective of readers in *Aristipp*, but such generic questions also seem tied to the issue of *Täuschung*. Parrhasius shows Aristippus two other paintings that surpass all that the latter has ever seen in illusive vivacity, "an täuschender Lebendigkeit" (34:85), and Kleonidas views works by Parrhasius and Timanthes, writing that their rival Zeuxis is admired for the illusion created by his coloring, "des Täuschenden seiner Färbung" (34:91), and that Timanthes has given Lais a painting that shows how artistic mimesis conveys an illusion of its sitter's spirit, "einen . . . täuschenden Widerschein des unsichtbaren Innern" (34:92). Kleonidas also asks Aristippus to educate Antipater by molding him as if he were a piece of marble, and Antipater both regards and describes Lais as if she were a statue, while Learchus notes that she refines art by modeling for painters and sculptors. She was once sold for the price of a statue, in fact, and just as she later poses for one of Venus sculpted by Scopas, her Thessalian lover sits for one of Achilles by Aristippus's friend Eufranor. On literal as well as metaphorical levels, then, numerous references to visual art in *Aristipp* confirm Lais's close association with illusion.

Explicit comparisons of visual and verbal art likewise suggest why Lais is so susceptible to *Täuschung*. Aristippus and his friends often link painting to poetry, reinforcing the role of imagination and illusion in narration such as hers. Phidias's inspiration for his statue of Jupiter is said to have come from reading the *Iliad*, and Socrates calls him a Homer among sculptors, "ein *Homer*, der, statt in Versen, in *Marmor* und *Elfenbein dichtet*" (33:247). Kleonidas similarly has a talent for verbal as well as visual art, being both a poet and a painter, and he explains Timanthes' portraits of Ajax and Iphigenia as allusions to Homer and Euripides. Timanthes adds that he never meant to leave anything to the imagination of his audience by hiding Agamemnon's face in the latter painting, saying that artists should be as clear about such things as they possibly can. The tricks played by imagination are subtler in Aristippus's closest analogy of verbal to visual art, which he draws when discussing Xenophon's *Anabasis*. This story of forlorn Greek soldiers' heroic retreat is not distorted or colored, he claims: "Alles erscheint in seiner eigenen Gestalt und Farbe" (34:190). Xenophon studiously avoids milking it for any extraordinary and marvelous effect, he adds, forgoing the opportunity to paint a prettier picture, "das Außerordentliche und Wunderbare der Thatsachen durch Kolorit und Beleuchtung geltend zu machen" (34:190). Such comments would not flatter a painter or poet, Aristippus knows, but they are the highest praise for a historian. Hippias says that Xenophon's apparent truthfulness is an illusion that fools the unsuspecting reader, an "angenehme Täuschung . . . , daß er, ohne allen Argwohn durch diesen Ton selbst getäuscht zu werden, immer die reinste Wahrheit zu lesen glaubt" (34:195–96). All readers are to blame if they are deceived by historians who try to tell the truth, he thinks, but Xenophon's account of himself as an ideal general is a *Täuschung* that smacks of poetry. Lais relates her affair with Arasambes, moreover, in detail that she finds typical of Herodotus, who Hippias says appeals to readers' imagination more openly. She also tells the story of Amor and Psyche in a way acclaimed for being both painterly and poetic, so her own narration implies such graphic illusion.

Qualities shared by visual and verbal art also help explain Lais's behavior when Aristippus cites various "canons" connected to extreme effects of some painting and sculpture. As historiography, he claims, Xenophon's *Anabasis* is comparable to the canon or standard of human beauty set by one of Polyclitus's statues. Filistus similarly writes a history of Sicily according to such a canon, taking his own point of view as a subjective but authentic angle on Dionysius. Diogenes calls every kind of philosophy an intellectual or ethical ideal or canon for someone, moreover, and Antipater remarks that Aristippus's skepticism hardly means that sensual lust alone is not deceptive, refusing to take such charges by his critics as the canon of truth. Aristippus himself clarifies such apparent contradictions between subjective impressions and objective standards when he objects to Plato's concept of beauty. The effect of light, color, shape, and texture results from the nature and structure of our sensory organs, he notes, so we have no choice but to take our sensations as the measure of beauty and ourselves as "den *Kanon der Natur*" (34:300). Plato's idea of beauty, by contrast, is the result of an illusion, "die Frucht einer *natürlichen Täuschung*" (34:303), since one can nearly always imagine objects being more beautiful than they appear. One could also imagine a moral character equivalent to Polyclitus's canon, he adds, but the notion that one can always think up something more beautiful than what is found in nature is pure illusion, "bloße Täuschung" (34:306). The consequences of taking such illusion too seriously are clear in two episodes about the effect of visual art. Aristippus appreciates the artful *Täuschung* briefly induced in him by a painting of his first encounter with Lais, an illusion that lasts far longer for a visiting Abderite, while young Chariton is seized with longing for the statue of Venus that Scopas modeled on Lais, with a passion for "ein bloßes Fantasiewerk des Künstlers" (35:105) that recalls not only Pygmalion but also Lais's fear of falling in love as hopelessly as

Xenophon's Araspes. Lais cures Chariton but cannot avoid later suc-
cumbing to her own idealistic, subjectively valid delusions.

Just as extreme effects of visual art are plain in the cases of Chariton
and the Abderite, that of verbal art is shown in remarks on Aristo-
phanes' *Clouds*. The play portrays Socrates as a casuistic quack, a
Sophist who charges a fortune to teach his students to twist facts, and it
is sometimes blamed for his trial in 399 B.C., when he was similarly ac-
cused of corrupting Athenian youth. Aristophanes is absolved of such
blame in *Aristipp*, but passages on his comedy underscore the illusory
force of fictional characters that troubles Lais. She herself reports how
Aristophanes is upset that Socrates' accusers take *The Clouds* seriously,
and Aristophanes explains that he only meant to criticize the Sophists'
newfangled pedagogy and deleterious influence, an intention com-
pletely misunderstood by whoever regards the play as satire aimed at
the actual Socrates. He distinguishes Socrates from his character of the
same name, adding that *The Clouds* is not responsible for whatever hap-
pens to the philosopher. These disclaimers seem aimed at Plato, who
thought Aristophanes morally irresponsible for slandering Socrates,
and *Aristipp* contains many allusions to *The Clouds* critical of Plato. If
some people, including Plato, take *The Clouds* too seriously, however,
Aristippus does not take it seriously enough, calling Socrates' trial a
comedy that will end as honorably for him as the play once did. Such
faith that one can laugh off real accusations as easily as those made in a
play is equally mistaken when Antipater describes how Lais has been
libelled by a rejected suitor, a poet, insisting that she need be no more
concerned by his attack than Socrates by *The Clouds*, since his caricature
resembles her as little as Aristophanes' Sophist did the actual Socrates.
This is ominous solace indeed, especially since one of Socrates' own ac-
cusers is such a minor poet. Aristippus and his protégé thus fail to fore-
see the powerful effect of fictional characters on people less aestheti-
cally disinterested than themselves. Especially since *The Clouds* favors
philosophy that is more like poetry than logic, praising education that
teaches morals from mythology, these characters' mistake reveals that
Lais is not alone in misconstruing the relationship of literature to life.

Lais herself considers aesthetic qualities of fiction wholly apart from
its more immediate effects in letters on Plato's *Phaedo*, a dialogue about
the immortality of the soul that shows Socrates surrounded by his dis-
ciples on his dying day. Three of them—Plato, Aristippus, and Kleom-
brotus—are absent, a fact that Plato mentions. In *Aristipp*, high-strung
Kleombrotus is haunted by his image of the dying Socrates. Plato sends
him a copy of *Phaedo*, telling him to read it, and Kleombrotus feels so

guilty for dallying with Lais in Socrates' hour of need that he commits suicide. Aristippus calls *Phaedo* the book that put Kleombrotus over the edge, "das Buch, das ihm den letzten Stoß gegeben hat" (34:67), and his suicide attests to the power of such fiction, for its author seems a poet, an even greater *Schwärmer* than Kleombrotus. Aristippus explains Plato's own absence by saying that he begged off sick in order to be free to have Socrates say whatever he, Plato, wanted. To this charge of poetic license, Aristippus adds that *Phaedo* is a prose poem and a "Mittelding von Dialektik und Poesie" (34:104), claiming that Plato would have been a poet if his natural talent for fabrication and allegory, his "Hang zum Fabulieren und Allegorisieren" (34:75), were not inhibited by his characteristic casuistry. This interpretation of *Phaedo* as fiction makes sense, for Plato's Socrates admits writing poetry, cites Homer as an authority on the heavens, and compares himself to a tragic character. Aristippus does not kill himself after reading it, though, less affected by such literature than Kleombrotus. Hippias is even cooler toward the dialogue, which he parodies, and Lais sounds almost callous in her praise. After briefly regretting Kleombrotus's death, she extols *Phaedo* as a story more beautiful than anything else ever written in Greek, admiring its psychological and narrative artistry. Such complete aesthetic detachment amounts to hubris, since Kleombrotus dies by throwing himself from a cliff, as Lais, refusing to love as blindly as Sappho, says she never would. Furthermore, Lais soon meets Arasambes, with whom she first discovers *Täuschung* caused by verbal and visual art, so her reaction to *Phaedo* highlights how hard she eventually falls.

Lais and her response to literary fiction change dramatically by the time she reads another of Plato's dialogues, his *Symposium*. It too is considered proof of Plato's gift for "poetry," for writing fiction as vivid as visual art, that is, but unlike Aristippus, who relates discussion of it in a matter-of-fact tone, Lais turns out to be a fanciful narrator herself, falling in love in a way that shows how deeply Plato's story moves her. Like *Phaedo*, *Symposium* strikes Aristippus as a cross between philosophy and poetry, a "Zwitter von Filosofie und Poesie" (35:129), and its author is once again credited with a knack for abstraction, a "Hang zum Sym[b]olisieren und Allegorisieren" (35:180), this time by the philosopher Praxagoras. Praising it in terms even higher than those Lais uses to describe *Phaedo*, in fact, Aristippus hails *Symposium* as a great step forward for Greek literature, as prose that could lead to the kind of formal model already supplied by Greek poets, sculptors, and architects. Eufranor takes such parallels between the arts even further, adding that Plato's portrayal of Alcibiades should be the canon for all poets describing people with an eye to both beauty and truth, the same problem that Wieland tries to solve in *Agathon*. Like its narrator, Aristippus calls his own style more sober, respecting *Symposium* as "eine Art von *Poem*" (35:150), but also proud of being "ein bloßer *Erzähler*" (35:151) in his own account of a dinner where Lais and her guests discuss it. Aristippus nonetheless lists "*Milesische Mährchen*" (35:129) among the narrative virtues of *Symposium*, and Lais has the last word by telling such a tall tale, the story of Amor and Psyche, a myth more incisive than Plato's abstractions. This is the tale later called poetic as well as painterly, "eines von den wenigen, wo die dichterische Darstellung mit der mahlerischen in Einem Punkte zusammentrifft" (35: 207–8), a tribute to its imaginative vividness, and her imagination plays a similar role when she falls for her Thessalian, since her attraction to him, as Aristippus explains, takes the erotic course plotted by Plato's Aristophanes in *Symposium*. In the end, then, the illusory effect of literary fiction on Lais seems downright fatal.

If various characters' comments on *Phaedo* and *Symposium* confirm the role of literary fictionality in Lais's *Täuschung*, Aristippus's exegesis of the *Republic* explains why he enjoys such illusion more cautiously. Asked for his opinion of this dialogue, "von dieser neuen *Dichtung* unsers erklärten *Dichterfeindes*" (36:34), he examines it as the work of a Plato opposed to poets, paradoxically considering it as a poetic work of art, "als dichterisches Kunstwerk" (36:126). Any such dialogue is an invention, composition, and imitation of nature that must observe the rules of verisimilitude and decorum, "des *Wahrscheinlichen* und *Schicklichen*" (36:35), he writes, but Plato breaks them by making Socrates the author of a story so long and detailed that it seems unlikely to have been told in a single day, as Plato claims. Worse than such poetic license, "alle diese Unwahrscheinlichkeiten" (36:38), is the disproportionate structure of the *Republic*, which has so many peripheral episodes that one often loses sight of its main point. A fictional dialogue should resemble as closely as possible an actual conversation among urbane, educated people, Aristippus notes, an artistic ideal that Plato seems to have ignored. Plato is a philosophical poet, then, "unser poetisierender Filosof oder filosofierender Dichter" (36:132), but one whose logic and literary urges are at odds. Even his philosophy strikes Aristippus as a fiction, however. Like a poet, he makes one marvelous thing seem credible by inventing others, building his house of cards out of thin air, Aristippus says, especially when he invents (*erdichtet*) the ideal of a just man at issue in the *Republic*, a figment of his imagination that results from letting his poetic fancy loose in the endless realm of ideas. Plato's story at the end of the *Republic* about the rewards awaiting such a just man after death is a similarly unbelievable and unnatural fiction, Aristippus adds. Its celestial images are impossible for readers to envision coherently, "in *Einem Gemählde*" (36:254), and it is a tale, "ein bloßes *Mährchen*" (36:256), too fantastic to be called poetry. Aristippus thus faults the style of the *Republic* as well as its substance, linking its literary and philosophical fictions.

This skepticism reflects Aristippus's ambivalence toward *Täuschung*. Averse to such illusion on an intellectual level, he accepts its use for aesthetic effect, which he thinks Plato fails to achieve. Platonic ideas are meant to transcend the world of phenomena and illusions, he knows, but he thinks the hero of Plato's story at the end of the *Republic* deceived (*getäuscht*) by seeing things that are really only symbols, and even Speusippus agrees that believing in Plato's ideas is probably an illusion: "Ob nicht in diesem Allen viel Täuschung seyn könne, oder wirklich sey, kann ich selbst kaum bezweifeln" (36:278). Aristippus admits that readers as easy to please as Socrates' small audience in the *Republic* can accept such illusion. By comparing his utopia to a painter's canon, a useful if impossible ideal, Aristippus explains, Plato lends it a kind of fictional reality, "eine Art von hypothetischer Realität . . . , woran wenigstens alle die Leser sich genügen lassen können, die der magischen Täuschung eben so willig und zutraulich als die beiden Söhne Aristons entgegen kommen" (36:197). Critical of such hypotheses, Aristippus adds that Plato deceives us by having his Socrates feign ignorance, even if others cannot see his sleights of hand, "daß er uns *täuscht*, wenn gleich nicht jeder Zuschauer ihm scharf genug auf die Finger sehen kann, um gewahr zu werden wie es damit zugeht" (36:145–46). Plato's Socrates, he reveals, initially plays his role "bis zum Täuschen" (36:52), but then plainly speaks for his idealistic author, who does not always heighten the illusion that Socrates himself is talking, "die Täuschung der Leser, als ob sie hier den berüchtigten *Eiron* wirklich reden hörten" (36:89). Plato can impersonate Socrates well enough that one feels inclined to wink at this illusion, but it lasts only briefly, for Plato's own voice is clearly audible behind his narrative mask: "Hinter dieser Larve sieht er zuweilen . . . dem wahren Sokrates so ähnlich, daß man einige Augenblicke getäuscht wird: aber seine *Stimme* kann oder *will* er vielmehr nicht so sehr verstellen, daß die Täuschung lange dauern könnte" (36:122). Indeed, Plato destroys this illusion, and his Socrates is often no more convincing than the "Pseudo-Sokrates" (36:137) of Aristophanes' *Clouds*. Even when read as purely literary fiction, the *Republic* thus fails to satisfy Aristippus, unable to make him feel sufficient aesthetic illusion.

Plato's narrative failure to put himself fully in Socrates' shoes is also tied to the notion of physiognomy. As in *Peregrinus Proteus*, this pseudo-science connotes *Täuschung*, and it clarifies the literary aspect of the attitudes toward such illusion taken by Aristippus and Lais. At times, Aristippus writes, Plato removes the mask that he wears to play Socrates in the *Republic*, revealing his own physiognomy instead: "Dieser scheint sogar von Zeit zu Zeit die unbequeme Larve ganz wegzuschieben, und uns auf einmahl mit seiner eigenen, von jener so stark abstechenden Fysionomie zu überraschen" (36:122). Aristippus likewise has intellectual profiles in mind when insisting that even he resembles Socrates "im Ganzen der Fysionomie" (34:309), but he also observes Socrates' facial features, along with those of Diagoras, Antisthenes, and Aristophanes, whose physiognomies he finds suited to their professions. He even asks if something in his own face repels Socrates: "Oder ist ihm irgend ein Zug in meiner Fysionomie zuwider?" (33:194). Socrates' face looks crude compared to his character, however, which Aristippus calls superior precisely for differing so markedly from his irregular appearance. This example of physiognomic fallibility seems cited to refute Lavater, who tried hard to find something good to say about Socrates' ugliness. In any case, it contrasts with the trust that Lais places in faces. She not only possesses one that Aristippus finds charming; she also observes that of Socrates, who similarly praises hers, and comments on facial features of both her protégée Lasthenia and the love-sick Chariton. She is also attracted to Plato, whom Kleonidas calls "eine der geistvollsten Fysionomien" (35:40), and whom she thinks will be a lady-killer if his physiognomy is as spirited and beautiful as Speusippus likewise claims. Aristippus suggests curing this fascination with Plato by having Lais come see for herself the "Schönheit seiner Fysionomie" (35:132), but she later has a dream inspired by *Phaedo*, one in which she envisions winged heads having various physiognomies, then meets Arasambes and Amor, and which makes her fear Araspes' extreme passion. Reacting to real as well as fictional physiognomies, then, Lais seems far more likely than Aristippus to mistake appearance for reality.

Considering Plato's poorly masked narrative voice in the *Republic* not only reveals how literary fiction can lead to *Täuschung* in much the same way that physiognomy does; it also shows *Aristipp* to be an artful argument against Plato's censorship of literary mimesis. Like Lais's many illusions, this argument turns on the issue of fictionality. Aristippus simply dismisses the infamous attack on all mimetic arts in Book 10 of the *Republic*, where Plato defines them as mere imitation of objects that in turn are only particular examples of universal ideas. Aristippus calls this notion nonsense bordering on madness, though he does not always belittle such ideas. In remarks on Plato's diatribe against poets

in Books 2 and 3 of the *Republic*, he notes that artists are not as danger-
ous as Plato thinks, but he praises this episode as one of the best in the
book, and though he argues that Plato's moralistic theory of the arts
should not be used as a universal canon, he calls it a principle valid in
a utopia meant to be a model of justice and moral perfection. Like
Wieland's Diogenes, Aristippus acknowledges such principles, as long
as no one actually applies them. Since he thus both defends poetic
mimesis and accepts Plato's basic assumption, if just for the sake of ar-
gument, Aristippus's critique of Plato's narration shows a heightened
awareness of fictionality. Indeed, in Book 3, Plato discusses two kinds
of narration by "fabulists or poets," which he defines in terms of narra-
tive voice. One is "pure" and found in lyric poetry, where poets speak
for themselves, while the other is achieved either wholly by imitation,
as in tragedy and comedy, or in combination with the first, as in epic
poetry. Plato welcomes narrative mimicry of virtuous acts and words,
but thinks it wrong to impersonate unworthy characters, and requires
keeping all imitation to a minimum. By mentioning his narrative mask,
Aristippus thus puts Plato on par with actors, favoring the kind of nar-
ration that Plato finds least desirable and disregarding the limits that
he imposes on poetry. Indeed, this mask recalls the dramatic form of
the "mime," the source of the term "mimesis." Aristippus's criticism of
Plato's Socrates in terms of physiognomy and *Täuschung* thus reflects
fundamental disagreements about the role of mimesis and acceptable
limits of fictionality.

   Given how Aristippus analyzes the *Republic*, criticizing both Plato's
ideas and his narration as fictions, one might wonder whether *Aristipp*
itself meets his aesthetic criteria. Does Wieland's own narration, that is,
induce aesthetic *Täuschung* more successfully than Plato's? One cannot
answer this question for other readers, of course, but Wieland does
avoid the faults that Aristippus finds with Plato, directly expressing his
views on the fictionality of his story, for example, only in the notes that
follow each volume of *Aristipp*. By thus banning any narrator from the
foregoing letters, he makes his *Quellenfiktion* seem marginal, but he of-
ten mentions the issues raised in remarks on such fictional sources in
his other novels. He thinks it unnecessary to document all cases of
historical fact, "alles, was in diesem Werke *historisch wahr* ist" (33:358),
or to explain events seeming merely probable, "wo es auf bloße Wahr-
scheinlichkeit ankommt" (33:358). This latter remark admits the possi-
bility that *Aristipp* is simply fiction, which he confirms when noting
a certain inaccuracy: "Ich sehe also weder wie dieser Knoten, wofern
unsre Aristippische Briefsammlung ächt seyn sollte, aufgelöset, noch
wie der Urheber derselben, falls sie erdichtet ist, von dem Vorwurf

einer groben Unwissenheit oder Nachlässigkeit frey gesprochen wer-
den könnte" (33:372). To his playful profession of ignorance here,
Wieland adds the request that readers simply imagine things to be as
they are wrongly reported, that they turn a blind eye to historical accu-
racy, that is, just as when he explains that the Antipater mentioned by
Diogenes Laertius need not be the same man as his own, fictional one:
"Ob es eben derselbe ist, den wir aus diesen Briefen kennen lernen,
oder nicht, kann uns gleichgültig seyn, wenn der unsrige nur gekannt
zu werden verdient" (35:358). Even this justification of fiction is sur-
passed, though, by a note telling how the historical Kleombrotus killed
himself after reading *Phaedo*, apparently because he wanted to see
whether his soul too was immortal. Wieland finds the reason given in
Aristipp, Kleombrotus's shame after reading that he was absent at
Socrates' death, far more probable or verisimilar (*wahrscheinlich*), a cri-
terion he elsewhere cites to justify his story in general.[21] Wieland thus
reveals having invented an important episode about the effect of liter-
ary fiction itself.

The same may also be said of *Aristipp* as a whole. In the many ways
adduced here, it too concerns the aesthetics of fiction like itself, refining
the concept of *Täuschung* considered in Wieland's other late novels as
well. This aesthetic concern seems fitting insofar as *Aristipp* is fiction
named for a philosopher who thought sensations the only source of
certain knowledge. Its title character is accordingly less susceptible to
fantasies and fictions than the enthusiastic Lais, a difference shown by
their responses to visual and verbal art, by their reactions to fictional
characters and narrative physiognomies in Xenophon, Aristophanes,
and Plato. This is not to say that Aristippus simply speaks for Wie-
land himself. Not only does he draw aesthetic conclusions shown to
be wrong, interpreting Parrhasius's *Demos* as allegory and failing to
foresee the deadly effect of Aristophanes' *Clouds* during the trial of
Socrates; just as the historical Aristippus of Cyrene based his ethics on
subjective sensations but did not think that they conveyed knowledge
of things in themselves, Wieland's fictional one also avoids seeing any-
thing more than *aesthetic* illusion in such art only at the cost of feeling
neither the heights nor the humiliation known to Lais, who succumbs
to *Täuschung* less wisely. Indeed, it is she, not Aristippus, who goes
to the extremes of rapture and ridicule familiar from the sublime
Schwärmerei of Wieland's earlier heroes—Don Sylvio, Agathon, Da-
nischmend, Peregrinus, and even the Abderites. *She* is the quintessen-
tial, quixotic character found over and over in Wieland's novels, the
one who, much like its model in Cervantes, lives and dies according to
grand delusions inspired by fictional literature. By contrast, Aristippus

seems safe but sorry, a commentator whose refined consciousness of *Täuschung* keeps him from being moved as deeply. Conveying such serious reservations about its title character, such strong ambivalence about theoretical awareness of literary illusion, *Aristipp* may indeed be read as Wieland's last word on the wider subject of fictionality.

Conclusion

Die Kunst aufzuhören, zu fühlen, was genug *ist, und*
nicht ein Wort mehr *zu sagen, nicht einen Strich*
mehr *zu thun, als nöthig ist damit die abgezielte*
Wirkung erfolge . . . ist für den Dichter wie für den
Mahler (und warum nicht für jeden *Schriftsteller?)*
eine große und schwere Kunst!
—Wieland, "Die Kunst aufzuhören" (1775)

With the neat explanations of aesthetic illusion given by the jaded title
figure of *Aristipp*, Wieland conveys thoughts on the subject of fictional-
ity that seem far removed from the naive experience of literary imagi-
nation gained by the juvenile hero of *Don Sylvio*. Aristippus sounds
more like a hardened literary critic, that is, than a hopelessly quixotic
reader of fairy tales. As the tragic example of Lais proves, however,
Wieland never lost interest in such avid readers' *Schwärmerei*. In his in-
tervening novels, he examines their enthusiasm from many angles, ty-
ing it not only to illusion and imagination but also to social ideals. In
each, he thereby explores the pros and cons of fictionality, which he re-
gards as both a distinctive feature of his stories themselves and a dis-
tinguishing characteristic of the fanciful notions, moral laws, political
utopias, religious beliefs, and artistic concepts that they describe. This
broad understanding of fictionality is best defined in terms of various
current theories. Such terms provide a logical, literary, and linguistic
context for evaluating Wieland's indirect and less systematic study of
the traits, referents, and truths of fiction. Indeed, the theoretical frame-
work established by recent research helps show how his nine novels
cohere, since all are informed by his insights into the nature of fiction-
ality, literary and otherwise. Those novels show why we should take
fictions seriously, yet not literally; how to suspend disbelief without
also suspending our judgment. The purpose of this study has been
not only to read Wieland's novels in light of recent literary theory,
however, but also to show how knowing them enriches such theory
in turn. With his reflections on their narrators' attitudes and tech-
niques, their characters' minds and manners, and their readers' expec-
tations and responsibilities, they suggest that grasping the concept of
fictionality is essential not only to making sense of all fictional litera-
ture but also to leading a meaningful human life. In their revelations of

the psychological, epistemological, and ontological aspects of fictionality thus defined, they also seem proof that its significance can be gauged only by analyzing narrative practice in careful detail. Reading Wieland closely thus helps us understand the larger issues involved in all "self-conscious" "metafiction."

As noted in the introduction, the concept of fictionality is inseparable from the modern novel, a genre met with much resistance in eighteenth-century Germany. Current theorists have been more receptive, ready to consider many semantic and aesthetic aspects of such texts, most notably the distinction between fiction and nonfiction now drawn in narratology, speech-act theory, linguistics, and reader-reception aesthetics; the question of reference posed in possible-worlds semantics; and the issue of fictional truth raised with the aid of analytic philosophy as well as semiotics. These aspects suggest how widely the concept of fictionality can be applied, not only in interpretation of fictional literature but also in the wider sense of philosophical fictionalism. Wieland's novels treat that concept both ways, as being pertinent to both his prose and actual people's lives. He thereby changed the history of the German novel, which had been more advanced in theory than in practice, overcoming many religious, moral, and aesthetic objections and using lessons that he learned from Bodmer and Breitinger, among others, who redefined verisimilitude, mimesis, and the marvelous. While some previous studies of his work mention fictionality, few examine its treatment in his novels and none has shown its significance as a thread that runs through them all. It pervades them in ways suggested by three of his own essays. "Unterredung mit dem Pfarrer von ***" considers moral aspects of the imagination needed by readers as well as authors of fiction, distinguishing romances from fictional "history" à la Fielding and refuting the accusation of moral laxness, citing Hogarth's satirical drawings. "Über die Ideale der Griechischen Künstler" addresses similar questions of human nature and artistic ideals, taking a sober attitude toward the ancients and a favorable one toward all artists' imagination. "Versuch über das deutsche Singspiel" defines aesthetic illusion as the result of a tacit contract between the creators of opera and its audience, a collusion sometimes encouraged in eighteenth-century fiction as well. Current theories of fictionality can thus be connected to the history and poetics of the novel in Wieland's Germany.

Imagination is the issue tied to fictionality considered most closely in his two early novels. In both, his fictional characters, bogus editors, and implied readers all show it to be an ambiguous attribute, one that makes its possessor ridiculous as well as sublime. In *Don Sylvio*, this ambiguity afflicts a reader of fairy tales whose puerile fancies are re-placed by purer sentiment. His wild imagination hardly seems unnat-ural, though, and his literary urge is shared by other characters, whose long debate about the patently fantastic "Biribinker" relates his avid reading to notions of fiction discussed by early adherents of possible-worlds semantics and by Gottsched. Wieland diagnoses Don Sylvio's imagination instead of deriding it, just as some contemporaries came to regard Don Quixote as a sympathetic figure rather than a fool. His nar-rator respects literary imagination and readily uses it himself, asking readers of *Don Sylvio* to do the same, advice that its initial reviews confirm was sorely needed. *Agathon* addresses this same problem more earnestly, treating controlled imagination as the mark of moral ideals and credible novels alike. Its story is meant to teach virtue and wisdom, which prove to be at odds, and Wieland's attempt to reconcile them re-quired three different endings. His forewords both cite a fictional source and define narrative truth in terms of verisimilitude and "his-tory," also admitting less objective evidence as well as scruples about describing human nature accurately. Links to Euripides' *Ion* and to Plato's dialogue of that name hint that his frame of reference is simply intertextual, signs of a poetic conundrum likewise clear from his am-bivalence toward imagination, fictional "history," and his spurious source as he puts his narrative theory into practice. Pleasures of the imagination prove dangerous yet desirable, a contradiction that Aga-thon feels more consciously than Don Sylvio and that besets Wieland's "editor" as well, most blatantly in the final scenes of his successive ver-sions, which first show ironic detachment from his happy ending, then satisfaction with well-meant autobiography, and finally a new accep-tance of fictionality in both his own narration and Archytas's Kantian ethics. A moral-literary "as-if," *Agathon* stresses both halves of the term *Bildungsroman*.

Just as Wieland's two early novels regard imagination from recipro-cal points of view, his four middle ones all express strong concern with ideals, a second issue connected to fictionality in his essays. Each shows Wieland debating Rousseau, whose *social* ideals they link to the reading and writing of fiction presented according to *artistic* ones found in the visual arts. The cynical hero of *Diogenes* is ironic in his "Republik," a parody of Rousseau's designs for returning to nature, critical of putting such utopian notions into practice. Irony informs the story of his life too, a fiction in which painting implies civilized deca-dence but can also convey social ideals sincerely. By comparing literary and visual images, Wieland tries to transcend the irony crucial to "self-conscious" novels. A similar attempt is made in *Der goldne Spiegel*, which shows a royal audience averse to fiction but intrigued by a Rousseauean hero, yet unwilling to introduce corresponding reforms. Both the fake annals of "Scheschian" and their explicit reception betray shifting attitudes toward the fictionality that Wieland's medium and message have in common. His allusions to visual art similarly hint that novels and social ideals are related, useful fictions. Difficulties translating fiction into action also occur in *Danischmend*, which shows how instilling social ideals can be like abusing imagination for less salutary reasons. It too concerns "Kinder der Natur," Rousseauean innocents whose survival seems offset by irony in luxuriant footnotes but is illustrated in a sentimental tableau vivant. The manipulation inherent in Wieland's storytelling is also exposed to readers and thus rendered moot. The effects of other arts seem especially clear in *Die Abderiten*, where Rousseau's social contract is replaced by the aesthetic one described in Wieland's essay on the *Singspiel*. As political animals, the Abderites are ridiculous, but they rightly submit to illusion in the theater, thus setting an example for readers of Wieland's satire, which is fiction like Fielding's comic prose and art like Hogarth's caricatures, not just an attack ad hominem. With their reliance on the visual arts to suggest social ideals, Wieland's middle novels thus convey indirect, increasing acceptance of the concept of fictionality, broadly defined and applied.

The aesthetic illusion treated so humorously in *Die Abderiten* is taken seriously in his three late novels, where it is an issue related to fictionality, one that their protagonists accept to different degrees and that accordingly has differing implications for reading them. In *Peregrinus Proteus*, such *Täuschung* is fatal, for its title character never knows that his erotic and religious adventures so often deceive him because he fails to comprehend their aesthetic character. His *Schwärmerei* causes him both happiness and humiliation when he overreacts to poetry, painting, sculpture, and theater. He is likewise fooled by appearances when he misinterprets physiognomy and figurative language, but Wieland's narration nonetheless encourages readers to credit the fictional nature of this subtly romantic *Roman*. How to accept the truth of such fiction without having to believe everything one reads is a problem more elegantly solved in *Agathodämon*. Its Apollonius uses *Täuschung* to educate people like Peregrinus, exploiting their religious superstition to enlighten them, but he doubts such deception and believes in supernatural worlds better represented by Pythagorean music than by visual art or verbal language. Wieland's narration likewise avoids reifying its referent, Jesus, thus suggesting an illusion that conveys its own antidote thanks to a kind of romantic irony. Such reflections are most deliberate in *Aristipp*, which repeatedly analyzes aesthetic pleasures. While Aristippus is skeptical but willing to accept *Täuschung*, Lais succumbs to it, affected by literary characters and acting like them, too. The novel discusses such strong effects of verbal as well as visual art, above all in long passages on Plato's *Republic* that criticize Socrates as a fictional character who fails to induce sufficient illusion because Plato's narrative voice is poorly masked. Wieland himself avoids this narrative fault, thereby breaking Plato's rules limiting literary mimesis, though his Aristippus seems prosaic compared to Lais. Thus taking *Täuschung* to mean both *il*lusion and *de*lusion, in life as well as literature, Wieland's late novels display a heightened awareness of fictionality along with its underlying ambiguities.

It might seem surprising that such general aspects of fictionality are apparent in the novels of an author who once insisted that execution, not invention, was the better part of his art.[1] As recent theories cited above attest, however, raw originality is but one measure of fiction, which has to do with far more than just belles lettres. The others involve various definitions of fictionality, a concept now applied not only to literary texts, to "feigned" written narratives about imaginary facts, but also to "fiction" more broadly considered. Indeed, fictionality has been defined as a product of narrative style, a result of semantic convention, an attribute of fictional literature as well as its referents, and an attitude toward the larger realm of the fictive. In these senses, it pertains not only to aesthetic consciousness but also to pragmatic communication, being a matter of logical propositions as well as linguistic assumptions. While some of these criteria are regarded as fixed, moreover, given once and for all, others seem fluid, changing with historical mentalities. Although he seldom mentions it in such explicit, abstract terms, Wieland treats the notion of fictionality in these suggestive ways, as the foregoing conclusions about his novels show. His most telling contribution to current discussions of that notion may well lie in his observations on arts other than literature, where his discourse shifts from musings on common narrative concerns to comments on the visual arts, the theater, and music. Those observations extend the reach of fictionality even beyond the other representational arts, a step that recent theorists have only begun to take. *Diogenes* and *Agathodämon* might thus be Wieland's most notable efforts, since they show him turning his attention to painting and music as further paradigms for remarks on fictional literature. In any case, such shifts are signs of how subtly the concept of fictionality informs his novels, where its social, epistemological, and anthropological aspects may be summed up—as the title of this study and its preface imply— as "noble lies," "slant truths," and "necessary angels."

With their revealing emphasis on the concept of fictionality in all its complexity, then, Wieland's novels show and tell a great deal about defining fiction, knowing its referents, and accepting its truths. They do so in part because many of their characters—Don Sylvio, Danischmend, Peregrinus Proteus, and even Apollonius and the Abderites— resemble Don Quixote, readers of fiction too avid to be satisfied with actual life. Making one's way in the "real" world, moreover, seems to involve exploring and explaining the possible ones that they posit. By raising these fundamental literary concerns while remaining between the extremes of "romantic" fantasy and enlightened satire, Wieland urges us to grasp the concept of fictionality yet to take novels seriously—precisely because it pervades them. Learning this lesson is crucial to making sense of *Agathon*, for example, since the end of its final version seems less stilted and abrupt if read as a logical outcome of the thoughts on fictionality developed in Wieland's other novels. A further reason why he entertained those thoughts seems obvious in a report of a meeting that occurred when Napoleon passed through Weimar in 1808. The emperor supposedly asked Wieland why *Agathon*, *Diogenes*, and *Peregrinus Proteus* were written in such an equivocal genre, one that easily leads to confusion because it mixes romance with history. According to the Prince de Talleyrand, Wieland answered that he had wanted to teach humanity useful lessons, and therefore required the authority of history, while he mixed the ideal with the romanesque in order to make the examples that he cited agreeable and easy to follow. He preferred good novels to human nature, however, remarking that thoughts sometimes seem worthier than deeds: "Les pensées des hommes valent quelquefois mieux que leurs actions, et les bons romans valent mieux que le genre humain."[2] If true, this report confirms the comprehensive faith in fictionality professed in Wieland's several novels. Besides, even if false, it demonstrates the depth that he lends their proverbial lesson: *se non è vero, è ben trovato*.

Notes

Introduction

1. See Ihwe and Rieser, "Normative and Descriptive Theory of Fiction," 63–84; see also *Poetics* 11 (1982).
2. See Henrich and Iser, *Funktionen des Fiktiven*; see also Kanyó, *Fictionality*.
3. Doležel, "Truth and Authenticity in Narrative," 7.
4. Heintz, "Reference and Inference in Fiction," 90.
5. Hamburger, *Die Logik der Dichtung*, 73; Woods, *The Logic of Fiction*, 12.
6. Doležel, "Truth and Authenticity in Narrative," 7, 8.
7. See Ulrich Keller, *Fiktionalität als literaturwissenschaftliche Kategorie*.
8. Assmann, *Die Legitimität der Fiktion*, 196.
9. Spittler, "Was ist Fiktionalität?," 107; Lüthe, "Fiktionalität als konstitutives Element literarischer Rezeption," 1–15; Hoops, "Fiktionalität als pragmatische Kategorie," 297, 298, 316–17.
10. Höger, "Fiktionalität als Kriterium poetischer Texte," 266, 281.
11. Walton, *Mimesis as Make-Believe*, 43, 36, 205, 208. See also Margolin, "The Nature and Functioning of Fiction," 101–17.
12. See Pelc, "On Fictitious Entities and Fictional Texts," 1; Costa Lima, *The Dark Side of Reason*, 4–11.
13. Von Wilpert, *Sachwörterbuch der Literatur*, 298–99.
14. See Rösler, "Die Entdeckung der Fiktionalität in der Antike," 284–85.
15. Jauss, "Zur historischen Genese der Scheidung von Fiktion und Realität," 423–31; Heinzle, "Die Entdeckung der Fiktionalität," 55.
16. Kleinschmidt, "Die Wirklichkeit der Literatur," 174–97.
17. McKeon, *The Origins of the English Novel*, 63.
18. See Hasselbeck, *Illusion und Fiktion*.
19. Doležel, *Occidental Poetics*, 33–52.
20. Heimrich, *Fiktion und Fiktionsironie*, 138.
21. See Berthold, *Fiktion und Vieldeutigkeit*.
22. Waugh, *Metafiction*, 2. See also Scholes, *Fabulation and Metafiction*; Hutcheon, *Narcissistic Narrative*; Christensen, *The Meaning of Metafiction*.
23. Federman, "Surfiction," 7.
24. Fluck, "Fiction and Fictionality in Popular Culture," 58–59.
25. Rowe, "Metavideo," 231.
26. Tom Wolfe, quoted in Lodge, *The Art of Fiction*, 208.
27. Kontje, *Private Lives in the Public Sphere*, 8, 162.
28. Wolterstorff, *Works and Worlds of Art*, 112.
29. See Uphaus, preface to *The Idea of the Novel*, vii–viii.
30. Hollander, *Melodious Guile*, ix.
31. Kermode, *The Sense of an Ending*, 131, 133.

32. Ibid., 128.

33. Genette, "Fictional Narrative, Factual Narrative," 770; Cohn, "Signposts of Fictionality," 776.

34. Pavel, "Between History and Fiction"; Lützeler, "Fictionality in Historiography and the Novel"; and Ryan, "Fictionality, Historicity, and Textual Authority."

35. Cohn, "Signposts of Fictionality," 775.

36. Gale, "The Fictive Use of Language"; Coleman, "A Few Observations on Fictional Discourse."

37. Smith, *On the Margins of Discourse*, 29.

38. Pratt, *Toward a Speech Act Theory of Literary Discourse*, 96.

39. See Mooij, "Fictionality and the Speech Act Theory." For a critique of fictionality as defined by speech-act theory, see Walton, "Fiction, Fiction-Making, and Styles of Fictionality."

40. Wildekamp, von Montfoort, and Ruiswijk, "Fictionality and Convention," 555.

41. Schmidt, "Fictionality in Literary and Non-Literary Discourse," 528. See also Swiggart, "Fictionality and Language Meaning."

42. Stempel, "Alltagsfiktion."

43. Anderegg, "Das Fiktionale und das Ästhetische," 155; Anderegg, *Fiktion und Kommunikation*, 122, 125. See also Pätzold, "Wie steht es eigentlich um die Fiktionalität literarischer Texte?," 621.

44. Berthold, *Fiktion und Vieldeutigkeit*, 191–214.

45. Coste, "*Lector in figura*," 15.

46. See Brooks, "Fiction and Its Referents," 74.

47. Harshaw, "Fictionality and Fields of Reference," 237, 238.

48. Henrich and Iser, "Entfaltung der Problemlage," 10.

49. Kerbrat-Orecchioni, "Le statut référentiel des textes de fiction," 133.

50. Collett, "Literature, Criticism, and Factual Reporting," 283.

51. Doležel, "Mimesis and Possible Worlds," 481.

52. Ibid., 484; see also Doležel, *Occidental Poetics*, 33–52.

53. Pelc, "Some Thoughts on Fictitious Entities," 84; Bernáth and Csúri, "On the Relevance of Possible-Worlds Semantics for Literary Theory," 124; Ishiguro, "Contingent Truths and Possible Worlds."

54. Pavel, *Fictional Worlds*, 43, 80.

55. Ibid., 64, 84.

56. Riffaterre, *Fictional Truth*, xi, xv.

57. Ibid., 30.

58. Ibid., 63.

59. Norris, *Deconstruction*, 131.

60. Hamburger, *Wahrheit und ästhetische Wahrheit*, 99, 94.

61. Wimsatt and Brooks, *Literary Criticism*, 686; Fricke, "Semantics or Pragmatics of Fictionality?," 440.

62. Doležel, "Truth and Authenticity in Narrative," 11.

63. Vaihinger, *Die Philosophie des Als Ob*, 18.

64. Kermode, *The Sense of an Ending*, 40.

65. Iser, *Das Fiktive und das Imaginäre*, 16, 145–57.

66. Ibid., 36. An earlier version of Iser's introduction was published as "Akte des Fingierens oder Was ist das Fiktive am fiktionalen Text?"

67. Lamarque, "Narrative and Invention," 135.

68. Pelc, "On Fictitious Entities and Fictional Texts," 1.

69. Crittenden, *Unreality*, 173.

70. Van Abbé, *Christoph Martin Wieland*, 89.

71. Lessing, *Werke*, 555.

72. Von Blanckenburg, *Versuch über den Roman*, 257.

73. Emmel, "Roman," 491.

74. Anonymous, "Ueber den dramatischen Roman," 165.

75. Weber, *Die poetologische Selbstreflexion*, 70–73, 124; Voßkamp, *Romantheorie in Deutschland*, 143.

76. Heidegger, *Mythoscopia romantica*, 55.

77. Gundling, review of *Mythoscopia romantica*, by Gotthard Heidegger, 59.

78. Gottsched, review of *Die asiatische Banise*, by Heinrich Anshelm von Ziegler und Kliphausen, 71, 72.

79. Gottsched, *Versuch einer Critischen Dichtkunst*, 198.

80. Wieland to Bodmer, 6 March, 1752, *Wielands Briefwechsel*, 1 : 49.

81. Bodmer, *Critische Betrachtungen über die Poetischen Gemählde der Dichter*, 548.

82. Ibid., 549.

83. Breitinger, *Critische Dichtkunst*, 1 : 271.

84. See Sauder, "Argumente der Fiktionskritik," 136; Nobis, *Phantasie und Moralität*, 255.

85. Hinderer, "Christoph Martin Wieland," 277; see also Hinderer, "Wielands Beiträge zur deutschen Klassik," 53, 56.

86. Vietta, *Literarische Phantasie*, 2, 182.

87. Tschapke, *Anmutige Vernunft*, 50, 111.

88. See Anger, "Rokokodichtung," 485.

89. Nobis, *Phantasie und Moralität*, 253–54; Preisendanz, "Wieland und die Verserzählung des 18. Jahrhunderts," 31.

90. See Fietz, "Fiktionsbewußtsein und Romanstruktur," 115–131.

91. Michelsen, *Laurence Sterne und der deutsche Roman des achtzehnten Jahrhunderts*, 191, 200–201.

92. Brenner, *Die Krise der Selbstbehauptung*, 61, 130.

93. Stahl, *Das Wunderbare als Problem und Gegenstand der deutschen Poetik*, 223, 233.

94. Oettinger, *Phantasie und Erfahrung*, 31, 51–52; see also Bracht, *Der Leser im Roman des 18. Jahrhunderts*, 76.

95. Thomé, *Roman und Naturwissenschaft*, 118–19.

96. See Müller-Solger, *Der Dichtertraum*.

97. Lange, "Erzählformen im Roman des achtzehnten Jahrhunderts," 484; Marchand, "Wieland's Style and Narratology"; Norbert Miller, *Der empfindsame Erzähler*, 88; Kleinschmidt, "Zur Ästhetik der Leserrolle im deutschen Roman," 58; Jørgensen, "Warum und zu welchem Ende schreibt man eine Vorrede?," 8, 14.

98. See Kurth, *Die zweite Wirklichkeit*.

99. Vormweg, "Die Romane Chr. M. Wielands," 320.

100. Matthecka, "Die Romantheorie Wielands und seiner Vorläufer."

101. Jacobs, *Wielands Romane*, 42–46.

102. Jan-Dirk Müller, *Wielands späte Romane*.

103. McCarthy, *Fantasy and Reality*.

104. Rogan, *The Reader in the Novels of C. M. Wieland*.

105. McCarthy, *Fantasy and Reality*, 156.

106. Jan-Dirk Müller, *Wieland späte Romane*, 156–57.

107. Beddow, *The Fiction of Humanity*, 5.

108. Meessen, "Wieland's 'Briefe an einen jungen Dichter.'" For remarks on Wieland's lecture, see Gardiner and Schmitt, "Christoph Martin Wieland."

109. McCarthy, "The Poet as Journalist and Essayist," 108; see also McCarthy, "Klassisch lesen," 420.

110. Unless otherwise noted, Wieland's works are quoted from the so-called "wohlfeile Ausgabe" of *C. M. Wielands Sämmtliche Werke*, 45 volumes.

111. Huet, *Traité de l'origine des romans*, 224–25.

112. Bobertag, "Wielands Romane," 23.

113. Robertson, "The Beginning of the German Novel," 192.

114. Johann Heinrich Voß, "Michaelis, 1772."

115. Cf. Kayser, *The Grotesque in Art and Literature*, 30–32.

116. See Lavater, *Physiognomische Fragmente*, 3:40–47; for further remarks on Lavater, see Shookman, *The Faces of Physiognomy*.

117. Sengle, *Wieland*, 327; Müller-Solger, *Der Dichtertraum*, 217; cf. Schostack, "Wieland und Lavater," 50; Stoll, *Christoph Martin Wieland*, 164.

118. Voßkamp, *Romantheorie in Deutschland*, 122.

119. S.v. "Wieland, Christoph Martin," *New Grove Dictionary of Music and Musicians*; see also s.v. "Wieland, Christoph Martin," *Die Musik in Geschichte und Gegenwart*.

120. Köhler, "Musikhistorische Skizzen zur Weimarer Klassik," 293.

121. Lessing, *Werke*, 282.

122. Goethe, "Frauenrollen auf dem römischen Theater durch Männer gespielt" (1788) and "Über Wahrheit und Wahrscheinlichkeit der Kunstwerke" (1798), in *Goethes Werke*, 1. Abtheilung, vol. 47, p. 272 and pp. 255–66.

123. Schiller, *Werke*, 6.

124. Heimrich, *Fiktion und Fiktionsironie*, 17; Albrecht, "Die milde Humanität des Priesters der Musen," 767.

125. Pfeiffer, "Fiction," 102.

Chapter 1

1. Kurth, "W. E. N.—Der teutsche Don Quichotte," 129.

2. Van Abbé, *Christoph Martin Wieland*, 95.

3. Stahl, *Das Wunderbare als Problem und Gegenstand der deutschen Poetik*, 225, 233.

4. Jahn, "Zu Wielands 'Don Sylvio,'" 308, 317.

5. Martini, afterword to *Christoph Martin Wieland: Werke*, 1:923.

6. Schönert, *Roman und Satire im 18. Jahrhundert*, 135.

7. McCarthy, *Fantasy and Reality*, 51, 53.

8. Norbert Miller, *Der empfindsame Erzähler*, 96.

9. Heimrich, *Fiktion und Fiktionsironie*, 75–76; Kurth, *Die zweite Wirklichkeit*, 156; Meid, "Zum Roman der Aufklärung," 96; see also Jacobs, *Prosa der Aufklärung*, 164.

10. Apel, *Die Zaubergärten der Phantasie*, 84, 86.

11. Sengle, *Wieland*, 182.

12. Stockhammer, *Leseerzählungen*, 110; Bracht, *Der Leser im Roman*, 69; Tarot, "Wieland: *Geschichte des Prinzen Biribinker*," 62.

13. Stern, "Saint or Hypocrite?," 101.

14. Gottsched, *Critische Dichtkunst*, 199–200.

15. Hillmann, "Wunderbares in der Dichtung der Aufklärung," 102, 107.

16. Fink, *Naissance et apogée du conte merveilleux en Allemagne*, 142, 145, 149.

17. Klotz, *Das europäische Kunstmärchen*, 100.

18. Nobis, *Phantasie und Moralität*, 97; Apel, *Die Zaubergärten der Phantasie*, 87.

19. Tronskaja, *Die deutsche Prosasatire der Aufklärung*, 124–26, 129.

20. Brenner, "Kritische Form," 180–83.

21. Julie von Bondeli to Wieland, 21 June 1764, *Wielands Briefwechsel*, 3:281.

22. Wieland, *Der teutsche Merkur* (August 1773), 120; quoted in Prather, "C. M. Wieland's Narrators, Heroes and Readers," 64.

23. Gottsched, *Critische Dichtkunst*, 183.

24. Bodmer, *Critische Betrachtungen*, 531.

25. Quoted in Kayser, "Die Anfänge des modernen Romans," 428.

26. Lim, *Don Sylvio und Anselmus*, 64.

27. Berger, "Don Quixote in Deutschland," 50.

28. Meyer, *Der Sonderling in der deutschen Dichtung*, 38–39; Lange, "Zur Gestalt des Schwärmers," 160–61.

29. Frenzel, "Mißverstandene Lektüre," 130, 132–33.

30. Cf. Berthold, *Fiktion und Vieldeutigkeit*, 70.

31. Prather, "Wieland's Narrators," 64.

32. Leopold, "Wieland's *Don Sylvio von Rosalva*," 37; Jacobs, *Prosa der Aufklärung*, 161.

33. Otto Keller, *Wilhelm Heinses Entwicklung zur Humanität*, 30; Matthecka, "Die Romantheorie Wielands," 97, 103.

34. Kimpel, *Der Roman der Aufklärung*, 94; Moser-Verrey, *Dualité et continuité*, 9.

35. Preisendanz, "Die Auseinandersetzung mit dem Nachahmungsprinzip," 84, 85.

36. Wieland to Geßner, 20 and 21 October 1763; Wieland to Johann Georg Zimmermann, 8 March 1764, *Wielands Briefwechsel*, 3:197, 198; 3:252.

37. Wieland to Geßner, 7 November 1763, *Wielands Briefwechsel*, 3:207.

38. McCarthy, "Shaftesbury and Wieland," 91.

39. Jørgensen, "Der unverheiratete Held," 343.

40. Müller-Solger, *Der Dichtertraum*, 140.

41. Wieland, *Der Sieg der Natur über die Schwärmerey, oder die Abentheuer des Don Sylvio von Rosalva*, a2.

42. Wieland to Julie von Bondeli, 16 July 1764, *Wielands Briefwechsel*, 3:289–90.

43. Von Poser, *Der abschweifende Erzähler*, 70.

44. Schings, *Melancholie und Aufklärung*, 197.

45. Wedel, "Zum Motiv der Schwärmerei in Chr. M. Wielands *Don Sylvio*," 220.

46. Rogan, *The Reader in the Novels of C. M. Wieland*, 67, 68. See also Rogan, "The Reader in Wieland's *Die Abenteuer des Don Sylvio von Rosalva*," 192, 193.

47. Seiler, "Die Rolle des Lesers in Wielands *Don Sylvio von Rosalva* und *Agathon*," 160.

48. Kleinschmidt, "Zur Ästhetik der Leserrolle im deutschen Roman," 61, 58; Marx, *Erlesene Helden*, 72.

49. Schönert, *Roman und Satire*, 141; Schönert, "Der satirische Roman von Wieland bis Jean Paul," 210.

50. Wilson, *The Narrative Strategy of Wieland's Don Sylvio von Rosalva*, 10.

51. Ibid., 111, 135, 137, 128.

52. Review of *Don Sylvio*, *Göttingsche Anzeigen von Gelehrten Sachen*, 933.

53. Review of *Don Sylvio*, "*Journal Encyclopédique.*"

54. Review of *Don Sylvio*, *Erlangsche gelehrte Anmerkungen und Nachrichten*, 388.

55. Review of *Don Sylvio*, *Allgemeine deutsche Bibliothek* 1: 105–6.

56. "Avertissement de l'éditeur," 6–7.

57. Jørgensen, Jaumann, McCarthy, and Thomé, *Christoph Martin Wieland*, 137; Jens Voß, ". . . das Bißchen Gärtnerey," 94; Heinz, "Von der Schwärmerkur zur Gesprächstherapie," 43.

58. Brunkhorst, "Vermittlungsebenen im philosophischen Roman," 137.

59. Sagmo, "Über die ästhetische Erziehung des Eros," 194.

60. Kurth-Voigt, *Perspectives and Points of View*, 134.

61. Winter, *Dialog und Dialogroman in der Aufklärung*, 92, 103; Kurth-Voigt, *Perspectives and Points of View*, 130, 135.

62. Wilson, *The Narrative Strategy of Wieland's Don Sylvio*, 26, 39.

63. Ibid., 47, 114, 120.

64. Michelsen, *Laurence Sterne*, 198.

65. Gruber, *C. M. Wielands Leben*, 1:363.

66. Kermode, *The Sense of an Ending*, 131.

67. Wolterstorff, *Works and Worlds of Art*, 356.

68. See Haslinger, "'Dies Bildnisz ist bezaubernd schön,'" 128.

69. Jacobs, *Prosa der Aufklärung*, 163–64; Vietta, *Literarische Phantasie*, 189, 190.

70. Marx, *Erlesene Helden*, 81; Gay, *The Enlightenment*, 179.

Chapter 2

1. Opitz, *Krise des Romans?*, 19; Meid, "Zum Roman der Aufklärung," 108.

2. Johne, "Wieland und der antike Roman," 45; Kurth-Voigt, "Wielands 'Geschichte des Agathon': Zur journalistischen Rezeption des Romans," 15.

3. Beddow, *The Fiction of Humanity*, 47, 58–59.

4. George Moir, *Foreign Quarterly Review* 2 (1828):459, quoted in Kurth-Voigt, "Wielands 'Geschichte des Agathon': Zur journalistischen Rezeption des Romans in England," 91.

5. See Shookman, "Intertextuality, *Agathon*, and *Ion*."

6. Ibid., 210–13.

7. Buddecke, C. M. *Wielands Entwicklungsbegriff*, 217.

8. Frick, *Providenz und Kontingenz*, 2:388–89.

9. Gabriel, *Fiktion und Wahrheit*, 69.

10. Schindler-Hürlimann, *Wielands Menschenbild*, 33.

11. Jacobs, *Prosa der Aufklärung*, 168.

12. Klaus-Detlef Müller, *Autobiographie und Roman*, 102.

13. Ibid., 101, 104.

14. Beißner, afterword to *Chr. M. Wieland: Ausgewählte Werke in drei Bänden*, 2:909, 911–12.

15. Steven R. Miller, *Die Figur des Erzählers in Wielands Romanen*, 137, 143.

16. Jørgensen, Jaumann, McCarthy, and Thomé, *Christoph Martin Wieland*, 123; Heimrich, *Fiktion und Fiktionsironie*, 9; Schrader, *Mimesis und Poiesis*, 31; Frick, *Providenz und Kontingenz*, 2:396.

17. See Kurth, "Historiographie und historischer Roman," 357.

18. Wieland, "Von den Requisitiis zur Glaubwürdigkeit eines Geschichtschreibers und von den Kennzeichen der historischen Wahrheit," in *Wielands gesammelte Schriften*, Abteilung I, vol. 4, p. 631.

19. See Lucian, *Wie man Geschichte schreiben soll*.

20. Hahl, *Reflexion und Erzählung*, 9, 77.

21. Voßkamp, *Romantheorie in Deutschland*, 186–87, 189–90.

22. Preisendanz, "Die Auseinandersetzung mit dem Nachahmungsprinzip," 92.

23. Prather, "Wieland's Narrators," 68.

24. Oettinger, *Phantasie und Erfahrung*, 84, 75–76.

25. Becker, *Der deutsche Roman um 1780*, 6; cf. Hemmerich, *Christoph Martin Wielands "Geschichte des Agathon,"* 24.

26. Emrich, "Literatur und Geschichte," 132.

27. Sahmland, *Christoph Martin Wieland und die deutsche Nation*, 334–35.

28. Jørgensen, "Der unverheiratete Held," 345.

29. Gabriel, *Fiktion und wahrheit*, 67; Lim, *Don Sylvio und Anselmus*, 66.

30. Jakob Hermann Obereit to Johann Jakob Bodmer, 25 January 1763; Johann Georg Zimmermann to Albrecht von Haller, 31 May 1766; quoted in Starnes, *Christoph Martin Wieland*, 1:226, 292.

31. Moir, quoted in Kurth-Voigt, "Wielands 'Geschichte des Agathon': Zur journalistischen Rezeption des Romans in England," 91.

202 Notes to Pages 62–67

32. Kurth-Voigt, "Wielands 'Geschichte des Agathon': Zur journalistischen Rezeption des Romans."

33. Iselin, review of *Agathon*, 191.

34. Martini, afterword to *Christoph Martin Wieland: Werke*, 1:943; Gillespie, "Wielands 'Agathon' als Bildungsroman zwischen Barock und Romantik," 349.

35. Wölfel, "Daphnes Verwandlungen," 233, 247; Kowatzki, "Die Funktion des konstituierenden Bewußtseins," 149.

36. Von Mücke, *Virtue and the Veil of Illusion*, 232, 238, 263.

37. Vietta, *Literarische Phantasie*, 201, 209.

38. Schrader, *Mimesis und Poiesis*, 26–27; cf. Perez, "Personengestaltung bei Christoph Martin Wieland," 174.

39. Schrader, *Mimesis und Poiesis*, 152.

40. Wieland, *Geschichte des Agathon*, in *Christoph Martin Wieland: Werke*, 1:827.

41. Ibid., 831.

42. Ibid.

43. Cf. Berthold, *Fiktion und Vieldeutigkeit*, 185.

44. Wieland to Johann Georg Zimmermann, 5 January 1762, *Wielands Briefwechsel*, 3:60.

45. Klaus-Detlef Müller, *Autobiographie und Roman*, 106; Jacobs, "Die Theorie und ihr Exempel," 36.

46. Sengle, *Wieland*, 195; Niggl, *Geschichte der deutschen Autobiographie*, 44.

47. Norbert Ratz, *Der Identitätsroman*, 44; Schaefer, "Das Problem der sozialpolitischen Konzeption in Wielands 'Geschichte des Agathon,'" 186.

48. Martini, afterword to *Geschichte des Agathon*, 665, 668; Sengle, *Wieland*, 196.

49. Grimminger, "Wieland's 'Agathon,'" 694.

50. Erhart, *Entzweiung und Selbstaufklärung*, 163, 164.

51. Stanzel, *Theorie des Erzählens*, 111.

52. Johnson, "On Fiction," 326.

53. Paulsen, *Christoph Martin Wieland*, 186; Schindler-Hürlimann, *Wielands Menschenbild*, 157.

54. Jørgensen, Jaumann, McCarthy, and Thomé, *Christoph Martin Wieland*, 130, 131; Erhart, "'In guten Zeiten gibt es selten Schwärmer,'" 180; Manger, in Wieland, *Christoph Martin Wieland: Geschichte des Agathon*, 946.

55. Jens Voß, ". . . das Bißchen Gärtnerey," 199; Schaefer, "Chr. M. Wielands Beitrag zur Revolutionsdebatte," 326–27; Mayer, *Der deutsche Bildungsroman*, 38.

56. Böhm, "Wielands 'Geschichte des Agathon,'" 26.

57. Wilson, "'Prächt'ge Vase' oder 'halber Topf'?," 667–68.

58. Schaefer, "Der Schluss von Ch. M. Wielands 'Geschichte des Agathon,'" 55.

59. Erhart, *Entzweiung und Selbstaufklärung*, 172.

60. Klaus-Detlef Müller, "Der Zufall im Roman," 270; Thomé, *Roman und Naturwissenschaft*, 238.

61. Oettinger, *Phantasie und Erfahrung*, 30.

62. Wolffheim, *Wielands Begriff der Humanität*, 26, 27–28; Bock, *Die ästhetischen Anschauungen Wielands*, 8.

63. Gruber, *Wielands Leben*, 4:205, 210.

64. Wieland to Karl Leonhard Reinhold, 18 September 1793; Jens Baggesen to Reinhold, 22 March 1795; quoted in Starnes, *Christoph Martin Wieland*, 2:318, 411.

65. Groß, *C. M. Wielands "Geschichte des Agathon,"* 95; Mayer, *Der deutsche Bildungsroman*, 37.

66. Schlagenhaft, *Wielands Agathon*, 170–71; Hemmerich, *Wielands "Geschichte des Agathon,"* 29–30, 82.

67. Grimminger, "Wielands 'Agathon,'" 695; Reichert, "The Philosophy of Archytas," 17; Frick, *Providenz und Kontingenz*, 466–83, 484.

68. Vietta, *Literarische Phantasie*, 255.

69. See Shookman, "Fictionality and the Bildungsroman."

70. Gerhard, *Der deutsche Entwicklungsroman*, 101.

71. Paulsen, *Christoph Martin Wieland*, 184; Saariluoma, *Die Erzählstruktur des frühen deutschen Bildungsromans*, 177.

72. Jacobs, *Wilhelm Meister und seine Brüder*, 60.

73. Jacobs, "Die Theorie und ihr Exempel," 40–41; Jacobs, "Wieland und der Entwicklungsroman des 18. Jahrhunderts," 175; Jacobs and Krause, *Der deutsche Bildungsroman*, 56.

74. Mayer, "Die Begründung des Bildungsromans durch Wieland," 31; Rogan, *The Reader in the Novels of C. M. Wieland*, 70, 71; Röder, *Glück und glückliches Ende im deutschen Bildungsroman*, 51; Kleinschmidt, "Zur Ästhetik der Leserrolle im deutschen Roman," 59; M. H. Würzner, "Die Figur des Lesers in Wielands 'Geschichte des Agathon,'" 400, 406.

75. Beddow, *The Fiction of Humanity*, 24.

76. Ibid., 33; Swales, *The German Bildungsroman*, 49.

77. See, for example, Schings, "Agathon—Anton Reiser—Wilhelm Meister"; Glockhamer, "The Apprenticeship of a Hetaera"; Thomé, "Menschliche Natur und Allegorie sozialer Verhältnisse"; Ernst Keller, "Agathons pietistisches Erbe"; Stettner, *Das philosophische System Shaftesburys und Wielands Agathon*; Wolff, *Die Weltanschauung der deutschen Aufklärung*, 207–25; Gössl, *Materialismus und Nihilismus*.

Chapter 3

1. See Baumann, *Die bildende Kunst im deutschen Bildungsroman*, 39; Kurth-Voigt, "Die 'Tabula Cebetis' und 'Agathon.'"

2. See Athenaeus, *The Deipnosophists*; Diogenes Laertius, *Lives of the Eminent Philosophers*; Epictetus, *The Discourses as Reported by Arrian, the Manual, and Fragments*; Lucian, "The Life of Demonax."

3. See Comenius, *Diogenes the Cynic*; Dancourt, *Diogène fabuliste*.

4. Niehues-Pröbsting, *Der Kynismus des Diogenes*, 40, 58, 228.

5. See Seiffert, "Zu einigen Fragen der Wieland-Rezeption und Wieland-Forschung," 427.

6. See Sengle, *Wieland*, 226; Klein, *Wieland und Rousseau*, 26; McCarthy, *Christoph Martin Wieland*, 92; Süßenberger, *Rousseau im Urteil der deutschen Publizistik*, 235. For another source of Wieland's remarks on Rousseau, see his "Briefe an einen Freund über eine Anekdote aus J. J. Rousseaus geheimer Geschichte seines Lebens" (1780) in C. M. *Wielands Sämmtliche Werke*, 15: 167–251.

7. Mielke, "Wieland contra Swift und Rousseau—und Wezel," 22–23, 25.

8. Bracht, *Der Leser im Roman*, 74; Niehues-Pröbsting, "Wielands Diogenes und der Rameau Diderots," 81.

9. See Samuel, "Wieland als Gesellschaftskritiker," 49; Schönert, "Der satirische Roman von Wieland bis Jean Paul," 207.

10. See Langfelder, introduction to *Wieland: Die Dialogen des Diogenes von Sinope*, 14–17.

11. Martini, afterword to *Christoph Martin Wieland: Werke*, 2:851; Bäppler, *Der philosophische Wieland*, 41.

12. Mähl, "Die Republik des Diogenes," 69.

13. Ibid., 70; see Seiffert, "Die Idee der Aufklärung bei Christoph Martin Wieland," 686.

14. Wieland to Sophie von La Roche, 20 March 1770; Wieland to Johann Wilhelm Ludwig Gleim, 18 November 1770; Wieland to Johann Georg Jacobi, 20 March 1773, *Wielands Briefwechsel*, 4:112, 225, and 5:100.

15. Wieland to Rijklof Michael van Goens, 21 August 1769; Wieland to Johann Wilhelm Ludwig Gleim, 2 October 1769; Wieland to Sophie von La Roche, 31 January 1770, *Wielands Briefwechsel*, 4:18, 38, 80. For remarks on Wieland in Erfurt, see Schulze-Maizier, *Wieland in Erfurt*, and Schelle, "Zur Biographie des Erfurter Wieland."

16. Wieland to Sophie von La Roche, 17 February 1770, *Wielands Briefwechsel*, 4:92; see also Starnes, *Christoph Martin Wieland*, 2:453, 568, and 3:172.

17. Wieland to Damian Friedrich Dumeiz, 16 June 1770, *Wielands Briefwechsel*, 4:157.

18. See Bäppler, *Der philosophische Wieland*, 44; Michelsen, *Laurence Sterne*, 206.

19. See Michelsen, *Laurence Sterne*, 207, 211; Mager, "Wielands 'Nachlass des Diogenes von Sinope' und das englische Vorbild"; Behmer, *Laurence Sterne und C. M. Wieland*.

20. See Bäppler, *Der philosophische Wieland*, 49, 57.

21. Wilson, "Wieland's *Diogenes* and the Emancipation of the Critical Intellectual," 175.

22. See Sengle, *Wieland*, 226, 228; Martini, afterword to *Christoph Martin Wieland: Werke*, 2:843.

23. A mistaken allusion to classical mythology by Diogenes in this moment of anger has been cited to suggest that he is an unreliable narrator. See Kurth, "Unzuverlässige Sprecher und Erzähler in deutscher Dichtung."

24. Wilson, "Wieland's *Diogenes* and the Emancipation of the Critical Intellectual," 158–59.

25. Review of *Diogenes, Allgemeine deutsche Bibliothek*, 606, 602.

26. Ibid., 602, 605.

27. L. G. [?], review of *Diogenes*, 137; also in *Mannigfaltigkeiten: Eine gemeinnützige Wochenschrift*, 611–14.

28. Goethe to Philipp Erasmus Reich, 20 February 1770, *Goethes Werke*, 4. Abtheilung, vol. 1, p. 230.

29. Frederick the Great to Lord Georg Keith, 1 September 1762, quoted in Niehues-Pröbsting, *Der Kynismus des Diogenes*, 168.

Chapter 4

1. See Biesterfeld, *Die literarische Utopie*, 68; Schneider, "Staatsroman und Fürstenspiegel," 171; Aurich, *China im Spiegel der deutschen Literatur*, 134.

2. See Benjamin, "Christoph Martin Wieland," 487; Höhle, "Wieland und die verpönte Gattung des Staatsromans," 51.

3. Schings, "Der Staatsroman im Zeitalter der Aufklärung," 166; Bersier, *Wunschbild und Wirklichkeit*, 193; Naumann, *Politik und Moral*, 179, 189.

4. See Höhle, "Wieland und die verpönte Gattung des Staatsromans," 41; Biesterfeld, "The *Mirror of Princes* Turns Into a Novel," 925.

5. See Matthecka, "Die Romantheorie Wielands," 192–93, 196.

6. Hohendahl, "Zum Erzählproblem des utopischen Romans," 101; Dedner, *Topos, Ideal und Realitätspostulat*, 119 n. 17, 121.

7. Hohendahl, 114.

8. See Götz Müller, "Der verborgene Prinz," 77, 78; Götz Müller, *Gegenwelten*, 104–13; Hofmann La Torre, "Vision et construction," 101.

9. Jørgensen, "Vom Fürstenspiegel zum *Goldenen Spiegel*," 370; Spies, *Politische Kritik, psychologische Hermeneutik, ästhetischer Blick*, 108, 116.

10. Jørgensen, Jaumann, McCarthy, and Thomé, *Christoph Martin Wieland*, 89.

11. For remarks on Wieland's use of the term "edle Einfalt" prior to Winckelmann's, see Clark, "Christoph Martin Wieland and the Legacy of Greece," 43.

12. See Ketzer, "Einige Bemerkung zu Wielands Rousseau-Aneignung," 268, 270; Bersier, "The Education of the Prince," 5, 9.

13. See Walter, "'Keine Zeichen von guter Vorbedeutung,'" 38.

14. See Schings, "Der Staatsroman im Zeitalter der Aufklärung," 168; Bruford, *Culture and Society in Classical Weimar*, 23.

15. Kurth-Voigt, *Perspectives and Points of View*, 172; see Vormweg, "Die Romane Chr. M. Wielands," 124; Michel, *C.-M. Wieland*, 471.

16. Sengle, *Wieland*, 260; see Schönert, "Der satirische Roman von Wieland bis Jean Paul," 211–12; Jaumann, afterword, 882.

17. Fohrmann, "Utopie, Reflexion, Erzählung," 41; Jaumann, afterword, 872.

18. See Herchner, "Die Cyropädie in Wielands Werken," part 2, 18; see also

Vogt, *"Der goldene Spiegel" und Wielands politische Ansichten*, 22; Breucker, "Wielands 'Goldner Spiegel,'" 172.

19. Seuffert, "Wielands Berufung nach Weimar," 353.

20. Von Eichendorff, *Der deutsche Roman des achtzehnten Jahrhunderts*, 173.

21. Merck, review of *Der goldne Spiegel*, 568.

22. See Wilson, "Intellekt und Herrschaft," 479, 489.

23. See McNeely, "Historical Relativism in Wieland's Concept of the Ideal State," 275; Hans Würzner, "Christoph Martin Wieland," 67.

24. Wieland, "Der Herausgeber an den Leser," in *Wieland: Der goldne Spiegel*, 730.

25. Ibid., 731.

26. Wieland, *"Der goldene Spiegel, oder die Könige von Scheschian, eine wahre Geschichte, aus dem Scheschianischen übersetzt,"* in *Wieland: Der goldne Spiegel*, 734.

27. Starnes, *Christoph Martin Wieland*, 2:568–69, 698.

28. Crown Prince Karl August to Wieland, 23 July 1772, *Wielands Briefwechsel*, 4:582.

29. See Wieland's "Über die Behauptung, daß ungehemmte Ausbildung der menschlichen Gattung nachtheilig sey," an essay written 1770 and published along with his essays on Rousseau, and "Reise des Priesters Abulfauaris ins innere Afrika," and "Auszüge aus Jacob Forsters Reise um die Welt" (1778), in *C. M. Wielands Sämmtliche Werke*, 14:237–88; 15:1–28; and *Supplemente*, 5: 175–246.

30. Wieland to Johann Wilhelm Ludwig Gleim, 4 May 1772, *Wielands Briefwechsel*, 4:489.

31. Wieland to Sophie von La Roche, 22 June 1772, *Wielands Briefwechsel*, 4:545.

Chapter 5

1. See Jaumann, afterword to *Christoph Martin Wieland*, 887.

2. Jean Paul, *Vorschule der Aesthetik*, 127. See also Schillemeit, review of *Das Zitat in der Erzählkunst*, by Herman Meyer, 97–99.

3. Meyer, *Das Zitat in der Erzählkunst*, 92, 98, 100.

4. See Brenner, *Die Krise der Selbstbehauptung*, 191; see also Schönert, "Der satirische Roman von Wieland bis Jean Paul," 221.

5. Ibid.

6. See Matthecka, "Die Romantheorie Wielands," 198, 202; Jacobs, *Wielands Romane*, 38; Klein, "Wieland and Rousseau," 427, 130.

7. "Histoire de la belle Arouja," 219.

8. Cf. Stamm, "Wieland and Sceptical Rationalism," 25.

9. See Meyer, *Das Zitat in der Erzählkunst*, 104–5.

10. See Kausch, "Die Kunst der Grazie," 21.

11. Quoted in Wieland, *Christoph Martin Wieland: Der goldne Spiegel und andere politische Dichtungen*, 794.

Chapter 6

1. Manger, "Universitas Abderitica," 402.
2. See Kleinschmidt, "Die ungeliebte Stadt," 40; Klotz, *Die erzählte Stadt*, 67.
3. See Rotermund, "Massenwahn und ästhetische Therapeutik," 417; see also Weyergraf, *Der skeptische Bürger*, 72–73.
4. See Staiger, afterword to *Geschichte der Abderiten*, 322; see also Bohnert, "Der Weg vom Wort zur Tat," 552.
5. See Kleinschmidt, "Die ungeliebte Stadt," 43; see also Promies, *Der Bürger und der Narr*, 162.
6. See Edelstein, "Wielands 'Abderiten' und der deutsche Humanismus," 446, 452.
7. See Clark, "Wieland and Winckelmann," 2; Clark, "Wieland contra Winckelmann?," 8, 13; see also von Bülow, "Das historische Vorbild für Wielands Abdera," 99.
8. See Martini, "Wieland: 'Geschichte der Abderiten,'" 160; Elkhadem, *Sechs Essays über den deutschen Roman*, 16; Mauser, "Wielands 'Geschichte der Abderiten,'" 169.
9. See Martini, afterword to *Christoph Martin Wieland: Werke*, 2:871; Staiger, afterword to *Geschichte der Abderiten*, 323.
10. Jørgensen, Jaumann, McCarthy, and Thomé, *Christoph Martin Wieland*, 138.
11. See Bohnert, "Der Weg vom Wort zur Tat," 548.
12. See Schönert, "Der satirische Roman von Wieland bis Jean Paul," 217.
13. See Rudolph, "Einige Aspekte des Antike- und Zeitbezugs in Wielands Roman 'Geschichte der Abderiten'"; Rudolph, "Abderitismus und Aufklärung in Wielands Roman 'Geschichte der Abderiten,'" 222–23.
14. Mauser, "Wielands 'Geschichte der Abderiten,'" 172.
15. See Klotz, *Die erzählte Stadt*, 67; Kleinschmidt, "Die ungeliebte Stadt," 44.
16. See Matthecka, "Die Romantheorie Wielands," 215.
17. See ibid., 217; Dreger, *Wielands "Geschichte der Abderiten,"* 27, 32.
18. Rabener, "Vom Mißbrauche der Satire," 61.
19. Bayle, "Abdera," 14.
20. See Lucian, *Wie man Geschichte schreiben soll*, 95–97, 169.
21. See Schulze-Maizier, *Wieland in Erfurt*, 51–52.
22. See Knüfermann, "C. M. Wieland: Geschichte der Abderiten," 32, 36.
23. See Behmer, *Laurence Sterne*, 56.
24. Addison, "On the Pleasures of the Imagination," 542.
25. See Hogarth, *The Analysis of Beauty*.
26. Fielding, *Joseph Andrews*, 4–6.
27. Ibid., 168.
28. See Starnes, *Christoph Martin Wieland*, 1:627 and 2:410, 569, and 604; see also Sengle, *Wieland*, 338.
29. See Flaherty, *Opera in the Development of German Critical Thought*, 279; Mauser, "Wielands 'Geschichte der Abderiten,'" 167.

30. Bodmer, *Die Discourse der Mahlern*, 26.

31. *Der teutsche Merkur*, 1 January 1774, quoted in *Christoph Martin Wieland: Werke*, 2:729.

32. Thomsen, *Das Groteske im englischen Roman des 18. Jahrhunderts*, 33 n. 65; see also Kayser, *The Grotesque in Art and Literature*, 67.

33. *Der teutsche Merkur*, 1 January 1774, quoted in *Christoph Martin Wieland: Werke*, 2:729.

34. Ibid., 1 July 1774, quoted in *Christoph Martin Wieland: Werke*, 2:734.

35. "Auszug aus einem Schreiben an einen Freund in D*** über die Abderiten," *Der teutsche Merkur*, September 1778, quoted in *Christoph Martin Wieland: Werke*, 2:743.

36. Ibid., 744.

37. Ibid., 743.

38. *Der teutsche Merkur*, 1 January 1774, quoted in *Christoph Martin Wieland: Werke*, 2:729.

39. "Auszug aus einem Schreiben an einen Freund in D*** über die Abderiten," 744.

40. See Hermann, *Wielands Abderiten und die Mannheimer Theaterverhältnisse*; see also Manger, "Universitas Abderitica," 400.

41. See Pröhle, introduction to *Geschichte der Abderiten*, ii; see also Fuchs, *Geistiger Gehalt und Quellenfrage in Wielands Abderiten*, 16; Hermann, 23.

42. Sterne, *A Sentimental Journey*, 34.

43. See Fuchs, *Geistiger Gehalt und Quellenfrage in Wielands Abderiten*, 2, 11; see also Flaherty, *Opera in the Development of German Critical Thought*, 269, 276.

44. Yuill, "Abderitis and Abderitism," 84, 86.

45. See Mauser, "Wielands 'Geschichte der Abderiten,'" 170; Dreger, *Wielands "Geschichte der Abderiten,"* 27; von Poser, *Der abschweifende Erzähler*, 79.

46. Bracht, *Der Leser im Roman*, 83–84.

47. See McCarthy, *Christoph Martin Wieland*, 125; Schönert, "Der satirische Roman," 218.

48. See Manger, "Universitas Abderitica," 401.

49. See von Wilpert, *Der verlorene Schatten*, 8; Cases, *Stichworte zur deutschen Literatur*, 253–76; see also Whiton, "Sacrifice and Society in Wieland's Abderiten," 221, 228; Bohm, "Ancients and Moderns in Wieland's 'Proceß um des Esels Schatten,'" 659.

50. Fielding, *Joseph Andrews*, 7.

51. Ibid., 4.

Chapter 7

1. See Rutledge, *The Dialogue of the Dead*; see also Weinreich, *Der Trug des Nektanebos*, 87.

2. See Raab, "Studien zu Wielands Romane 'Peregrinus Proteus,'" 13–14, 30.

3. See Starnes, *Christoph Martin Wieland*, 2:256, 404, and 521.

4. See Sengle, *Wieland*, 482; Starnes, review of *Fantasy and Reality*, by John McCarthy, 280; Mickel, "Peregrinus Proteus oder die Nachtseite der Pädagogischen Revolution," 835; Schostack, "Wieland und Lavater," 116–29.

5. See Thorand, "Zwischen Ideal und Wirklichkeit," 91–93, and Höhle, "Die Auseinandersetzung mit der Großen Französischen Revolution," 7–9.

6. Braunsperger, *Aufklärung aus der Antike*, 241.

7. Voges, *Aufklärung und Geheimnis*, 420, 445.

8. See Mickel, "Peregrinus Proteus," 826.

9. See Immerwahr, "'Romantic' and Its Cognates," 56, 60; see also Kistler, "Dionysian Elements in Wieland," 83, 85–86.

10. See Sengle, *Wieland*, 472, 479–80; see also Viering, *Schwärmerische Erwartung*, 10, 289.

11. See Matthecka, "Die Romantheorie Wielands," 222, 227.

12. See Jan-Dirk Müller, *Wielands späte Romane*, 136, 33, 44, 182.

13. McCarthy, *Fantasy and Reality*, 112, 154.

14. Strauss, "Wieland's Late Novel *Peregrinus Proteus*," 51–52.

15. Voges, *Aufklärung und Geheimnis*, 416.

16. Ibid., 436.

17. Viering, *Schwärmerische Erwartung*, 95, 96.

18. Cf. Sträßner, *Tanzmeister und Dichter*, 160.

19. See Schostack, "Wieland und Lavater," 123.

20. Wieland, "Ueber die Glaubwürdigkeit Lucians in seinen Nachrichten vom Peregrinus," 93, 107.

Chapter 8

1. See Copleston, *A History of Philosophy*, 190–94.

2. Starnes, *Christoph Martin Wieland*, 2:707, 3:49.

3. See Martini, afterword to *Christoph Martin Wieland: Werke*, 2:883; see also Hans Würzner, "Christoph Martin Wieland," 125, 130.

4. Thomé, "Religion und Aufklärung in Wielands *Agathodämon*," 118, 120.

5. Ihlenburg, "Wielands Agathodämon," 19, 36, 65.

6. Jan-Dirk Müller, *Wielands späte Romane*, 15, 175.

7. Voges, *Aufklärung und Geheimnis*, 452, 455.

8. See Albrecht, "'Agathodämon,'" 107, 102.

9. See Teesing, "Wielands Verhältnis zur Aufklärung im *Agathodämon*," 24, 30, 31.

10. Voges, *Aufklärung und Geheimnis*, 471; Thomé, "Religion und Aufklärung in Wielands *Agathodämon*," 95, 120.

11. Martini, afterword to *Christoph Martin Wieland: Werke*, 2:876, 877, 878.

12. Beißner, afterword to *Chr. M. Wieland*, 3:855; Sengle, *Wieland*, 488.

13. Albrecht, "'Agathodämon,'" 119; Albrecht, "Wielands 'Agathodämon,'" 602.

14. Mellinger, "Wielands Auffassung vom Urchristentum," 51–52.

15. Thomé, "Religion und Aufklärung in Wielands *Agathodämon*," 93–94; Albrecht, "'Agathodämon,'" 118.

16. Matthecka, "Die Romantheorie Wielands," 235; Jan-Dirk Müller, *Wielands späte Romane*, 177.

17. Voges, *Aufklärung und Geheimnis*, 465, 466.

18. Ibid., 466.

19. Ibid., 471.

20. Quoted in Beißner, afterword to *Chr. M. Wieland*, 3:856.

21. See Philostratus, *Apollonius von Tyana*, 388–89; Philostratus, *The Life of Apollonius of Tyana* 1:xii.

22. Lüderwald, *Anti-Hierocles*, 35, 129, 158.

23. Mellinger,"Wielands Auffassung vom Urchristentum," 11, 55.

24. Ihlenburg, "Wielands Agathodämon," 103; Martini, afterword to *Christoph Martin Wieland: Werke*, 2:887.

25. Hecker, *Wieland*, 164–65.

26. Sengle, *Wieland*, 486; Beißner, afterword to *Chr. m. Wieland*, 3:856, 858. The translation noted by Beißner is Johann Lorenz Mosheim's *Systema Intellectuale hujus Universi* (1733).

27. Dinkel, "Herder und Wieland," 86; cf. Alfred E. Ratz, "C. M. Wieland: Toleranz, Kompromiß und Inkonsequenz," 503.

28. See Albrecht, "'Agathodämon,'" 110–11; Kistler, "Dionysian Elements," 88–90; Spitzer, *Classical and Christian Ideas of World Harmony*, 10–11.

Chapter 9

1. See Pröhle, introduction to *Aristipp*, 33; Paulsen, *Wielands Aristipp als Roman*, 25.

2. See Paulsen, "Die emanzipierte Frau in Wielands Weltbild," 165; Phelan, "Ironic Lovers," 105–6.

3. See Beutin, *"Als eine Frau lesen lernte,"* 72–73, 87; Dufner, "The Tragedy of Lais," 64.

4. Wieland to Johann Gottfried Gruber, 25 February 1799, and to Georg Joachim Göschen, 14 December 1799, quoted in Jan-Dirk Müller, *Wielands späte Romane*, 9; Schiller to Christian Gottfried Körner, 5 January 1801, quoted in Jan-Dirk Müller, *Wielands späte Romane*, 8.

5. Pröhle, introduction to *Aristipp*, 30, 33; Sengle, *Wieland*, 502, 507.

6. Sinnwell, "Wielands 'Liebling,'" 99.

7. Pröhle, introduction to *Aristipp*, 25; Sinnwell, "Wielands 'Liebling,'" 107, 103.

8. Kind, "Christoph Martin Wieland und die Entstehung des historischen Romans in Deutschland," 165; Mewes, "'Man sieht den Wald vor lauter Bäumen nicht,'" 131.

9. Höhle, "Revolution, Bürgerkrieg und neue Verfassung in Cyrene," 601, 599, 603.

10. Mewes, "Wielands 'Aristipp,'" 44.

11. Voss, "Erzählprobleme des Briefromans," 262; Jan-Dirk Müller, *Wielands späte Romane*, 26; Neuhaus, *Typen multiperspektivischen Erzählens*, 69–70; Emmel, "Formprobleme des Romans," 268.

12. Barthel, *Das "Gespräch" bei Wieland*, 122, 63; Albrecht, "Die milde Humanität des Priesters der Musen," 760.

13. Jan-Dirk Müller, *Wielands späte Romane*, 100; Matthecka, "Die Romantheorie Wielands," 248.

14. Mewes, "'Man sieht den Wald vor lauter Bäumen nicht,'" 132, 133.

15. Thomé, "'Utopische Diskurse,'" 505, 508, 515.

16. Manger, *Klassizismus und Aufklärung*, 45, 35, 72; see also Manger, "Wielands klassizistische Poetik," 331, 345, 353.

17. Matthecka, "Die Romantheorie Wielands," 244; Gerke, "Wielands 'Aristipp,'" quoted in Mewes, "Wielands 'Aristipp,'" 30; Sengle, *Wieland*, 506; Reemtsma, *Das Buch vom Ich*, 133–34, 153, 156.

18. Sengle, *Wieland*, 506, 503.

19. Albrecht, "Die milde Humanität des Priesters der Musen," 767–68; Jan-Dirk Müller, *Wielands späte Romane*, 191, 193, 194.

20. Manger, *Klassizismus und Aufklärung*, 76–77; Manger, "Wieland und Raffael," 34–36.

21. Starnes, *Christoph Martin Wieland*, 2:758.

Conclusion

1. Wieland to Carl August Böttiger, 17 January 1800, quoted in Starnes, *Christoph Martin Wieland*, 3:3.

2. Charles Maurice de Talleyrand-Périgord, *Mémoires*, quoted in Starnes, *Christoph Martin Wieland*, 3:303–4.

Bibliography

Abbé, Derek Maurice van. *Christoph Martin Wieland (1733–1813): A Literary Biography.* London: Harrap, 1961.

Abbt, Thomas. Review of *Don Sylvio. Allgemeine deutsche Bibliothek* 1 (1765): 97–107.

Addison, Joseph. "On the Pleasures of the Imagination." *The Spectator,* no. 412 (23 June 1712). Quoted in *The Spectator,* ed. Donald F. Bond, vol. 3, 540–44. Oxford: Clarendon Press, 1965.

Albrecht, Wolfgang. "Die milde Humanität des Priesters der Musen: Wielands Dichtungsverständnis und seine Auffassung vom Dichterberuf nach 1780." *Weimarer Beiträge* 30 (1984): 753–76.

———. "Wielands 'Agathodämon': Wege der Aufklärung im Glauben an Humanität und Fortschritt." *Weimarer Beiträge* 33 (1987): 599–615.

———. "'Agathodämon'—Bilanz und Credo eines Aufklärers." In Höhle, *Das Spätwerk Christoph Martin Wielands,* 101–24.

Anderegg, Johannes. *Fiktion und Kommunikation: Ein Beitrag zur Theorie der Prosa.* Göttingen: Vandenhoeck & Ruprecht, 1973.

———. "Das Fiktionale und das Ästhetische." In Henrich and Iser, 154–72.

Anger, Alfred. "Rokokodichtung." *Reallexikon der deutschen Literaturgeschichte.* 2d ed. Vol. 3, 480–90.

Apel, Friedmar. *Die Zaubergärten der Phantasie: Zur Theorie und Geschichte des Kunstmärchens.* Heidelberg: Winter, 1978.

Assmann, Aleida. *Die Legitimität der Fiktion: Ein Beitrag zur Geschichte der literarischen Kommunikation.* Munich: Fink, 1980.

Athenaeus. *The Deipnosophists.* Trans. Charles Burton Gulick. Cambridge: Harvard University Press, 1941.

Aurich, Ursula. *China im Spiegel der deutschen Literatur des 18. Jahrhunderts.* Berlin: Ebering, 1935.

"Avertissement de l'éditeur." In *Le cabinet des fées,* 36: 5–10.

Bäppler, Klaus. *Der philosophische Wieland: Stufen und Prägungen seines Denkens.* Bern: Francke, 1974.

Barthel, Marga. *Das "Gespräch" bei Wieland: Untersuchungen über Wesen und Form seiner Dichtung.* Frankfurt am Main: Diesterweg, 1939.

Baumann, Hanny Elisabeth. *Die bildende Kunst im deutschen Bildungsroman.* Turbenthal: Rob. Furrers Erben, 1933.

Bayle, Pierre. "Abdera." In *Herrn Peter Baylens . . . Historisches und critisches Wörterbuch.* Ed. Johann Christoph Gottsched. Vol. 1, 14. Leipzig: Breitkopf, 1741–44.

Becker, Eva D. *Der deutsche Roman um 1780.* Stuttgart: Metzler, 1964.

Beddow, Michael. *The Fiction of Humanity: Studies in the Bildungsroman from Wieland to Thomas Mann.* Cambridge: Cambridge University Press, 1982.

Behmer, Carl August. *Laurence Sterne und C. M. Wieland*. Munich: Haushalter, 1899; Hildesheim: Gerstenberg, 1976.

Beißner, Friedrich. Afterwords to *Chr. M. Wieland: Ausgewählte Werke in drei Bänden*. Ed. Friedrich Beißner. 3 vols. Munich: Winkler, 1964–65.

Benjamin, Walter. "Christoph Martin Wieland: Zum zweihundertsten Jahrestag seiner Geburt." In *Angelus Novus: Ausgewählte Schriften 2*, 482–93. Frankfurt am Main: Suhrkamp, 1966.

Berger, Tjard W. "Don Quixote in Deutschland und sein Einfluss auf den deutschen Roman: 1613–1800." Diss., Heidelberg, 1908.

Bernáth, A., and K. Csúri. "On the Relevance of Possible-Worlds Semantics for Literary Theory." In Kanyó, 115–39.

Bersier, Gabrielle. *Wunschbild und Wirklichkeit: Deutsche Utopien im 18. Jahrhundert*. Heidelberg: Winter, 1981.

———. "The Education of the Prince: Wieland and German Enlightenment at School with Fénelon and Rousseau." *Eighteenth-Century Life*, n.s., 10 (January 1986): 1–13.

Berthold, Christian. *Fiktion und Vieldeutigkeit: Zur Entstehung moderner Kulturtechniken des Lesens im 18. Jahrhundert*. Tübingen: Niemeyer, 1993.

Beutin, Heidi. *"Als eine Frau lesen lernte, trat die Frauenfrage in die Welt"*. Hamburg: Bormann & von Bockel, 1990.

Biesterfeld, Wolfgang. *Die literarische Utopie*. 2d ed. Stuttgart: Metzler, 1982.

———. "The *Mirror of Princes* Turns Into a Novel: Fictional Literature as a Vehicle for Political Ideas in the Eighteenth Century." *Studies on Voltaire and the Eighteenth Century* 264 (1989): 923–26.

Blanckenburg, Friedrich von. *Versuch über den Roman*. 1774. Stuttgart: Metzler, 1965.

Bobertag, Felix. "Wielands Romane: Ein Beitrag zur Geschichte und Theorie der Dichtung." In *Realschule erster Ordnung zum heiligen Geist in Breslau: Jahres-Bericht über das Schuljahr 1870/71*, 1–25.

Bock, Werner. *Die ästhetischen Anschauungen Wielands*. Berlin: Fleischel, 1921.

Bodmer, Johann Jacob. *Die Discourse der Mahlern, Zwanzigster Diskurs des ersten Theils* (1721). Quoted in *Meisterwerke deutscher Literaturkritik*, ed. Hans Mayer, 21–26. Berlin: Rütten & Loening, 1956.

———. *Critische Betrachtungen über die Poetischen Gemählde der Dichter*. Zurich: Orell, 1741.

Bohm, Arnd. "Ancients and Moderns in Wieland's 'Proceß um des Esels Schatten.'" *Modern Language Notes* 103 (1988): 652–61.

Böhm, Hans. "Wielands 'Geschichte des Agathon,' dritte Fassung, 1794: Zum Menschenbild in der Spätaufklärung." In Höhle, *Das Spätwerk Christoph Martin Wielands*, 20–28.

Bohnert, Christiane. "Der Weg vom Wort zur Tat: Maßstab und Wirklichkeitsbezug der Satire 1774–1792." *German Quarterly* 60 (1987): 548–66.

Bracht, Edgar. *Der Leser im Roman des 18. Jahrhunderts*. Frankfurt am Main: Lang, 1987.

Braunsperger, Gerhard. *Aufklärung aus der Antike: Wielands Lukianrezeption in seinem Roman "Die geheime Geschichte des Philosophen Peregrinus Proteus."* Frankfurt am Main: Lang, 1993.

Breitinger, Johann Jacob. *Critische Dichtkunst.* 2 vols. Zurich: Orell, 1740; Stuttgart: Metzler, 1966.

Brenner, Peter J. "Kritische Form: Zur Dialektik der Aufklärung in Wielands Roman 'Don Sylvio von Rosalva.'" *Jahrbuch der deutschen Schillergesellschaft* 20 (1976): 162–83.

———. *Die Krise der Selbstbehauptung: Subjekt und Wirklichkeit im Roman der Aufklärung.* Tübingen: Niemeyer, 1981.

Breucker, Gustav. "Wielands 'Goldner Spiegel.'" *Preußische Jahrbücher* 22 (1888): 149–74.

Brooks, Peter. "Fiction and Its Referents: A Reappraisal." *Poetics Today* 4 (1983): 73–75.

Bruford, W. H. *Culture and Society in Classical Weimar.* Cambridge: Cambridge University Press, 1962.

Brunkhorst, Martin. "Vermittlungsebenen im philosophischen Roman: *Candide, Rasselas* und *Don Sylvio.*" *Arcadia* 14 (1979): 133–47.

Buddecke, Wolfram. *C. M. Wielands Entwicklungsbegriff und die Geschichte des Agathon.* Göttingen: Vandenhoeck & Ruprecht, 1966.

Bülow, Gerda von. "Das historische Vorbild für Wielands Abdera." In Kunze, 95–99.

Cases, Cesare. *Stichworte zur deutschen Literatur.* Trans. Friedrich Kollmann. Vienna: Europa Verlag, 1969.

Christensen, Inger. *The Meaning of Metafiction: A Critical Study of Selected Novels by Sterne, Nabokov, Barth and Beckett.* Bergen: Universitetsforlaget, 1981.

Clark, William H. "Christoph Martin Wieland and the Legacy of Greece: Aspects of His Relation to Greek Culture." Diss., Columbia, 1954.

———. "Wieland and Winckelmann: Saul and the Prophet." *Modern Language Quarterly* 17 (1956): 1–16.

———. "Wieland contra Winckelmann?" *Germanic Review* 34 (1959): 4–13.

Cohn, Dorrit. "Signposts of Fictionality: A Narratological Perspective." *Poetics Today* 11 (1990): 775–804.

Coleman, Francis X. J. "A Few Observations on Fictional Discourse." In *Language and Aesthetics: Contributions to the Philosophy of Art,* ed. Benjamin R. Tilghman, 31–42. Lawrence: University Press of Kansas, 1973.

Collett, Alan. "Literature, Criticism, and Factual Reporting." *Philosophy and Literature* 13 (October 1989): 282–96.

Comenius, Jan Amos. *Diogenes the Cynic, Back from the Grave.* Trans. Michael C. Mittelstadt. New York: Czechoslovak Society of Arts and Sciences in America, c. 1970.

Copleston, Frederick. *A History of Philosophy.* Vol. 1, *Greece & Rome,* part 2. New York: Image Books, 1962.

Costa Lima, Luiz. *The Dark Side of Reason: Fictionality and Power.* Trans. Paulo Henriques Britto. Stanford: Stanford University Press, 1992.

Coste, Didier. "*Lector in figura*: Fictionalité et rhétorique générale." In *Lectures, systèmes de lecture*, ed. Jean Bessière, 13–26. Paris: Presses Universitaires de France, 1984.

Crittenden, Charles. *Unreality: The Metaphysics of Fictional Objects*. Ithaca: Cornell University Press, 1991.

Dancourt, L. H. *Diogène fabuliste, comédie-épisodique en un acte et en vers*. Paris: Cailleau, 1783.

Dedner, Burghard. *Topos, Ideal und Realitätspostulat: Studien zur Darstellung des Landlebens im Roman des 18. Jahrhunderts*. Tübingen: Niemeyer, 1969.

Dinkel, Herbert. "Herder und Wieland." Diss., Munich, 1959.

Diogenes Laertius, *Lives of the Eminent Philosophers*. Trans. R. D. Hicks. London: Heinemann, 1931.

Doležel, Lubomír. "Truth and Authenticity in Narrative." *Poetics Today* 1 (1980): 7–25.

———. "Mimesis and Possible Worlds." *Poetics Today* 9 (1988): 475–96.

———. *Occidental Poetics: Tradition and Progress*. Lincoln: University of Nebraska Press, 1990.

Dreger, Johannes-Heinrich. *Wielands "Geschichte der Abderiten": Eine historisch-kritische Untersuchung*. Göppingen: Kümmerle, 1973.

Dufner, Max. "The Tragedy of Lais in C. M. Wieland's 'Aristipp.'" *Monatshefte* 50 (1960): 63–70.

Edelstein, Ludwig. "Wielands 'Abderiten' und der deutsche Humanismus." *University of California Publications in Modern Philology* 26 (1950): 441–72.

Eichendorff, Joseph von. *Der deutsche Roman des achtzehnten Jahrhunderts in seinem Verhältnis zum Christenthum*. Leipzig: Brockhaus, 1851.

Elkhadem, Saad. *Sechs Essays über den deutschen Roman*. Bern: Lang, 1969.

Emmel, Hildegard. "Zur Gestalt von Wielands spätem Roman 'Aristipp.'" In Schelle, *Christoph Martin Wieland*, 109–16. First published as "Formprobleme des Romans im Spätwerk Wielands und Goethes" in *Stil- und Formprobleme in der Literatur*, ed. Paul Böckmann, 267–72. Heidelberg: Winter, 1959.

———. "Roman." *Reallexikon der deutschen Literaturgeschichte*. 2d ed. Vol. 3, 490–519.

Emrich, Berthold. "Literatur und Geschichte." *Reallexikon der deutschen Literaturgeschichte*. 2d ed. Vol. 2, 111–43.

Epictetus. *The Discourses as reported by Arrian, the Manual, and Fragments*. Trans. W. A. Oldfather. London: Heinemann, 1926.

Erhart, Walter. *Entzweiung und Selbstaufklärung: Christoph Martin Wielands "Agathon"-Projekt*. Tübingen: Niemeyer, 1991.

———. "'In guten Zeiten gibt es selten Schwärmer': Wielands 'Agathon' und Hölderlins 'Hyperion.'" *Hölderlin-Jahrbuch* 28 (1992–93): 173–91.

Federman, Raymond. "Surfiction—Four Propositions in Form of an Introduction." In *Surfiction: Fiction Now . . . and Tomorrow*, ed. Raymond Federman, 5–15. Chicago: Swallow Press, 1975.

Fehn, Ann, Ingeborg Hoesterey, and Maria Tatar, eds. *Neverending Stories: Toward a Critical Narratology*. Princeton: Princeton University Press, 1992.

Fielding, Henry. *The History of the Adventures of Joseph Andrews.* London: Oxford University Press, 1970.

Fietz, Lothar. "Fiktionsbewußtsein und Romanstruktur in der Geschichte des englischen und amerikanischen Romans." In *Gestaltungsgeschichte und Gesellschaftsgeschichte*, ed. Helmut Kreuzer, 115–31. Stuttgart: Metzler, 1969.

Fink, Gonthier-Louis. *Naissance et apogée du conte merveilleux en Allemagne 1740–1800.* Paris: Belles Lettres, 1966.

Flaherty, Gloria. *Opera in the Development of German Critical Thought.* Princeton: Princeton University Press, 1978.

Fluck, Winfried. "Fiction and Fictionality in Popular Culture: Some Observations on the Aesthetics of Popular Culture." *Journal of Popular Culture* 21 (Spring 1988): 49–62.

Fohrmann, Jürgen. "Utopie, Reflexion, Erzählung: Wielands *Goldner Spiegel.*" In *Utopieforschung: Interdisziplinäre Studien zur neuzeitlichen Utopie*, ed. Wilhelm Voßkamp, vol. 3, 24–49. Stuttgart: Metzler, 1982.

Frenzel, Elisabeth. "Mißverstandene Lektüre: Musäus' *Grandison der Zweite* und Wielands *Die Abenteuer des Don Sylvio von Rosalva*—zwei deutsche Donquichottiaden des 18. Jahrhunderts." In *Gelebte Literatur in der Literatur: Studien zu Erscheinungsformen und Geschichte eines literarischen Motivs*, ed. Theodor Wolpers, 110–33. Göttingen: Vandenhoeck & Ruprecht, 1986.

Frick, Werner. *Providenz und Kontingenz: Untersuchungen zur Schicksalssemantik im deutschen und europäischen Roman des 17. und 18. Jahrhunderts.* 2 vols. Tübingen: Niemeyer, 1988.

Fricke, Harald. "Semantics or Pragmatics of Fictionality? A Modest Proposal." *Poetics* 11 (1982): 439–52.

Fuchs, Albert. *Geistiger Gehalt und Quellenfrage in Wielands Abderiten.* Paris: Belles Lettres, 1934.

Gabriel, Gottfried. *Fiktion und Wahrheit: Eine semantische Theorie der Literatur.* Stuttgart: Frommann-Holzboog, 1975.

Gale, Richard M. "The Fictive Use of Language." *Philosophy* 46 (October 1971): 324–40.

Gardiner, Jeffrey B., and Albert R. Schmitt. "Christoph Martin Wieland: 'Theorie und Geschichte der Red-Kunst und Dicht-Kunst. Anno 1757': An Early Defense of Shakespeare." *Lessing Yearbook* 5 (1973): 219–41.

Gay, Peter. *The Enlightenment: An Interpretation. The Rise of Modern Paganism.* New York: Knopf, 1966; New York: Norton, 1977.

Genette, Gerard. "Fictional Narrative, Factual Narrative." *Poetics Today* 11 (1990): 755–74.

Gerhard, Melitta. *Der deutsche Entwicklungsroman bis Goethes 'Wilhelm Meister.'* Halle: Niemeyer, 1926.

Gerke, Karl. "Wielands 'Aristipp.'" Diss., Berlin, 1926.

Gillespie, Gerald. "Wielands 'Agathon' als Bildungsroman zwischen Barock und Romantik." In *Jahrbuch für Internationale Germanistik*, Reihe A, Band 8 (*Akten des VI. Internationalen Germanisten-Kongresses Basel 1980.* Teil 3), ed. Heinz Rupp and Hans-Gert Roloff, 344–52. Bern: Lang, 1980.

Glockhamer, Heidi. "The Apprenticeship of a Hetaera: Gender and Socialization in Wieland's *Geschichte des Agathon.*" *German Quarterly* 61 (1988): 371–86.

Goethe, Johann Wolfgang. *Goethes Werke.* 133 vols. Weimar: Böhlau, 1887–1918.

Gössl, Sybille. *Materialismus und Nihilismus: Studien zum deutschen Roman der Spätaufklärung.* Würzburg: Köngishausen and Neumann, 1987.

Gottsched, Johann Christoph. Review of *Die asiatische Banise,* by Heinrich Anshelm von Ziegler und Kliphausen. In *Beyträge Zur Critischen Historie Der Deutschen Sprache, Poesie und Beredsamkeit . . . Sechstes Stück.* Leipzig, 1733. Quoted in Lämmert, 71–72.

———. *Versuch einer Critischen Dichtkunst.* 4th ed. Leipzig: Breitkopf, 1751.

Grimminger, Rolf. "Wieland's 'Agathon': Erfahrungspsychologie und Bildungsidee im Roman der Hoch- und Spätaufklärung." In *Hansers Sozialgeschichte der deutschen Literatur vom 16. Jahrhundert bis zur Gegenwart,* vol. 3, *Deutsche Aufklärung bis zur Französischen Revolution 1680–1789,* ed. Rolf Grimminger, 690–701. Munich: Hanser, 1980.

Groß, Erich. *C. M. Wielands "Geschichte des Agathon": Entstehungsgeschichte.* Berlin: Ebering, 1930.

Gruber, J. G. *C. M. Wielands Leben.* 4 vols. Leipzig: Göschen, 1827–28; Hamburg, 1984.

Gundling, Nicolaus Hieronymus. Review of *Mythoscopia romantica,* by Gotthard Heidegger. In *Neuer Unterredungen Dritter Monat oder Martius.* Lützen, 1702. Quoted in Lämmert, 58–61.

Hahl, Werner. *Reflexion und Erzählung: Ein Problem der Romantheorie von der Spätaufklärung bis zum pragmatischen Realismus.* Stuttgart: Kohlhammer, 1971.

Hamburger, Käte. *Die Logik der Dichtung.* Stuttgart: Klett, 1957.

———. *Wahrheit und ästhetische Wahrheit.* Stuttgart: Klett-Cotta, 1979.

Harshaw (Hrushovski), Benjamin. "Fictionality and Fields of Reference: Remarks on a Theoretical Framework." *Poetics Today* 5 (1984): 227–51.

Haslinger, Adolf. "'Dies Bildnisz ist bezaubernd schön': Zum Thema 'Motiv und epische Struktur' im höfischen Roman des Barock." *Literaturwissenschaftliches Jahrbuch im Auftrage der Görres-Gesellschaft,* n.s., 9 (1968): 83–140.

Hasselbeck, Otto. *Illusion und Fiktion: Lessings Beitrag zur poetologischen Diskussion über das Verhältnis von Kunst und Wirklichkeit.* Munich: Fink, 1979.

Hecker, Jutta. *Wieland: Die Geschichte eines Menschen in der Zeit.* Weimar: Kiepenheuer, 1958.

Heidegger, Gotthard. *Mythoscopia romantica: oder Discours Von den so benanten Romans.* Zurich, 1698. Quoted in Lämmert, 52–56.

Heimrich, Bernhard. *Fiktion und Fiktionsironie in Theorie und Dichtung der deutschen Romantik.* Tübingen: Niemeyer, 1968.

Heintz, John. "Reference and Inference in Fiction." *Poetics* 8 (1979): 85–99.

Heinz, Jutta. "Von der Schwärmerkur zur Gesprächstherapie—Symptomatik und Darstellung des Schwärmers in Wielands 'Don Sylvio' und 'Peregrinus Proteus.'" *Wieland-Studien* 2 (1994): 33–53.

Heinzle, Joachim. "Die Entdeckung der Fiktionalität: Zu Walter Haugs 'Literaturtheorie im deutschen Mittelalter.'" *Beiträge zur Geschichte der deutschen Sprache und Literatur* 112 (1990): 55–80.

Hemmerich, Gert. *Christoph Martin Wielands "Geschichte des Agathon": Eine kritische Werkinterpretation.* Nuremberg: Carl, 1979.

Henrich, Dieter, and Wolfgang Iser, eds. *Funktionen des Fiktiven.* Munich: Fink, 1983.

———. "Entfaltung der Problemlage." In Henrich and Iser, 9–14.

Herchner, Hans. "Die Cyropädie in Wielands Werken." Parts 1, 2. *Wissenschaftliche Beilage zum Programm des Humboldts-Gymnasiums zu Berlin* (1892, 1896): 3–28, 3–24.

Hermann, Ernst. *Wielands Abderiten und die Mannheimer Theaterverhältnisse.* Mannheim: Löffler, 1885.

Hillmann, Heinz. "Wunderbares in der Dichtung der Aufklärung: Untersuchungen zum französischen und deutschen Feenmärchen." *Deutsche Vierteljahrsschrift für Literaturwissenschaft und Geistesgeschichte* 43 (1969): 76–113.

Hinderer, Walter. "Wielands Beiträge zur deutschen Klassik." In *Deutsche Literatur zur Zeit der Klassik,* ed. Karl Otto Conrady, 44–64. Stuttgart: Reclam, 1977.

———. "Christoph Martin Wieland." In *Deutsche Dichter,* vol. 3, *Aufklärung und Empfindsamkeit,* ed. Gunter E. Grimm and Frank Rainer Max, 266–93. Stuttgart: Reclam, 1988.

"Histoire de la belle Arouja." In *Les milles et un jours: Contes Persans,* trans. Petis de la Croix. In *Le cabinet des fées,* 15:189–231.

Hofmann La Torre, Gabriela. "Vision et construction: Louis-Sebastien Mercier, *L'An 2440*—Christoph Martin Wieland, *Le Miroir d'Or.*" In *De l'Utopie à l'Uchronie: Formes, Significations, Fonctions,* ed. Hinrich Hudde and Peter Kuon, 99–108. Tübingen: Narr, 1988.

Hogarth, William. *The Analysis of Beauty: Written with a View of Fixing the Fluctuating Ideas of Taste.* London: Reeves, 1753.

Höger, Alfons. "Fiktionalität als Kriterium poetischer Texte." *Orbis Litterarum* 26 (1971): 262–83.

Hohendahl, Peter Uwe. "Zum Erzählproblem des utopischen Romans im 18. Jahrhundert." In *Gestaltungsgeschichte und Gesellschaftsgeschichte,* ed. Helmut Kreuzer, 79–114. Stuttgart: Metzler, 1969.

Höhle, Thomas. "Wieland und die verpönte Gattung des Staatsromans." In Höhle, *Wieland-Kolloquium,* 41–60.

———. "Die Auseinandersetzung mit der Großen Französischen Revolution in den späten Romanen Christoph Martin Wielands." In Höhle, *Das Spätwerk Christoph Martin Wielands,* 5–19.

———. "Revolution, Bürgerkrieg und neue Verfassung in Cyrene: Betrachtungen zu Wielands 'Aristipp' und den Nachspielen der Französischen Revolution." In *"Sie, und nicht Wir": Die Französische Revolution und ihre Wirkung auf das Reich,* ed. Arno Herzig, Inge Stephan, and Hans G. Winter, vol. 2, 591–605. Hamburg: Dölling and Galitz, 1989.

———, ed. *Wieland-Kolloquium Halberstadt 1983.* Halle: Martin-Luther-Universität, 1983.

————, ed. *Das Spätwerk Christoph Martin Wielands und seine Bedeutung für die deutsche Aufklärung*. Halle: Martin-Luther-Universität, 1988.

Hollander, John. *Melodious Guile: Fictive Pattern in Poetic Language*. New Haven: Yale University Press, 1988.

Hoops, Wiklef. "Fiktionalität als pragmatische Kategorie." *Poetica* 11 (1979): 281–317.

Huet, Pierre-Daniel. *Traité de l'origine des romans*. Ed. Arend Kok. Amsterdam: Swets & Zeitlinger, 1942.

Hutcheon, Linda. *Narcissistic Narrative: The Metafictional Paradox*. Waterloo, Ontario: Wilfrid Laurier University Press, 1980.

Ihlenburg, Karl Heinz. "Wielands Agathodämon." Diss., Greifswald, 1957.

Ihwe, Jens F., and Hannes Rieser. "Normative and Descriptive Theory of Fiction: Some Contemporary Issues." *Poetics* 8 (1979): 63–84.

Immerwahr, Raymond. "'Romantic' and its Cognates in England, Germany, and France before 1790." In *"Romantic" and Its Cognates: The European History of a Word*, ed. Hans Eichner, 17–97. Toronto: University of Toronto Press, 1972.

Iselin, Isaac. Review of *Agathon*. *Allgemeine deutsche Bibliothek* 6 (1768): 190–211.

Iser, Wolfgang. "Akte des Fingierens oder Was ist das Fiktive am fiktionalen Text?" In Henrich and Iser, 121–52.

————. *Das Fiktive und das Imaginäre: Perspektiven literarischer Anthropologie*. Frankfurt am Main: Suhrkamp, 1991.

Ishiguro, Hide. "Contingent Truths and Possible Worlds." In *Leibniz: Metaphysics and Philosophy of Science*, ed. R. S. Woolhouse, 64–76. Oxford: Oxford University Press, 1981.

Jacobs, Jürgen. *Wielands Romane*. Bern: Francke, 1969.

————. *Wilhelm Meister und seine Brüder: Untersuchungen zum deutschen Bildungsroman*. Munich: Fink, 1972.

————. *Prosa der Aufklärung: Kommentar zu einer Epoche*. Munich: Winkler, 1976.

————. "Die Theorie und ihr Exempel: Zur Deutung von Wielands 'Agathon' in Blanckenburgs 'Versuch über den Roman.'" *Germanisch-romanische Monatsschrift*, n.s., 31 (1981): 32–42.

————. "Wieland und der Entwicklungsroman des 18. Jahrhunderts." In *Handbuch des deutschen Romans*, ed. Helmut Koopmann, 170–83. Düsseldorf: Bagel, 1983.

Jacobs, Jürgen, and Markus Krause. *Der deutsche Bildungsroman: Gattungsgeschichte vom 18. bis zum 20. Jahrhundert*. Munich: Beck, 1989.

Jahn, Wolfgang. "Zu Wielands 'Don Sylvio.'" In Schelle, *Christoph Martin Wieland*, 307–21. First published in *Wirkendes Wort* 18 (1968): 320–28.

Jaumann, Herbert, ed. Afterword to *Christoph Martin Wieland: Der goldne Spiegel und andere politische Dichtungen*, 859–89. Munich: Winkler, 1979.

Jauss, Hans Robert. "Zur historischen Genese der Scheidung von Fiktion und Realität." In Henrich and Iser, 423–31.

Jean Paul. *Werke*. Ed. Norbert Miller. Rev. ed. Abteilung 1. 6 vols. Munich: Hanser, 1980–89.

Johne, Renate. "Wieland und der antike Roman." In Kunze, 45–54.

Johnson, Samuel. "On Fiction." *The Rambler*, no. 4 (31 March 1750). Quoted in *Critical Theory since Plato*, ed. Hazard Adams, 324–27. San Diego: Harcourt Brace Jovanovich, 1971.

Jørgensen, Sven-Aage. "Warum und zu welchem Ende schreibt man eine Vorrede?" *Text und Kontext* 4 (1976): 3–20.

———. "Der unverheiratete Held." *Orbis Litterarum* 42 (1987): 338–52.

———. "Vom Fürstenspiegel zum *Goldenen Spiegel*." In *Europäische Barock-Rezeption*, ed. Klaus Garber, 365–75. Wiesbaden: Harrasowitz, 1991.

Jørgensen, Sven-Aage, Herbert Jaumann, John A. McCarthy, and Horst Thomé, eds. *Christoph Martin Wieland: Epoche, Werk, Wirkung*. Munich: Beck, 1994.

Kanyó, Zoltán, ed. *Fictionality*. Studia Poetica 5. Szeged: n.p., 1984.

Kausch, Karl Heinz. "Die Kunst der Grazie: Ein Beitrag zum Verständnis Wielands." *Jahrbuch der deutschen Schillergesellschaft* 2 (1958): 12–42.

Kayser, Wolfgang. "Die Anfänge des modernen Romans im 18. Jahrhundert und seine heutige Krise." *Deutsche Vierteljahrsschrift für Literaturwissenschaft und Geistesgeschichte* 28 (1954): 417–46.

———. *The Grotesque in Art and Literature*. Trans. Ulrich Weisstein. Bloomington: Indiana University Press, 1963 [1957].

Keller, Ernst. "Agathons pietistisches Erbe." In *Antipodische Aufklärungen: Festschrift für Leslie Bodi*, ed. Walter Veit, 201–11. Frankfurt am Main: Lang, 1987.

Keller, Otto. *Wilhelm Heinses Entwicklung zur Humanität: Zum Stilwandel des deutschen Romans im 18. Jahrhundert*. Bern: Francke, 1972.

Keller, Ulrich. *Fiktionalität als literaturwissenschaftliche Kategorie*. Heidelberg: Winter, 1980.

Kerbrat-Orecchioni, Catherine. "Le statut référentiel des textes de fiction." *Fabula* 2 (October 1983): 131–38.

Kermode, Frank. *The Sense of an Ending*. New York: Oxford University Press, 1966.

Ketzer, Hans-Jürgen. "Einige Bemerkung zu Wielands Rousseau-Aneignung und deren Beurteilung durch die Stürmer und Dränger." In Höhle, *Wieland-Kolloquium*, 267–72.

Kimpel, Dieter. *Der Roman der Aufklärung*. Stuttgart: Metzler, 1967.

Kind, Helmut. "Christoph Martin Wieland und die Entstehung des histori-schen Romans in Deutschland." In *Gedenkschrift für Ferdinand Josef Schneider*, ed. Karl Bischoff, 158–72. Weimar: Böhlau, 1956.

Kistler, Mark O. "Dionysian Elements in Wieland." *Germanic Review* 35 (1960): 83–92.

Klein, Timotheus. *Wieland und Rousseau*. Berlin: Duncker, 1903.

———. "Wieland and Rousseau." *Studien zur vergleichenden Literaturgeschichte* 3, 4 (1903, 1904): 425–80, 129–74.

Kleinschmidt, Erich. "Zur Ästhetik der Leserrolle im deutschen Roman zwischen 1750 und 1780." *Deutsche Vierteljahrsschrift für Literaturwissenschaft und Geistesgeschichte* 53 (1979): 49–73.

———. "Die ungeliebte Stadt: Umrisse einer Verweigerung in der deutschen Literatur des 18. Jahrhunderts." *LiLi: Zeitschrift für Literaturwissenschaft und Linguistik* 12 (1982): 29–49.

———. "Die Wirklichkeit der Literatur: Fiktionsbewußtsein und das Problem der ästhetischen Realität von Dichtung in der Frühen Neuzeit." *Deutsche Vierteljahrsschrift für Literaturwissenschaft und Geistesgeschichte* 56 (1982): 174–97.

Klotz, Volker. *Die erzählte Stadt: Ein Sujet als Herausforderung des Romans von Lesage bis Döblin.* Munich: Hanser, 1969.

———. *Das europäische Kunstmärchen: Fünfundzwanzig Kapitel seiner Geschichte von der Renaissance bis zur Moderne.* Stuttgart: Metzler, 1985.

Knüfermann, Volker. "C. M. Wieland: Geschichte der Abderiten: Sprachbewußtsein und Dichtungsstruktur." *Journal of the Australasian Universities Language and Literature Association* 35 (1971): 27–40.

Köhler, Karl-Heinz. "Musikhistorische Skizzen zur Weimarer Klassik: Zur Beziehung von Dichtung und Musik im Schaffen von Goethe, Wieland und Schiller." *Musik und Gesellschaft* 35 (1985): 290–96.

Kontje, Todd. *Private Lives in the Public Sphere: The German "Bildungsroman" as Metafiction.* University Park: Pennsylvania State University Press, 1992.

Kowatzki, Irmgard. "Die Funktion des konstituierenden Bewußtseins in einem 'Studium für die Seelenmaler': Die phänomenologische Studie einer Erzählphase in M. C. Wielands 'Geschichte des Agathon.'" *Analecta Husserliana* 4 (1976): 149–64.

Kunze, Max, ed. *Christoph Martin Wieland und die Antike.* Stendal: Winckelmann-Gesellschaft, 1986.

Kurth[-Voigt], Lieselotte E. "Historiographie und historischer Roman: Kritik und Theorie im 18. Jahrhundert." *Modern Language Notes* 79 (1964): 337–62.

———. "W. E. N.—Der teutsche Don Quichotte, oder die Begebenheiten des Marggraf von Bellamonte: Ein Beitrag zur Geschichte des deutschen Romans im 18. Jahrhundert." *Jahrbuch der deutschen Schillergesellschaft* 9 (1965): 106–30.

———. *Die zweite Wirklichkeit: Studien zum Roman des achtzehnten Jahrhunderts.* Chapel Hill: University of North Carolina Press, 1969.

———. "Unzuverlässige Sprecher und Erzähler in deutscher Dichtung." In *Traditions and Transitions: Studies in Honor of Harold Jantz,* ed. Lieselotte Kurth-Voigt et al., 105–24. Munich: Delp, 1972.

———. *Perspectives and Points of View: The Early Works of Wieland and Their Background.* Baltimore: Johns Hopkins University Press, 1974.

———. "Die 'Tabula Cebetis' und 'Agathon.'" *Jahrbuch der deutschen Schillergesellschaft* 23 (1979): 222–49.

———. "Wielands 'Geschichte des Agathon': Zur journalistischen Rezeption des Romans." *Wieland-Studien* 1 (1991): 9–42.

————. "Wielands 'Geschichte des Agathon': Zur journalistischen Rezeption des Romans in England." *Wieland-Studien* 2 (1994): 54–96.

L. G. [?] Review of *Diogenes. Beytrag zu den Erlangischen gelehrten Anmerkungen*, 3 March 1770, 137–38.

————. Review of *Diogenes. Mannigfaltigkeiten: Eine gemeinnützige Wochenschrift*, 26 May 1770, 611–14.

Lamarque, Peter. "Narrative and Invention: The Limits of Fictionality." In *Narrative in Culture: The Uses of Storytelling in the Sciences, Philosophy, and Literature*, ed. Cristopher Nash, 131–53. London: Routledge, 1990.

Lämmert, Eberhard, et al., eds. *Romantheorie 1620–1880: Dokumentation ihrer Geschichte in Deutschland*. Frankfurt am Main: Athenäum, 1988.

Lange, Victor. "Erzählformen im Roman des achtzehnten Jahrhunderts." In *Zur Poetik des Romans*, ed. Volker Klotz, 32–47. Darmstadt: Wissenschaftliche Buchgesellschaft, 1965. First published in *Anglia* 76 (1958): 129–44.

————. "Zur Gestalt des Schwärmers im deutschen Roman des 18. Jahrhunderts." In *Festschrift für Richard Alewyn*, ed. Herbert Singer and Benno von Wiese, 151–64. Cologne: Böhlau, 1967.

Langfelder, Paul, ed. Introduction to *Wieland: Die Dialogen des Diogenes von Sinope*, 5–26. Bucharest: Literatur-Verlag, 1963.

Lavater, Johann Caspar. *Physiognomische Fragmente, zur Beförderung der Menschenkenntniß und Menschenliebe*. 4 vols. Leipzig and Winterthur, 1775–78; Zurich: Orell Füssli, 1968–69.

Le cabinet des fées, ou collection choisie des contes des fées, et autres contes merveilleux. 41 vols. Geneva: Barde, Manget & Compagnie, 1786–89.

Leopold, Keith. "Wieland's *Don Sylvio von Rosalva*: The First Modern German Novel?" In *Keith Leopold: Selected Writings*, ed. Manfred Jurgensen, 31–40. New York: Lang, 1985. First published in *Festschrift for Ralph Farrell*, ed. Anthony Stephens, H. L. Rogers, and Brian Coghlan. Bern: Lang, 1977.

Lessing, Gotthold Ephraim. *Werke*. Vol. 4., *Dramaturgische Schriften*. Ed. Karl Eibl. Munich: Hanser 1973.

Lim, Jeong-Taeg. *Don Sylvio und Anselmus: Untersuchung zur Gestaltung des Wunderbaren bei C. M. Wieland und E. T. A. Hoffmann*. Frankfurt am Main: Lang, 1988.

Lodge, David. *The Art of Fiction*. New York: Penguin, 1994 [1992].

Lucian. "The Life of Demonax." In *The Works of Lucian of Samosata*. Trans. H. W. Fowler and F. G. Fowler. Oxford: Clarendon Press, 1905.

————. *Wie man Geschichte schreiben soll*. Ed. and trans. H. Homeyer. Munich: Fink, 1965.

Lüderwald, Johann Balthasar. *Anti-Hierocles: oder Jesus Christus und Apollonius von Thyana in ihrer großen Ungleichheit vorgestellt*. Halle: Buchhandlung des Waisenhauses, 1793.

Lüthe, Rudolf. "Fiktionalität als konstitutives Element literarischer Rezeption." *Orbis Litterarum* 29 (1974): 1–15.

Lützeler, Paul Michael. "Fictionality in Historiography and the Novel." In Fehn, Hoesterey, and Tatar, 29–44.

McCarthy, John A. *Fantasy and Reality: An Epistemological Approach to Wieland.* Bern: Lang, 1974.

————. "Shaftesbury and Wieland: The Question of Enthusiasm." *Studies in Eighteenth-Century Culture* 6 (1977): 79–95.

————. *Christoph Martin Wieland.* Boston: Twayne, 1979.

————. "The Poet as Journalist and Essayist: Ch. M. Wieland." Parts 1, 2. *Jahrbuch für Internationale Germanistik* 12, 13 (1980, 1981): 104–38, 74–137.

————. "Klassisch lesen: Weimarer Klassik, Wirkungsästhetik und Wieland." *Jahrbuch der deutschen Schillergesellschaft* 36 (1992): 414–32.

McKeon, Michael. *The Origins of the English Novel 1600–1740.* Baltimore: Johns Hopkins University Press, 1987.

McNeely, James A. "Historical Relativism in Wieland's Concept of the Ideal State." *Modern Language Quarterly* 22 (1961): 269–82.

Mager, A[dolf]. "Wielands 'Nachlass des Diogenes von Sinope' und das englische Vorbild." In *Marburg a. d. Drau, Staats- und Oberrealschule, Abhandlung zum 20. Jahresbericht* (1890), 1–15.

Mähl, Hans-Joachim. "Die Republik des Diogenes: Utopische Fiktion und Fiktionsironie am Beispiel Wielands." In *Utopieforschung: Interdisziplinäre Studien zur neuzeitlichen Utopie,* ed. Wilhelm Voßkamp, vol. 3, 50–85. Stuttgart: Metzler, 1982.

Manger, Klaus. "Universitas Abderitica: Zu Wielands Romankonzeption." *Euphorion* 77 (1983): 395–406.

————. "Wieland und Raffael." *Jahrbuch des freien deutschen Hochstifts* (1984): 34–56.

————. "Wielands klassizistische Poetik als Kunst des Mischens." In *Literarische Klassik,* ed. Hans-Joachim Simm, 327–53. Frankfurt am Main: Suhrkamp, 1988.

————. *Klassizismus und Aufklärung: Das Beispiel des späten Wieland.* Frankfurt am Main: Klostermann, 1991.

Marchand, James W. "Wieland's Style and Narratology." In *Christoph Martin Wieland: North American Scholarly Contributions on the Occasion of the 250th Anniversary of His Birth,* ed. Hansjörg Schelle, 1–32. Tübingen: Niemeyer, 1984.

Margolin, Uri. "The Nature and Functioning of Fiction: Some Recent Views." *Canadian Review of Comparative Literature/Revue Canadienne de Littérature Comparée* 19 (1992): 101–17.

Martini, Fritz. Afterwords to *Christoph Martin Wieland: Werke.* 5 vols. Ed. Fritz Martini and Hans Werner Seiffert. Munich: Hanser, 1964–68.

————. "Wieland: 'Geschichte der Abderiten.'" In Schelle, *Christoph Martin Wieland,* 152–87. First published in *Der deutsche Roman: Vom Barock bis zur Gegenwart,* ed. Benno von Wiese, 64–94, 414–17. Düsseldorf: Bagel, 1963.

————. Afterword to *Geschichte des Agathon.* Ed. Fritz Martini and Reinhard Döhl, 643–79. Stuttgart: Reclam, 1979.

Marx, Friedhelm. *Erlesene Helden: Don Sylvio, Werther, Wilhelm Meister und die Literatur.* Heidelberg: Winter, 1995.

Matthecka, Gerd. "Die Romantheorie Wielands und seiner Vorläufer." Diss., Tübingen, 1956.

Mauser, Wolfram. "Wielands 'Geschichte der Abderiten.'" *Innsbrucker Beiträge zur Kulturwissenschaft* 15 (1969): 165–77.

Mayer, Gerhart. "Die Begründung des Bildungsromans durch Wieland: Die Wandlung der 'Geschichte des Agathon.'" *Jahrbuch der Raabe-Gesellschaft* (1970): 7–36.

———. *Der deutsche Bildungsroman: Von der Aufklärung bis zur Gegenwart.* Stuttgart: Metzler, 1992.

Meessen, H. J. "Wieland's 'Briefe an einen jungen Dichter,'" *Monatshefte* 47 (April–May 1955): 193–208.

Meid, Volker. "Zum Roman der Aufklärung." In *Aufklärung: Ein literaturwissenschaftliches Studienbuch*, ed. Hans-Friedrich Wessels, 88–115. Königstein: Athenäum, 1984.

Mellinger, Johanna. "Wielands Auffassung vom Urchristentum mit hauptsächlicher Berücksichtigung seines Romans Agathodämon." Diss., Munich, 1911.

Merck, Johann Heinrich. Review of *Der goldne Spiegel. Frankfurter gelehrte Anzeigen* 86 (27 October 1772). Quoted in *Deutsche Literaturdenkmale des 18. Jahrhunderts*, ed. Bernhard Seuffert, vol. 8, *Frankfurter gelehrte Anzeigen vom Jahr 1772, zweite Hälfte*, 565–69. Stuttgart: Göschen, 1883.

Mewes, Knuth. "'Man sieht den Wald vor lauter Bäumen nicht'—Ausblicke für ein Verständnis von Wielands 'Aristipp'?!" In Höhle, *Das Spätwerk Christoph Martin Wielands*, 125–38.

———. "Wielands 'Aristipp'—ein unbewältigter Forschungsgegenstand." *Hallesche Studien zur Wirkung von Sprache und Literatur* 17 (1989): 20–47.

Meyer, Herman. *Das Zitat in der Erzählkunst: Zur Geschichte und Poetik des europäischen Romans.* Stuttgart: Metzler, 1961.

———. *Der Sonderling in der deutschen Dichtung.* Munich: Hanser, 1963.

Michel, Victor. *C.-M. Wieland: La formation et l'évolution de son esprit jusqu'en 1772.* Paris: Boivin, 1938.

Michelsen, Peter. *Laurence Sterne und der deutsche Roman des achtzehnten Jahrhunderts.* Göttingen: Vandenhoeck & Ruprecht, 1962.

Mickel, Karl. "Peregrinus Proteus oder die Nachtseite der pädagogischen Revolution." *Sinn und Form* 35 (1983): 814–35.

Mielke, Andreas. "Wieland contra Swift und Rousseau—und Wezel." *Colloquia Germanica* 20 (1987): 15–37.

Miller, Norbert. *Der empfindsame Erzähler: Untersuchungen an Romananfängen des 18. Jahrhunderts.* Munich: Hanser, 1968.

Miller, Steven R. *Die Figur des Erzählers in Wielands Romanen.* Göppingen: Kümmerle, 1970.

Mooij, J. J. A. "Fictionality and the Speech Act Theory." In *Fiction, Narratologie, Texte, Genre*, ed. Jean Bessière, 15–22. New York: Lang, 1989.

Moser-Verrey, Monique. *Dualité et continuité du discours narratif dans Don Sylvio, Joseph Andrews et Jacques le Fataliste.* Bern: Lang, 1976.

Mücke, Dorothea E. von. *Virtue and the Veil of Illusion: Generic Innovation and the Pedagogical Project in Eighteenth-Century Literature.* Stanford: Stanford University Press, 1991.

Müller, Götz. "Der verborgene Prinz: Variationen einer Fabel zwischen 1768 und 1820." *Jahrbuch der Jean-Paul Gesellschaft* 17 (1982): 71–89.

———. *Gegenwelten: Die Utopie in der deutschen Literatur.* Stuttgart: Metzler, 1989.

Müller, Jan-Dirk. *Wielands späte Romane: Untersuchungen zur Erzählweise und zur erzählten Wirklichkeit.* Munich: Fink, 1971.

Müller, Klaus-Detlef. *Autobiographie und Roman: Studien zur literarischen Autobiographie der Goethezeit.* Tübingen: Niemeyer, 1976.

———. "Der Zufall im Roman: Anmerkungen zur erzähltechnischen Bedeutung der Kontingenz." *Germanisch-romanische Monatsschrift*, n.s., 28 (1978): 265–90.

Müller-Solger, Hermann. *Der Dichtertraum: Studien zur Entwicklung der dichterischen Phantasie im Werk Christoph Martin Wielands.* Göppingen: Kümmerle, 1970.

Naumann, Dietrich. *Politik und Moral: Studien zur Utopie der deutschen Aufklärung.* Heidelberg: Winter, 1977.

Neuhaus, Volker. *Typen multiperspektivischen Erzählens.* Cologne: Böhlau, 1971.

Niehues-Pröbsting, Heinrich. *Der Kynismus des Diogenes und der Begriff des Zynismus.* Munich: Fink, 1979.

———. "Wielands Diogenes und der Rameau Diderots: Zur Differenz von Kyniker und Zyniker in der Sicht der Aufklärung." In *Peter Sloterdijks "Kritik der zynischen Vernunft,"* 73–109. Frankfurt am Main: Suhrkamp, 1987.

Niggl, Günter. *Geschichte der deutschen Autobiographie im 18. Jahrhundert.* Stuttgart: Metzler, 1977.

Nobis, Helmut. *Phantasie und Moralität: Das Wunderbare in Wielands "Dschinnistan" und der "Geschichte des Prinzen Biribinker."* Kronberg: Scriptor, 1976.

Norris, Christopher. *Deconstruction: Theory and Practice.* Rev. ed. London: Methuen, 1988.

Oettinger, Klaus. *Phantasie und Erfahrung: Studien zur Erzählpoetik Christoph Martin Wielands.* Munich: Fink, 1970.

Opitz, Roland. *Krise des Romans? Drei Essays.* Halle: Mitteldeutscher Verlag, 1984.

Pätzold, Jörg. "Wie steht es eigentlich um die Fiktionalität literarischer Texte?" *Neuphilologische Mitteilungen* 89 (1988): 619–24.

Paulsen, Wolfgang. *Wielands Aristipp als Roman.* Biberach an der Riß: Thomae, 1973.

———. *Christoph Martin Wieland: Der Mensch und sein Werk in psychologischen Perspektiven.* Bern: Francke, 1975.

———. "Die emanzipierte Frau in Wielands Weltbild." In *Die Frau als Heldin und Autorin*, ed. Wolfgang Paulsen, 153–74. Bern: Francke, 1979.

Pavel, Thomas G. *Fictional Worlds.* Cambridge: Harvard University Press, 1986.

———. "Between History and Fiction: On Dorrit Cohn's Poetics of Prose." In Fehn, Hoesterey, and Tatar, 17–28.

Pelc, Jerzy. "Some Thoughts on Fictitious Entities." In Kanyó, 73–86.

————. "On Fictitious Entities and Fictional Texts." *Recherches Sémiotiques/ Semiotic Inquiry* 6 (1986): 1–35.

Perez, Hertha. "Personengestaltung bei Christoph Martin Wieland." *Études Germaniques* 40 (April–June 1985): 161–74.

Pfeiffer, K. Ludwig. "Fiction: On the Fate of a Concept between Philosophy and Literary Theory." In *Aesthetic Illusion: Theoretical and Historical Approaches*, ed. Frederick Burwick and Walter Pape, 92–104. Berlin: de Gruyter, 1990.

Phelan, Tony. "Ironic Lovers: Wieland's *Aristipp und einige seiner Zeitgenossen.*" *German Life and Letters* 29 (1975): 97–108.

Philostratus. *Apollonius von Tyana.* Trans. Eduard Baltzer. Rudolstadt: Hartung, 1883.

————. *The Life of Apollonius of Tyana.* Trans. F. C. Conybeare. 2 vols. London: Heinemann, 1912.

Poser, Michael von. *Der abschweifende Erzähler: Rhetorische Tradition und deutscher Roman im achtzehnten Jahrhundert.* Bad Homburg: Gehlen, 1969.

Prather, Charlotte C. "C. M. Wieland's Narrators, Heroes and Readers." *Germanic Review* 55 (1980): 64–73.

Pratt, Mary Louise. *Toward a Speech Act Theory of Literary Discourse.* Bloomington: Indiana University Press, 1977.

Preisendanz, Wolfgang. "Wieland und die Verserzählung des 18. Jahrhunderts." *Germanisch-romanische Monatsschrift,* n.s., 12 (1962): 17–31.

————. "Die Auseinandersetzung mit dem Nachahmungsprinzip in Deutschland und die besondere Rolle der Romane Wielands." In *Nachahmung und Illusion,* ed. H. R. Jauß, 72–95. Munich: Eidos, 1963.

Pröhle, Heinrich. Introduction to *Geschichte der Abderiten.* In *Deutsche National-Litteratur,* vol. 53, *Wielands Werke: Dritter Theil,* ed. Joseph Kürschner, i–xvii. Berlin: Spemann, c. 1885.

————. Introduction to *Christoph Martin Wieland: Aristipp und einige seiner Zeitgenossen.* Ed. Heinrich Pröhle. Frankfurt am Main: Insel, 1984.

Promies, Wolfgang. *Der Bürger und der Narr oder das Risiko der Phantasie: Sechs Kapitel über das Irrationale in der Literatur des Rationalismus.* Munich: Hanser, 1966.

Raab, Karl. "Studien zu Wielands Romane 'Peregrinus Proteus.'" *Prag-Altstadt, Staats-Gymnasium mit deutscher Unterrichtssprache, Jahresbericht* (1908–9), 3–32.

Rabener, Gottlieb Wilhelm. "Vom Mißbrauche der Satire" (1751). Quoted in *Meisterwerke deutscher Literaturkritik,* ed. Hans Mayer, 27–61. Berlin: Rütten & Loening, 1956.

Ratz, Alfred E. "C. M. Wieland: Toleranz, Kompromiß und Inkonsequenz: Eine kritische Betrachtung." *Deutsche Vierteljahrsschrift für Literaturwissenschaft und Geistesgeschichte* 42 (1968): 493–514.

Ratz, Norbert. *Der Identitätsroman: Eine Strukturanalyse.* Tübingen: Niemeyer, 1988.

Reemtsma, Jan Philipp. *Das Buch vom Ich: Christoph Martin Wielands Aristipp und einige seiner Zeitgenossen.* Zurich: Haffmans, 1993.

Reichert, H. W. "The Philosophy of Archytas in Wieland's *Agathon.*" *Germanic Review* 24 (1949): 8–17.

Review of *Diogenes. Allgemeine deutsche Bibliothek* 13 (1770): 601–6.

Review of *Don Sylvio. Erlangsche gelehrte Anmerkungen und Nachrichten.* 27 November 1764, 387–89.

Review of *Don Sylvio. Göttingsche Anzeigen von Gelehrten Sachen.* 13 October 1764, 993–95.

Review of *Don Sylvio. "Journal Encyclopédique."* August 1764. Quoted in *Wielands Briefwechsel*, 3:312.

Riffaterre, Michael. *Fictional Truth.* Baltimore: Johns Hopkins University Press, 1990.

Robertson, J. G. "The Beginning of the German Novel." *Westminster Review* (July–December 1894): 183–95.

Röder, Gerda. *Glück und glückliches Ende im deutschen Bildungsroman: Eine Studie zu Goethes "Wilhelm Meister."* Munich: Hueber, 1968.

Rogan, Richard G. *The Reader in the Novels of C. M. Wieland.* Las Vegas: Lang, 1981.

———. "The Reader in Wieland's *Die Abenteuer des Don Sylvio von Rosalva.*" *German Studies Review* 4 (May 1981): 177–93.

Rösler, Wolfgang. "Die Entdeckung der Fiktionalität in der Antike." *Poetica* 12 (1980): 283–319.

Rotermund, Erwin. "Massenwahn und ästhetische Therapeutik bei Christoph Martin Wieland: Zu einer Neuinterpretation der 'Geschichte der Abderiten.'" *Germanisch-romanische Monatsschrift*, n.s., 28 (1978): 417–51.

Rowe, John Carlos. "Metavideo: Fictionality and Mass Culture in a Postmodern Economy." In *Intertextuality and Contemporary American Fiction*, ed. Patrick O'Donnell and Robert Con Davis, 214–35. Baltimore: Johns Hopkins University Press, 1989.

Rudolph, Wilfried. "Einige Aspekte des Antike- und Zeitbezugs in Wielands Roman 'Geschichte der Abderiten.'" In Kunze, 89–94.

———. "Abderitismus und Aufklärung in Wielands Roman 'Geschichte der Abderiten.'" In Höhle, *Wieland-Kolloquium*, 222–27.

Rutledge, John. *The Dialogue of the Dead in Eighteenth-Century Germany.* Bern: Lang, 1974.

Ryan, Judith. "Fictionality, Historicity, and Textual Authority: Pater, Woolf, Hildesheimer." In Fehn, Hoesterey, and Tatar, 45–61.

Saariluoma, Liisa. *Die Erzählstruktur des frühen deutschen Bildungsromans: Wielands "Geschichte des Agathon." Goethes "Wilhelm Meisters Lehrjahre."* Helsinki: Suomalainen Tiedeakatemia, 1985.

Sagmo, Ivar. "Über die ästhetische Erziehung des Eros: Zu Wielands Roman *Don Sylvio von Rosalva.*" *Text & Kontext* 9 (1981): 185–97.

Sahmland, Irmtraut. *Christoph Martin Wieland und die deutsche Nation: Zwischen Patriotismus, Kosmopolitismus und Griechentum.* Tübingen: Niemeyer, 1990.

Samuel, Richard. "Wieland als Gesellschaftskritiker: eine Forschungsaufgabe." *Seminar* 5 (Spring 1969): 45–53.

Sauder, Gerhard. "Argumente der Fiktionskritik 1680–1730 und 1960–1970." *Germanisch-romanische Monatsschrift,* n.s., 26 (1976): 129–40.

Schaefer, Klaus. "Das Problem der sozialpolitischen Konzeption in Wielands 'Geschichte des Agathon' (1766/67)." *Weimarer Beiträge* 16 (1970): 171–96.

————. "Chr. M. Wielands Beitrag zur Revolutionsdebatte in der Endfassung seines Romans 'Die Geschichte des Agathon' (1794)." *Zeitschrift für Germanistik,* n.s., 1 (1991): 323–29.

————. "Der Schluss von Ch. M. Wielands 'Geschichte des Agathon'—Ein Werk in der Wandlung." *Wieland-Studien* 1 (1991): 43–57.

Schelle, Hansjörg. "Zur Biographie des Erfurter Wieland." *Lessing Yearbook* 18 (1986): 209–26.

————, ed. *Christoph Martin Wieland.* Darmstadt: Wissenschaftliche Buchgesellschaft, 1981.

Schillemeit, Jost. Review of *Das Zitat in der Erzählkunst,* by Herman Meyer. *Göttingsche gelehrte Anzeigen* 216 (1964): 81–100.

Schiller, Friedrich. *Schillers Werke.* Vol. 8, *Wallenstein.* Ed. Hermann Schneider and Lieselotte Blumenthal. Weimar: Böhlau, 1949.

Schindler-Hürlimann, Regine. *Wielands Menschenbild: Eine Interpretation des Agathon.* Zurich: Atlantis, 1963.

Schings, Hans-Jürgen. *Melancholie und Aufklärung: Melancholiker und ihre Kritiker in Erfahrungsseelenkunde und Literatur des 18. Jahrhunderts.* Stuttgart: Metzler, 1977.

————. "Der Staatsroman im Zeitalter der Aufklärung." In *Handbuch des deutschen Romans,* ed. Helmut Koopmann, 151–69. Düsseldorf: Bagel, 1983.

————. "Agathon—Anton Reiser—Wilhelm Meister: Zur Pathogenese des modernen Subjekts im Bildungsroman." In *Goethe im Kontext: Kunst und Humanität, Naturwissenschaft und Poetik von der Aufklärung bis zur Restauration,* ed. Wolfgang Wittkowski, 45–57. Tübingen: Niemeyer, 1984.

Schlagenhaft, Barbara. *Wielands Agathon als Spiegel aufklärerischer Vernunft- und Gefühlsproblematik.* Erlangen: Palm & Enke, 1935.

Schmidt, Siegfried J. "Fictionality in Literary and Non-Literary Discourse." *Poetics* 9 (1980): 525–46.

Schneider, Helmut J. "Staatsroman und Fürstenspiegel." In *Deutsche Literatur: Eine Sozialgeschichte,* ed. Horst Albert Glaser, vol. 4, *Zwischen Absolutismus und Aufklärung: Rationalismus, Empfindsamkeit, Sturm und Drang,* ed. Ralph-Rainer Wuthenow, 170–84. Hamburg: Rowohlt, 1980.

Scholes, Robert. *Fabulation and Metafiction.* Urbana: University of Illinois Press, 1979.

Schönert, Jörg. *Roman und Satire im 18. Jahrhundert: Ein Beitrag zur Poetik.* Stuttgart: Metzler, 1969.

————. "Der satirische Roman von Wieland bis Jean Paul." In *Handbuch des deutschen Romans,* ed. Helmut Koopmann, 204–25. Düsseldorf: Bagel, 1983.

Schostack, Renate. "Wieland und Lavater: Beitrag zur Geschichte des ausgehenden 18. Jahrhunderts." Diss., Freiburg, 1964.

Schrader, Monika. *Mimesis und Poiesis: Poetologische Studien zum Bildungs-roman.* Berlin: de Gruyter, 1975.

Schulze-Maizier, Friedrich. *Wieland in Erfurt.* Erfurt: Villaret, 1919.

Seiffert, Hans Werner. "Die Idee der Aufklärung bei Christoph Martin Wieland." *Wissenschaftliche Annalen* 2 (1953): 678–89.

———. "Zu einigen Fragen der Wieland-Rezeption und Wieland-Forschung," *Modern Language Notes* 99 (1984): 425–36.

Seiler, Christiane. "Die Rolle des Lesers in Wielands *Don Sylvio von Rosalva* und *Agathon.*" *Lessing Yearbook* 9 (1977): 152–65.

Sengle, Friedrich. *Wieland.* Stuttgart: Metzler, 1949.

Seuffert, Bernhard. "Wielands Berufung nach Weimar." *Vierteljahrschrift für Litteraturgeschichte* 1 (1888): 342–435.

Shookman, Ellis. "Fictionality and the Bildungsroman: Wieland's *Agathon.*" *Michigan Germanic Studies* 13 (Fall 1987): 156–68.

———. "Intertextuality, *Agathon,* and *Ion*: Wieland's Novel, Euripides's Tragedy, Plato's Dialogue." *Lessing Yearbook* 22 (1990): 199–217.

———, ed. *The Faces of Physiognomy: Interdisciplinary Approaches to Johann Caspar Lavater.* Columbia, S.C.: Camden House, 1993.

Sinnwell, Armin P. "Wielands 'Liebling': Zur Genese des Romans *Aristipp und einige seiner Zeitgenossen.*" *Colloquia Germanica* 21 (1988): 99–110.

Smith, Barbara Herrnstein. *On the Margins of Discourse: The Relation of Litera-ture to Language.* Chicago: University of Chicago Press, 1978.

Spies, Bernhard. *Politische Kritik, psychologische Hermeneutik, ästhetischer Blick: Die Entwicklung bürgerlicher Subjektivität im Roman des 18. Jahrhunderts.* Stuttgart: Metzler, 1992.

Spittler, Horst. "Was ist Fiktionalität? Erläuterungen zu einem literaturwis-senschaftlichen Begriff." In *Kleine Studien,* ed. Reinhard Düchting and Adolf Schulte, 103–8. Witten: Krüger, 1983.

Spitzer, Leo. *Classical and Christian Ideas of World Harmony: Prolegomena to an Interpretation of the Word "Stimmung."* Baltimore: Johns Hopkins University Press, 1963.

Stahl, Karl-Heinz. *Das Wunderbare als Problem und Gegenstand der deutschen Poetik des 17. und 18. Jahrhunderts.* Frankfurt am Main: Athenaion, 1975.

Staiger, Emil. Afterword to *Geschichte der Abderiten.* Frankfurt am Main: Fischer, 1961.

Stamm, Israel S. "Wieland and Sceptical Rationalism." *Germanic Review* 33 (1958): 15–29.

Stanzel, Franz K. *Theorie des Erzählens.* 3d ed. Göttingen: Vandenhoeck & Ruprecht, 1985.

Starnes, Thomas. Review of *Fantasy and Reality: An Epistemological Approach to Wieland,* by John McCarthy. *Lessing Yearbook* 8 (1976): 279–80.

———. *Christoph Martin Wieland: Leben und Werk.* 3 vols. Sigmaringen: Thor-becke, 1987.

Stempel, Wolf-Dieter. "Alltagsfiktion." In *Erzählen im Alltag,* ed. Konrad Ehlich, 385–402. Frankfurt am Main: Suhrkamp, 1980.

Stern, Guy. "Saint or Hypocrite? A Study of Wieland's 'Jacinte Episode.'" *Germanic Review* 29 (1954): 96–101.

Sterne, Laurence. *A Sentimental Journey through France and Italy.* London: Oxford University Press, 1968.

Stettner, Leo. *Das philosophische System Shaftesburys und Wielands Agathon.* Halle: Niemeyer, 1929.

Stockhammer, Robert. *Leseerzählungen: Alternativen zum hermeneutischen Verfahren.* Stuttgart: M & P Verlag für Wissenschaft und Forschung, 1991.

Stoll, Karin. *Christoph Martin Wieland, Journalistik und Kritik: Bedingungen und Maßstab politischen und ästhetischen Räsonnements im "Teutschen Merkur" vor der Französischen Revolution.* Bonn: Bouvier, 1978.

Sträßner, Matthias. *Tanzmeister und Dichter: Literatur-Geschichte(n) im Umkreis von Jean Georges Noverre: Lessing, Wieland, Goethe, Schiller.* Berlin: Henschel, 1994.

Strauss, D. Pieter. "Wieland's Late Novel *Peregrinus Proteus.*" Diss., Cornell, 1972.

Süßenberger, Claus. *Rousseau im Urteil der deutschen Publizistik bis zum Ende der Französischen Revolution: Ein Beitrag zur Rezeptionsgeschichte.* Frankfurt am Main: Lang, 1974.

Swales, Martin. *The German Bildungsroman from Wieland to Hesse.* Princeton: Princeton University Press, 1978.

Swiggart, Peter. "Fictionality and Language Meaning." *Language & Communication* 2 (1982): 285–302.

Tarot, Rolf. "Christoph Martin Wieland: *Geschichte des Prinzen Biribinker.*" In *Kunstmärchen: Erzählmöglichkeiten von Wieland bis Döblin,* ed. Rolf Tarot, 37–63. Bern: Lang, 1993.

Teesing, H. P. H. "Wielands Verhältnis zur Aufklärung im *Agathodämon.*" *Neophilologus* 21 (1936): 23–35.

Thomé, Horst. *Roman und Naturwissenschaft: Eine Studie zur Vorgeschichte der deutschen Klassik.* Frankfurt am Main: Lang, 1978.

———. "Menschliche Natur und Allegorie sozialer Verhältnisse: Zur politischen Funktion philosophischer Konzeptionen in Wielands 'Geschichte des Agathon' (1766/67)." *Jahrbuch der deutschen Schillergesellschaft* 22 (1978): 205–34.

———. "'Utopische Diskurse': Thesen zu Wielands *Aristipp und einige seiner Zeitgenossen.*" *Modern Language Notes* 99 (1984): 503–21.

———. "Religion und Aufklärung in Wielands *Agathodämon*: Zu Problemen der 'kulturellen Semantik' um 1800." *Internationales Archiv für Sozialgeschichte der deutschen Literatur* 15 (1990): 93–122.

Thomsen, Christian W. *Das Groteske im englischen Roman des 18. Jahrhunderts: Erscheinungsformen und Funktionen.* Darmstadt: Wissenschaftliche Buchgesellschaft, 1974.

Thorand, Brigitte. "Zwischen Ideal und Wirklichkeit—Zum Problem des Schwärmertums im 'Peregrinus Proteus.'" In Höhle, *Das Spätwerk Christoph Martin Wielands,* 91–100.

Tronskaja, Maria. *Die deutsche Prosasatire der Aufklärung.* Berlin: Rütten & Loening, 1969.

Tschapke, Reinhard. *Anmutige Vernunft: Christoph Martin Wieland und die Rhetorik.* Stuttgart: Heinz, 1990.

"Ueber den dramatischen Roman." *Neue Bibliothek der schönen Wissenschaften und der freyen Künste* 44 (1791). Quoted in Lämmert, 165–72.

Uphaus, Robert W. Preface to *The Idea of the Novel in the Eighteenth Century,* ed. Robert W. Uphaus, vii–x. East Lansing, Mich.: Colleagues Press, 1988.

Vaihinger, Hans. *Die Philosophie des Als Ob: System der theoretischen, praktischen und religiösen Fiktionen der Menschheit auf Grund eines idealistischen Positivismus.* 3d ed. Leipzig: Meiner, 1918.

Viering, Jürgen. *Schwärmerische Erwartung bei Wieland, im trivialen Geheimnisroman und bei Jean Paul.* Cologne: Böhlau, 1976.

Vietta, Silvio. *Literarische Phantasie: Theorie und Geschichte.* Stuttgart: Metzler, 1986.

Voges, Michael. *Aufklärung und Geheimnis: Untersuchungen zur Vermittlung von Literatur- und Sozialgeschichte am Beispiel der Aneignung des Geheimbundmaterials im Roman des späten 18. Jahrhunderts.* Tübingen: Niemeyer, 1987.

Vogt, Oskar. *"Der goldene Spiegel" und Wielands politische Ansichten.* Berlin: Duncker, 1904.

Vormweg, Heinrich. "Die Romane Chr. M. Wielands: Zeitmorphologische Reihenuntersuchung." Diss., Bonn, 1956.

Voss, Ernst Theodor. "Erzählprobleme des Briefromans dargestellt an vier Beispielen des 18. Jahrhunderts." Diss., Bonn, 1960.

Voß, Jens. *". . . das Bißchen Gärtnerey": Untersuchungen zur Garten- und Naturmotivik bei Christoph Martin Wieland.* Frankfurt am Main: Lang, 1993.

Voß, Johann Heinrich. "Michaelis, 1772." *Göttinger Musenalmanach* (1775): 209. Quoted in *Christoph Martin Wieland: Werke,* ed. Martini and Seiffert, 3:848.

Voßkamp, Wilhelm. *Romantheorie in Deutschland: Von Martin Opitz bis Friedrich von Blanckenburg.* Stuttgart: Metzler, 1973.

Walter, Michael. "'Keine Zeichen von guter Vorbedeutung': Zur Textbedeutung des Schlußkapitels vom 'Goldnen Spiegel.'" In Höhle, *Das Spätwerk Christoph Martin Wielands,* 29–41.

Walton, Kendall L. "Fiction, Fiction-Making, and Styles of Fictionality." *Philosophy and Literature* 7 (Spring 1983): 78–88.

———. *Mimesis as Make-Believe: On the Foundations of the Representational Arts.* Cambridge: Harvard University Press, 1990.

Waugh, Patricia. *Metafiction: The Theory and Practice of Self-Conscious Fiction.* London: Methuen, 1984.

Weber, Ernst. *Die poetologische Selbstreflexion im deutschen Roman des 18. Jahrhunderts: Zu Theorie und Praxis von "Roman", "Historie" und pragmatischem Roman.* Stuttgart: Kohlhammer, 1974.

Wedel, Alfred R. "Zum Motiv der Schwärmerei in Chr. M. Wielands *Don Sylvio*: Illusion—Desillusion; Platonismus—Erotismus." In *Aufnahme— Weitergabe: Literarische Impulse um Lessing und Goethe: Festschrift für Heinz*

Moenkemeyer zum 68. Geburtstag, ed. John A. McCarthy and Albert A. Kipa, 219–32. Hamburg: Buske, 1982.

Weinreich, Otto. *Der Trug des Nektanebos*. Berlin: Teubner, 1911.

Weyergraf, Bernd. *Der skeptische Bürger: Wielands Schriften zur Französischen Revolution*. Stuttgart: Metzler, 1972.

Whiton, John. "Sacrifice and Society in Wieland's *Abderiten*." *Lessing Yearbook* 2 (1970): 213–34.

Wieland, Christoph Martin. *Der Sieg der Natur über die Schwärmerey, oder die Abentheuer des Don Sylvio von Rosalva, Eine Geschichte worinn alles Wunderbare natürlich zugeht*. Ulm: Bartholomäi, 1764.

———. "Ueber die Glaubwürdigkeit Lucians in seinen Nachrichten vom Peregrinus." In *Lucians von Samosata Sämmtliche Werke*, trans. Christoph Martin Wieland, 93–110. Leipzig: Weidmann, 1788.

———. *C. M. Wielands Sämmtliche Werke*. 45 volumes. Leipzig: Göschen, 1794–1811; Hamburg, 1984.

———. *Wielands gesammelte Schriften*. Ed. Bernhard Seuffert et al. 23 vols. to date. Berlin: Weidmann, 1909–54; Akademie-Verlag, 1954–.

———. *Wielands Briefwechsel*. Ed. Hans Werner Seiffert. 12 vols. to date. Berlin: Akademie-Verlag, 1963–.

———. *Christoph Martin Wieland: Werke*. Ed. Fritz Martini and Hans Werner Seiffert. 5 vols. Munich: Hanser: 1964–68.

———. *Christoph Martin Wieland: Der goldne Spiegel und andere politische Dichtungen*. Ed. Herbert Jaumann. Munich: Winkler, 1979.

———. *Christoph Martin Wieland: Geschichte des Agathon*. Ed. Klaus Manger. Frankfurt am Main: Deutscher Klassiker Verlag, 1986.

"Wieland, Christoph Martin." *Die Musik in Geschichte und Gegenwart: Allgemeine Enzyklopädie der Musik*. Vol. 14, 593–99.

"Wieland, Christoph Martin." *New Grove Dictionary of Music and Musicians*. Vol. 20, 403.

Wildekamp, Ada, Ineke von Montfoort, and Willem van Ruiswijk. "Fictionality and Convention." *Poetics* 9 (1980): 547–67.

Wilpert, Gero von. *Der verlorene Schatten: Varianten eines literarischen Motivs*. Stuttgart: Kröner, 1978.

———. *Sachwörterbuch der Literatur*. 7th ed. Stuttgart: Kröner, 1989.

Wilson, W. Daniel. "'Prächt'ge Vase' oder 'halber Topf'? Horatian Poetics in Wieland's *Agathon*." *Modern Language Notes* 95 (1980): 664–69.

———. *The Narrative Strategy of Wieland's Don Sylvio von Rosalva*. Bern: Lang, 1981.

———. "Intellekt und Herrschaft: Wielands *Goldner Spiegel*, Joseph II. und das Ideal eines kritischen Mäzenats im aufgeklärten Absolutismus." *Modern Language Notes* 99 (1984): 479–502.

———. "Wieland's *Diogenes* and the Emancipation of the Critical Intellectual." In *Christoph Martin Wieland: North American Scholarly Contributions on the Occasion of the 250th Anniversary of His Birth*, ed. Hansjörg Schelle, 149–79. Tübingen: Niemeyer, 1984.

Wimsatt, William K., and Cleanth Brooks. *Literary Criticism: A Short History*. New York: Knopf, 1957.

Winter, Hans Gerhard. *Dialog und Dialogroman in der Aufklärung: Mit einer Analyse von J. J. Engels Gesprächstheorie*. Darmstadt: Thesen Verlag, 1974.

Wölfel, Kurt. "Daphnes Verwandlungen: Zu einem Kapitel in Wielands *Agathon*." In Schelle, *Christoph Martin Wieland*, 232–50. First published in *Jahrbuch der deutschen Schillergesellschaft* 8 (1964): 41–56.

Wolff, Hans M. *Die Weltanschauung der deutschen Aufklärung in geschichtlicher Entwicklung*. Bern: Francke, 1949.

Wolffheim, Hans. *Wielands Begriff der Humanität*. Hamburg: Hoffmann und Campe, 1949.

Wolterstorff, Nicholas. *Works and Worlds of Art*. Oxford: Clarendon Press, 1980.

Woods, John. *The Logic of Fiction*. The Hague: Mouton, 1974.

Würzner, Hans. "Christoph Martin Wieland: Versuch einer politischen Deutung." Diss., Heidelberg, 1957.

Würzner, M. H. "Die Figur des Lesers in Wielands 'Geschichte des Agathon.'" In Schelle, *Christoph Martin Wieland*, 399–406. First published in *Dichter und Leser: Studien zur Literatur. Utrechter Beiträge zur Allgemeinen Literaturwissenschaft* 14 (1972): 151–55.

Yuill, W. E. "Abderitis and Abderitism: Some Reflections on a Novel by Wieland." In *Essays in German Literature 1*, ed. F. Norman, 72–91. London: Institute of Germanic Studies, 1965.

Index

Abbt, Thomas, 43
Addison, Joseph, 70; "On the Pleasures of the Imagination," 60–61, 121
Arabian Nights, 88, 90–91, 114
Aristophanes, 171, 172, 187; *The Clouds*, 181, 184, 187
Aristotle, 52; concept of poetry, 1, 6, 10, 50, 57, 70; *Poetics*, 12. *See also* Mimesis: Plato's and Aristotle's concepts of

Baggesen, Jens, 68
Baumgarten, Alexander, 4
Bayle, Pierre, 118
Bildungsroman, 5, 16, 47, 68–69, 71, 191
Blanckenburg, Friedrich von, 12
Bodmer, Johann Jakob: and possible worlds, 4; and mimesis, 13–14, 160; Wieland as student of, 14, 86, 190; and the marvelous, 22, 30, 32, 140, 144, 164; and illusion, 23; and *Don Quixote*, 35–36; and sister arts, 75, 83, 86, 90; and taste, 120, 131; and allegorical interpretation, 122–23
Bondeli, Julie von, 33, 175
Borges, Jorge Luis, 9, 67
Brecht, Bertolt, 24
Breitinger, Johann Jakob, 4, 14, 32, 85, 130. *See also* Bodmer, Johann Jakob
Brentano, Sophie, 125

Cervantes Saavedra, Miguel de, 1, 30, 38, 42, 71, 98, 187; *Don Quixote*, 28, 34, 35–37, 40, 107, 139, 141, 160, 191, 194
Chiaroscuro, 124–25, 142, 163
Congreve, William, 3
Crébillon, Claude Prosper Jolyot de, 19, 53

Eichendorff, Joseph von, 101
Euripides, 70, 115–31 passim, 176, 179; *Ion*, 48, 53, 191

Fichte, Johann Gottlieb, 154, 177
Fiction: and nonfiction, 6–7; and the fictive, 8, 44

Fictionalism, 11, 12, 44–45, 47, 67, 71, 190
Fictionality: and modern novel, 1, 2–3; concept of, 1, 189, 193–94; current approaches to, 2–3, 6–10, 189–90, 193; history of, 3–4, 5; extent of, 4, 10–12; and fictivity, 7; and visual art, 10, 16, 110, 115, 123–25, 131, 177, 191–92, 193; and previous studies of Wieland's novels, 15, 16; and music, 170, 193
Fictional source. *See Quellenfiktion*
Fictional worlds. *See* Possible worlds
Fictions, legal, 11
Fielding, Henry, 66, 115, 121–22, 123, 131, 190, 192; *Tom Jones*, 18, 46, 54; *Joseph Andrews*, 19, 122, 130, 131; *David Simple*, 36
Figurative language, 7, 85, 110, 136, 147–48, 169, 192
Frederick II, "the Great" (king of Prussia), 86

Geschichte, 46, 55–58, 63–64, 65, 66, 69, 70, 79, 191. *See also* Historiography
Geßner, Salomon, 27
Gleim, Johann Ludwig Wilhelm, 102–3
Gluck, Christoph Willibald, 22
Goethe, Johann Wolfgang, 22, 24, 86, 168
Gottsched, Johann Christoph, 4, 13–14, 22, 36, 120, 191; *Critische Dichtkunst*, 13, 32, 35
Greuze, Jean Baptiste, 111–12, 114, 129

Hegel, Georg Wilhelm Friedrich, 12
Heidegger, Gotthard, 13
Heinse, Wilhelm, 81
Herder, Johann Gottfried, 168
Historiography, 6, 13–14, 51, 57, 191. See also *Geschichte*
Hogarth, William, 19, 20, 41, 115, 121, 190, 192
Homer, 3, 49, 129, 141, 151, 152, 160, 164, 179
Huet, Pierre-Daniel, 13, 18

University of North Carolina
Studies in the Germanic Languages
and Literatures

78 OLGA MARX AND ERNST MORWITZ, TRANS. *The Works of Stefan George*. 2nd, rev. and enl. ed. 1974. Pp. xxviii, 431.

96 G. RONALD MURPHY. *Brecht and the Bible: A Study of Religious Nihilism and Human Weakness in Brecht's Drama of Mortality and the City*. 1980. Pp. xi, 107.

99 JOHN M. SPALEK AND ROBERT F. BELL, EDS. *Exile: The Writer's Experience*. 1982. Pp. xxiv, 370.

100 ROBERT P. NEWTON. *Your Diamond Dreams Cut Open My Arteries: Poems by Else Lasker-Schüler*. Translated and with an Introduction. 1982. Pp. x, 317.

For other volumes in the "Studies" see p. ii.

Send orders to:
The University of North Carolina Press, P.O. Box 2288
Chapel Hill, NC 27515–2288

Several out-of-print titles are available in limited quantities through the UNCSGLL office. These include:

58 WALTER W. ARNDT, PAUL W. BROSMAN, JR., FREDERIC E. COENEN, AND WERNER P. FRIEDRICH, EDS. *Studies in Historical Linguistics in Honor of George Sherman Lane*. 1967. Pp. xx, 241.

68 JOHN NEUBAUER. *Bifocal Vision: Novalis' Philosophy of Nature and Disease*. 1971. Pp. x, 196.

70 DONALD F. NELSON. *Portrait of the Artist as Hermes: A Study of Myth and Psychology in Thomas Mann's "Felix Krull."* 1971. Pp. xvi, 146.

72 CHRISTINE OERTEL SJÖGREN. *The Marble Statue as Idea: Collected Essays on Adalbert Stifter's "Der Nachsommer."* 1972. Pp. xiv, 121.

73 DONALD G. DAVIAU AND JORUN B. JOHNS, EDS. *The Correspondence of Schnitzler and Auernheimer, with Raoul Auernheimer's Aphorisms*. 1972. Pp. xii, 161.

74 A. MARGARET ARENT MADELUNG. *"The Laxdoela Saga": Its Structural Patterns*. 1972. Pp. xiv, 261.

75 JEFFREY L. SAMMONS. *Six Essays on the Young German Novel*. 2nd ed. 1975. Pp. xiv, 187.

76 DONALD H. CROSBY AND GEORGE C. SCHOOLFIELD, EDS. *Studies in the German Drama: A Festschrift in Honor of Walter Silz*. 1974. Pp. xxvi, 255.

77 J. W. THOMAS. *Tannhäuser: Poet and Legend*. With Texts and Translation of His Works. 1974. Pp. x, 202.

80 DONALD G. DAVIAU AND GEORGE J. BUELOW. *The "Ariadne auf Naxos" of Hugo von Hofmannsthal and Richard Strauss*. 1975. Pp. x, 274.

81 ELAINE E. BONEY. *Rainer Maria Rilke: "Duinesian Elegies."* German Text with English Translation and Commentary. 2nd ed. 1977. Pp. xii, 153.

82 JANE K. BROWN. *Goethe's Cyclical Narratives: "Die Unterhaltungen deutscher Ausgewanderten" and "Wilhelm Meisters Wanderjahre."* 1975. Pp. x, 144.

83 FLORA KIMMICH. *Sonnets of Catharina von Greiffenberg: Methods of Composition.* 1975. Pp. x, 132.

84 HERBERT W. REICHERT. *Friedrich Nietzsche's Impact on Modern German Literature.* 1975. Pp. xxii, 129.

85 JAMES C. O'FLAHERTY, TIMOTHY F. SELLNER, AND ROBERT M. HELMS, EDS. *Studies in Nietzsche and the Classical Tradition.* 2nd ed. 1979. Pp. xviii, 278.

87 HUGO BEKKER. *Friedrich von Hausen: Inquiries into His Poetry.* 1977. Pp. x, 159.

88 H. G. HUETTICH. *Theater in the Planned Society: Contemporary Drama in the German Democratic Republic in Its Historical, Political, and Cultural Context.* 1978. Pp. xvi, 174.

89 DONALD G. DAVIAU, ED. *The Letters of Arthur Schnitzler to Hermann Bahr.* 1978. Pp. xii, 183.

91 LELAND R. PHELPS AND A. TILO ALT, EDS. *Creative Encounter: Festschrift for Herman Salinger.* 1978. Pp. xxii, 181.

92 PETER BAULAND. *Gerhart Hauptmann's "Before Daybreak."* Translation and Introduction. 1978. Pp. xxiv, 87.

93 MEREDITH LEE. *Studies in Goethe's Lyric Cycles.* 1978. Pp. xii, 191.

94 JOHN M. ELLIS. *Heinrich von Kleist: Studies in the Character and Meaning of His Writings.* 1979. Pp. xx, 194.

95 GORDON BIRRELL. *The Boundless Present. Space and Time in the Literary Fairy Tales of Novalis and Tieck.* 1979. Pp. x, 163.

97 ERHARD FRIEDRICHSMEYER. *Die satirische Kurzprosa Heinrich Bölls.* 1981. Pp. xiv, 223.

98 MARILYN JOHNS BLACKWELL, ED. *Structures of Influence: A Comparative Approach to August Strindberg.* 1981. Pp. xiv, 309.

Orders for these titles only should be sent to Editor, UNCSGLL, CB#3160 Dey Hall, Chapel Hill, NC 27599–3160.

Volumes 1–44, 46–50, 52, 60, and 79 of the "Studies" have been reprinted. They may be ordered from AMS Press, Inc., 56 E. 13th Street, New York, NY 10003.

For complete list of reprinted titles write to the Editor.